Social Capital, Corporate Social Responsibility, Economic Behaviour and Performance

Social Capital, Corporate Social Responsibility, Economic Behaviour and Performance

Edited by

Lorenzo Sacconi

and

Giacomo Degli Antoni

First published 2011 by
PALGRAVE MACMILLAN

Palgrave Macmillan in the UK is an imprint of Macmillan Publishers Limited,
registered in England, company number 785998, of Houndmills, Basingstoke,
Hampshire RG21 6XS.

Palgrave Macmillan in the US is a division of St Martin's Press LLC,
175 Fifth Avenue, New York, NY 10010.

Palgrave Macmillan is the global academic imprint of the above companies
and has companies and representatives throughout the world.

Palgrave® and Macmillan® are registered trademarks in the United States,
the United Kingdom, Europe and other countries.

ISBN 978–0–230–23568–7 hardback

This book is printed on paper suitable for recycling and made from fully
managed and sustained forest sources. Logging, pulping and manufacturing
processes are expected to conform to the environmental regulations of the
country of origin.

A catalogue record for this book is available from the British Library.

Library of Congress Cataloging-in-Publication Data
Social Capital, Corporate Social Responsibility, Economic Behaviour and
    Performance / Edited By Lorenzo Sacconi and Giacomo Degli Antoni.
        p.   cm
    Includes bibliographical references and index.
    ISBN 978–0–230–23568–7 (hardback)
    1. Social capital (Sociology)   2. Social responsibility of business.
    3. Economics—Psychological aspects.   I. Sacconi, Lorenzo, 1956– ,
    editor of compilation.   II. Antoni, Giacomo Degli, editor of compilation.
    III. Frey, Bruno S., 1941– Plea for unconventional economics.
    HM708.S6517 2011
    302.3′5—dc22   2010042404

10   9   8   7   6   5   4   3   2   1
20 19 18 17 16 15 14 13 12 11

Printed and bound in Great Britain by
CPI Antony Rowe, Chippenham and Eastbourne

Contents

v

Part III The Economic Effect of Social Capital and Other-regarding Preferences: Experimental and Empirical Evidence

Part IV Social Capital and Sustainable Economic Development: the Macro Approach

List of Tables and Figures

Tables

Figures

Notes on Contributors

Masahiko Aoki is the Henri and Tomoye Takahashi Professor Emeritus of Japanese Studies in the Economics Department, and a Senior Fellow of Stanford Institute of Economic Policy Research (SIEPR) and Freeman Spogli Institute for International Studies (FSI) at Stanford University. He is also the Director of the Virtual Center for Advanced Studies in Institutions (VCASI) at the Tokyo Foundation.

Stefano Bartolini is Associate Professor of Economics at the University of Siena.

Leonardo Becchetti is Professor of Economics at the University of Rome 'Tor Vergata', and Member of EconomEtica Scientific Committee.

Sergio Beraldo is Assistant Professor of Economic Policy at the University of Naples Federico II.

Luigi Bonatti is Professor of Economic Policy at the University of Trento.

Carlo Borzaga is Professor of Economic Policy at the University of Trento and Chairman of the European Research Institute on Cooperative and Social Enterprises (Euricse).

Giacomo Degli Antoni is Assistant Professor of Economics at the Department of Sociology and Social Research of the University of Milano-Bicocca, and Research Fellow at EconomEtica, Italy.

Sara Depedri is Research Fellow at the University of Trento.

Marco Faillo is Assistant Professor of Economic Policy at the University of Trento.

Bruno S. Frey is Professor of Economics at the University of Zurich, Distinguished Professor of Behavioral Science at the Warwick Business School at the University of Warwick, UK, and Research Director of CREMA-Centre for Research in Economics, Management and the Arts, Switzerland. He is Managing Editor of *Kyklos*.

Gianluca Grimalda is Assistant Professor at the University Jaume I of Castellon, Spain; Research Associate of IN+ Center for Innovation, Technology, and Policy Research, Instituto Superior Tecnico of Lisbon, Portugal; Research Associate of the Centre for the Study of Globalisation and Regionalisation, University of Warwick, UK.

Catalina Holguin is Ph.d Candidate at the London School of Economics and Political Science.

Robert Leonardi is Director of the ESOCLAB, LSE Enterprise, London School of Economics and Political Science and Visiting Professor at LUISS-Rome.

Steffen Lippert is Senior Lecturer in Economics at Massey University, New Zealand.

Luigi Mittone is Professor of Economics at the University of Trento and Director of the Computable and Experimental Economics Laboratory (CEEL).

Raffaella Nanetti is Professor of Urban Planning and Policy in the College of Urban Planning and Public Affairs, University of Illinois at Chicago.

Martin Paldam is Professor at the School of Economics and Management, Aarhus University and Honorary Professor at Deakin University, Melbourne.

Vittorio Pelligra is Assistant Professor of Economics at the University of Cagliari and Member of Centre for North South Economic Research (CRENoS).

Lorenzo Sacconi is Professor of Economics, Unicredit Chair in Economic Ethics and Corporate Social Responsibility at the Department of Economics of Trento University, and Director of EconomEtica, Inter-University Centre of Research at the University of Milano-Bicocca, Italy.

Ermanno Tortia is Assistant Professor of Economic Policy at the University of Trento.

Gilberto Turati is Assistant Professor of Public Economics at the University of Turin.

Introduction

Lorenzo Sacconi and Giacomo Degli Antoni

1. About the general subjects of the book

Over the last few years, economics has experienced significant changes. These have concerned both new substantive subjects of research and new theories, methodologies and analytical tools. As regards subjects, the interest of economists has been increasingly attracted by matters – such as intrinsic adherence to social norms, other-regarding preferences and non-instrumental reciprocity – previously considered to be 'non-economic' phenomena (and the exclusive competence of other disciplines: psychology and sociology, and perhaps moral philosophy). As regards theories, methodologies and tools, new approaches characterized by high interdisciplinarity – such as behavioral economics and behavioral law and economics, experimental economics, 'psychological' games, and more generally behavioral game theory – have been developed and have spread throughout the economics profession. Substance, theory, methods and tools are closely interwoven because new approaches have been developed and/or applied in the analysis of new topics (for example, the experimental approach has been widely used to explain the extensive evidence of deviations from the behavior predicted on the basis of standard microeconomic models; deviations associated with what we may intuitively call social reciprocity, conformity with norms, not strictly selfish behavior, trust and trustworthiness, etc.).

To be sure, these elements have not yet given rise to a radical change in the dominant microeconomic paradigm, given that the core idea of rational behavior as the maximization of an expected utility function remains unquestioned. Moreover, these changes are still not bold enough with respect to evidence, or to items of theoretical research, delivered by adjoining fields (for example, artificial intelligence, soft computing and cognitive sciences). Indeed, experimentally observed anomalies extend across the entire standard model of the *maximizing instrumentally rational* and *selfish homo oeconomicus*. It is difficult to believe that such systematic anomalies can be circumscribed and directed only against the type of *motivation* (the

1

selfish behavior typically represented by the model) without considering that they may also involve the definition of *rationality* (i.e. the kind of *reasoning* that economic agents carry out, which the standard theory somewhat ironically assumes to equate with finding the mathematical solution of the model, that is, for each agent *maximizing* an expected utility function). In fact, such deviations concern both (i) *the cognitive sphere* (i.e. systematic probability biases – excessive optimism and self-confidence – and probabilistic judgment mistakes, framing effects and violations of independence postulates, violations of logical omniscience assumptions), and (ii) *the motivational sphere* (i.e. voluntary compliance with social norms without apparent material returns, non-egoistic behavior exhibited in voluntary participation in non-profits and commons management, corporate social responsibility advocacy even when there is no self-interested material advantage in doing so, for example, activism by responsible consumers and investors, etc.). All these are phenomena not easily explainable as simple variations of the selfish rational maximizer of the utility model; at least, they are not so as long as the model is not made completely tautological and devoid of any empirical content (in principle, in fact, the outcomes for an individual could be understood as also encapsulating any perfectly 'altruistic' effect whatsoever; and in this case, as far as it is rational, preferring such 'altruistic' consequences would be 'selfish' in a completely tautological way).

Besides the casual observation of relevant social facts, laboratory experiments systematically and accurately reveal deviations from the standard model of the *homo oeconomicus*. They employ simple experimental games such as the Ultimatum Game, the Prisoner's Dilemma, the Dictator Game, the Trust Game, the Public Good Game or the recently introduced 'Exclusion Game' (see Sacconi and Faillo 2010). Such experimental games gather a large amount of evidence suggesting that players behave more cooperatively, more fairly and less selfishly than the standard theory would predict. These experiments can be taken as methods with which to test specific predictions of standard game theory, or also predictions deriving from slight modifications of its postulates. Under minor variations of the game form, incorporated as small adaptations of the experimental design, they may also be considered as heuristically useful means with which to establish on which part (hypothesis) of the theory the *modus tollens* must be *first* directed.

Behavioral economics is thus a source of demand for new economic modeling – both theoretically and experimentally grounded – in two respects. *First*, it suggests modeling the choices of boundedly rational agents – not logically omniscient ones characterized by specific logics of approximate reasoning – able to encapsulate relevant cognitive constraints. The most important challenge in this regard is how to account for reasoning procedures that are boundedly rational but nevertheless intelligent economic agents adopt in the awareness that they are unable to predict and envisage all possible future contingences (states of the world). This is more a matter of reasoning under conditions of vagueness and indeterminacy than of statistical uncertainty. It consequently concerns the thought processes which a boundedly rational but nevertheless aware reasoner uses intentionally or simply de facto in order to circumvent such problems – for example, by resorting to general principles, mental models, framings, and so on. For example, *fuzzy logic* and *default reasoning* may be logical tools better suited to realistic representation of the reasoning process that underlies decisions taken by a boundedly rational agent who is still able to make albeit fallible inferences and is faced with such vague and indeterminate decision situations (Sacconi 2007; Sacconi and Moretti 2008).

Second, the behavioral turn in economics suggests that models of choice should be devised which yield understanding of motivations and practical reasons different from those typically represented by standard rational self-interest and consequentialist models of choice – that is, utility maximization as seeking the best self-regarded consequence materially accruing to the agent him/herself. Most important in this respect are not 'social preferences' – a broadening of the description of consequences, including the well-being of others or, worse, the enrichment of the personal utility function's arguments so as also to include the utilities of other people as an object – but rather accounting for different patterns of preference and motivation that give different practical reasons for acting: for example, preference patterns underlying behaviors like deontology or rule-following, voluntary compliance with social norms, or the 'sense of justice'. This suggests considering agreed or shared norms or principles per se as reasons for acting or having a preference that induce economic agents to make decisions. This also would create room for the role of mutual expectations – concerning norm compliance – as a specific basis for motivation and preference to act, so that preference depends directly on beliefs and expectations. The other agents' expected reciprocity may thus be a basis for the first agent's reciprocity (one reciprocates *just because* of the others' expected reciprocity; not necessarily for mutual advantage or instrumentally for any material payoff, but simply because the first agent expects the other party to reciprocate). Psychological games provide models for such motivations and the ensuing interactions (Geanakoplos et al. 1989; Rabin 1993).

In general, this richer way to model complex motivations is grouped together with other behavioral game models under the umbrella of a research agenda consisting of numerous alternative extensions of the individual's utility function, which aim to make sense of different, not strictly selfish, modes of motivation. In order to safeguard or even augment empirical and predictive power with respect to classical models, these extensions must not introduce too many ad hoc parameters into the utility function. In fact, predictive power can be taken as a positive function of the *ratio* {accurate predictions/simplicity of assumptions}, so that introducing too many new parameters into the utility function would reduce the explanatory power of the theory.

This research strategy is *piecemeal*. It maintains the utility maximizing model of the economic agent while admitting different motivations, represented by variations in some components of the utility function appropriately defined, in order to make sense of the peculiarity of different reasons to act and different modes of preference: that is to say, it gives rise to a model of a 'fully rational' agent endowed with complex and not merely selfish preferences. However, sooner or later bounded rationality will enter these models of motivational complexity as well. In fact, as previously said, the most interesting of them are concerned with mutual beliefs and expectations that directly affect preferences (as in reciprocity models and psychological games). But where do these beliefs come from? Current psychological game models assume that in equilibrium each player derives such beliefs from the individual's infinite hierarchy of expectations (mutually consistent with other individuals' hierarchies) that conclusively enable each player (say player 1) to predict exactly the other player's behavior (say player 2), while player 2 predicts 1's behavior as well; and this is also predicted through second-order beliefs by player 1 – and so on in an infinite regress where each prediction layer of a player is derived from a higher-order layer of beliefs about beliefs, and so on. But beliefs formation in a behavioral model should account for the lack of logical omniscience and the limited capacity to outguess another's reasoning (i.e. the ability to draw inferences from a higher-order beliefs-layer to all the possible lower-level belief-layers cannot be endless and usually does not extend further than three layers).

The experimental evidence strongly counsels for the integration of the *motivational* and the *cognitive* lines of inquiry. In some experiments, subjects are observed as jumping by default from the fact that they have, *ex ante*, agreed on a principle to the shared belief that they will comply: that is, the belief that supports reciprocity, and hence compliance with the agreement reached in the pre-play situation, even though there is no logical justification for doing so (see Faillo et al. 2008; Sacconi and Faillo 2010). What are the cognitive mechanisms at work in these situations? 'We thinking', understood as group-identification through 'framing effects' (see Bacharach 2006)? Simple *default reasoning* (see Sacconi and Moretti 2008) or a combination of the two (Faillo and Sacconi 2008)? Answering these questions would typically introduce bounded rationality (as limited reasoning) considerations into the explanation of the relevant evidence.

However, even in the current context of a less than radical reorientation of economic theory, it can be said that the ongoing changes are of some relevance to the philosophical understanding and intuitive conceptualization of individual and strategic economic behavior. Types of social behavior that would once have been considered 'irrational' or at least 'non-economic' are now explained by means of substantial reformulations of the basic concept of utility function which, while they safeguard the mathematics of expected utility maximization, create substantial room for different intentions, reasons and motivations to operate. Importantly, this is not the typical reductionist approach of economics whereby every kind of behavior is reduced to a self-interest-based explanation because an interpretive model is set out that makes it possible to identify the self-dealing component of any given social behavior. On the contrary, the new theories introduce models of preference that are consistent with the intuitive understanding of the intentions of agents observed acting for reasons other than seeking to satisfy their best material interests. Thus, there is not reduction of unselfish behavior to some variant of individual maximization of a utility function representing self-interest, that is something that would be quite different from what can be intuitively and reasonably described as non-egoistic behavior.

In certain contexts, moreover, the new behavioral economic models predict 'new facts': that is, interaction outcomes that would have been excluded as inconsistent with traditional theories and would have therefore been unpredictable. Examples are the success of commons' management by large non-hierarchical groups of individuals, which 'should' be ruled out by some versions of the free-rider problem; or quite successful decisions to contribute voluntarily to the production of a local public good; or participation in non-profit organizations producing welfare services, with no evidence of either managers and employees resorting to substantial rent seeking or any effectiveness of reputation effects (long-run game repetition with learning parties); or compliance by professionals with codes of professional ethics not understood as means to restrict competition but simply as they are – statements of fiduciary duties to clients and the profession.

The truly novel aspect of these results resides in their normative implications for institutional and organization design, and for policy-making. In fact, according to such explanations, it is not necessary to superimpose on each domain of economic interaction and transaction the model of economic incentives represented by some sort of competitive market in order to curb personal self-interests and make them consistent with social efficiency. Nor is it necessary to frame all contractual relationships in terms of the principal-agent model whereby the principal provides self-interested incentives (incurring agency costs) to the agent in order to induce him/her to do what his/her contract could already oblige him/her to do. Often, institution designs of this kind, in order to make the incentive mechanisms work properly, first require a motivational and cognitive reorientation of the participating players' behavior rules that makes them truly selfish agents – as was required by a socially accepted behavioral standard of greediness. This happens, for example, when mangers once understood as fiduciaries of a large array of stakeholders are then (by means of a stock-options plan) transformed into self-dealing proprietors who seek to maximize the value of their own holdings, which form the largest part of their remuneration.

As easily predictable, the new models have consequences markedly different from those of the neoclassical models in terms of social philosophy and institutional policy reforms and design. According to whether it is possible to design choice situations that are cognitively and motivationally favorable to engendering relevant not-simply-selfish kinds of behavior, non-market institutions and economic organizations can be introduced in order to achieve social outcomes more beneficial than those yielded by market-like institutions and organizations, or those of traditional principal-agent models based on self-interested monetary incentives.

2. An overview on the book's contents

However, even in the less-than-revolutionary perspective that concerns us in this book, much remains to be done before the potential of the ongoing changes has been fully exploited. One possible methodological development suggested by this book is a closer interaction among behavioral and experimental economics, psychological game theory and network analysis in order to study subjects that only recently have attracted the attention of economists and seem to be characterized by several links, which are still unexplored. A good example, one that will concern us for most of this book, is the link between social capital and socially responsible behavior of economic agents and organizations in terms of social norms, management standards and good practices of corporate social responsibility (CSR). These concepts have been widely used in the past two decades: the former in socioeconomics, in order to study the effects of trust, trustworthiness and ethical norms of reciprocity and cooperation within communities, social groups and local economic systems; the latter in business ethics, corporate governance, law and economics and the theory of the firm, in order to study similar phenomena in the business and entrepreneurial context. Although they seem to be linked by numerous common elements relative to the quantity and quality of social relations among agents, their connections have not yet been thoroughly investigated (but see Sacconi and Degli Antoni 2009). This book focuses on the relationship between these two concepts (and the underlying phenomena) – social capital, and socially responsible behavior of economic agents with particular regard to the notion of corporate social responsibility – and it contributes to the economic literature on these concepts in two main ways. *First*, it shows that these two notions have several interconnections, understanding of which may clarify the determinants and the effects of both social capital and the socially responsible behavior of individual and corporate actors in light of a behavioral perspective that does not necessarily disconnect them from self-interest but certainly does not explain them as merely driven by it. The concept of social capital is discussed by taking account of its multidimensional nature. It is studied by considering its cognitive and structural dimensions, and it is approached at both a micro and a macro level. The notion of CSR is interpreted from a multi-stakeholder perspective. Also examined are the instrumental, normative and intrinsic reasons which may explain a firm's decision to be socially responsible toward all its stakeholders, instead of only the shareholders.

Second, the contributions collected in this book adopt methodological approaches that range from the psychological game theory to behavioral and experimental analysis – approaches that are somewhat original in the social capital literature and definitely uncommon in the CSR literature – and they also contribute to the relevant literatures in general. In fact, while the present book's main subjects are social capital, CSR, and their possible relationships, it is more generally concerned with (as Frey's chapter puts it) the advancement of 'unconventional' economics wherein agents' motivations to act are considered more complex than mere self-interest aimed at maximizing material payoffs. Indeed, other regarding preferences, well-being and psychological payoffs are linking themes among the book's chapters. They are considered from the perspective of the economic theory of institutions in the first part of the book, where the complexity of agents' preferences is of key importance in understanding how cooperative and responsible behaviors by agents (both firms and individuals) increase social welfare and prevent market failures. In this regard, the book adds something in particular to the theory of economic institutions by explaining the emergence of economic organizations that improve market and social efficiency by deviating from the standard *homo oeconomicus* neoclassical view. The same approaches are employed in the second part of the book, where behavioral game theory is used in connection with network analysis, this being viewed as a basic tool for understanding social capital. Again, advancement in the same broad line of inquiry is achieved in the third and fourth parts by adopting the experimental and empirical approach, and then a macro perspective, respectively.

Although the papers collected in this book have been brought together within a unified framework, they are also grouped into four parts according to their themes and methodology. The four parts are:

Part I. New Perspectives on the Economic Theory of Institutions, Individual Preferences and Social Norms
Part II. Social Capital and Corporate Social Responsibility: a Game Theoretical and Network Analysis Approach
Part III. The Economic Effect of Social Capital and Other-Regarding Preferences: Experimental and Empirical Evidence
Part IV. Social Capital and Sustainable Economic Development: the Macro Approach

Part I – New perspectives on the economic theory of institutions, individual preferences and social norms

The motivational complexity of agents operating in a socio-economic and political environment characterized by increasing complexity is the 'picklock' for entry into the chapters included in the first part of this collection. Study is made of economic and non-economic institutions, which deviate in their behavior from the orthodox economic model of the *homo oeconomicus*. The idea behind this part of the book is not only that, as Bruno Frey says in Chapter 1, neoclassics is important as a background theory into which unorthodox elements can be introduced, but also that neoclassical economics may not provide realistic descriptions of economic systems and reliable predictions of their behavior, because it fails to take account of the important cognitive, emotional and psychological factors stressed by the 'unconventional' economic approaches developed in the past few years. Intrinsic motivations, trust, reciprocity, processes affecting belief formation, and ideal utility must be considered when seeking to explain not only the emergence of otherwise non-understandable institutions but also their contribution to the efficiency of markets and to the creation of social welfare. In the broad perspective of the 'unconventional economics' that deviates from the 'straitjacket' of orthodox neoclassical theory, this part of the book contributes to the explanation and design of four economic institutions that can be envisaged according this new approach: (i) the democratic provision of public goods beyond national borders; (ii) corporate social responsibility as an extended model of corporate governance based on extended fiduciary duties owed to all the corporate stakeholders; (iii) microcredit institutions providing financial services to so-called 'unbankable' people; (iv) the emergence of non-market institutions aimed at providing market transactions with the necessary amount of social capital and trust that they require for their proper functioning.

First, in Chapter 1, Bruno Frey discusses institutional innovations desirable for the organization of the public sector and of democratic institutions in an increasingly interconnected socio-economic and political international context. Such institutional innovations should be based on the concepts of flexible political units and flexible citizenship. Flexible democratic political institutions should be able to adjust to the 'geography of problems', instead of being restricted by traditional frontiers among political units. FOCJ (*Functional, Overlapping, and Competing Jurisdictions*) are democratic governmental units with authority (e.g. the power to tax) over their citizens. They should provide one or some public services for a certain geographical area (so as to exploit economies of scale) and only residents in that area should pay for that or those services (no spillover effect). FOCJ are in competition with each other because citizens may opt to leave a specific FOCUS, and FOCJ may overlap, that is, two FOCJ may cater to different functions, or also the same function, in the same territory. In regard to the idea of flexible citizenship, Frey notes that a new approach to citizenship is required by the process of globalization, which decreases communication and transportation costs. For this purpose, national citizenship should be extended (here the author introduces the concepts of temporary, multiple and partial citizenship) and citizenship should concern organizations of various types, that is, a subject should be allowed to become a citizen of an organization other than the nation. Second, Frey deals with three selected contributions from *Psychological Economics*: 1) the complexity of human motivations, referring to the idea of intrinsic motivations in relation to the extrinsic ones; 2) the usefulness of conducting surveys on subjective well-being or happiness in order to approximate individual utility; 3) the importance of considering utility as deriving not only from the consequences of actions but also from procedural aspects relative to *how* the outcomes are determined. Frey's chapter is thus 'a plea for unconventional economics'. Although various factors (homogenized doctoral programs, which in many cases rule out non-orthodox approaches, and the need to publish in refereed journals) help to explain the continuing dominance of conventional economics, 'only those scholars will be able to play a prominent role in future academic economics who are coming forth with innovative ideas'.

In Chapter 2, Lorenzo Sacconi provides a definition of CSR as a multi-stakeholder governance model *whereby those who run a firm (entrepreneurs, directors, managers) have responsibilities that range from fulfillment of fiduciary duties toward the owners to fulfillment of analogous – even if not identical – fiduciary duties toward all the firm's stakeholders.* The basic idea is that such an institutional model, provided it is not obstructed by statutory company law, which imposes a single-stakeholder fiduciary model and objective function on companies, is self-sustaining as a social norm and self-regulatory standard, which can then be easily enacted by the legal order. The relevant perspective is that of an institution in Aoki's sense (a self-sustaining system of shared beliefs about a salient way in which a game is repeatedly played) completed with the idea of a *social contract* reached, in a Rawlsian hypothetical situation, 'under a veil of ignorance' between the firm and its stakeholders. This chapter is the third part of a comprehensive essay on the Rawlsian view of corporate social responsibility (for Parts I and II see Sacconi 2010a; 2010b). The Rawlsian social contract on an explicit CSR norm performs four essential functions in implementation of this very broad idea of multi-stakeholder corporate governance: 1) the *constructive role*; 2) the *normative role*; 3) the *motivational role*; 4) the *predictive role*. While the first two functions are discussed in Parts I and II of the essay respectively, the third part, included in this volume, focuses on the third and fourth aspects. Hence, after answering the question as to what pattern of interaction the firm and its stakeholders would *ex ante* select on an *ex ante* impartial agreement from the set of possible equilibria, this chapter addresses the problem concerning the players' incentives to respect the *ex ante* agreement reached under the social contract once they exit from the original-position-and-veil-of-ignorance situation and consider the entire set of their preferences and motivations to act. This point is discussed by adopting a behavioral approach drawn from psychological game theory, where ideal motivations to act in conformity with an agreed impartial principle of fairness have a central role. In particular, the analysis of the CSR model's self-sustainability is conducted by supposing that the *ex ante* agreement on an impartial norm by itself affects incentives and beliefs in the *ex post* perspective: that is, it integrates the players' preferences defined over the set of admissible equilibria of the game of life relevant in the *ex post* (outside the veil of ignorance) perspective.

This happens because of two interlocked behavioral hypotheses. The *first* is that an *ex ante* agreement generates additional motivational (i.e. preferential) forces precisely because it has been chosen 'behind the veil of ignorance'. It consequently adds a further psychological component to the players' payoff functions. This component works so that only those equilibria wherein conditional and reciprocal conformity is positively expected are reinforced psychologically. The main result of this chapter is the following: whereas when the interaction between a series of stakeholders and a firm is modeled as a repeated Trust Game, numerous Nash equilibria are possible solutions of the game, on the contrary, under the hypothesis that an *ex ante* impartial (apparently cheap-talk) agreement induces conformist preferences, there are only *two* possible psychological equilibria: the one in which the agreement is fully respected, and the one in which, because the stakeholders expect to be abused by the firm, they do not allow any deviation from the principle to occur by staying out of the interaction. All the other Nash equilibria, especially those in mixed strategies, are deleted. This is a very strong and unexpected consequence of what can be considered the 'sense of justice' (the Rawlsian idea encapsulated in this behavioral theory). The *second* behavioral hypothesis is that of a framing mechanism such that agreeing 'behind the veil' also influences beliefs about other parties' behavior *ex post*: that is, it induces a state of shared beliefs whereby what was chosen behind the veil will be also believed to be implemented *ex post*. This facilitates and makes quite likely – even if it is not sufficient for a logical implication to be drawn – that the fully compliant with the agreed principle equilibrium will be selected *ex post*.

While socially responsible corporate governance enables organizations to avoid economic inefficiency due to suboptimal investments by non-controlling stakeholders when they are at risk of authority abuse, other contract failures concern information asymmetry in the financial sector. Chapter 3 by Vittorio Pelligra focuses on some of these market failures and adopts a behavioral approach to explain and interpret possible solutions. Because of its assumptions of self-interested behavior and asymmetric information, the neoclassical explanatory framework applied to the credit market predicts opportunistic behavior, adverse selection and, consequently, credit rationing. Credit will be provided only to borrowers able to back it with collateral. The success of micro-credit initiatives around the world demonstrates that there is something lacking in the standard interpretation based on traditional rational choice theory. Not only are 'unbankable' poor people trustworthy, but the loan recovery rate is surprisingly high. Pelligra uses the tools of psychological game theory to interpret the behavior of lenders and borrowers involved in micro-credit programs by supplementing the usually considered explanation based, for example, on joint liability and reputation, with a behavioral explanation based on the concept of trust responsiveness, and according to which lenders' expectations to be repaid have a key role in fostering trustworthy behavior by borrowers.

Is competition a sufficient condition for a trustworthy economy (i.e. 'an economy in which buyers' expectations that sellers always deliver high-quality commodities are fulfilled') to come about, or do external interventions and regulation have a fundamental role in making the competitive mechanism able to sustain an acceptable level of trust and trustworthiness? Sergio Beraldo and Gilberto Turati's Chapter 4 tackles this issue by developing a formal analysis, which brings to light the main stylized facts characterizing this issue in an historical perspective. While before the Industrial Revolution the conditions for competition to be sufficient in sustaining trust and trustworthiness were probably fulfilled (the bulk of trade consisted of *local exchanges*, consumers and suppliers knew each other, and the quality of commodities could be generally verified either before or after consumption), Beraldo and Turati argue that the increasing complexity of economic systems (mainly due to concentration and mass production entailing a separation between consumers and producers, and technological advancements obstructing the determination of product quality) makes competition alone inadequate for sustaining an acceptable level of trust. This requires a new set of market- or non market-based institutions designed to deal with the problem in a more complex context. In this perspective, authors point out that existing institutions, either market-based (e.g. based on investments in firm-specific and non-recoverable assets such as promotion of *brand names* through *advertisements*) or ultimately rooted in public regulation, have limitations that would also characterize possible solutions based on self-regulation by firms.

Part II – Social capital and corporate social responsibility: a game theoretical and network analysis approach

Social capital, corporate social responsibility and their relationship, analyzed by means of the tools of psychological game theory and network analysis, are the protagonists of Part II of the volume.

Masahiko Aoki's Chapter 5 discusses the relationship between social capital and socially responsible behavior by firms. In particular, it challenges the orthodox view that 'corporations do not need to do anything beyond legal obligations in order to serve stockholders interests' by suggesting an analytical approach, which endogenizes the relevance of social constructs such as (individual) social capital, norms and status ascriptions to the economic behavior of firms within an expanded framework of game-theoretic thinking. In order to endogenize the role of social values into the economic analysis of firm's behavior, Aoki explicitly considers the domain of economic-transaction games, that of social-exchange games, and the link between them. The two domains are characterized by different instruments (action choices), languages and intentions (payoffs), but each player coordinates his or her own strategies across the two domains in a unified manner, that is, by considering trade-offs between hedonistic payoffs and social payoffs. Social capital is defined within the social-exchange game domain and represents agents' expected capacity to derive positive net emotional payoffs over time, as well as to use them to derive benefits in other domains. Corporate social responsibility is considered according to a multi-stakeholder approach. By applying the notion of individual social capital to corporate players within the framework just described, this chapter discusses how corporate social capital accumulated through corporate social responsibility programs can compensate the pecuniary costs of CSR programs, how the former can nonetheless indirectly complement the accumulation of the latter, and how the former can become an insurance against an institutional change in environmental rights distribution.

Steffen Lippert in Chapter 6 proposes an original formalization of the concept of social capital based on the theory of networks of relations, which is applied to define individual social capital in the spirit of Bourdieu and Coleman, and to aggregate social capital in the spirit of Putnam. Lippert studies different network structures where pairs of adjacent players situated at the network's nodes are involved in bilateral repeated strategy games, such as the Prisoner's Dilemma. The nature of links in the networks determines whether or not players are able to support their bilateral cooperative relations. There are, however, some networks where bilateral cooperative relations are deficient (i.e. there is no bilateral strategy able to support mutual cooperation). Nevertheless, the structure of the entire network may provide a multilateral strategy that allows sustaining cooperation in pairs of relations because of the possibility that other players located elsewhere in the network may sanction deviation from cooperation within relations in which they do not directly participate. Thus, at a micro level, the social capital that two agents can rely on by being members of a social network equals the sanction power of the network usable to enforce cooperation-compliance in bilateral interactions between pairs of members that by themselves would be unable to sustain cooperation. Because the sanctioning members are not those directly involved in the deficient cooperative relationships, social capital at micro level proves to be a governance mechanism operating by means of a multilateral punishment strategy involving a social network. At a macro level, social capital corresponds to the average pair-specific micro-level social capital of agents within the social network. By considering different network configurations, characterized by different payoff structures and information conditions (with public and non-public information), Lippert shows that the amount of social capital depends on the structure of the underlying social network, and that denser social networks do not necessarily provide higher social capital.

In Chapter 7, Giacomo Degli Antoni and Lorenzo Sacconi use a formal model to investigate the idea of a virtuous circle between the amount of social capital and the diffusion of CSR social norms and practices – which is the idea that gave origin to this book on the linkages between these two subjects of study. Social capital is defined by taking account of both its cognitive (disposition to cooperate and belief in others' behavior) and structural (cooperative network of relation) dimensions. Corporate social responsibility is defined according to the contractarian approach (as understood in Sacconi's Chapter 2, *infra*). The idea behind this chapter is to show how the level of endogenous sustainability of mutual relations of cooperation and trust within networks – wherein bilateral relations between pairs of players involved in repeated games may be deficient (unable to sustain cooperation) – in fact changes dramatically when the relations among a few members of the network are modeled as a repeated psychological game, which not only modifies the behaviors of the pairs of players directly involved, but also induces different behaviors in other parts of the network where somewhat distant network members are located. The result is the creation of a network of sustainable cooperative relationships (structural social capital) based on what may be understood as cognitive social capital related to the adoption of socially responsible norms of behavior in a quite precise sense. Degli Antoni and Sacconi introduce a psychological game model where the psychological payoffs of agents – endowed with conformist preferences – depends on their contribution to fulfillment of an agreed principle of fair distribution coincident with a CSR norm, and their mutual beliefs about reciprocity in compliance. This agreement concerns the behavior of a player – a firm – in regard to different members of the network in which it is embedded, some of them being strong stakeholders and others weak stakeholders. In particular, the psychological game based on conformist preferences involves the firm and its strong stakeholders. The chapter shows that the level of stakeholders' cognitive social capital – understood as the combination of strong stakeholders' conformist dispositions plus their expectations concerning the firm's reciprocity in compliance with the agreed CSR norm – is a positive economic incentive for firms to also adopt and respect CSR practices in regard to weak stakeholders – which entails the creation of a network of cooperative relations (structural social capital). The adoption of a CSR norm, in fact, allows the formation of stakeholders' beliefs on the firm's behavior. The disposition to conform, the effective implementation of CSR practices and the resulting mutual beliefs enable the formation of structural social capital in terms of cooperative relationships between the firm and all its stakeholders, which would not be sustainable otherwise.

Part III – The economic effect of social capital and other-regarding preferences: experimental and empirical evidence

The chapters in this part of the book focus on the economic effect of other-regarding preferences. They allow a step forward to be taken in our knowledge concerning the role that relational goods, generalized trust and organizations characterized by a pro-social nature may perform in reducing selfish behavior and improving socio-economic performance.

Leonardo Becchetti, Giacomo Degli Antoni and Marco Faillo's Chapter 8 adopts an experimental approach to show that other-regarding preferences may arise as a consequence of the possibility offered to players to generate and consume relational goods with their counterparts. In particular, the chapter summarizes interesting experimental evidence from two treatments on an investment game and a traveler's dilemma, respectively, both of which were characterized by the possibility for players to decide if they wanted to meet their counterpart after the game. Before playing the game, the players were aware of the fact that the meeting would take place only if both players wanted it, and they were informed about their opponent's choice concerning the meeting only at the end of the experiment. The mere possibility of meeting the counterpart both in the investment game and in the traveler's dilemma reduced selfish behavior in players who opted for the meeting. By comparing experimental results when the meeting option was available, when it was not available or when the meeting was a compulsory characteristic of the game (this last only in the traveler's dilemma game), the authors give an original interpretation to their results in terms of *relational goods*. The willingness to affect the counterpart's disposition in regard to the creation of relational goods through the meeting affects players' strategies in the game and reduces selfish behavior.

In the next chapter (Chapter 9), Gianluca Grimalda and Luigi Mittone combine survey and experimental evidence to investigate at a micro level the relationship between individual trust in others (measured by three different questions referring to three aspects of generalized trust) and other individual-level variables, and how these are reflected in the propensity to cooperate with others in public-good game experiments. The experimental evidence is obtained from: a linear Public Goods Game (PGG) with people from the same locality; a nested PGG with people from the same locality and other parts of the country; a nested PGG with people from the same locality and other parts of the world. Grimalda and Mittone's aim is to test three main hypotheses: 1) participation in voluntary associations fosters generalized trust; 2) associational membership generates economic returns by increasing cooperation; 3) individual generalized trust enhances economic performance (for example, because it increases institutional capacity to produce public goods). While the data provide only mixed support for the first hypothesis (associational membership seems to positively affect only generalized trust when it is measured using the classic GSS question: '*Generally speaking, would you say that most people can be trusted or that you can't be too careful in dealing with people?*') they seem to confute the second hypothesis. Conversely, some support is forthcoming for the third hypothesis, in that individuals stating that they trusted others seemed more inclined to cooperate in the experiments than others, although there were differences among different measures of generalized trust.

Chapter 10, the last in this part of the book, by Carlo Borzaga, Sara Depedri and Ermanno Tortia focuses on other-regarding and social preferences but shifts the emphasis from the individual to the organizational level. The aim of the contribution is to analyze the intentional and unintended effects of social enterprises on social welfare, with particular reference to poor and weak socio-demographic groups. The analysis is based on an original database comprising data on a representative sample of 320 Italian social cooperatives, their managers and 4134 paid workers. In regard to intentional effects, the authors show that a significant role assigned by the interviewees to cooperatives as social enterprises concerned the over-production and over-distribution of output compared with the contractual obligation undertaken by these enterprises with those parties that represented the paying demand. This feature takes the form of some services being distributed for free or at a price below the production costs and furnished to all the clients, or free services for poor people. According to the authors, these features of over-production by social enterprises may arise mainly because these enterprises – given their specific characteristics also concerning the social and ideological involvement of their members – do not fully remunerate the production factors (labour and capital) and are able to gather additional non-market resources, such as more or less intense labour donations (voluntarism) and financial donations (giving). Unintended effects – also considered in this chapter – regard the capacity of social enterprises to affect social capital in terms of relationships, trust with stakeholders and implementation of social norms.

Part IV – Social capital and sustainable economic development: the macro approach

The fourth part of the book collects three original contributions which investigate the relationship between social capital as a macro variable (declined according to various dimensions envisaged by the literature) and sustainable economic development. This relationship is considered at both theoretical and different empirical levels.

Stefano Bartolini and Luigi Bonatti, in Chapter 11, focus on a possible trade-off between output growth and long-run individual well-being related to the accumulation of social capital and social relationships. This trade-off is shown by developing a theoretical model which provides a set-up in which to analyze the effects of two kinds of policy: one aimed at accelerating endogenous technical progress, which promotes inputs efficiency in the production of market goods; the other intended to engender incentives alleviating the negative impacts of social commons over-consumption and environmental resources deployment, by increasing the time devoted by households to activities that positively affect social cohesion and community ties, or by promoting the adoption of new technologies that reduce the negative effects of consumer activities on the natural environment. The chapter shows that policies which stimulate technical progress can lead to an increase of output growth by augmenting the efficiency of the inputs used in the production of market goods, but they may also have a negative effect on individual social welfare due to a detrimental impact of higher levels of consumption on social and environmental assets, which represent important sources of people's welfare. Moreover, the declining quality of social and environmental assets is bound to worsen even further, because agents will be induced by this social and environmental decline to devote more and more time to the accumulation of private assets, and to increase their work effort so as to have access to more market goods. By contrast, policies creating incentives for a more sober lifestyle have a positive effect on long-run welfare, even though they tend to decrease productivity and output growth by inducing economic agents to allocate less efforts and resources to enhancing the production of market goods.

Moving to an empirical approach to social capital and its effect on development, Martin Paldam in Chapter 12 wonders whether social capital, understood as generalized trust, is a univocally primary determinant (in the sense that it causes, but is not caused by) of institutional progress and economic development. The analysis is based on data from the World Value Surveys and considers as underlying model useful to organize and analyse data the 'Grand Transition theory', namely the process whereby poor countries become wealthy. Both by considering the dynamic of trust within the same country (also in respect to countries that have undergone transition from socialism) and by analyzing the relationship between generalized trust, income, life satisfaction, the Transparency International's honesty/corruption index, the Gini coefficient measuring the distribution of income and the *Polity* index of democracy/dictatorship, the author concludes that generalized trust is not a primary factor for the univocal determination of economic and institutional development. It enters into a complex interconnection characterizing the socio-economic variables, which change during the Grand Transition process, and it seems to be related to economic and institutional development in an indirect way through other variables.

Moving from international comparison to a more locally oriented approach, Chapter 13 by Raffaella Nanetti, Robert Leonardi and Catalina Holguin approaches the concept of social capital by investigating the policies and strategies able to increase the stock of social capital in a particular community and to generate sustainable development outcomes. This contribution refers to a successful experimental policy program started in 1996 and aimed at generating development through social capital formation in Pianura, one of twenty neighborhoods of Naples characterized by significant social and economic problems. The Pianura neighborhood Development Program was designed as a set of integrated measures covering five interrelated sub-programs – transport, environmental safety, community services, production and commercial activities, and the mandated evaluation – and constructed around nine operational measures concerning, for example, the local road system, the hydro-geological securing of hillsides, and parks and green spaces. The data clearly show the incremental growth of social capital in Pianura over the course of the Program, together with significant improvements in the neighborhood's physical and service infrastructure and economic opportunities. The experience documented in the chapter demonstrates that creating social capital through ad hoc programs is possible, and that if strategies and programmes aimed at developing social capital are to be successful, they must be longitudinal, since this makes it possible to weather inevitable delays in their implementation and events which may give the impression of unfulfilled promises.

Acknowledgements

This edited collection stems from the International Workshop on 'Social Capital, Corporate Social Responsibility and Sustainable Economic Development', which was held in Trento, Italy, on 24 and 25 July 2007 and organized by EconomEtica, the interuniversity Centre for Economic Ethics and Corporate Social Responsibility located at the Milano-Bicocca University and the LaSER (Laboratory for Social responsibility, Ethics and Rationality) of the Department of Economics, Trento University. Organizational and financial support by both these institutions is gratefully acknowledged.

Moreover, we gratefully acknowledge the financial support received from the Italian Ministry of University and Research under the two national research projects (PRIN) n. 2007B8SC7A and n. 20085BHY5T that aided us in the research activity for the revision and production of the final version of these texts.

References

M. Bacharach (2006) *Beyond Individual Choice, Teams and Frames in Game Theory*, edited by N. Gold and R. Sugden (Princeton, NJ: Princeton University Press).

M. Faillo and L. Sacconi (2008) 'Norm Compliance: The Contribution of Behavioral Economics Models', in A. Innocenti and P. Sbriglia (eds), *Games, Rationality and Behavior* (London: Palgrave Macmillan).

M. Faillo, S. Ottone and L. Sacconi (2008) 'Compliance by Believing: An Experimental Exploration on Social Norms and Impartial Agreements', working paper N. 10/2008, Dipartimento di Economia dell'Università di Trento.

J. Geanakoplos, D. Pearce and E. Stacchetti (1989) 'Psychological Games and Sequential Rationality', *Games and Economic Behavior*, 1, 60–79.

A. Rabin (1993) 'Incorporating Fairness into Game Theory', *American Economic Review*, 83(5), 1281–1302.

L. Sacconi (2007) 'Incomplete Contracts and Corporate Ethics: A Game Theoretical Model under Fuzzy Information', in F. Cafaggi, A. Nicita and U. Pagano (eds), *Legal Orderings and Economic Institutions* (London: Routledge).

L. Sacconi (2010a) 'A Rawlsian View of Corporate Social Responsibility (Part I): The Multistakeholder Model of Corporate', in L. Sacconi, M. Blair, R.E. Freeman and A. Vercelli (eds), *Corporate Social Responsibility and Corporate Governance: The Contribution of Economic Theory and Related Disciplines* (London: Palgrave Macmillan).

L. Sacconi (2010b) 'A Rawlsian View of CSR and the Game Theory of its Implementation (Part II): Fairness and Equilibrium', in L. Sacconi, M. Blair, R.E. Freeman and A. Vercelli (eds), *Corporate Social Responsibility and Corporate Governance: The Contribution of Economic Theory and Related Disciplines* (London: Palgrave Macmillan).

L. Sacconi and G. Degli Antoni (2009) 'A Theoretical Analysis of the Relationship between Social Capital and Corporate Social Responsibility: Concepts and Definitions', in S. Sacchetti and R. Sugden (eds), *Knowledge in the Development of Economies. Institutional Choices under Globalisation* (London: Edward Elgar Publishing Ltd).

L. Sacconi and M. Faillo (2010) 'Conformity, Reciprocity and the Sense of Justice. How Social Contract-based Preferences and Beliefs Explain Norm Compliance: The Experimental Evidence', *Constitutional Political Economy*, 21(2), 171–201.

L. Sacconi and S. Moretti (2008) 'A Fuzzy Logic and Default Reasoning Model of Social Norms and Equilibrium Selection in Games under Unforeseen Contingencies', *International Journal of Uncertainty, Fuzziness and Knowledge Based Systems*, 16(1), 59–81.

Part I

New Perspectives on the Economic Theory of Institutions, Individual Preferences and Social Norms

1
A Plea for Unconventional Economics

Bruno S. Frey

1. Neoclassics and unconventional economics

This chapter endeavors to convince the reader that *unconventional economics* is helpful to better understand issues concerned with social capital, corporate social responsibility and sustainable development. I hasten to add that this does *not* mean that standard neoclassical economics is superfluous and a waste of effort. Quite the contrary, neoclassics is important as a background theory into which the unorthodox elements can be introduced. Thus, the basic tenet of neoclassics, the strictly individualistic approach in which individuals seek to maximize their utility and are restricted by all sorts of economic (such as income or time) and institutional (such as the organization of industry or the governance of the state) constraints, is accepted and followed. Indeed, I presume standard neoclassics to be known by the reader both with respect to its fundamental features as well as to its specific theories and results.

I see the future of economics in approaches to the study of specific issues that deviate from what may be seen as the 'straitjacket' of orthodox economics as taught, for example, in graduate schools all over the world. I want to emphasize, that over the years many different economists have brought forth new ideas that are incompatible with standard economics, but I leave it to the respective authors to propagate them. The concrete unconventional ideas proposed here are only hinted at rather than thoroughly discussed. The goal is to provide a broad survey of what an unconventional economics might look like. I intend to present *concrete* unconventional ideas with respect to content and way of analysis. This is based on my conviction that methodological discussions normally are of no avail and have no noticeable effect on how economics proceeds in the future. The unconventional ideas presented here are the results of studies undertaken together with my co-workers. These ideas are presented because I happen to believe them to be interesting and potentially relevant.

Section 2 discusses *institutional innovations* for the organization of the public sector and of democratic institutions: flexible political units and flexible citizenship. Section 3 deals with three selected contributions from *Psychological Economics*: extrinsic and intrinsic human motivation, insights from happiness research and procedural utility. The last section concludes that unconventional economics may indeed contribute much to modern economics and should, therefore, be assigned a larger role in teaching and research.

2. Institutional innovations: Organization of the public sector and democratic institutions

There are many different areas in which new institutions can be devised with the purpose of making the public sector more efficient and responsive to the preferences of the citizens. Here, the discussion is restricted to two specific innovations. The first suggests flexibility with respect to political units, the second flexibility with respect to citizenship.

2.1. Flexible political institutions

Most politicians are convinced that the modern world requires larger political units. This has, for example, been one reason, though not the only one, for European unification. Many economists agree with this view, pointing out the existence of economies of scale. Other economists emphasize that the provision of public goods is more efficient when supply is decentralized because it allows preferences varying over the geographical space to be taken into account. Moreover, competition between political suppliers raises efficiency. These economists suggest federalism, in which the local units have taxing power and the right to allocate expenditures as they see fit.

The two proposals can only be combined by a compromise. The suggested size of a political unit is too small to fully exploit the economies of scale, and too large to fully exploit the advantages of decentralization.

The dilemma may be overcome by establishing *more flexible democratic political institutions*. They must be able to adjust to the 'geography of problems' instead of being restricted by traditional frontiers between political units. The idea of FOCJ[1] presents an alternative institution; an institution that is able to enjoy both the advantages of centralization and decentralization. FOCJ stands for 'Functional, Overlapping, and Competing Jurisdictions'.

The federal units proposed here thus have four essential characteristics:

Functional

A particular public service that benefits only a certain geographical area should be financed by the people living in that area, that is, there should be no spillover. The various governmental units providing different functions can cater to regional differences in the populations' preferences or, more precisely, to its demands. To minimize costs, these units have to exploit economies of scale in production. As the latter may strongly differ between functions (e.g. between schools, police, hospitals, power plants and defense), there is an additional reason for uni-functional (or few-functional) governmental units of different sizes. This is the central idea of *'fiscal equivalence'*, as proposed by Olson (1969) and Oates (1972). This endogeneity of the size of governmental units constitutes an essential part of FOCJ. However, fiscal equivalence theory has been little concerned with decision-making within functional units. The supply process is either left unspecified or it is assumed that the mobility of persons (and of firms, a fact rarely mentioned) automatically induces these units to cater for individual preferences.

Overlapping

FOCJ may overlap in two respects: (a) FOCJ catering to different functions may overlap; (b) two or more FOCJ catering for the same function may geographically intersect (e.g. a multitude of school FOCJ may exist in the same geographical area). An individual or a political community normally belongs to various FOCJ at the same time. FOCJ need not be physically contiguous, and they need not have a monopoly over a certain area of land. Thus, this concept completely differs from archaic nationalism with its fighting over pieces of land. It also breaks with the notion of federalist theory that units at the same level may not overlap. On the other hand, it is in this respect similar to Buchanan's (1965) *'clubs'*, which may intersect.

Competing

The heads of FOCJ are induced to conform closely to their members' preferences by two mechanisms: while the individuals' and communities' possibilities to *exit* mimics market competition (Hirschman 1970), their right to *vote* establishes political competition (see Mueller 2003). It should be noted that migration is only one means of exit; often, membership in a particular FOCUS (as the singular of FOCJ is called) can be discontinued without changing one's location. Exit is not restricted to individuals or firms; as said before, political communities as a whole, or parts of them, may also exercise this option. Moreover, exit may be total or only partial. In the latter case, an individual or community only participates in a restricted set of FOCUS activities.

For FOCJ to establish competition between governments, exit should be as unrestrained as possible. In contrast, entry needs not necessarily be free. As for individuals in Buchanan-type clubs, jurisdictions and individuals may be asked to pay a price if they want to join a particular FOCUS and benefit from its public goods. The existing members of the particular FOCUS have to democratically decide whether a new member pays an adequate entry price and is thus welcome.

Competition also needs to be furthered by political institutions, as the exit option does not suffice to induce governments to act efficiently. Citizens should elect the persons managing the FOCJ directly, and should be given the right to initiate popular referenda on specific issues. These democratic institutions are known to raise efficiency in the sense of caring well for individual preferences (for elections, see Downs 1957; Mueller 2003; for referenda Frey and Stutzer 2006).

Jurisdictions

A FOCUS is a democratic governmental unit with authority over its citizens, including the power to tax. According to the two types of overlap, two forms of membership can be distinguished: (i) The lowest political unit (normally the community is a member), and all corresponding citizens automatically become citizens of the FOCJ to which their community belongs. In that case, an individual can only exit via mobility; (ii) Individuals may choose freely whether they want to belong to a particular FOCUS, but while they are one of its citizens, they are subject to its authority. Such FOCJ may be non-voluntary in the sense that one must belong to a FOCUS providing for a certain function, for example, to a school FOCUS, and must pay the corresponding taxes (an analogy here is health insurance, which in many countries is mandatory but individuals are allowed to choose an insurance company). The citizens of such a school FOCUS may then decide that everyone must pay taxes in order to finance the particular school, irrespective of whether one has children. With respect to FOCJ providing functions with significant redistributive effects, a minimal regulation by the central government may be in order so that, for example, citizens without children cannot join 'school FOCJ', that do not, in fact, offer any schooling and have correspondingly low (or zero) taxes. In this respect, Buchanan-type clubs differ from FOCJ, because they are always voluntary while membership in a FOCUS can be obligatory.

Flexible institutions in history and today

Decentralized, overlapping political units have been an important feature of European *history*. The competition between governments in the Holy Roman Empire of German Nations, especially in today's Italy and Germany, has been intensive. Many of these governments were small. Many scholars attribute the rise of Europe to this diversity and competition of governmental units, which fostered technical, economic and artistic innovation (see, e.g. Hayek 1960; Jones 1987; Rosenberg and Birdzell 1986; Weede 1993). The unification of Italy and Germany in the nineteenth century, which has often been praised as a major advance, partially ended the stimulating competition between governments and led to deadly struggles between nation states. Some smaller states escaped unification; Liechtenstein, Luxembourg, Monaco, San Marino and Switzerland stayed politically independent, and at the same time grew rich.

The above-mentioned governmental units were not FOCJ in the sense outlined in this contribution, but they shared the characteristic of competing for labor and capital (including artistic capital) among each other. However, history also reveals examples of jurisdictions even closer to FOCJ. The highly successful Hanse prospered from the twelfth to the sixteenth century, and comprised inter alia Lübeck, Bremen, Köln (today German), Stettin and Danzig (today Polish), Kaliningrad (today Russian), Riga, Reval and Dorpat (today parts of the Baltic republics) and Groningen and Deventer (today Dutch); furthermore, London (England), Bruges and Antwerp (today Belgian) and Novgorod (today Russian) were *Handelskontore* or associated members. It was clearly a functional governmental unit providing for trade rules and facilities and was not geographically contiguous.

There are also *contemporary examples* of institutions similar to FOCJ. In two countries, functional, overlapping and competing jurisdictions exist to some degree. They do not in all cases meet all the requirements of FOCJ specified above but they nevertheless show that democratic functional jurisdictions are viable.

Single-purpose governments, called *special districts*, play a significant role in the *American* federalist system. Their number has increased more quickly than other types of jurisdictions (Zax 1988). There are both autonomous and democratically organized as well as dependent special districts (e.g. for fire prevention, recreation and parks). Empirical research suggests that the former type is significantly more efficient (Mehay 1984). Existing jurisdictions tend to oppose the formation of special districts. In order not to threaten the monopoly power of existing municipalities, statutes in 18 states prohibit new municipalities within a specified distance of existing municipalities; in various states there is a minimum population size required and various other administrative restrictions have been introduced (see, e.g. Nelson 1990). Empirical studies reveal that these barriers tend to reduce the relative efficiency of the local administration (Deno and Mehay 1985; Di Lorenzo 1981), and tend to boost local government expenditures (Martin and Wagner 1978).

Many cantons in *Switzerland* have a structure of overlapping and competing functional jurisdictions that share many features of FOCJ. For example, in canton Zurich (with a population of 1.2 million, a size of 1700 km^2 and a tax revenue of CHF 2800 million) there are 171 political communes (with a tax revenue of CHF 3900 million), which in themselves are composed of three to six independently managed, democratically organized communes devoted to specific functions and raising their own taxes. Examples of such types of functional communes cannot only be found in the canton of Zurich but also in the cantons of Glarus and Thurgau (for the latter, see Casella and Frey 1992). Cantonal bureaucracy and politicians have made various efforts to suppress this diversity of functional communes. However, most of these attempts were thwarted because the population is most satisfied with the public services provided. The example from Switzerland – which is generally considered to be a well organized and administered country – shows that a multiplicity of functional jurisdictions under democratic control is not a theorist's wishful thinking but has worked out well in reality.

2.2. Flexible citizenship

Traditionally, citizenship is a relationship between an individual and a state, in which an individual owes allegiance to that state and in turn is entitled to its protection.

Three aspects of this definition have to be noted:

- The actors involved are the citizens and the state. Today, citizenship is a unique and monopolistic relationship between an individual and a particular nation. It is strongly shaped geographically because most of the government services involved are only provided to residents, that is, citizens living within the boundaries of the respective state.
- The citizens have both rights and obligations. The rights refer to the political sphere (i.e. the citizens have the right to vote and to hold public office), to the economic sphere (i.e. the citizens have the right to become economically active as employees or employers), as well as to the social sphere (i.e. the citizens are protected against economic hardship within the welfare state).
- The relationship between an individual and the state goes well beyond an exchange of taxes for public services. Rather, the citizen 'owes allegiance' to the state. The citizens are expected to be public spirited and to exhibit civic virtue. The relationship is thus partly non-functional and relies on the intrinsic motivation (see next section) of the citizens and the community of people who share loyalty and identity. This aspect distinguishes the new type of citizenship proposed here from being purely a customer or member of an organization, as theoretically analyzed in the Economic Theory of Clubs (Buchanan 1965).

The process of globalization, which brings a decrease in communication and transportation costs, undermines the geographically based concept of citizenship for two reasons: first, with increasing mobility of individuals, a rising number of individuals are living in countries of which they are not citizens. Often, they live in a country only for a short period of time. Then they enjoy part of the rights of citizens, but do not have to carry the respective obligations. Second, the transaction costs for delivering government services to non-residents are decreasing dramatically. An example is education, which can be increasingly supplied via the Internet to non-residents. Thus, government institutions are becoming more and more virtual (see Colander 2000).

The existing concept of citizenship can be generalized by making citizenship more flexible (see more fully Frey 2003).

Extending national citizenship

- *Temporary Citizenship.* An individual should be able to choose for a predetermined period to become a citizen of a particular political unit, for instance because he or she is working and living in a country for a specific period of time.
- *Multiple Citizenships.* For persons simultaneously working and living in various countries, a good solution might be to split up the citizenship into various parts. The rights going with the citizenship must be adjusted accordingly. In particular, the voting rights are to reflect the fact that a person chooses to split up citizenship among several nations. In the computer age, there is no problem whatsoever in allowing for fractional votes.
- *Partial Citizenship.* An individual might be a citizen of a political unit with respect to one particular function, while being a citizen of another political unit with respect to other functions. In referenda, the voting rights should accordingly only extend to issues referring to the respective function.

Citizenship in various types of organizations

A person may become a citizen of an organization other than the nation. The following possibilities are conceivable:

- *Levels of government.* Citizenship might refer to the national level – which is the rule – but also to a lower level, such as the region, province or commune (the latter being the case in Switzerland) or to a higher level, such as the European Union.
- *Governmental sub-organizations.* Individuals might choose to become a citizen of only part of a government, such as the diplomatic service, the military or the social security administration.
- *Quasi-governmental organizations.* There are many organizations close to the public sector in which individuals might become citizens. Universities are such an example. Indeed, the concept of the *'Universitätsbürger'* (university citizen) is well known in the German-speaking academic system. It obviously means much more than being an 'employee' of a university. Rather, it means that one is prepared to commit oneself to the academic life beyond considerations of short-term, purely personal benefits and costs.

- *Non-governmental organizations* (NGOs). Citizenship may be of organizations such as churches, clubs (e.g. the Rotary Club, the Boy Scouts or even sport clubs such as Manchester United or FC Barcelona), action groups (e.g. the World Wildlife Fund, 'Médecins sans Frontières' or the Red Cross) and functional organizations (e.g. ICANN, the 'Internet Cooperation for Assigned Names and Numbers'). Yet other organizations for which citizenship may be considered are profit-oriented firms. Citizens of firms have a special relationship, which goes beyond just being a customer or employee or stakeholder. Shareholders have the power to influence a decision according to their number of shares, while stakeholders have no formal voting right at all, but exert pressure outside of established channels, for example via the media or demonstrations. In contrast, each citizen of a firm has a vote according to generally accepted democratic principles. While these principles differ, they are not necessarily incompatible with each other. Citizenship in firm can exist quite well along with shareholder rights.

Citizenship in the broadest sense proposed here is based on voluntary contracts between the persons aspiring toward citizenship in a particular organization and the organization offering the possibility of citizenship. These contracts establish a special bond and are necessarily incomplete because it is impossible to state all the contingencies the future might hold.

An essential feature of citizenship is that an organization can expect a measure of allegiance and loyalty from its members. Citizens are prepared to abstain from exploiting all short-term advantages. 'Citizenship' means that the members have an intrinsically based motivation to support 'their' organization beyond personal calculations. This also means that citizens are prepared to cooperate in the provision of public goods, even when pure egoists would try to free ride.

3. Innovations from economics and psychology

Over the past decade or so, social psychology and economics have established increasingly close interactions. In previous times, there were certainly some economists interested in integrating theories and concepts from social psychology into their own discipline but they had no impact on the field. Only very few economists such as Duesenberry (1949), Easterlin (1974) or Scitovsky (1976) received some attention for a limited time, but their contributions did not become part of economic doctrine. The situation today is very different. Economics and Psychology – or as it is also sometimes misleadingly called Behavioral Economics – has become one of the 'hot' fields in economics and attracts scholars from the best universities. Accordingly, the state of knowledge has been surveyed various times (e.g. Frey and Benz 2007; Frey and Stutzer 2001, 2007; Mullainathan and Thaler 2000; Rabin 1998).

This section focuses on three areas – *Human Motivation and Crowding Theory* (subsection 3.1), *Subjective Well-being* or *Happiness* (subsection 3.2) and *Procedural Utility* (subsection 3.3). In these areas unconventional approaches have brought new insights and impulses into standard economic theory. There are certainly other fields where this could also be demonstrated, in particular behavioral anomalies or paradoxes.[2] But orthodox economics was not sustainedly affected by these insights after all. It seems, or that is at least what I hope, that the inputs into economics from social psychology with respect to motivation and well-being are able to have a more lasting effect.

3.1. Human motivation

Standard homo oeconomicus with extrinsic incentives

Standard economics has a generally accepted rational theory to explain human behavior. Individuals are assumed to maximize their own utility subject to a set of constraints, most importantly income. Preferences are taken to be constant. It follows that individuals react systematically to changes in relative prices. In particular, they reduce an activity (for instance the consumption of a particular good or service) when its cost (or price) rises compared to other activities, keeping other influences constant (*ceteris paribus*). Economists accordingly predict changes in behavior by observing the measurable changes in costs. Thus, for instance, when the cost of polluting the environment rises (for instance because a tax has been imposed on the exhaust of pollutants), individuals and firms are expected to emit less. They have a selfish incentive to change their behavior (in this case to switch to a car or a production process with less pollution). Econometric analyses with many different real life data have indeed demonstrated that this model of behavior applies under a wide set of conditions.

This model has successfully been extended to areas outside the economy. Economists have, for instance, made noteworthy contributions to decisions in the family, especially on marriage, the number of children, abortion and divorce (Becker et al. 1977), on drug addiction (Becker and Murphy 1988) or on religious practices (Iannaccone 1998). This 'economic' or 'rational choice' approach to the social sciences (Becker 1976; Frey 1999, 2001; Lazear 2000) has influenced other social sciences considerably, most notably political science (Public Choice), sociology and jurisprudence (Law and Economics).

One of the great advantages of this model of human behavior is that it is simple and robust and can therefore be applied to many conditions and areas of study. It provides an overarching, generally accepted theory to economics. In contrast, (social) psychology has identified a great number of detailed effects relating to human behavior. But it is, at least from the point of view of an economist, difficult to see which effect applies when, and what happens if the effects are contradictory. The absence of an overarching and generally accepted socio-psychological theory does not help to determine which effect applies in one area but not in another one. Economists consider the use of a simple, and generally accepted, theory of human behavior a decisive advantage of their science, and it seems to me that social psychology could in this respect learn from economics.

The economic model of behavior is simple – sometimes *too* simple. Most importantly, it has been proved impossible to explain the empirical observation that individuals contribute considerably to a public good even though free riding is the rational choice (under anonymity and in one-shot situations). For instance, the expected punishment for tax evasion in most countries is so small that even risk-averse individuals should cheat much more than is actually observed (e.g. Alm et al. 1992).

Crowding theory with intrinsic and extrinsic incentives

To solve the puzzles mentioned, social psychology has proved to be of great help in the past and is likely to be so also in the future. Economists have long considered only *one* motivational force, namely *extrinsic incentives*, often – but not necessarily – in the form of monetary rewards. Social psychologists have taught us that it is useful to also consider *intrinsic motivation*. A pertinent example is tax morale. But as long as the two motivations are independent of each other, no major problem arises for economic theory. The dynamic relationship between extrinsic and intrinsic motivation in psychology, often called 'hidden costs of rewards' (Lepper and Greene 1978) or 'self-determination theory' (Deci and Ryan 2000), introduces a new element. When an external intervention strongly undermines intrinsic motivation, the relative price effect is counteracted and the outcome may be the *exact opposite* of the normal prediction by economists. This may be very relevant for economics. For instance, inducing employees to put in more effort by offering them higher compensation may backfire if the employees targeted are thereby also led to reduce their work morale, a specific kind of intrinsic motivation (see Frey and Osterloh 2002).

The systematic relationship between extrinsic and intrinsic motivation has been introduced into economics as '*Crowding Theory*' (Frey 1992, 1997). It is taken into account that there may be 'crowding out' as well as 'crowding in'. This import from social psychology has proved to be useful far beyond the analysis of pay for performance systems. An example is the siting of locally unwanted projects such as a nuclear plant where offering monetary compensation tends to *reduce*, rather than to increase, the willingness of the local population to accept it. Another important example is the compensation of managers geared to 'performance', which has led to an explosion of their incomes (Frey and Osterloh 2002, 2005). Considerable empirical evidence has been collected for many different areas (see Frey and Jegen 2001 for a survey). Such research should be of interest to social psychologists because the applications extend to important real life situations, which have so far not been treated by them. However, such transfer of results from economics to psychology seems to be rather slow, if it takes place at all.

3.2. Happiness economics: Measuring subjective well-being

Macroeconomics, the analysis of economic variables such as production, employment or inflation, works with highly aggregate data. The skilful reduction of the multiple dimensions of these variables into a single one, by using the monetary evaluation by market prices, has allowed economists to develop empirically testable theories of economic growth and fluctuations. Aggregate income, or gross national product (GNP), has become a generally accepted measure of economic activity used by virtually everyone dealing with economic affairs. This is no small achievement and it might serve as an example to social psychology.

Since the beginning of the 1930s economists used utility as a unit to be maximized but thought that the concept was not measurable. Economic theory simply *assumed* that whatever individuals do is the result of maximizing their own utility. Following this approach, even suicide is a utility maximizing act: it is *revealed* to be superior to any other alternative because otherwise this voluntary act would not have been undertaken.

Insights from social psychology have strongly changed this view recently. Evidence has accumulated showing that not all behavior is in the individual's own best interest. But to make progress, a measure of utility independent of behavior is needed. Psychologists have convincingly demonstrated that it is indeed possible to approximate individual utility in a useful way by surveys on subjective well-being or happiness (e.g. Diener et al. 1999; Kahneman et al. 1999). This enables economics to leave the self-imposed straitjacket of solely revealed preferences and to analyze the determinants of well-being. This is of central importance for economics because it is agreed that the ultimate aim of economic activity is to promote individual happiness (Frey and Stutzer 2002a, 2002b; Frey et al. 2008).

Research on happiness has become a truly transdisciplinary endeavor. What has been aimed at in many other areas has here been achieved in a natural way serving as a shining example. Economists have, above all, learned that the use of self-reported data presents a most useful addition to the data sets prepared by statistical offices and normally used by them. They have, moreover, gained insights into how perceptions and expectations can be dealt with. An example is the rising aspiration level spurred by increasing income.

Some of the results of happiness research support the conventional economic views while others clearly contradict the standard assumption of economics. The standard assumption that the higher an individual's income is, the higher is his or her utility, but at a marginally decreasing rate, conforms to standard theory. In contrast, the fact that over time per capita national income rises but reported subjective well-being stays about the same (Easterlin 1974) strongly *contradicts* conventional economics. Another instance refers to the evaluation of unemployment. Following the 'New Classical Macroeconomics' as well as other parts of standard economics, unemployment is voluntary. People choose to go out of employment because they find the burden of work and the wages unattractive compared to having leisure as an unemployed person and receiving unemployment compensation. In contrast to this view, but in line with much psychological evidence, happiness research has convincingly established that being unemployed causes significant stress and reduces well-being in a magnitude similar to divorce (e.g. Clark and Oswald 1994).

3.3. Procedural utility

Procedural utility means that people not only value actual outcomes, that is, the '*what*', but also the conditions and processes which lead to these outcomes, that is, the '*how*'. Procedural utility thus represents a completely different approach to human well-being than the standard approach applied in economics. The economic concept of utility as generally applied today is outcome-oriented: individual utility is seen as a result of benefits and costs associated with instrumental outcomes. In contrast, procedural utility refers to the non-instrumental pleasures and displeasures of processes.

Procedural utility is seen as an important determinant of human well-being that has to be incorporated more widely into economic theory and empirical research (see, more fully, Frey et al. 2004). So far, this has been largely neglected.

The concept

Economic analysis has focused on instrumental outcomes ever since the positivistic movement in economics in the 1930s. Without doubt, this was of paramount importance for the success of the economic approach to behavior in the social sciences. Obviously, individuals do care a lot about instrumental outcomes as reflected in the costs and benefits of available alternatives; economics has derived a powerful model of human behavior based on this insight.

Paradoxically, the positivistic movement in economics in itself did not imply such a focus on instrumental outcomes. In fact, since then economics has been deliberately vague about how human preferences are defined. In the 1930s, economists just gave up on the idea that utility could be observed directly and adopted the view that the only way to infer utility was from revealed behavior. But in principle, what individuals value could be anything. Economics is thus also potentially open to the idea that individuals enjoy procedural utility.

Procedural utility, however, presents a challenge to the concept of utility as it is *practically* used in much of economics. The existing theoretical cornerstones of economics, for instance, expected utility theory or game theory, generally define preferences over monetary payoffs. Thus, economics models as applied today often adopt a narrow view of human utility by focusing on instrumental outcomes. The notion that instrumental outcomes are not the only source of utility and not the only driving force behind behavior has become almost completely obsolete in economic analysis.[3] Procedural utility, in contrast, means that there is something beyond instrumental outputs as they are captured in a traditional economic utility function. People may have preferences about *how* instrumental outcomes are generated. These preferences about processes generate procedural utility.

Building blocks

Procedural utility rests on three foundations, which deviate in important respects from the utility concept normally applied in economics:

- Procedural utility emphasizes utility as *well-being*. Utility is understood in a broad sense as pleasure and pain, positive and negative affect or life satisfaction.[4] This reinstates the original economic idea that utility consists of everything that individuals value.
- Closely connected with this first point, procedural utility focuses on *non-instrumental* determinants of utility. It is not exclusively concerned with instrumental outcomes that are brought about by, for example, different decision-making procedures. Rather, processes and institutions under which people live and act are seen as independent sources of utility.[5]
- Procedural utility emerges because people have a *sense of self*. The concept thus incorporates a central tenet of social psychology into economics, namely that people care about how they perceive themselves as human beings and how they are perceived by others (see, e.g. Baumeister 1998 for a survey).[6] Procedural utility exists because procedures provide important feedback information to the self. Specifically, they address innate psychological needs of self-determination differently. Psychologists have identified three such psychological needs to be paramount: autonomy, relatedness and competence. The desire for autonomy encompasses the experience to self-organize one's own actions or to be causal. The need for relatedness refers to the desire to feel connected to others in love and care, and to be treated as a respected group member within social groups. And the need for competence refers to the propensity to control the environment and experience oneself as capable and effective. Different procedures can be expected to provide different procedural goods serving these innate needs; in this respect they contribute to individual well-being irrespective of instrumental outcomes traditionally studied by economists.

Procedural utility thus can be defined as the well-being people gain from living and acting under institutionalized processes as they contribute to a positive sense of self, addressing innate needs of autonomy, relatedness and competence.

Procedural fairness as a special case

The general concept of procedural utility can be illustrated with one of the most prominent studies in the field of *procedural fairness*, which can be considered as the best investigated aspect of procedural utility (e.g. Lind and Tyler 1988). Lind et al. (1993) investigate a situation in which actual litigants are involved in an arbitration process. At the end of arbitration, the court orders an award; the parties can decide whether they want to accept this award or reject it and go to trial. Economists would typically study such a situation by considering the costs and benefits of accepting an award. Indeed, their likely predictions are borne out: award acceptance depends on instrumental outcomes like the ratio between the actual award and the amount originally demanded, or the litigants evaluation of whether the outcome was favorable or unfavorable (which can be seen as a good proxy for the expected net benefit of going to trial). But overall, the fairness of the arbitration procedure is found to be much more important for acceptance than instrumental outcomes. Litigants who judge the arbitration process as fair are much more likely to accept the court-ordered award, irrespective of instrumental outcomes. This result emerges because procedures convey important feedback information to the self, thereby affecting individuals' well-being. Procedures seen as fair are, for example, those that give individuals 'voice'. Being given a say in issues concerning oneself generates procedural utility because it addresses innate needs of self-determination such as autonomy and competence, and, because it is an important signal about one's standing in a group, it affects innate needs of relatedness.

Applications to institutions

The value of the concept of procedural utility can be illustrated by applying it to the economic analysis of institutions as undertaken by New Institutional Economics. This approach studies institutions as decision-making mechanisms that lead to different instrumental outcomes for the parties involved. The category of procedural utility, in contrast, allows one to highlight aspects disregarded by this kind of analysis, namely that institutions also directly contribute to people's well-being when they serve innate needs of autonomy, relatedness and competence. This, in turn, has potentially important implications for the design of institutions. If individuals' overall evaluation of a situation (in the sense of overall satisfaction or utility) depends on utility from instrumental outcomes as well as utility from the procedure used, one cannot just focus on instrumental outcomes alone. An unfavorable instrumental outcome is more likely to be accepted if the procedure applied was 'good', and a favorable outcome might provide little overall satisfaction if the procedure that brought it about was 'bad'. The concept of procedural utility thus sheds new light on the study of institutions.

Sources of procedural utility

The sources of procedural utility can be classified into two broad categories:

- Procedural utility that people get from institutions as such. People have preferences about how allocating and redistributive decisions are taken. At the level of society, the most important formal systems for reaching decisions are the price system (market), democracy, hierarchy and bargaining (Dahl and Lindblom 1953). People may gain procedural utility from these institutions because they express judgments about the people involved. For example, a constitution that secures civil liberties like freedom of speech may greatly contribute to people's self-worth. In contrast, a constitution that denies offenders their political rights may be deeply disturbing to the people's sense of self, irrespective of instrumental outcomes. Institutions thus have a direct effect on individuals' well-being by addressing innate needs of autonomy, relatedness and competence.
- Procedural utility is involved with the interactions between people. People evaluate actions toward them not only by their consequences, but also by how they feel treated by other persons. Institutions shape such treatment significantly; they provide examples for people in interrelationships on how to treat each other in everyday interactions. For instance, labor law and company statutes are shaping the interaction between managers and employees. Or, the organization of the health care system is guiding the relationship between medical suppliers and patients. Institutions thus also have an indirect effect on individuals' well-being through motivation and through restrictions in the issue of how people are treated, thereby affecting their sense of self.

There is, of course, often a smooth transition between the two categories. Institutions, on the one hand, select and motivate people and guide them in how to treat their fellow workers, citizens and consumers. On the other hand, people who evaluate institutions, processes or authorities usually base their judgment on the treatment experienced by the specific people involved.

Procedural utility thus may emerge at different, and sometimes hard to distinguish, levels. Nevertheless, the multitude of sources does not mean that the concept could be applied arbitrarily. Whether procedural utility emerges from institutions like the market mechanism, democratic decision-making or hierarchy as such, or whether it stems from procedural differences on a smaller scale, for example, from procedural differences within an organization, a political system or a legal framework, there is a common ground to all these channels of impact: individuals judge processes positively to the extent that they address innate needs of self-determination. Theoretical hypotheses can therefore be derived. With respect to procedural differences on a smaller scale, there is a clear understanding from the large literature on 'procedural fairness' or 'procedural justice' about what constitutes good procedure (e.g. Lind and Tyler 1988). As procedures on this level often involve how authority is exercised in organizations, public administrations or legal contexts, innate needs are mainly affected by relational information that procedures convey, such as assessments of impartiality, trustworthiness of superiors and authorities, the extent to which individuals feel they are treated with dignity and the extent to which individuals are given voice. When institutions on a larger scale are considered, like democracy or hierarchy, one can derive similar hypotheses. For example, democracy can be expected to have positive procedural utility effects because it enhances individuals' perception of self-determination. Hierarchy, in contrast, is likely to produce procedural disutility because it interferes with individuals' self-determination.

4. Toward an unconventional economics

This chapter has made a plea for unconventional economics. The deviations from standard neoclassical economics have been shown to be in two directions: proposing institutional innovations and introducing insights from other social sciences, in particular psychology. Flexible political units (FOCJ) and flexible citizenship have been given as examples of the first direction. Extensions of human motivations beyond extrinsic incentives, the measurement of utility in happiness research and introducing procedural utility are examples for the second direction. It must be emphasized again that these are only a few selected cases in an area in which the author has long been involved. For other instances of leaving the straitjacket of strict neoclassics, the corresponding literature has been referred to.

Despite these many interesting and relevant innovations in economics, there cannot be any doubt that conventional economics is still absolutely dominant. One reason is the introduction of homogenized doctoral programs that tend to follow the received doctrines and treat unconventional ideas lightly, and in many cases not at all. While such programs undoubtedly help to raise the average standard of what it considered 'good' or 'competent' economics, it is less helpful to bring together economics with other disciplines, and it threatens to lead to stagnation. The doctoral students accumulate an extensive capital stock of conventional neoclassical knowledge, which they are unlikely to throw overboard later in their careers. A similar process takes place in contemporary economic research because the need to publish in refereed journals forces young (and potentially particularly innovative) scholars to play safe and to follow the conventions of the received doctrine. If they do not yield to the demands of the two to four referees – who almost by necessity agree only with the conventional neoclassical view – they find it nearly impossible to publish.

As a result of these two forces, standard economics is able to retain a dominant position. But there is a strong counterforce. Only those scholars who are coming forth with innovative ideas such as Schumpeter and Keynes in the past, or Akerlof and Sen in the present will be able to play a prominent role in future academic economics. This strategy not only requires ingenuity but also a willingness to take the risk of deviating from the crowd.

Notes

1. See, more extensively, Frey and Eichenberger (1999, 2004). A critical discussion is provided by Vanberg (2000) and Blatter and Ingram (2000). Kyriacou (2006) discusses and applies FOCJ to a topical issue, the management of ethnic conflicts.
2. The work of social psychologists, above all the article by Kahneman and Tversky (1979) and the collection of essays in Kahneman et al. (1982), for some time received considerable attention by economists, e.g. Schoemaker (1982), Machina (1987), Thaler (1991), Frey and Eichenberger (1994).
3. An exception may be the utility gained from gambling, which was already considered by Pascal (1670), and later by Marschak (1950) and by Von Neumann and Morgenstern (1944) to be incompatible with expected utility maximization. The most prominent economist, who has repeatedly argued that economic choice models should combine preferences for outcome with those for processes, is Sen (1995, 1997).
4. Kahneman has coined the term 'experienced utility' for this notion of utility, in contrast to traditional 'decision utility' (e.g. Kahneman et al. 1997).
5. Non-instrumental human motives of people who are self-aware and who self-reflect have previously entered economic analysis, for example in the form of identity (e.g. Akerlof and Kranton 2000), respect, self-esteem and pride (e.g. Khalil 1996; Köszegi 2002a, 2002b; Lea and Webley 1997), self-signaling, goal completion, mastery and meaning (e.g. Loewenstein 1999) or status (e.g. Frank 1985).
6. An alternative way of describing that individuals have a reflexive consciousness is that beliefs about oneself enter the utility function directly (e.g. Akerlof and Dickens 1982).

References

G.A. Akerlof and W.T. Dickens (1982) 'The Economic Consequences of Cognitive Dissonance', *American Economic Review*, 72(3), 307–319.

G.A. Akerlof and R.E. Kranton (2000) 'Economics and Identity', *Quarterly Journal of Economics*, 115(3), 715–753.

J. Alm, G. McClelland and W.D. Schulze (1992) 'Why Do People Pay Taxes?', *Journal of Public Economics*, 48, 21–38.

R.F. Baumeister (1998) 'The Self' in D.T. Gilbert, S.T. Fiske and G. Lindzey (eds), *The Handbook of Social Psychology, vol. 1* (New York and Oxford: Oxford University Press), pp. 680–740.

G.S. Becker (1976) *The Economic Approach to Human Behavior* (Chicago: Chicago University Press).

G.S. Becker, E.M. Landes and R.T. Michael (1977) 'An Economic Analysis of Marital Instability', *Journal of Political Economy*, 85(6), 1141–1187.

G.S. Becker and K.M. Murphy (1988) 'A Theory of Rational Addiction', *Journal of Political Economy*, 96(August), 675–700.

J. Blatter and H. Ingram (2000) 'States, Markets and Beyond: Governance of Transboundary Water Resources', *Natural Resources Journal*, 40, 439–473.

J.M. Buchanan (1965) 'An Economic Theory of Clubs', *Economica*, 32(125), 1–14.

A. Casella and B.S. Frey (1992) 'Federalism and Clubs: Towards an Economic Theory of Overlapping Political Jurisdictions', *European Economic Review*, 36, 639–646.

A.E. Clark and A.J. Oswald (1994) 'Unhappiness and Unemployment', *Economic Journal*, 104, 424, 648–659.

D. Colander (2000) 'New Millenium Economics: How Did It Get This Way, and What Way Is It?', *Journal of Economic Perspectives*, 14(1), 121–132.

R.A. Dahl and C.E. Lindblom (1953) *Politics, Economics and Welfare: Planning and Politico-Economic Systems Resolved into Basic Social Processes* (Harper: New York).

E.L. Deci and R.M. Ryan (2000) 'The "What" and "Why" of Goal Pursuits: Human Needs and the Self-Determination of Behavior', *Psychological Inquiry*, 11, 227–268.

K.T. Deno and S.L. Mehay (1985) 'Institutional Constraints on Local Jurisdiction Formation', *Public Finance Quarterly*, 13, 450–463.

E. Diener, E.M. Suh, R.E. Lucas and H.L. Smith (1999) 'Subjective Well-Being: Three Decades of Progress', *Psychological Bulletin*, 125(2), 276–303.

T.J. Di Lorenzo (1981) 'Special Districts and Local Public Services', *Public Finance Quarterly*, 9, 353–367.

A. Downs (1957) *An Economic Theory of Democracy* (New York: Harper & Row).

J.S. Duesenberry (1949), *Income, Savings and the Theory of Consumer Behavior* (Cambridge, MA: Harvard University Press).

R.A. Easterlin (1974) 'Does Economic Growth Improve the Human Lot? Some Empirical Evidence' in P.A. David and M.W. Reder (eds), *Nations and Households in Economic Growth: Essays in Honor of Moses Abramowitz* (New York: Academic Press), pp. 89–125.

B.S. Frey (1992) 'Tertium Datur: Pricing, Regulating and Intrinsic Motivation', *Kyklos*, 45(2), 161–184.

B.S. Frey (1997) *Not Just for The Money. An Economic Theory of Personal Motivation* (Cheltenham, UK, and Brookfield, USA: Edward Elgar).

B.S. Frey (1999) *Economics as a Science of Human Behaviour*, 2nd rev. and extended edn. (Boston and Dordrecht: Kluwer).

B.S. Frey (2001) *Inspiring Economics: Human Motivation in Political Economy* (Cheltenham, UK, and Northampton, USA: Edward Elgar).

B.S. Frey (2003) 'Flexible Citizenship for a Global Society', *Politics, Philosophy & Economics*, 2(1), 93–114.

B.S. Frey and M. Benz (2007) 'Die psychologischen Grundlagen des Marktmodells (homo oeconomicus)' in L. von Rosenstiel und D. Frey (eds), *Enzyklopädie der Psychologie. Marktpsychologie* (Göttingen, Bern, Toronto, Seattle: Hogrefe).

B.S. Frey, M. Benz and A. Stutzer (2004) 'Introducing Procedural Utility: Not Only What, but Also How Matters', *Journal of Institutional and Theoretical Economics*, 160(3), 377–401.

B.S. Frey and R. Eichenberger (1994) 'Economic Incentives Transform Psychological Anomalies', *Journal of Economic Behavior and Organisation*, 23, 215–234.

B.S. Frey and R. Eichenberger (1999) *The New Democratic Federalism for Europe: Functional, Overlapping and Competing Jurisdictions* (Cheltenham, UK: Edward Elgar).

B.S. Frey and R. Eichenberger (2004) 'The New Democratic Federalism for Europe: Functional, Overlapping and Competing Jurisdictions' in J.G. Backhaus and D. Doering (eds), *The Political Economy of Secession* (Zürich: Verlag Neue Zürcher Zeitung).

B.S. Frey and R. Jegen (2001) 'Motivation Crowding Theory: A Survey of Empirical Evidence', *Journal of Economic Surveys*, 5, 589–611.

B.S. Frey and M. Osterloh (2002) (eds) *Successful Management by Motivation. Balancing Intrinsic and Extrinsic Incentives* (Berlin, Heidelberg, New York: Springer Verlag).

B.S. Frey and M. Osterloh (2005) 'Yes, Managers Should Be Paid Like Bureaucrats', *Journal of Management Inquiry*, 14(1), 96–111.

B.S. Frey and A. Stutzer (2001) 'Economics and Psychology: From Imperialistic to Inspired Economics', *Revue de Philosophie économique*, 4(2), 5–22.

B.S. Frey and A. Stutzer (2002a) *Happiness and Economics. How the Economy and Institutions Affect Human Well-Being* (Princeton, NJ: Princeton University Press).

B.S. Frey and A. Stutzer (2002b) 'What Can Economists Learn from Happiness Research?', *Journal of Economic Literature*, 40(2), 402–435.

B.S. Frey and A. Stutzer (2006) 'Direct Democracy: Designing a Living Constitution' in R.D. Congleton and B. Swedenborg (eds), *Democratic Constitutional Design and Public Policy. Analysis and Evidence* (Cambridge, MA and London, U.K.: MIT Press), pp. 39–80.

B.S. Frey and A. Stutzer (eds) (2007) *Economics and Psychology. A Promising New Cross-Disciplinary Field* (Cambridge, MA, and London, UK: MIT Press).

B.S. Frey, A. Stutzer, M. Benz, S. Meier, S. Luechinger and C. Benesch (2008) *Happiness: A Revolution in Economics* (Cambridge, MA: MIT Press).

R.H. Frank (1985) *Choosing the Right Pond. Human Behavior and the Quest for Status* (New York and Oxford: Oxford University Press).

F.A. Hayek (1960) *The Constitution of Liberty* (London: Routledge and Kegan Paul).

A.O. Hirschman (1970) *Exit, Voice and Loyalty* (Cambridge, MA: Harvard University Press).

L.R. Iannaccone (1998) 'Introduction to the Economics of Religion', *Journal of Economic Literature*, 36(3), 1465–1495.

E.L. Jones (1987) *The European Miracle.* 2nd edn (Cambridge, UK: Cambridge University Press).

D. Kahneman, E. Diener and N. Schwarz (eds) (1999) *Well-Being: The Foundations of Hedonic Psychology* (New York: Russell Sage Foundation).

D. Kahneman, P. Slovic and A. Tversky (eds) (1982) *Judgement under Uncertainty: Heuristics and Biases* (Cambridge: Cambridge University Press).

D. Kahneman and A. Tversky (1979) 'Prospect Theory: An Analysis of Decision under Risk', *Econometrica*, 47(2), 263–291.

D. Kahneman, P.P. Wakker and R. Sarin (1997) 'Back to Bentham? Explorations of Experienced Utility', *Quarterly Journal of Economics*, 112(2), 375–405.

E.L. Khalil (1996) 'Respect, Admiration, Aggrandizement: Adam Smith as Economic Psychologist', *Journal of Economic Psychology*, 17(5), 555–577.

B. Köszegi (2002a) 'Ego Utility and Information Acquisition', Mimeo, University of California at Berkeley.

B. Köszegi (2002b) 'Ego Utility, Overconfidence, and Task Choice' Mimeo. University of California at Berkeley.

A.P. Kyriacou (2006) 'Functional, Overlapping, Competing, Jurisdictions and Ethnic Conflict Management', *Kyklos*, 59(1), 63–83.

E. Lazear (2000) 'Economic Imperialism', *Quarterly Journal of Economics*, 115(1), 99–146.

S.E. Lea and P. Webley (1997) 'Pride in Economic Psychology', *Journal of Economic Psychology*, 18(2–3), 323–340.

M.R. Lepper and D. Greene (eds) (1978) *The Hidden Costs of Reward: New Perspectives on Psychology of Human Motivation* (Hillsdale, NY: Erlbaum).

E.A. Lind, C.T. Kulik, M. Ambrose and M.V. De Vera Park (1993) 'Individual and Corporate Dispute Resolution: Using Procedural Fairness as a Decision Heuristic', *Administrative Science Quarterly*, 38(2), 224–251.

E.A. Lind and T.R. Tyler (1988) *The Social Psychology of Procedural Justice* (New York: Plenum Press).

G. Loewenstein (1999) 'Because It Is There: The Challenge of Mountaineering for Utility Theory', *Kyklos*, 52(3), 315–343.

M.J. Machina (1987) 'Choice Under Uncertainty: Problems Solved and Unsolved', *Journal of Economic Perspectives*, 1(1), 121–154.

J. Marschak (1950) 'Uncertain Prospects, and Measurable Utility', *Econometrica*, 18, 111–141.

D. Martin and R. Wagner (1978) 'The Institutional Framework for Municipal Incorporation: An Economic Analysis of Local Agency Formation Commissions in California', *Journal of Law and Economics*, 21(2), 409–425.

S.L. Mehay (1984) 'The Effect of Governmental Structure on Special District Expenditures', *Public Choice*, 44, 339–348.

D.C. Mueller (2003) *Public Choice III* (Cambridge, UK: Cambridge University Press).

S. Mullainathan and R. Thaler (2000) 'Behavioral Economics', Massachusetts Institute of Technology, Department of Economics Working Paper: 00/27.

M.A. Nelson (1990) 'Decentralization of the Subnational Public Sector: An Empirical Analysis of the Determinants of Local Government Structure in Metropolitan Areas in the U.S.', *Southern Economic Journal*, 57, 443–457.

W.E. Oates (1972) *Fiscal Federalism* (New York: Harcourt Brace Jovanovich).

M. Olson (1969) 'The Principle of "Fiscal Equivalence": The Division of Responsibilities among Different Levels of Government', *American Economic Review*, 59(2), 479–487.

B. Pascal (1670) *Pensées* (Paris: Port-Royal).

M. Rabin (1998) 'Psychology and Economics', *Journal of Economic Literature*, 36 (March), 11–46.

N. Rosenberg and L.E. Birdzell (1986) *How the West Grew Rich: The Economic Transformation of the Industrial World* (London: I.B. Tauris).

P.J. Schoemaker (1982) 'The Expected Utility Model: Its Variants, Purposes, Evidence and Limitations', *Journal of Economic Literature*, 20(June), 529–563.

T. Scitovsky (1976) *The Joyless Economy: An Inquiry into Human Satisfaction and Dissatisfaction* (Oxford: Oxford University Press).

A.K. Sen (1995) 'Rationality and Social Choice', *American Economic Review*, 85(1), 1–24.

A.K. Sen (1997) 'Maximization and the Act of Choice', *Econometrica*, 65(4), 745–779.

R.H. Thaler (1991) *Quasi-Rational Economics* (New York: Russell Sage).

V.J. Vanberg (2000) 'Functional Federalism: Communal or Individual Rights?', *Kyklos*, 53(3), 363–386.

J. Von Neumann and O. Morgenstern (1944) *Theory of Games and Economic Behavior* (Princeton: Princeton University Press).

E. Weede (1993) 'The Impact of Interstate Conflict on Revolutionary Change and Individual Freedom', *Kyklos*, 46, 473–495.

J.S. Zax (1988) 'The Effects of Jurisdiction Types and Numbers on Local Public Finance' in H.S. Rosen (ed.), *Fiscal Federalism: Quantitative Studies* (Chicago and London: The University of Chicago Press).

2
A Rawlsian View of CSR and the Game Theory of its Implementation (III): Conformism, Equilibrium Refinement and Selection

Lorenzo Sacconi

1. Introduction

This is the third part of a comprehensive essay on the Rawlsian view of corporate social responsibility (CSR), seen as an extended model of corporate governance, and the corresponding firm's objective function.[1] In the first part of this essay (Sacconi, 2010a), I provided the following definition of CSR as a multi-stakeholder governance model (see also Sacconi 2006a, 2006b, 2007a, 2009):

> *CSR is a model of extended corporate governance whereby those who run a firm (entrepreneurs, directors, managers) have responsibilities that range from fulfillment of fiduciary duties toward the owners to fulfillment of analogous – even if not identical – fiduciary duties toward all the firm's stakeholders.*

This definition has been articulated and defended as an institutional model of corporate governance implementable through explicitly expressed norms of self-regulation based on company/stakeholders social dialog – which means that CSR is neither a matter of managerial discretion nor one of external regulation enforced though statutory laws. The basic idea is that such a model of self-regulation, provided it is not obstructed by statutory company law, which imposes a single-stakeholder fiduciary model and objective function on companies, is self sustaining. Hence the relevant perspective from which to understand the normative nature of CSR is that of an institution in Aoki's sense (see Aoki 2001, Aoki 2007a, Aoki 2007b and Sacconi 2010a). Let us summarize Aoki's definition:

> *An institution is a self-sustaining system of shared beliefs about a salient way in which a game is repeatedly played; it is based on a summary representation*

of compressed information about the equilibrium strategy combination which is currently being played in the repeated game characteristic of a given social domain.

(cf. Aoki 2001)

However, the addition of a social contract perspective essentially completes the definition of 'institution' (Sacconi 2010a). The aim of this addition is to account for the crucial role that not just regularities of behavior and descriptive beliefs but also of norms and normative beliefs play as inherent parts of the beliefs system characterizing an institution as an equilibrium supported by a consistent system of expectations. To explain the role of the social contract on explicitly expressed self-regulatory norms of corporate governance, I take the game theoretic perspective of a repeated game between the firm – or those who occupy positions of authority within the hierarchical control structure of the firm – and the series of its stakeholders (see Sacconi 2000, Sacconi 2007b, and also Posner 2000) as the typical game in the 'corporate governance domain' (Aoki 2001).

Within this context, four roles played by a Rawlsian social contract have been identified in the first part of this essay in determining the equilibrium institution that satisfies the normative requirement of CSR. They are at the same time able to meet the main game theoretical challenges for the emergence of such an institution.

- The *cognitive-constructive role*, which answers the question on *how* the firm *works out* the *set* of commitments that it *can* undertake with respect to generic states of the world it is aware of not being able to predict in any detail, and therefore *what* types of *possible* equilibrium behavior the firm can work out so that stakeholders may entertain expectations about them;
- The *normative role*, which answers the question on what (if any) pattern of interaction the firm and its stakeholders must a priori *select* from the set of possible equilibria to be carried out *ex post* (according to the answer given to the first question), if they adopt an *ex ante* standpoint enabling an agreement to be reached impartially;
- The *motivational role*, which answers the question on *what* and *how many* equilibrium patterns of behavior, amongst those that may emerge *ex post* from the interaction between firm and stakeholder, would retain *their motivational force* if firm and stakeholder were able to agree in an *ex ante* perspective on a CSR norm along the lines of the second question;
- The *cognitive-predictive role* concerning how the *ex ante* agreement on a CSR norm *affects* the beliefs formation process whereby a firm and its stakeholders cognitively converge on a system of mutually consistent expectations, such that they reciprocally predict from each another the execution of a given equilibrium in their *ex post* interaction (given

that more than one equilibrium point still retains motivational force according to the answer to the third question). The question to be answered by this function is thus 'does the norm shape the expectation formation process so that in the end it will coincide with what the *ex ante* agreed principle would require of firm and stakeholders?'

The first two roles have been examined at length in Parts I and II respectively. In particular, it was seen in Part II (see Sacconi 2010b) that, from the *ex ante* perspective, a Rawlsian social contract is able to solve the *normative* equilibrium selection problem, that is, to choose a governance structure through a decision procedure that satisfies elementary conditions of impersonality, impartiality and empathy (Harsanyi 1977). At the same time, it resulted in the egalitarian solution, consistent with the Rawlsian maximin principle, not just because of those ethical assumptions, but precisely because it internalizes the requirement of self-sustainability and implementation in equilibrium (Rawls 1971). This takes us to the typical Rawlsian maximization of the worst-off participant seen as a criterion for the constitutional choice of the firm's governance structure, which is basically consistent with both justification and realistic implementation (Binmore 1991, Binmore 2005). Nevertheless, roles three and four still need to be explained. In fact, although the social contract is able to select *ex ante* a reasonable equilibrium, *ex post* we are again faced with the problem of the incentives to which players will respond when they exit from the original-position-and-veil-of-ignorance thought experiment and return to 'the game of life' (see again Binmore 2005), where they play according to the entire set of their preferences and motivations to act. This requires discussion of the equilibrium selection problem from the *ex post* perspective.

To gain better understanding of where we stand, consider that the appropriate game representation of the firm/stakeholders interaction is the iterated Trust Game, with the following stage-game (see Figure 2.1, section 3): player A (the stakeholder) will enter (or not) by trusting (or not) player B (who runs the firm) and by carrying out a specific investment. Player B decides whether to appropriate player A's investment by abusing or not. If s/he chooses non-abuse the surplus is shared in an equitable way. Otherwise, the stakeholder is deprived of any benefit from entrance (including the endowment that s/he would possess if s/he did not invest), while the party who runs the firm gains a large profit. Note, however, that this mode of interaction is intuitively understood as socially inefficient in a utilitarian sense – that is, admitted utility comparability, the firm still prefers individually to abuse, but the fair sharing in the case of non-abuse would yield a larger amount of interpersonal social welfare. However, notwithstanding any consideration of social efficiency, the only Nash equilibrium is the strategy pair such that B abuses and A stays out. The mutually beneficial outcome (4, 4) cannot be sustained in equilibrium as long as the game is played one shot (see again Figure 2.1).

But now consider the equilibrium set of the repeated Trust Game between the long-run firm B, who receives the average payoff from all his/her participations into the infinite series of stage-games, and the 'average' stakeholder (call him/her again A because this is useful for considering the average payoff of an infinite series of short-run stakeholders that enter or otherwise the position of the one-shot A player at each repetition), who enters each stage-game (or refuses to enter). Under the usual assumptions for reputation games (see Part I), the repeated Trust game will display a convex payoff space (constituted by all the average discounted payoff vectors obtainable from pairs of repeated strategies) coinciding with the convex envelope of the one-stage pure payoff vectors (see section 4.1, Figure 2.2 for more details).

Within this payoff space, every point above the dotted line corresponds to an equilibrium strategy profile such that player A 'enters' with a given frequency and player B abuses or not with the appropriate probability mixture (Fudenberg 1991; Fudenberg and Levine 1989). Of course, the most relevant equilibria are those where player A never enters because player B will always abuse, with average discounted payoffs (1,1), and the equilibrium with average discounted payoffs (4,4) where player B never abuses and hence player A enters each time. But also remarkable is the *Stackelberg equilibrium*, where the firm B is believed to make a commitment on the mixed strategy $(0.75a, 0.25 \neg a)$ (see again Figure 2.2, section 4.1). In fact, B may develop a reputation for being this type by playing the two pure strategies with the attached probability throughout all the repetitions of the game. Thus each stakeholder in the role of player A necessarily enters, since his/her payoff is the same as staying out (namely 1) – that is, s/he is indifferent between entering and staying out (if player B were to give him/her an infinitesimal additional positive utility ε by reducing his/her abuse probability correspondingly, 'entrance' would be certain). This gives B an average expected payoff of 4.75, which is the best payoff that player B can obtain in equilibrium. Then player B's best response is to stick to this type/commitment whenever s/he is able to convince player A that s/he is this type so that A responds with his/her best response to this type's mixed strategy (see also Andreozzi 2010, for a discussion of the relevance of this fact in the game theoretical explanation of CSR).

There is some evidence of this behavior in real life relationships between companies and their stakeholders. An example is provided by companies that claim to be socially accountable because they publish a social report and announce a code of ethics, but nevertheless are not accurate in reporting all the relevant social and environmental impacts of their conduct on all the concerned stakeholders, and comply in only few cases, or to a minimal extent, with the declared code. Thus, a company may acquire a reputation for abusing the trust of its employees, customers, suppliers, investors, capital-lenders and local communities wherein it operates – but only to the extent that makes them indifferent between maintaining their relations with the firm and withdrawing from them.

However, there is also evidence of stakeholder activism that refuses to acquiesce and actively countervails such hypocritical corporate conduct. In fact, stakeholder activism is a growing component of market behavior. Examples are phenomena such as responsible consumerism, socially responsible finance, human rights advocacy through active participation in shareholders meetings, brand boycotts in the case of environmental disasters and allegations of human rights violations or discrimination against employees by companies (especially when operating plants relocated to developing countries). Further examples of the same behaviors are corporate bankruptcies decreed by investors through the mass liquidation of stocks after ethical scandals (as in the case of Arthur Andersen after the Enron scandal). These companies – evidently responsible for intentional breaches of their ethical commitments – are doomed by their shareholders to collapse more dramatically than would be 'rational' according to those shareholders' self-interest (i.e. their share-value-maximization). All these examples illustrate behaviors by active stakeholders that cannot be captured in terms of their mere self-interest and cannot be understood as mere defense of their own material interest (see also Frey 1997).

Admittedly, some of these behaviors can be understood as reflecting a concern for other stakeholders' well-being, rather than the well-being of the active stakeholders themselves. More exactly, however, they express the stakeholders' attachment to impersonal principles of justice, that is, a desire to conform with socially accepted norms of fair treatment – even when such conformity concerns not so much the active stakeholder itself but mostly the well-being of third parties. Hence, only disinterested (from the egoistic point of view) motivations may be of relevance in explaining such action. A proper understanding of these third-parties-concerned non-egoistic behaviors in terms of norm compliance based on conformist preferences has been the focus of previous works on this topic (see Grimalda and Sacconi 2005; Sacconi and Grimalda 2007). Here I shall try to make sense of the evidence by focusing on the basic firm/stakeholders bilateral strategic relationships. This perspective is also a basis for extending the explanation to larger firms/stakeholders networks, where the creation of social capital and support for non-egoistically profitable trust relationships is at stake (see Degli Antoni and Sacconi 2010, *infra*; Sacconi and Degli Antoni 2009).

How does the social contract approach account for these apparently 'irrational' but unselfish actions, given that acquiescence would be the stakeholder's best response? In Part II (Sacconi 2010b) the focus was on the *ex ante* agreement on CSR norms and standards of behavior as a useful collective decision device for the unique selection of an equilibrium point. The concern now is with how stakeholders react to the discovery that in the game of life the firm has strong incentives to behave in a way quite different from strict compliance with the *ex ante* agreed equilibrium, and *de facto it prefers to* deviate from it. As a consequence it seeks to develop a reputation for being a type of player who systematically adopts a sophisticated abuse behavior that, if it was taken for granted, would induce stakeholders to abandon the *ex ante* agreed equilibrium point and adapt to the less than fully compliant equilibrium profile.

This can be understood as a struggle for the *ex post* equilibrium selection amongst the many still possible. What we are in fact facing are two tightly connected but nevertheless distinct game theoretical problems. First, *ex ante* equilibrium selection by agreement does not necessarily work well as an *ex post* equilibrium selection mechanism. Even though it ensures that the decision taken 'behind the veil of ignorance' could be self-enforceable if there were a system of expectations that predicted that decision as the effective *ex post* behavior of the parties, it does not ensure that these expectations will de facto emerge, and therefore that selection will be *ex post* effective. There is no logical *necessity* linking *ex ante* equilibrium selection to the emergence of the shared knowledge condition required for the unicity of the solution in the *ex post* perspective. But, second, this also raises the compliance problem again. Given multiple *ex post* equilibria, why should the player comply with the agreement by carrying out exactly the equilibrium chosen under the veil of ignorance? The problem is that, in the presence of multiple equilibria, each with some motivating force conditional on existence of a system of expectations consistent with it, no particular equilibria has any reason to be carried out, and thus the one corresponding to the *ex ante* agreement need not have any incentive effect on compliance.

A different answer could be given if the *ex ante* selective function of an impartial agreement by itself performed a *causal* role in changing incentives and beliefs on the set of admissible equilibria of the game of life relevant in the *ex post* perspective. This can happen along two routes. The first is a behavioral mechanism according to which the agreed equilibrium carries additional motivational (i.e. preferential) force precisely because it has been selected 'behind the veil of ignorance'. The second is (again) a psychological mechanism according to which agreeing 'behind the veil' (as a *matter of fact about reasoning*, but without logical necessity) also influences beliefs about other parties' behavior *ex post*: that is, it induces a state of shared beliefs whereby what was chosen behind the veil will be also implemented *ex post*. These two behavioral hypotheses are interlocked (i.e. beliefs formation must be granted in order to introduce the psychological preferences). Some empirical evidence for them can be found in related experimental works (Faillo et al. 2008; Sacconi and Faillo 2010). We discuss the first hypothesis in the next few sections by introducing a Rawlsian idea of the sense of justice and the corresponding model of conformist preferences. The latter hypothesis will be shortly addressed in section 5.

2. The true Rawlsian theory of norm compliance

An original approach to the institutional compliance problem was suggested by John Rawls in the *Theory of Justice* (1971), where he proposed the 'sense of justice' as a solution for the stability problem of a well-ordered society – that is, a society whose institutions are arranged according to the principles of justice (norms in our sense) chosen under a 'veil of ignorance'. This solution, however, was long overlooked by economists and game theorists because it was at odds with the methodology of rational choice in that it resorted to socio-psychological assumptions common in theories on moral learning.

However, given the behaviorist turn in microeconomics, it is time to reconsider this neglected solution and to acknowledge that it may suggest an illuminating explanation of why (sometimes) some of us comply with just institutions even if we have some direct material incentive not to do so. The rest of this section thus summarizes Rawls' argument about how a sense of justice is engendered in a well-ordered society, and finally suggests the relevant features of Rawls' theory captured in the conformist preferences model.

Justice as fairness, Rawls says, understood as the set of principles of justice chosen 'under a veil of ignorance' – once the principles are assumed to shape the institutions of a well-ordered society – provides its own support to the stability of just institutions. In fact, when institutions are just (here it is clear that we are taking the *ex post* perspective, that is, once the constitutional decision from the *ex ante* position has already been taken and for some reason has been successful), those who take part in the arrangement develop a sense of justice that carries with it the desire to support and maintain that arrangement. The idea is that motives to act are now enriched with a new motivation able to overcome the counteracting tendency to injustice. Note that instability is clearly seen in term of a Prisoner's Dilemma-like situation: institutions may be unstable because complying with them may not result in the best response of each participant to other members' behavior. However, the sense of justice, once developed, overcomes incentives to cheat and transforms fair behavior into each participant's best response to the other individuals' behaviors.

To understand how this is possible, it is necessary to consider the definition of 'sense of justice'. Although it presupposes the development of lower-level moral sentiments of love and trust, understood as feelings of attachment to lower-level institutions (families and just associations), if these institutions are perceived to be just, it is noticeable that the sense of justice is a desire to act upon general and abstract principles of justice as such, once they have been chosen under a veil of ignorance as the shaping principles of institutions, and hence have proved beneficial to ourselves in practice. Note that it is not the case that we act upon the principles insofar as they are beneficial only to concrete persons with whom we have direct links and emotional involvements. Once the level of a morality of principles has been reached, our desire to act upon the principles does not depend on other people's approbation or on other contingent facts such as satisfaction of the interests of some particular concrete person. On the contrary, it is the system of principles of justice in itself that constitutes the object of the sense of justice.

The question to be answered thus becomes how it is possible that principles themselves are capable of influencing our affections – that is, of generating the sense of justice as a relatively self-contained 'desire to conform with the principles'. The answer is twofold.

First, the sense of justice is not independent of the *content* of principles. These are principles that we could have decided to agree upon under a veil of ignorance as expressions of our rationality as free and equal moral persons. These principles are mutually advantageous and hence impartially acceptable by a rational choice, even if it is made from an impartial perspective, for they promote our interests and hence have some relation with our affections (preferences). Thus, in order for a sense of justice to develop, principles cannot be arbitrary. They must be those principles that would have been chosen by a rational impartial agreement.

Second, despite the intellectual effect of recognizing that principles are rationally acceptable, the basic fact about the sense of justice is that it is by nature a moral sentiment inherently connected to natural attitudes. Moral sentiments are systems of dispositions interlocked with the human capability to realize natural attitudes. Thus moral liability for lacking moral sentiments has a direct counterpart in the lack of certain natural attitudes, which result in affective responses like a sense of guilt, indignation or shame. Hence, even though the thought experiment of a decision under the veil of ignorance merely aids us in the *intellectual* recognition of principles acceptability, the sense of justice retains a motivational force on its own, which can be only traced back to its nature as a moral sentiment or desire not entirely reducible to the experience of its intellectual justification.

The proper functioning of the sense of justice can be understood, however, as the third level of a process of moral learning, which in its first two steps already cultivates moral sentiments of love for parents and trust and friendship vis-à-vis the members of just associations in which the individual already takes part – and which s/he re-elaborates on those pre-existing sentiments. '*Given that a person's capacity for fellow feeling has been realized by forming attachment in accordance with the first two... [levels] and given that a society's institutions are just and are publicly known to be just, then this person acquires the correspondent sense of justice as he recognized that he and those for whom he cares are the beneficiaries of these arrangements*' (Rawls 1971: 491).

As seems clear, reciprocity is a basic element in this definition. In fact reciprocity is understood as a deep-lying psychological fact of human nature amounting to the tendency to 'answer in kind'. The sense of justice '*arises from the manifest intention of other persons to act for our good. Because they recognize they wish us well we care for their well being in return. Thus we acquire attachment to persons and institutions according to how we perceive our good to be affected by them. The basic idea is one of reciprocity, a tendency to answer in kind*' (p. 494). Two aspects are to be noted concerning the other person's 'manifest intention', which elicits the tendency to 'answer in kind'. We recognize that the caring for our good derives from other people acting consistently with the principles of justice. Hence reciprocity is elicited not from the mere coherence of institutions with the principles of justice, but from the fact that other people make our good by acting intentionally upon those principles. What matters is not just reciprocity in accepting the principles, but the intention displayed by other players' concretely acting upon the principles for our well-being. Second, this intention cannot be a direct intention from concrete person toward us as particular persons. By complying with principles, our good is pursued in an unconditional way – that is, impersonally and not conditionally on any particular description of us based on contingent characteristics or positions.

It also makes it immediately evident that the sense of justice is a force that typically emerges and stabilizes a well-ordered society only *ex post*, when institutions are already 'out there' operating through some level of compliance by the members of society. Thus the question arises of where compliance with principles arises from at the very first step of their implementation, when it cannot be said that there is an history of well-ordered society institutions already operating.

The following elements taken from Rawls's analysis and incorporated into the model of conformist preference explained in the next section are important here (see also Sacconi and Faillo 2010).

i) First, there is an exogenous disposition in our motivational system of drives to action – the capacity of a desire to act upon principles or the agent's duties. This derives from learning about the justice of lower-level institutions (family, associations) or the widespread operating of the institutions of a well-ordered society (such that if these conditions are not fully satisfied this exogenous motivational factor cannot be assumed to have an overwhelming force in general, and thus must balance with other motivational drives).

ii) Second, the foregoing element defines just a capacity for the sense of justice, but its proper formation depends upon conditions relative only to the principles of justice and their compliance, as follows:

    a. agents construe and justify norms as the result of an impartial agreement under the 'veil of ignorance', that is, before considering conformity, different states of affairs resulting from compliant or non-compliant actions must be assessed in term of their consistency with the fair principles – compliance is not arbitrary;

    b. each agent knows that also others justify the norm and assess compliance decisions in a similar way;

    c. we know, or have the reasoned belief that other agents are effectively playing their part in carrying out the principles, and this behavior, because of the content of the principles it conforms with, expresses an intention to be beneficial to us in impartial terms. Thus, by playing our part in compliance we may be understood as reciprocating other agents' intentions – that is, our compliance is conditional on theirs;

d. owing to the hypothesis of public knowledge, other agents are also predicted as having (and we know that they have) the reasoned belief that we do our part in benefiting them in an impartial manner by acting upon the principles, and thus they may be seen as reciprocating our intention expressed by our compliance with the principles – hence our compliance is conditional on their reciprocity as well.

e. When these conditions are satisfied, our capacity to form a 'sense of justice' becomes effective and translates into a motivational force able to counteract incentives to act unjustly in situation like the Prisoner's Dilemma game – that is, a psychological preference for complying overcomes the preference for personal advantages gained by not complying and opportunistically exploiting other agents' cooperation.

What we will see in the next section is how conformist preferences derived from the Rawlsian idea of a sense of justice may affect compliance with the social contract amongst the firm and its stakeholders. Preferences incorporating the sense of justice will affect compliance by selecting as admissible the only subset of equilibria which are compatible with compliance with the agreed principles.

3. The motivational role of social contract: conformist preferences in the Trust Game

Any equilibrium point exerts a (limited) motivational force able to command actual behavior, which is effective in so far as each player believes that other players will play their strategy components of the same equilibrium. One may wonder whether the fact that a norm has been agreed from an *ex ante* (pre-play) perspective and exhibits various levels of consistency with different equilibria, may affect the motivational force exerted by different equilibria in a game. A positive answer would amount to a restriction on the number of equilibrium points that have motivational force over the players' behavior. In other words, one may ask whether norms can 'refine' the equilibrium set of a game in terms of the motivational strength of certain equilibria over other equilibria.

A voluntary CSR norm constraining the firm's discretion in the firm/ stakeholder interaction, would in fact perform a motivational function. It would restrict the admissible equilibrium set in the event that – having been chosen via a unanimous impartial agreement and granted that players expect reciprocal compliance with the norm – it generates an additional utility weight to be introduced into the payoffs of the players. The conjecture is that a preference for equilibrium strategies may in part depend not just on their outcomes, but also on the level of conformity that any equilibrium exhibits in regard to an agreed norm. A conformity level must be understood as conditional on beliefs – that is, conformity depends on one player's compliance, given his/her beliefs about the other players' behaviors, and about other players' reciprocity in compliance, given their beliefs. It follows that the additional psychological payoff involved by a given level of conformity is not just an exogenous parameter reflecting the absolute motivational force of the desire to be consistent with an agreed norm. The exogenous component is also conditioned by a function of beliefs concerning reciprocal behaviors.

Whatever the case, if the norm generates a modification in the players' payoffs in favor of situations in which no significant deviation from reciprocal conformity occurs, then it may be that the overall motivational strength reinforcing an equilibrium behavior may be integrated (relatively augmented or reduced) by an additional motivational factor that in the end confines overall motivational strength only to those equilibria that exhibit significant compliance levels with the norm.

The reference is of course to a different notion of equilibrium – the psychological Nash equilibrium (Geanakoplos et al. 1989) – based on conformist preferences (Grimalda and Sacconi 2005; Sacconi and Grimalda 2007).[2] This results from a modification of the players' utility functions through integration of preferences with an intrinsic component for norm compliance, seen not as unilateral and unconditioned, but as conditioned by beliefs about other players' reciprocal conformity. The 'refinement effect' on the admissible equilibria that this change in the equilibrium notion entails is surprising (and unexpected). As we will see, the equilibrium set of the repeated Trust Games under this revision of the utility function shrinks dramatically to the pure strategy equilibria of the repeated psychological Trust Game.[3]

To begin, let us illustrate the conformist preference model with reference to its application to the one-shot (stage) Trust Game (TG) involving a firm (player B) and its stakeholder (player A) (see Figure 2.1). Stakeholder and firm now have *two* kinds of preferences defined over states of affairs

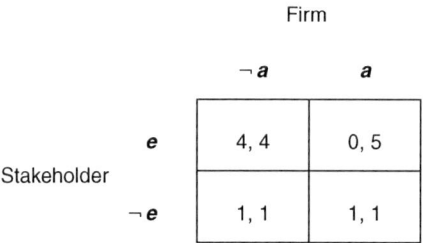

Figure 2.1   One-shot Trust Game

resulting from their interaction, which are both capable of motivating their actions. On one hand (more basic), the first kind of preferences is based on the description of states of affairs σ brought about by their interaction *as consequences*, and their preferences regarding consequences are called *consequentialist*. These may be not only typical self-interested preferences but also altruistic ones.

This part of the argument is by no means new. The new part instead concerns *conformist preferences*. Players also have preferences defined over states of the affairs σ resulting from their interaction but described as just *combination of actions*. To be clear the typical Trust Game – see again Figure 2.1 – identifies four possible states σ coinciding with cells of its normal form, where pairs of strategies are represented – (*e*, ¬*a*), (*e*, *a*), (¬*e*, ¬*a*), (¬*e*, *a*) – before attaching payoff over them. When these states of affairs are qualified in terms of their consistency with an *ex ante* agreed ethical norm, preference over them is *conformist* – where 'consistency' is defined as how far the players' strategy choices (jointly a state) are from the set of actions that would completely fulfill the agreed ethical norm of equity. By norm I mean a principle of justice for the distribution of material utilities coinciding with the stakeholders' social contract with the firm.

3.1. Conformist preferences

Let us assume that players have just agreed on a social contract concerning the principle of justice that should govern as a norm the distribution of the social surplus produced by means of their cooperation through the firm. Conformist preferences may now enter the picture. Intuitively speaking, a stakeholder will gain intrinsic utility from simply complying with the principle, if the same stakeholder expects that in doing so she will be able to contribute to fulfilling the distributive principle, and taking into account that she expects the other stakeholders (or the firm) also to contribute to fulfilling the same principle, given their expectations.

A complete measure of the player's preferences is an overall utility function combining material utility, derived from her consequentialist preferences, with the representation of her conformist preferences represented by the conformist-psychological component of her utility function (see Grimalda and Sacconi 2005). The overall utility function of player i with reference to the state σ (understood as a strategy combination of player i strategy σ_i and the other players' strategies σ_{-i}), is the following:

$$V_i(\sigma) = U_i(\sigma) + \lambda_i F[T(\sigma)] \tag{1}$$

where

   i. U_i is player i's material utility for the state σ;
  ii. λ_i is an exogenous parameter $\lambda_i \leq 0$;

iii. *T* is a fairness principle defined for the state σ;
iv. *F* is a compounded index expressing the agent *i*'s conditional conformity and her expectation of reciprocal by any other player *j* with respect to the principle *T* for each state σ

Let us concentrate on the conformist part of the utility function. *First* (as it can be seen within the most internal brackets), there is a norm *T*, a social welfare function that establishes a distributive principle of material utilities. Players adopt *T* by agreement in a pre-play phase and employ it in the generation of a consistency ordering over the set of possible states σ, each seen as a combination of individual strategies. The highest value of *T* is reached in a situation σ, where material utilities are distributed in such a way that they are mostly consistent with the distributive principle *T* within the available set of alternatives. Note that what matters to *T* is not 'who gets how much' material payoff (the principle *T* is neutral with respect to individual positions), but how utilities are distributed across players. Satisfaction of the distributional property is the basis for conformist preferences. As we are looking for a contractarian principle of welfare distribution, let us assume – according to what I have argued in Part II (Sacconi 2010b, sec.7) – that *T* coincides with the Nash bargaining function (Nash 1950) taking the stay-out outcome of the Trust Game as the *status quo*.

Agreed principle of fair welfare distribution T:

$$T(\sigma) = N(U_1, \ldots, U_n) = \prod_{i=1}^{n} (U_i - d_i) \tag{2}$$

Second, a measure of the extent to which, given the other agents' expected actions, the first player by her strategy choice contributes to a fully fair distribution of material payoffs in terms of the principle *T*. This may also be put in terms of the extent to which the first player is *responsible* for a fair distribution, given what (she expects that) the other player will do. It is a *conditional conformity index* assuming values from 0 (no conformity at all, when the first player chooses a strategy that minimizes the value of *T* given his/her expectation about the other strategy choice) to 1 (full conformity, when the first player chooses a strategy that maximizes the value of *T* given the other player's expected strategy choice) with the following form:

player's i conditional conformity index:

$$\left[1 + f_i\left(\sigma_{ik}, b_i^1\right) \right] \tag{3}$$

This index takes its values as a function of f_i, which in turn varies from 0 to -1 and measures player *i*'s *deviation degree* from the ideal principle *T* by making her choice conditional on her expectation about player *j*'s behavior *player's i deviation degree:*

$$f_i\left(\sigma_{ik}, b_i^{\,1}\right) = \frac{T\left(\sigma_{ik}, b_i^{\,1}\right) - T^{\text{MAX}}\left(b_i^{\,1}\right)}{T^{\text{MAX}}\left(b_i^{\,1}\right) - T^{\text{MIN}}\left(b_i^{\,1}\right)} \qquad (4)$$

where $b_i^{\,1}$ is player i's belief concerning player j's action, $T^{\text{MAX}}\left(b_i^{\,1}\right)$ is the maximum value of the function T due to whatever feasible strategy player i may choose given her belief about player j's choice, $T^{\text{MIN}}\left(b_i^{\,1}\right)$ is the minimum value of the function T due to whatever feasible strategy player i may choose, given her belief about player's j choice, and $T\left(\sigma_{ik}, b_i^{\,1}\right)$ is the actual value of T due to player i's adoption of her k-ary strategy σ_{ik} given her belief about player j's choice.

Third, a measure of the extent to which the *other* player (respectively the stakeholder or the firm) is expected to contribute to a fair payoff distribution in terms of the principle T, given what he is expected to expect from the first player's behavior. This may also be put in terms of the (expected) *responsibility* of the *other* player for generating a fair allocation of the surplus, given what he (is believed to) believes. This measure consists of a *reciprocally expected conformity index* assuming values from 0 (no conformity at all, when the *other* player is expected to choose a strategy that minimizes T given what he expects from the first player) to 1 (full conformity, when the *other* player is expected to maximize the value of T given what he expects from the first players). It is formally very similar to the conditional conformity index of the first player, that is,

player's j reciprocal expected conformity index:

$$\left[1 + \tilde{f}_j\left(b_i^{\,2}, b_i^{\,1}\right)\right]$$

In fact, it is as well a function of $\tilde{f}$, the *expected player j's degree of deviation* from the ideal principle T, which also varies from 0 to –1 as is also normalized by the magnitude of the difference between player j's full conformity and no conformity at all, given what he believes (and player i believes that he believes) about player i's choice, that is,

expected player j's degree of deviation:

$$\tilde{f}_j\left(b_i^{\,1}, b_i^{\,2}\right) = \frac{T\left(b_i^{\,1}, b_i^{\,2}\right) - T^{\text{MAX}}\left(b_i^{\,2}\right)}{T^{\text{MAX}}\left(b_i^{\,2}\right) - T^{\text{MIN}}\left(b_i^{\,2}\right)}$$

where $b_i^{\,1}$ is player i's *first order* belief about player j's action (that is, formally identical to a strategy of player j), $b_i^{\,2}$ is player i's *second order* belief about what player j believes about the action adopted by player i, while $T^{\text{MAX}}\left(b_i{}^2\right)$ and $T^{\text{MIN}}\left(b_i{}^2\right)$ are defined as above but in relation to second player i's second order belief.

Fourth, there is an exogenous parameter $\lambda(\lambda \geq 0)$ representing the motivational force of the agent's psychological disposition to act on the motive of reciprocal conformity with an agreed norm. This is a psychological parameter representing how strong the *sense of justice* or the 'desire to be just' has grown up for an individual in a given population; it may be taken as dependent on exogenous variables like the development of the affective capacity to act upon one's principles and duties that comes from lower level domain of interaction (as in Rawls' theory of moral development, the family and the circle of friends and small-scale associations). Notice, however, that in the model it doesn't operate as such but as only once the agreement over T is given and as it is weighted by the measure of reciprocal conformity.

In fact, steps *two* and *three* coalesce in defining an overall index F of conditional and expected reciprocal conformity for each player in each state of the game. This index operates as a *weight* on the parameter λ, deciding whether it will actually affect or not (and, if so, to what extent) the player's payoffs. Thus the complete psychological component of the utility function representing conformist preferences is

$$\lambda_i \left[1 + \tilde{f}_j\left(b_i{}^2, b_i{}^1\right)\right]\left[1 + f_i\left(\sigma_i, b_i{}^1\right)\right]$$

which reduces to the following cases: (i) $\lambda[(1 - x)\times(1 - y)] = \lambda$ since both x and y are 0, if player i doesn't deviate and expects that player j doesn't deviate at all from complete conformity; (ii) $\lambda[(1 - x) \times (1 - y)] = a\lambda < \lambda$, where $a < 1$ since at least one (or both) of x and y are $0 < x < -1$ and $0 < y < -1$, if player i partially deviates and/or expects player j to partially deviate from complete conformity; (iii) $a\lambda = 0$ since in the above expression at least one (or both) of x or y are -1, if player i does not conform at all and/or expects that player j doesn't conform at all.

Summing up the effect of the different components, if a stakeholder expects that the firm (or vice versa) is reciprocally responsible for the maximal value of T, given what the firm expects about that stakeholder's behavior, and the former is also responsible for a maximal value of T given the firm's (expected) behavior, then the motivational weight of conformity λ will entirely enter the stakeholder's utility function. In other words, in the player's preference, system λ will show all the force of the disposition to conform to agreed norms, so that complying with the principle will yield full conformist utility (in the psychological sense) in addition to the material payoff of the same strategy. In the one-shot Trust Game, this happens, for example, in the state of affairs where the stakeholder enters, the firm does not abuse, and they mutually predict these strategy choices.

3.2. Calculation of conformist psychological payoffs and equilibria in the one-shot Trust Game

To calculate conformist psychological payoffs and equilibria, let's consider the game matrix (a) below (that replicates Figure 2.1 for the reader convenience). Strategies combinations (state of affairs) and the relative material payoffs vectors are (*no-entry, abuse*) and (*no-entry, no-abuse*) with material payoffs (1,1); (*entry, abuse*) with material payoffs (0,5) and (*entry, no-abuse*) with material payoffs (4,4). This is helpful in understanding what is meant by calculating the level of conformity in the different states by applying the Nash bargaining solution, which requires maximizing the product of individual surpluses net of the *status quo*. In this particular case, the *status quo* coincides with the outcome of the no-entry strategy – (1,1) – which is the assurance level that player A can grant herself, for whatever player B's choice, included the case that B doesn't start any trust-based interaction. This payoff must then be subtracted from whatever payoff is used in the calculation of

	¬ *a*	*a*
e	4, 4	0, 5
¬ *e*	1, 1	1, 1

Matrix (a): TG normal form

	¬ *a*	*a*
e	$(4-1)(4-1)=9$	$(0-1)(5-1)=-4$
¬ *e*	$(1-1)(1-1)=0$	$(1-1)(1-1)=0$

Matrix (b): *T* values at each state

	¬ *a*	*a*
e	$(4+\lambda)=6,\ (4+\lambda)=6$	0, 5
¬ *e*	1, 1	$(1+\lambda)=3, (1+\lambda)=3$

Matrix (c): psychological TG with conformist utilities included with $\lambda=2$.

the Nash product annexed to any state of affair (strategy combination). The two further matrices (see below) show respectively (b) the Nash bargaining product calculated for each pure strategy combination needed to measure the consistency of each state with respect to the principle T and the players' relevant degrees of conditional and expected reciprocal conformity for each state, and (c) the overall payoffs resulting from the addition of the psychological conformist preference weight $\lambda = 2$ to the material payoffs where this addition is appropriate.

In order to understand the psychological payoffs reported in matrix (c), consider that if a player cannot do anything better to improve the 'collective' value of the principle T with respect to the *status quo* by means of her/his unilateral decision, given the expected strategy choice of the other player, then s/he will be considered completely compliant by choosing to keep the *status quo* (no deviation from maximal conformity can be ascribed to her/his responsibility since her/his choice cannot do any more to maximize T than keeping to the status quo). This feature of the model depends on considering compliance in a non-cooperative *ex post* context, wherein players are able to deviate unilaterally from an agreed norm, and second, by considering conformity as conditional on the other player's expected level of compliance. Hence, in cases like the Trust Game, if the firm is expected to abuse, the stakeholder cannot do anything to improve the value of T on the status quo and, therefore, the stakeholder will be considered fully compliant with the principle by deciding to stay out. (As a matter of fact she could only worsen the T value by entering.) At the same time, the firm predicting that the stakeholder will stay out – given she believes that the firm shall abuse – cannot modify the value of T with respect to the status quo. Thus whatever the firm's strategy choice, it is fully compliant in this case. The result is that also in the (*no-entry, abuse*) equilibrium point of the basic Trust Game, the conformity weight λ adds to the players' payoffs. In this respect, there is no difference between the case (*no-entry, abuse*) and the case of the stakeholder entering because she predicts that the firm is going not to be abusive and the firm refraining from being abusive because it predicts that the stakeholder will enter (*entry, no-abuse*) – which is obviously the case in which both players unconditionally maximize T and hence, necessarily, the weight λ enters their payoffs as they are fully compliant.

By contrast, if the stakeholder enters when the firm is unilaterally predicted to abuse, she would minimize T with reference to the alternative choice open to her of not entering, which scores a higher level of T. At the same time, the firm misses the opportunity to maximize T given the stakeholder's decision to enter, and hence the latter will be considered as not complying at all. This implies that when the firm unilaterally and successfully abuses its stakeholder, none of the conformist preferences can add value to the players' material payoffs.

Lastly, if the firm chooses a mixed strategy whereby the stakeholder's decision between entry or non-entry has no influence on the T value, the stakeholder, whether she decides to enter or not, would be unable to improve the value of T. Therefore, by staying out she maximizes T as well. If, however, the stakeholder still stays out, no firm's strategy can do any better in maximizing T than the one just described, and thus the firm does as well when it is completely compliant as when it abuses. Hence, a firm's mixed strategy responded to by the stakeholder's no-entry strategy implies that conformist weights are added to the player's payoffs. On the contrary, were the stakeholder willing to enter when the firm adopts the mixed strategy (so that by entering she is equally compliant as when staying out), the firm would become responsible for a sharp deviation from full compliance, for he could have chosen not to abuse at all. In that case, he would not have maximized the value of T as he possibly could have. This may not be the minimum value for T, but he has nonetheless produced a significant deviation from full compliance (proportional to the distance from the maximum value of T conditional on the stakeholder's choice). Thus, in this case the motivational weight of conformity cannot enter the utility functions of both players in all its strength.

The previous discussion illustrates a particularity in the way the firm's conditional conformity index and reciprocally expected conformity index (as seen in the stakeholders' eyes) behave in games like the Trust Game, and in general in games where the strategy of one player would induce the same result whatever the behavior of the second player. The stakeholder's strategy $\neg e$ (the trustor's strategy in the Trust Game in general), in fact, causes the same pair of payoffs whatever the reply of the firm (the *trustee*). Hence the firm by its behavior can't make any difference about the two pair of the players' payoffs that are possible when stakeholder-player chooses $\neg e$, which both will be necessarily $(1,1)$. Since T is a function of the material payoffs, the value of T is also thus invariant in the two states compatible with stakeholder's strategy $\neg e$. (Notice that in the sequential version of the Trust Game this is quite natural: by playing $\neg e$ the stakeholder, player A, stays out of the interaction and thus prevents the firm from having any influence over the outcome of the game, which in fact is only one, whatever the decision of player B could have been.) This means that, in this case, the firm, given the stakeholder's strategy $\neg e$ *cannot* do any better than to witness the first player bringing about the value 0 of function T representing the distribution principle of social welfare. In other words, in case the stakeholder doesn't enter, no value higher than $T = 0$ does exist that can be obtained through a choice of the firm. So, whatever the strategic choice deliberated by the firm, it cannot induce any deviation from the maximum possible value of T, given $\neg e$. Neither of the firms' choices – let it be a or $\neg a$ – may deviate at any rate from the maximin possible value of $T(= 0)$ given that the stakeholder's choice is $\neg e$. Thus, for both the firm's strategy choices, conformity will be as high as possible given the stakeholder's choice $\neg e$.

In terms of determinants of the firm's conditional conformity index and expected reciprocity index (as seen in the stakeholder's eyes) the differences between the T values determined by any firm's strategy choice and the maximum possible value of T (conditional on the given the stakeholder's choice $\neg e$) are thus zero:

$$T(a, \neg e) - T^{\text{MAX}}(\neg e) = 0, \qquad T(\neg a, \neg e) - T^{\text{MAX}}(\neg e) = 0.$$

This is true for any pure or mixed strategy of the firm (e.g. including any probabilistic combination of a and $\neg a$), granted that the stakeholder stays out.

This entails – and here we point out the peculiarity in how the indexes behave – that the firm's conditional deviation degree and the firm's expected reciprocal deviation degree in the case under consideration are indefinite. In fact, as far as no strategy of the firm, given $\neg e$, may induce any difference with respect the value of T, this also entails that the max and min value of function T are even, given $\neg e$ (i.e. $T^{\text{MAX}}(\neg e) = T^{\text{MIN}}(\neg e) = 0$). Therefore, their difference reported at the denominator is nil (i.e. neither the numerator nor denominator may report any distance from the maximum value of T given $\neg e$). Hence, both the deviation degree and the reciprocally expected deviation degree are necessarily 0/0, namely indefinite. But, of course, this occurs because there is no proper sense in normalizing the measure of deviation from the max value of T given $\neg e$ with respect to the interval from 0 to -1, by taking it as a fraction of the distance between the maximum and the minimum value of T in cases where this distance is nil. In these cases the fraction is simply meaningless.

Thus in this and all the analogous cases in which, given a certain adversary's choice, the maximum and minimum value of T determined by a player's choice scores a difference equal to zero, we will assume that the degree of deviation from the maximum value of T due to this player's choices is simply represented by the *absolute value* of the difference between the T value determined by the player's choice (given the adversary's choice) and the maximum T value possible given that adversary's choice. Notice, however, that, because the T value is identical for all this player's choices given the adversary's behavior, the deviation is necessarily nil for that player and hence also this deviation measure – even without normalization – is necessarily 0. Thus the conformity indexes cannot be but 1.

Coming back to the Trust Game of matrix (a), by considering first the psychological utilities of the firm, when the stakeholder is predicted to play $\neg e$, then the firm would score full conformity both playing a or $\neg a$. But it is only when the firm believes that the stakeholder predicts that he (the firm) plays a that the stakeholder's reciprocal conformity would be full by using $\neg e$. In fact, in case the firm believed to be predicted to use $\neg a$, then the stakeholder's not entering choice would minimize T, and then the stakeholder's reciprocally expected conformity would be 0. Thus, under the strategy combination ($\neg e$, a), represented through first and second order

beliefs of the firm, the firm's conformity index and the stakeholder's reciprocal expected conformity index equal 1. Therefore, the weight λ fully enters
the psychological payoff of the firm. On the contrary, under the combination (¬*e*, ¬*a*) – again seen through the firm's beliefs – the stakeholder's
reciprocal conformity index equals zero, what would nullify the weight λ in
the firm's psychological payoff.

As well, coming now to the stakeholder's psychological utilities, if the
firm is predicted to use the strategy *a*, then the stakeholder's strategy ¬*e*
scores full conditional conformity, since by playing *e* the stakeholder would
induce a lower *T* value and no other stakeholder strategy other than ¬*e*
can induce a higher *T* value. Otherwise, if the stakeholder believes that
the firm predicts that she uses ¬*e*, then the firm's reciprocal conformity
expected in case the firm is predicted to use *a* or ¬*a* *is even (as high as possible in these contingencies)*, that is, the firm's reciprocally expected conformity
equals 1. Thus, given these stakeholder's conditional conformity and firm's
expected reciprocal conformity indexes for the combination (¬*e*, *a*), as seen
through the stakeholder beliefs, the weight λ enters the psychological payoff
of the stakeholder. This would not be the case if the stakeholder predicted
that the firm was to use ¬*a*. In fact, as far as the stakeholder plays ¬*e*, it
is true that the firms' expected reciprocal conformity index (as seen by the
stakeholder) is even (and equal 1) for both the choices *a* and ¬*a*. But if
she predicts ¬*a*, the stakeholder's conditional conformity of choosing ¬*e*
would be minimal (set to 0). So that the weight λ would be canceled in the
stakeholder's psychological utility function for the (¬*e*, ¬*a*) combination.
Summing up, taking the game matrix line corresponding to the strategy ¬*e*,
the weight λ enters the psychological payoffs of both the players only in the
state represented by the bottom right cell.

What has been said till now is by no means conclusive about the existence
of psychological equilibria based on conformist preferences in the one-shot
Trust Game. However, it helps to understand how the psychological payoffs
behave under different strategic and beliefs configurations. Psychological
equilibria (in pure strategies) are then simply calculable. Inspection of matrix
(b) shows that if the firm is predicted to play strategy *a*, the stakeholder maximizes *T* by playing strategy ¬*e*. If this is known, the firm also maximizes *T*
by playing *a*, since neither strategy is better or worse than *a* in order to maximize *T* from the firm's point of view. Hence, in the bottom right cell of
matrix (c) the psychological weight λ adds to each player's material payoff.
On the other hand, if the firm is predicted to play ¬*a*, then the stakeholder
maximizes *T* by choosing *e*. If this choice is also predicted by the firm, his
choice for maximizing *T* is ¬*a* as well. Consequently, in the top left cell of
matrix (c) psychological weights λ are also present. If the firm plays abuse
(*a*), the stakeholder will minimize *T* by entering (*e*), which is also true if
the same result is seen the other way round (given *e*, the firm minimizes
T by abusing with *a*). No weights must then be added in the top right cell

of matrix (c). Lastly, if the firm is predicted as not abusing, the stakeholder minimizes T by staying out with $\neg e$. Consequently, even though the firm is maximizing T when he plays $\neg a$, a zero index of individual conformity (the stakeholder's) is sufficient to nullify the overall level of conformity. Moreover, when this is the case, no psychological conformity weights are implied in the players' payoffs (see bottom left cell of the (c) matrix).

Summing up, given the value $\lambda = 2$, we may see that, as far as only pure strategies are concerned, two Nash psychological equilibria do exists (e, $\neg a$) and ($\neg e$, a). Thus, even in the one-shot game, the situation is ameliorated for not only the 'bad' equilibrium is now possible, but from the point of view of the solution determinateness the situation is also worsened as it isn't unique. I won't go into, here, the existence of mixed-strategy-psychological-Nash equilibria in the one-shot Trust Game as they are mostly relevant to our argument in the context of the repeated Trust Game considered in the next section (where many standard Nash equilibria are also possible). It is within the perspective of the repeated Trust Game that we have to verify whether conformist preferences with an *ex ante* agreed principle of justice will simplify the equilibrium selection problem.

4. Mixed strategies and refinement of the equilibrium set in the iterated Trust Game

4.1. Mixed strategies

Now let us consider the repeated Trust Game (TG). Recall that its payoff space in terms of material utilities is the convex hull of all the linear (probability) combinations of the three payoff vectors generated out of the pure strategy pairs of the basic Trust Game (see Figure 2.2). This is the same as representing the expected payoffs of every possible pair of pure and mixed strategies of the two players in the basic Trust Game. In fact, the player's i expected payoff for a mixed strategy is formally the same as the *average payoff* of the player's i repeated strategy that employs alternatively the two player's i pure strategies of the stage-game with a given frequency, generating the three stage-game outcomes (1,1,), (4,4), (0,5) according to the frequency of the two players' choices. The cumulative payoff of this repeated strategy, given a certain pure (or mixed) response by the second player, can be equated to the average payoff of a cycle during which player i gets each of the three stage-game payoffs a given number of times out of the total number of times defining the cycle (granted, of course, that during the game each repeated strategy pairs used by any player repeatedly enters a cycle with the same pattern of outcomes and the same average payoff value for the player that adopts it). It is thus simple to see that a firm's mixed strategy that employs the two pure strategies $\neg a$ and a with probability 0.25 and 0.75, respectively, against – to keep things simple – the stakeholder's pure entry strategy e, affords the firm and the stakeholder expected the payoffs ($0.25 \times 4 + 0.75 \times 5 = 4.75$) and ($0.25 \times 4 + 0.75 \times 0 = 1$) respectively. This is equal to the average

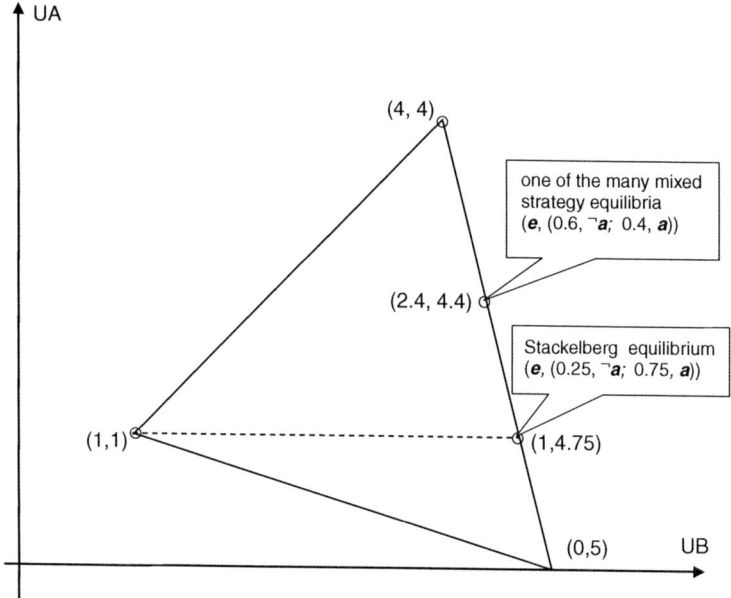

Figure 2.2 Repeated Trust Game between the long-run firm B and the 'average' stakeholder A

values attached to a repeated strategy whereby the firm plays the stage-game strategy ¬*a* 75 percent of the time and the stage-game strategy *a* 25 percent of the time, assuming – to keep things simple again – that the stakeholder always responds with the stage-game strategy *e*. It is obvious to see that in the one-shot Trust Game, no mixed strategy exists as a best response for the firm. In the repeated Trust Game, however, one knows that this is no longer true. In fact, the firm may create a reputation (along, for example, the first *N* repetitions of the game) to be a *type* that uses *the strategies* ¬*a* and *a* in a given frequency, such that the stakeholder's best response is 'always *e*', until by repeated observations he realizes that the frequency is respected, but sanctioning by '¬*e* forever' were it to become clear that the frequency is not respected. This induces the firm to stick to its repeated strategy, mixing *a* and ¬*a* according to the given frequency.

One must, however, consider the payoff space of the repeated psychological game, which can be generated from that of the Trust Game when all of the expected payoffs of mixed strategy pairs are accounted for. This repeated psychological Trust Game in pure and mixed strategies has the same material payoff space as the repeated TG, wherein the average payoffs of each repeated strategy – which employs the pure strategies of a player in a given frequency – is identical to the expected utility of the mixed strategy using the corresponding probability mixtures. Hence, one may ask what happens (under the psychological extension) to the mixed strategy equilibrium points of the corresponding standard repeated Trust Game.

Before answering that question, one must define a way to calculate the expected psychological utility of any mixed strategy. Let us take the point of view of the stakeholder (call him *A*) when she predicts that the firm (call it *B*) will choose a mixed strategy, for example:

$$\sigma_B^{0.6} = \{(0.6, \neg a); (0.4, a)\}.$$

A believes that if she enters by playing the pure strategy *e*, two states (*e*, *¬a*) and (*e*, *a*) may occur, so that two different values of the principle *T* – namely (9) and (−4) – can arise, each of them weighted with the probabilities 0.6 and 0.4 of the respective states. Hence, the expected Nash bargaining product generated by *B*'s mixed strategy $\sigma_B^{0.6}$, given *A*'s entrance, is $0.6 \times 9 + 0.4 \times (-4) = 3.9$, whereas if *A* does not enter, the expected *T* value is 0 as usual. Given $\sigma_B^{0.6}$, player *A*'s strategy *e* maximizes *T* in respect to any other pure or mixed strategy by *A*, whereas *¬e* minimizes it. It turns out that player *A*'s conformity indexes are 1 and 0 for her pure strategies, respectively.

On the other hand, player *B*'s conformity indexes are the following. Assuming that *B* believes *A* will enter, *B* does not maximize *T* by playing the strategy $\sigma_B^{0.6}$, because it is obvious that no-abuse would do better in terms of *T*. Nor does playing the mixed strategy minimize *T*, which in fact would happen by playing *a*. As a result, *B*'s conformity index for strategy $\sigma_B^{0.6}$ is a somewhat intermediate value 0.61. But, assuming that *B* believes that player *A* will not enter by *¬e*. Then *B*'s mixed strategy $\sigma_B^{0.6}$ will maximize *T* no less than any other strategy by *B*. *B*'s conformity index under this hypothesis is thus 1. To conclude the example, consider *A*'s respective expected material payoffs from playing *e* or *¬e* against the mixed strategy $\sigma_B^{0.6}$.

$$EU_A\left(e, \sigma_B^{0.6}\right) = 2.4, \qquad EU_A\left(\neg e, \sigma_B^{0.6}\right) = 1$$

Similarly, player *B*'s expected material payoffs from playing the mixed strategy against the two pure strategies of player *A* are

$$EU_B\left(e, \sigma_B^{0.6}\right) = 4.4, \qquad EU_B\left(\neg e, \sigma_B^{0.6}\right) = 1$$

Since the conformity indexes of players *A* and *B* for the strategy pair $\left(e, \sigma_B^{0.6}\right)$ are 1 and 0.61 respectively, the psychological conformity weight λ will enter the players' utility functions accordingly, that is, by a value (1)(0.61)λ. Given λ = 2, the weight of the conformist motivation is 1.22, and the overall utility payoffs of players *A* and *B* are 3.62 and 5.62, respectively.

In the repeated psychological Trust Game, these payoffs correspond to the following pair of player *B* and player *A*'s repeated strategies: player *B* employs his pure strategies *¬a* and *a* repeatedly, with frequency 0.6 and 0.4

respectively. By this repeated strategy, he tries to convince player *A* (or the sequence of short-run players who participate in the repeated game in the position of *A*) that he will stick to this frequency forever. Player *A* decides to play repeatedly her entry strategy *e* as long as she does not see player *B* employing *abuse* with a frequency higher than 0.4, but if this frequency is exceeded she will switch to '¬*e* forever'.

Since player *A*'s threat seems convincing, player *B* plays *ad infinitum* his above-defined mixed repeated strategy. Assume that exactly 100 times are sufficient to say that the required frequency has been verified so that – if the players adopt the pair of repeated strategies described above – 100 times is a cycle that repeats more and more along the repeated game with always the same proportion of stage-games with outcomes (*e*, *a*) and stage-games with outcomes (*e*, ¬*a*). The average payoffs for this pair of repeated strategies – including the psychological component – is the vector (3.62, 5.62). It would seem to be a good incentive for player *A* to yield to player *B*'s mixed abuse strategy, but I will come back to this point a little later.

Following the method mentioned above, under the hypothesis $\lambda = 2$, it is in fact possible to account for the entire payoff space of the psychological Trust Game, including mixed strategies as well (see Figure 2.3).

First, let us note that the status quo point $(1,1)$ – the only Nash equilibrium of the *basic one-shot* TG and, moreover, an equilibrium of the *repeated* TG – is translated in the north-east direction along the bisector to a point with overall utilities $(3,3)$, which is also a psychological equilibrium of the new game. At the same time, thanks to the motivational conformist weights $\lambda = 2$, the outcome $(4,4)$ where the Nash bargaining product is maximized translates in the north-east direction to the point $(6,6)$, which is also a psychological equilibrium. Let us recall that both these psychological equilibria correspond to Nash equilibria of the repeated Trust Game, so that these two Nash equilibria are sure to be preserved under the payoff change provided by conformist preferences.

In regard to player *B*'s mixed strategies, it can be seen that the entry strategy *e* of player *A* cannot be rewarded with any additional psychological conformist utility until the expected Nash bargaining product – the expected value of *T* associated with any particular probability mixture of the two pure strategies ¬*a* and *a* – is no longer positive, granted player *A* uses *e*. This necessarily happens until a mixed strategy associates the pure strategy ¬*a* with a probability high enough to give the respective *T* value (9) a weight able to counterbalance the *T* value of *a* (−4), so that the *T* expected value exceeds the *T* level fixed by the 'status quo' no-entry strategy (which is 0). Hence, within player *B*'s continuous set of probability mixtures of two pure strategies ¬*a* and *a*, the relevant threshold is fixed by player *B*'s mixed strategy that scores an expected Nash product no different from the *T* value of staying out. As long as this threshold is not exceeded, psychological payoffs do not add any values to the material payoffs of both players *A* and *B*, because

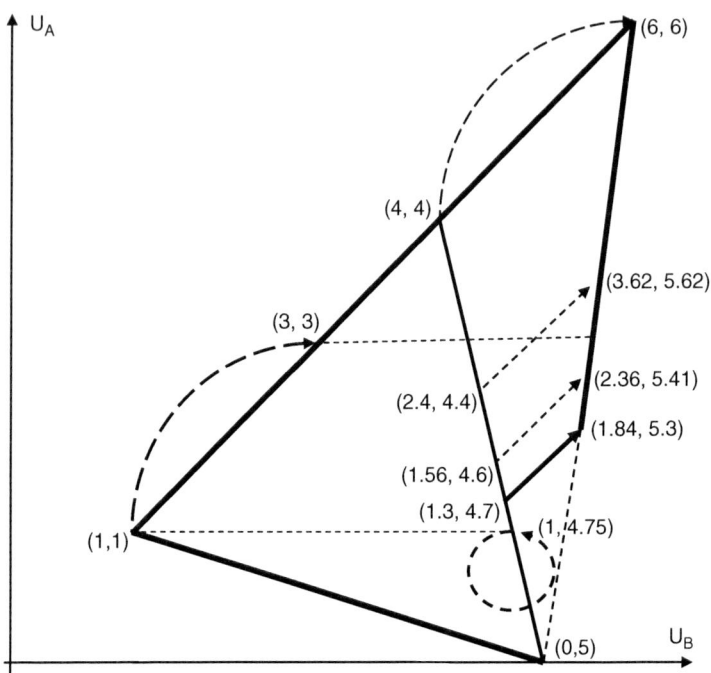

Figure 2.3   The payoff space of the iterated psychological TG. Payoffs of pure and mixed strategies and their translations into the psychological game payoff space are represented. Up to the mixed strategy $\sigma_B^{0.39}$ no psychological utilities accrue to players and hence a region of the basic TG payoff space does not translate into the psychological payoff space

entering by e minimizes the T value and exhibits zero conformity level. This is true also when player B adopts a mixed strategy that makes him partially, and hence positively, compliant. In fact, until player A's choice to enter by e exhibits a zero conformity index, the overall conformity level is also nil for both players and no psychological payoffs can be added to their material payoffs.

This does not mean that psychological utilities are not at work for these mixed strategies. Simply, the psychological component adds to the payoffs of strategy pairs such as (*no entry, mixed strategy*), which is the same as for the strategy pair (*no entry, abuse*) namely (3,3). This means that the best responses for these cases is ¬e, which gives player A an overall payoff 3, whereby player B's mixed strategies and his pure strategy a become indifferent as they both give B the same overall payoff 3.

As an example, consider the mixed strategy $\sigma_B^{0.25} = \{(0.25, \neg a); (0.75, a)\}$. The expected Nash bargaining product (the T value) is negative (-0.75) for the pair $(e, \sigma_B^{0.25})$, whereas T is 0 if player A chooses ¬e. It is thus obvious that A maximizes T by choosing $\neg e$, with conformity index 1, whereas the conformity index for choosing e is 0. As a result, by entering with e, player A can only get the expected overall payoff 1, which – due to the probability mixture provided by $\sigma_B^{0.25}$ – is no different from the *material* payoff of staying out. By staying out with $\neg e$, however, he gets an *overall* payoff 3, because the psychological conformist weight 2 now adds to this strategy's material payoff. Thus, A's best response is obviously to stay out. As far as player B is concerned, the mixed strategy $\sigma_B^{0.25}$ against e gives a payoff equal to its material payoff 4.75. When player A does not enter against $\sigma_B^{0.25}$, B's payoff benefits from the psychological conformist component (becoming 3) as well as for any other choice (abusing or not abusing) by B when he knows that A will play no-entry.

Note the importance of the mixed strategy $\sigma_B^{0.25}$. This is player B's Stackelberg mixed strategy that would correspond to the preferred (by the firm) equilibrium strategy of the repeated Trust Game. It identifies the equilibrium point of the repeated TG that would be the most obvious choice from the point of view of player B were he able to select the solution of the game by himself. It is noticeable, however, that the pair $\left(e,\ \sigma_B^{0.25}\right)$ is not an equilibrium in the psychological TG, even if player B's material payoff is high. Given the mixed strategy $\sigma_B^{0.25}$, player A's best response is not e, nor is player B's material payoff 4.75 sufficient to make the strategy $\sigma_B^{0.25}$ preferred than a when A plays e, simply because, due to a sufficiently high λ associated with the psychological equilibrium in pure strategies (*entry, no-abuse*), playing $\neg a$ pays B more (namely 6).

The threshold that allows mixed strategies to gain support from psychological conformist utility is reached at the mixed strategy $\sigma_B^{0.307} = \{(0.307,\ \neg a);\ (0.693,\ a)\}$. Given this mixed strategy, the expected value of T is zero for any strategy choice by A, so that A is fully conformist by choosing either e or $\neg e$.[4] At the same time, playing the mixed strategy is partially conformist also for player B, because the minimization of the T value, given A's entrance, would be obtained by playing a. Hence, under the pair $\left(e,\ \sigma_B^{0.307}\right)$, psychological utilities add to both the players' material payoffs (1.3, 4.7) generating an overall payoff vector (1.84, 5.31). It is important to note, however, that adding a bit of psychological utility does not mean that this strategy combination becomes a psychological equilibrium. Although it is true that player B's mixed strategy $\sigma_B^{0.307}$ grants a positive overall payoff to A's entry strategy, player A's overall payoff from no-entry (i.e. 3) is still higher than the overall payoff (1.84) from giving in to player B's mixed strategy. This is due to the incomplete conformity level of strategy $\sigma_B^{0.307}$ when player A chooses e. In fact, B's full conformity would be reached by the strategy $\neg a$, whereas $\sigma_B^{0.307}$ scores only the modest conformity index 0.31. This affects the psychological conformist component of player A's overall payoff for strategy e, which is lower than for $\neg e$.

Now let us consider mixed strategy $\sigma_B^{0.39} = \{(0.0.39, \neg a); (0.61, a)\}$. With this small increase in the probability of strategy $\neg a$, things finally seem to change. Player A, with overall payoff 2.36, benefits substantially from the psychological conformist utility of her entry strategy e'. At the same time, as typically happens when a pure strategy is surpassed in its conformity index, player A's conformity index of no-entry drops to zero, since choosing $\neg e$ given $\sigma_B^{0.39}$ would minimize the value of T in respect to the alternative entry strategy (and also any other mixed strategy). Hence, player A's overall utility for the no-entry strategy $\neg e$ also dramatically drops to 1 (the material payoff only). Moreover, for the pair $(e, \sigma_B^{0.39})$, player B's overall payoff contains a substantial psychological conformist component such that his overall payoff now reaches 5.41. If player A were to choose $\neg e$, however, player B's payoff would be reduced just to his material payoff 1, since the conformity index of player A's strategy $\neg e$ is zero (though B's index remains positive). Note, nonetheless, that this does not imply that one has reached an equilibrium point. Even though entry is player A's best reply to player B's mixed strategy $\sigma_B^{0.39}$, this strategy is not reciprocally player B's best response. The perfectly compliant strategy $\neg a$ would do better in terms of conformity index, scoring an overall payoff 6 higher than the mixed strategy.

This suggests a general fact about the model. Let us consider again the mixed strategy $\sigma_B^{0.6} = \{(0.6, \neg a); (0.4, a)\}$.

As we know, player A's conformity index if she uses strategy e against $\sigma_B^{0.6}$ is 1, whereas the mixed strategy's conformity index is 0.61. The annexed overall payoffs are (3.62, 5.62), respectively. Even though high psychological conformist utility enters both the players' payoffs, this is not enough to define reciprocal best responses at $(e, \sigma_B^{0.6})$ since, given player A's entry strategy, player B's best reply is again no-abuse at all with its overall payoff 6.

4.2. Equilibrium set of the psychological repeated Trust Game

In order to give a general assessment of the two players' best reply sets in the psychological Trust Game, let us assume that λ is high enough for the pure strategy equilibrium $(e, \neg a)$ to exist. Let us call $E^{n|e}(\Pi_{A,B})$ the expected Nash bargaining product corresponding to player B's n-ary mixed strategy σ_B^n (where the index n corresponds to the probability weight assigned to the pure strategy $\neg a$) given player A's strategy e. Hence, let $\Pi_{A,B}$ denote a generic Nash bargaining product. Lastly, let's call 'status quo' the material payoff granted by A's pure strategy $\neg e$. The relevant facts about the psychological Trust Game are the following:

- *Case 1*, $\forall \sigma_B^n$ with $n \geq 0$ s.t. $E^{n|e}(\Pi_{A,B}) < 0$, such that the pure strategy $\neg e$ induces $\Pi_{A,B} = 0 > E(\Pi_{A,B})^n$, the pure strategy e does not add any psychological conformist utility to player A's material payoff, whereas the pure strategy $\neg e$ adds the psychological conformity weight λ to the 'status quo' material payoff. Hence, player A's best reply is $\neg e$ whereby *any* mixed strategy in this case is as good as strategy a to player B. The equilibrium for this case is the psychological equilibrium point $(\neg e, a)$. This equilibrium is weak since every mixed strategy in this case gives player B the same overall payoff of a.

- *Case 2*, $\forall \sigma_B^n$ with $0 < n < 1$ s.t. $E^{n|e}(\Pi_{A,B}) > 0$, such that the pure strategy $\neg e$ induces $\Pi_{A,B} = 0 < E(\Pi_{A,B})^n$. Each pair (e, σ_B^n) adds some psychological conformity utility to both players' material payoffs, whereas the pure strategy $\neg e$ reduces player A to the 'status quo' material payoff. This follows from the minimal conformity index of strategy $\neg e$, while in this case mixed strategies σ_B^n have positive conformity indexes strictly less than 1. Thus for both players A and B, there is an intermediate overall index F of conditional and expected reciprocal conformity. In this case, player A's best reply is strategy e. Nevertheless, against strategy e, player B's best is $\neg a$. In other words, as little as player B's psychological conformist utility of a mixed strategy σ_B^n is positive, player B's pure strategy $\neg a$ against e (or whatever mixed strategy by player A) induces a psychological conformist payoff higher than σ_B^n, so that player B has an incentive to deviate from σ_B^n to $\neg a$. When this occurs, player A obviously has no reason to change her choice, and the equilibrium point is $(e, \neg a)$.

- *Case 3*, for a single $0 < n < 1$ $\exists$ σ_B^n such that $E^{n|e}(\Pi_{A,B}) = 0$, such that the pure strategy $\neg e$ induces $\Pi_{A,B} = 0 = E^{n|e}(\Pi_{A,B})$. In this case, both the strategy pairs (e, σ_B^n) and $(\neg e, \sigma_B^n)$ add positive psychological conformist utility to the material payoffs of both the players A and B. Nevertheless, player A's overall payoff gained from $(\neg e, \sigma_B^n)$ strictly dominates her overall payoff gained from (e, σ_B^n) since, whereas the two pure strategies e and $\neg e$ score the same conformity index, the case of player B's conformity indexes is different. Player B against $\neg e$ cannot do any better than play σ_B^n with conformity index 1, but given e, the strategy σ_B^n conformity index is strictly less than 1, which is the conformity index of his pure strategy $\neg a$. Since the strictly less than 1 conformity index of strategy σ_B^n directly depends on the required probability value n, which also affects the expected material utility of player A for (e, σ_B^n), this correlation is crucial in this case. It turns out that the greater player A's payoff gained from $(e, \neg a)$ is, the smaller the probability required for the $\Pi_{A,B}$ indifference, but also the smaller the resulting player B's conformity index for σ_B^n. Thus, player B's small conformity index at the same time affects negatively (via a small probability) player A's material expected utility – since a small probability of $(e, \neg a)$ will counterbalance its high payoff – and also makes the strategy e psychological utility increasingly lower than the strictly dominant psychological utility of strategy $\neg e$. The resulting equilibrium point of this case is still $(\neg e, a)$.

Boundaries between the three cases are established by the distribution of the material payoffs associated with any mixed strategy, and in particular how much surplus it assigns to player A. As long as a mixed strategy overwhelmingly advantages player B in relation to player A, the T expected value of the mixed strategy pair (e, σ_B^n) cannot exceed that of player A's staying out. This is not just because A is dissatisfied with his/her material outcome, but because of the insufficient conformity index of such mixed strategies. When a mixed strategy σ_B^n instead offers a substantial share of the material surplus to player A, it becomes the most conformist solution, and then provides psychological utility to both the players against a loss of material payoff to B. At this point, however, player B is able to compare the psychological utility of incomplete conformity against that of full conformity. It is evident that if the parameter λ is high enough to guarantee the existence of the psychological equilibrium in pure strategies, then it is also true that player B will always prefer the pure strategy of full conformity.

This also depends, of course, largely on the λ exogenous parameter of the two players (granted they are symmetric, which is not necessarily true). Were λ too low, the situation would not change in regards to the basic TG and the repeated TG. If, however, λ is greater than player B's payoff difference between abusing and not abusing (given player A's entry), its motivational effectiveness necessarily becomes maximal for the strategy of full conformity. In general, it biases the game toward excluding mixed strategies from giving rise to psychological equilibria. A look at the payoff space reveals a single north-east vertex where both payers have higher payoffs than anywhere on the eastern frontier where all the expected payoffs generated by mixed strategies lie. In short, given its overall payoffs, the pair $(e, \neg a)$ strictly dominates any other strategy pair involving a mixed strategy σ_B^n and player A's entry strategy e. We have argued enough to state the following:

Proposition I

Given a Trust Game with pure and mixed strategies, whereby a psychological game with conformist preferences is defined so that the motivational exogenous parameter λ is great enough to guarantee the existence of a psychological equilibrium in correspondence to $(e, \neg a)$, the game's psychological equilibria are only the two in pure strategy $(e, \neg a)$ and $(\neg e, a)$, and no equilibrium points in mixed strategies exist. In particular, none of player B's mixed strategies are the best reply to player A's pure entry strategy e, even if the entry strategy e is player A's best reply to some player B's mixed strategy.

From this proposition comes the following:

Corollary

In the repeated psychological Trust Game, psychological equilibria 'refine' the equilibrium set of the corresponding repeated TG in a discontinuous way as a function of the increase in the motivational exogenous parameter λ.

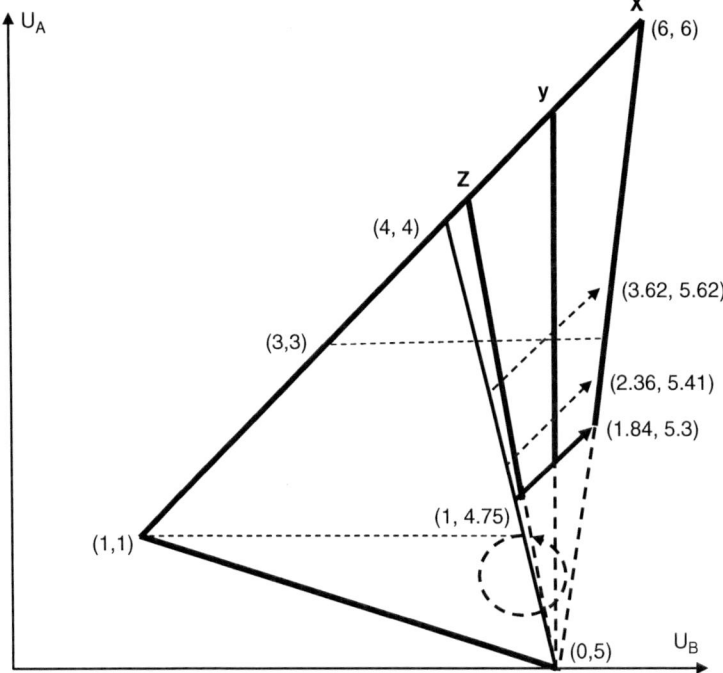

Figure 2.4 Payoff spaces of the repeated psychological TG under three values of the parameter λ.
λ < 1 implies the NE frontier Z; λ = 1 implies the NE frontier Y; λ = 2 implies the NE frontier X

- Given any λ such that in the one-shot psychological TG, there is no psychological equilibrium in correspondence with the pair (*e*, ¬*a*), the psychological equilibrium set of the repeated game is the same as the equilibrium set of the standard repeated TG due to the sole effect of material payoffs (see north-east boundary Z in Figure 2.4).
- If the value of λ is such that in the one-shot psychological TG player *B*'s overall payoff derived from the strategy combination (*e*, ¬*a*) is no different from the overall payoff derived by *B* from the strategy combination (*e*, *a*) – so that a weak psychological equilibrium exists for (*e*, ¬*a*) – then in the corresponding psychological repeated TG the psychological equilibria constituted by any mixed strategy σ_B^n and the pure strategy *e* have all the same player *B* expected payoffs, and thus they are all weak equilibria. Given the continuity of the probability mixture set over the two pure strategies ¬*a* and *a*, the value of λ such that this is true is unique (see north-east boundary Y in Figure 2.4).

- If λ is such that in the psychological one-shot TG in correspondence to the pair (*e*, ¬*a*) there is a strong psychological equilibrium, then in the repeated psychological TG there are no psychological equilibria in mixed strategies and the psychological equilibrium set dramatically shrinks to the only two pure strategy equilibrium points (*e*, ¬*a*) and (¬*e*, *a*). (See north-east boundary X of Figure 2.4).

The corollary is important, because it is in this context that we see our result. As far as the payoff space of a one-shot basic TG is concerned, mixed strategies are not equilibria. If *B* adopts a mixed strategy that induces *A* to enter, *B* immediately has an incentive to deviate to the abuse strategy since the mixed strategy is not the best reply to *A*'s choice to enter. On the contrary, if the payoff space is seen (as in the corollary) as the convex set of all the average payoffs for repeated strategies in a repeated TG, then represented within this space may be the average payoffs of player *B*'s repeated strategies mixing the two pure strategies *a* and ¬*a* according to some pre-established frequencies.

Thus, if player *B* is able to accumulate a reputation of being a player that unfailingly plays one such strategy, he will have no reason to deviate if player *A* adopts a conditioned strategy of entrance like 'as long as my observations are compatible with the hypothesis that *B* is playing *a* and ¬*a* according to the given pre-established frequency, I will continue to enter by *e*, but if I find that my observations are incompatible with that frequency, I will switch to ¬*e* forever'. In fact, given player *A*'s conditioned entrance strategy, player *B* verifies that maintaining his reputation of being the type of player who uses the repeated strategy 'abuse no more than *x* per cent of the time, and no abuse for the rest of the time' is profitable since it allows him to gain a certain portion of the surplus. Summing up, player *B* has the incentive to keep abuses at a certain frequency in order to support his reputation of being the relevant type.

The situation changes significantly, however, when the repeated psychological TG is considered. In this case, a payoff space identical to the convex hull of all the payoff pairs deriving from pure strategy combinations in the one-shot psychological TG is not completely generated by taking the set of all the *average* payoff pairs given by combinations of the two players' (pure and mixed) repeated strategies (in fact payoffs spaces of Figures 2.3 and 2.4 have a non convex region along the dotted line from the payoff pair (0,5) to the payoff pair (1.84, 5.3)). What happens is that if player *B* has chosen a repeated mixed strategy whereby he has been able to accumulate a positive reputation that induces player *A* to enter for the first time, then he immediately recognizes the incentive to switch to a strategy that employs ¬*a* with higher frequency. This feature of the repeated psychological TG completely changes the best response structure with regard to the standard repeated TG. In the standard case, player *B* has a clear incentive to maintain his strategy once he has been able to build up a reputation for being a mixed *type*, since abusing less would give away a larger part of the surplus to player A, while abusing more would induce player A to carry out her sanction. At the same time, player A has a strong incentive to monitor and sanction the relevant possible deviation by player B. In the repeated psychological TG, by contrast, player B's best reply to player A's entry is to deviate from any mixed strategy σ_B^n to $\neg a$. If, however, player B deviates to a strategy more concessive to him, A does not have any reason to punish him. Thus, the repeated mixed strategy equilibrium of the basic repeated TG is destabilized. Summing up, any mixed strategy by player B that induces player A to enter, according to player B's point of view is dominated by the pure strategy 'always $\neg a$', so that a rational player B would never strive after a reputation such as being committed to the mixed strategy σ_B^n. From the outset, he would prefer to develop the dominant reputation of being an 'always $\neg a$' player.

From this, the conclusion follows that even though generating a psychological game from a basic Trust Game enables us to determine new equilibrium points (in other words, to pass from only one equilibrium to at least two), when the change involves a step from the one-shot TG to the repeated TG, transforming the payoff space by means of conformist preferences has a powerful effect in reducing the psychological equilibria to a subset of the Nash equilibria. It remains, however, that the equilibria are two. Which of the two is to be selected?

5. Social contract-based *ex ante* beliefs

It is a somewhat disturbing truth in the foundation of game theory that even the existence of 'one sole' Nash equilibrium point, save for the case it is in dominant strategies, does not assure *per se* sufficient conditions for deducing the rational solution of the game (see Bacharach 1987, Bacharach 2006). In order to predict that rational players will carry out their equilibrium strategies, something more is needed: the system of reciprocally consistent expectations that justify the prediction that players will adopt exactly *that* combination of equilibrium strategies. A player rationally chooses an equilibrium strategy only when s/he has formed the backing expectation that the other players will also play the equilibrium strategy components of the same equilibrium point, so that his/her choice is rationally justified as his/her best response to them. Moreover, this backing expectation must be consistent with the assumption that the other players also act with similar backing expectations. Hence, in order to be considered as a *solution* that each player will *rationally* play, an equilibrium point even if unique needs *previously* to be predicted as the set of strategies that every player will play. In other words, it must be *previously known* by each player as the description of strategies that all the other players will effectively carry out, given that they all expect exactly these strategies from one another (this amounts to the somewhat circular statement that a Nash equilibrium is a solution as far as the solution – the equilibrium point to be the solution – is common knowledge).

Where can this *previous knowledge* come from? The simple existence of an equilibrium does not entail that it will be played since, again, in order to infer that it will actually be put into practise a player needs some reason to believe that other players besides him/herself have already formed the expectation that everybody will play it. In other words, a process of expectation formation converging on this mutually consistent system of beliefs and prediction must be worked out even in the apparently simple case that 'one sole' equilibrium point exists. Indubitably, therefore, a more pressing problem of expectations formation exists if the possible equilibrium points are many. Without answering the question as to which of them is mutually expected by players to be the actual solution of the game, there is no way to say that players have any incentive to play a particular strategy combination, even if it is an equilibrium point of the game.

To return to our context, recall that the foregoing section concluded that *at most two* Nash psychological equilibria remain as solution candidates once the game has been transformed into a psychological game through the *ex ante* agreement on a CSR norm and the introduction of conformist motivations. *Two*, however, are enough to create significant uncertainty about the actual solution. Though one of these equilibria properly corresponds to the *ex ante* agreement on a fairness principle (the Nash bargaining solution is maximized by the outcome (4,4)), this is not enough to say that it is the predicted solution of the *ex post* game.

In order to solve the problem, the *ex ante* 'should-be' agreed solution should also be known as the *ex post de facto* implemented set of strategy choices. Any player knows that a strategy combination is implemented only if this knowledge is consistent with the prediction that any other player also believes that everybody will in fact play that equilibrium. Could the fact that one has *ex ante* agreed on a principle corresponding to an equilibrium be sufficient to create this general expectation? It could, but it is important to realize that there is no necessity in this inference. What one decides to do in order to be impartial in the *ex ante* perspective is not necessarily what one will actually do in the *ex post* perspective. Moreover, it is not necessarily what other players will do in the *ex post* situation. This inference would be unwarranted from a logical point of view. Let us recall that the motivational force of conformist preference – driving players to conform with an *ex ante* agreed principle – also operates conditionally on the previous expectations that the counterparty will reciprocate compliance. Hence, the existence of a previous system of mutual expectations must also be granted in the context of psychological equilibria.

Here one appreciates the role that norms play in a cognitive process of belief formation converging on the mutual prediction across players that a given psychological equilibrium will be *de facto* executed. This role consists in a two-tiered answer. At a first stage, it is suggested that if each player has actually adopted a unanimous impartial agreement in the *ex ante* perspective, then s/he will get to hold at least one *mental model* of a decision maker (at least *himself*) who plans at a moment in time to act in accordance with the terms of the agreed course of action (for mental models see Johnson-Laird 1986, Johnson-Laird and Byrne 1991, Dezau and Northon 1984).

Notwithstanding the genuineness of the intention, agreeing on a set of actions to be carried out later in fact implies making a plan on some ensuing action, which is simply the behavioral content of the statement of agreement. In order to stipulate that 'we will act in a certain way later on' – which may be seen as the content of a generic agreement – each player at least must have in mind the mental model of an agent *who will act in that certain way later on*, where the 'way' is the one *signed* in the agreement. What could otherwise be meant by finding a strategy combination that is an equilibrium solution invariant under the players' position replacement, but having in mind a model of an agent who, without going against his/her incentives, behaves *ex post* exactly in the *same* way whatever his/her position in the game?

This is not a reason to say that if this mental model is admitted, then it follows that the player will actually carry out the correspondent action, nor is it a reason to say that if the existence of such a mental model is true for other players, then they will, in fact, carry out the corresponding actions. This is a matter of *approximate* and *default* reasoning, not one of pure logic or necessity (Reiter 1980, Bacharach 1994; Sacconi 2007b). The model is derived from introspection, because the player him/herself is a rational agent who has been able to plan action in accordance with the behavioral content of the statement of agreement. The paradigmatic case whereby the model is derived by generalization is that of the agent him/herself. Let us therefore simply state that a player holds in his/her mind the mental model of a rational agent (himself) who acts according to the behavioral content of the statement, which is the term of agreement (Faillo and Sacconi 2007).

Assume, moreover, that mental models are necessarily used in order to figure out possible situations and predict them (that is, no future behavior can be outguessed without a mental model of an agent performing the corresponding behavior). Let us hypothesize that at a point in time no further mental model of a rational agent comes to the mind of our players but that of an agent who *will act in a certain way later on*. If no contrary evidence is thus far forthcoming about the actual behavior of other players, the only way that an agent can simulate the other players' choice is to resort by default to his/her own mental model of a rational agent. By default, then, the same mental model is used to simulate every players' reasoning and behavior. This simulation can be recursive, so that a player uses his/her mental model not only to predict another player's behavior, but also in order to simulate the other player's reasoning and beliefs, so that a *shared mental model* of all the rational agents results in them all conforming to the terms of agreement (see Sacconi and Moretti 2008).

This explains, if not justifies, why the agent may categorize or recognize this situation (until proof of the contrary) as an element of the class wherein agents conform to the norm. If a player has agreed on a fairness principle s/he *normally* has a mental model of an agent who carries out the corresponding commitment, for this is the behavioral content of the principle he has agreed to. Moreover, nothing in his/her knowledge base (until proof or evidence to the contrary) contradicts that an agent who subscribed to an agreement on the principle will carry out the corresponding commitment (assume this is provisionally true). This produces, as a matter of description of how players *de facto* reason (not as a matter of deduction from whatever absolute logical principle), the state of reciprocal beliefs that justifies the decision of any player to carry out the strategies consistent with the psychological equilibrium wherein the principle *T reaches its absolute highest value* – in the Trust Game the pair $(e, \neg a)$.[5]

6. Concluding remarks

This concludes the explanation of the initially suggested four roles of voluntary, yet explicit, CSR norms based on a Rawlsian social contract. These norms make it possible to describe strategies and equilibrium points, even when the equilibria are multiple, in a game played under unforeseen contingencies among the firm and its stakeholders (see Part I, Sacconi 2010a). A CSR norm allows for the *ex ante* selection of the equilibrium point that meets the requirements of an impartial choice (see Part II, Sacconi 2010b). An explicit agreement on a contractarian norm is, moreover, a way of introducing psychological conformist equilibria and, surprisingly, of deriving the important result that mixed strategy equilibria are absent from a psychological repeated Trust Game (see section 4). Thus the only admitted psychological equilibria correspond to (*enter, not abuse*) and (*not enter, abuse*) in the Trust Game. Moreover, according to the logic of default reasoning, the *ex ante* agreement makes it reasonable that the players beliefs over which of the two remaining equilibria will constitute the solution of the game will converge on believing that the solution of the psychological game is the (*entry, no abuse*) – namely the one where the agreed principle *T* is mostly satisfied. The game theory of endogenous implementation of the normative model of multi-stakeholder fiduciary duties is thus complete.

Notes

1. Parts I and II of this essay (Sacconi 2010a, 2010b) appear in a parallel book edited by L. Sacconi, M. Blair, R.E. Freeman and A. Vercelli, *Corporate Social Responsibility and Corporate Governance: The Contribution of Economic Theory and Related Disciplines*, Palgrave: London, 2010.
2. Relevant literature on psychological games and reciprocity also includes Rabin (1993), Chareness and Dufwenberg (2006) and Segal and Sobel (2007).
3. The extensive literature on equilibrium refinements (see Van Damme 1987) may be seen as an indirect approach to equilibrium selection in the sense that by

specifying additional requirements on the solution concept it reduces admissible elements of the Nash equilibria set. By contrast, psychological games are not usually seen as 'refinements', for they seem to enlarge the equilibrium set with reference to the Nash equilibrium set. This refinement effect is thus a peculiar and somewhat surprising result of the conformist preferences model within the Trust Game context.

4. When the minimum and maximin T values are even, what happens here, given the mixed strategy under consideration for both player A's strategies e and $\neg e$, the measure of deviation from full conformity cannot be taken as equal to the ratio $T\left(.\left|\sigma_B^{0.307}\right.\right) - T^{\text{Max}}\left(\sigma_B^{0.307}\right) / T^{\text{Max}}\left(\sigma_B^{0.307}\right) - T^{\text{Min}}\left(\sigma_B^{0.307}\right)$ for this case it is 0/0, i.e. it is indefinite. It is needed here to take as the proper index of deviation the simple absolute number $T\left(.\left|\sigma_B^{0.307}\right.\right) - T^{\text{Max}}\left(\sigma_B^{0.307}\right)$, which is necessarily zero. See, for this point, what has been said at pp. 59–60 *infra*.

5. Of course, it may be the case that it comes to the player's mind that an agent also does not comply with the agreed principle and, until proof to the contrary, this alternative mental model can also be assigned by default to other players in order to simulate their choice as far as there is not contrary evidence. Thus, to the player's mind may come *two* mental models that are both *contingently* true according to two different incomparable mental *framings* of the situation. Considered separately, these mental models allow for a default inference in the format, 'it is not inconsistent with the base of knowledge that ...'. But taken together they are inconsistent. If the player is *aware* enough about his/her own possible different mental models (what asks for an higher level of reflection than the usual case studied by cognitive scientists) he may realize enough to be in a state of uncertainty about the context he is playing in. Then, aware-enough players could have a common prior probability distribution representing such uncertainty about which of the two possible equilibrium points – each supported by one of the two possible mental models – is to be taken as the solution of the game. This suggests that in such a situation an 'eductive' equilibrium selection process (for 'eductive' see Binmore 1987/8) such as Harsanyi and Selten's traducing procedure may be employed to single out the unique solution of the game (see Harsanyi 1975; Harsanyi and Selten 1988). It is a remarkable result that in our case the resulting solution would be the psychological equilibrium $(e, \neg a)$, i.e. the one where the Nash bargaining product (i.e. the principle T) takes its maximum value unconditionally (for this result see Sacconi 2008).

References

L. Andreozzi (2010) 'When Reputation is not Enough: Justifying Corporate Social Responsibility', in L. Sacconi, M. Blair, R.E. Freeman and A. Vercelli (eds), *Corporate Social Responsibility and Corporate Governance: The Contribution of Economic Theory and Related Disciplines*, London: Palgrave Macmillan.

M. Aoki (2001) *Toward a Comparative Institutional Analysis*, Cambridge, MA: MIT Press.

M. Aoki (2007a) 'Three-Level Approach to the Rules of the Societal Game: Generic, Substantive and Operational' paper presented at the conference on 'Changing Institutions (in developed countries): Economics, Politics and Welfare' Paris, 24–25 May 2007.

M. Aoki (2007b) 'Endogenizing Institutions and Institutional Change', *Journal of Institutional Economics*, **3**, pp. 1–39.

Bacharach (1987) 'A Theory of Rational Decisions in Games', *Erkenntnis*, **27**, pp. 17–55.

M. Bacharach (1994) 'The Epistemic Structure of a Game', *Theory and Decisions*, **37**, pp. 7–48.

M. Bacharach (2006) *Beyond Individual Choice, Teams and Frames in Game Theory*, edited by N. Gold and R. Sugden, Princeton, N.J.: Princeton University Press.

K. Binmore (1987) 'Modeling Rational Players', *Economics and Philosophy*, **1** (3), pp. 9–55 and **2** (4), pp. 179–214.

K. Binmore (1991) 'Game Theory and the Social Contract', in R. Selten (ed.), *Game Equilibrium Models II, Methods, Morals, Markets*, Berlin: Springer Verlag.

K. Binmore (2005) *Natural Justice*, Oxford: Oxford University Press.

S. Chareness and M. Dufwenberg (2006) 'Promises and Partnership', *Econometrica*, **74** (6), pp. 1579–1601.

G. Degli Antoni and L. Sacconi (2010) *infra* 'Modeling Cognitive Social Capital and Corporate Social Responsibility (CSR) as Preconditions for Sustainable Networks of Relations', in L. Sacconi and G. Degli Antoni (eds), *Social Capital, Corporate Social Responsibility, Economic Behaviour and Performance*, Basingstoke: Palgrave MacMillan.

A. Dezau and D. North (1994), 'Shared Mental Models: Ideologies and Institutions', *Kyklos*, **47** (1), pp. 1–31.

M. Faillo and L. Sacconi (2007) 'Norm Compliance: The Contribution of Behavioral Economics Models', in A. Innocenti and P. Sbriglia (eds), *Games, Rationality and Behavior*, London: Palgrave Macmillan.

M. Faillo, S. Ottone and L. Sacconi (2008) *Compliance by Believing: An Experimental Exploration on Social Norms and Impartial Agreements*, University of Trento – Department of Economics Working paper; online available at: http://papers.ssrn.com/sol3/papers.cfm?abstract_id=1151245.

B.S. Frey (1997) *Not Just for the Money*, Cheltenham: Edward Elgar.

D. Fudenberg (1991) 'Explaining Cooperation and Commitment in Repeated Games', in J.J. Laffont (ed.), *Advances in Economic Theory, 6th World Congress*, Cambridge: Cambridge University Press.

D. Fudenberg and D. Levine (1989) 'Reputation and Equilibrium Selection in Games with a Patient Player', *Econometrica*, **57**, pp. 759–778.

J. Geanakoplos, D. Pearce and E. Stacchetti (1989) 'Psychological Games and Sequential for Non-Cooperative Games', *International Journal of Game Theory*, **5** (1975), pp. 61–94.

G. Grimalda and L. Sacconi (2005) 'The Constitution of the Not-for-Profit Organisation: Reciprocal Conformity to Morality', *Constitutional Political Economy*, **16** (3), pp. 249–276.

J.C. Harsanyi and R. Selten (1988) *A General Theory of Equilibrium Selection*, Cambridge, MA: MIT Press.

J.C. Harsanyi (1975) 'The Tracing Procedure. A Bayesian Approach to Defining a Solution', *International Journal of Game Theory*, **4** (2), pp. 61–94.

J.C. Harsanyi (1977) *Rational Behaviour and Bargaining Equilibrium in Games and Social Situations*, Cambridge, MA: Cambridge University Press.

P.N. Johnson-Laird and R.M.J. Byrne (1991) *Deduction*, Hove and London: Lawrence Erlbaum Associates.

P.N. Johnson-Laird (1986) *Mental Models Towards A Cognitive Science of Language, Inference and Consciousness*, Cambridge: Cambridge University Press.

J. Nash (1950) 'The Bargaining Problem', *Econometrica*, **18**, pp. 155–162.

E.A. Posner (2000) *Law and Social Norms*, Cambridge, MA: Harvard University Press.

M. Rabin (1993) 'Incorporating Fairness into Game Theory', *American Economic Review*, **83** (5), pp. 1281–1302.

J. Rawls (1971) *A Theory of Justice*, Oxford: Oxford University Press.

R. Reiter (1980) 'A Logic for Default Reasoning', *Artificial Intelligence*, **13**, pp. 81–132.

L. Sacconi (2000) The Social Contract of the Firm, Berlin: Springer Verlag.

L. Sacconi (2006a) 'CSR As A Model of Extended Corporate Governance, An Explanation Based on the Economic Theory of Social Contract, Reputation and Reciprocal Conformism', in F. Cafaggi (ed.), *Reframing Self-Regulation in European Private Law*, London: Kluwer Law International.

L. Sacconi (2006b) 'A Social Contract Account For CSR as Extended Model of Corporate Governance (Part I): Rational Bargaining and Justification', *Journal of Business Ethics*, **68** (3), pp. 259–81.

L. Sacconi (2007a) 'A Social Contract Account for CSR as Extended Model of Corporate Governance (Part II): Compliance, Reputation and Reciprocity', *Journal of Business Ethics*, **75**, pp. 77–96.

L. Sacconi (2007b) 'Incomplete Contracts and Corporate Ethics: A Game Theoretical Model under Fuzzy Information', in F. Cafaggi, A. Nicita and U. Pagano (eds), *Legal Orderings and Economic Institutions*, London: Routledge.

L. Sacconi (2008) 'CSR as Contractarian Model of Multi-Stakeholder Corporate Governance and the Game-Theory of its Implementation, University of Trento – Department of Economics Working paper N. 18.

L. Sacconi (2009) 'Corporate Social Responsibility: Implementing a Contractarian Model of Multi-stakeholder Corporate Governance trough Game Theory', in J.P. Touffut and R. Solow (eds), *Does Company Ownership Matter?*, London: Centre for economic Studies Series, Edward Elgar Publishing Ltd.

L. Sacconi (2010a) 'A Rawlsian view of CSR and the Game Theory of its Implementation (Part I): The Multistakeholder Model of Corporate Governance', in L. Sacconi, M. Blair, R.E. Freeman and A. Vercelli (eds), *Corporate Social Responsibility and Corporate Governance: The Contribution of Economic Theory and Related Disciplines*, London: Palgrave Macmillan.

L. Sacconi (2010b) 'A Rawlsian view of CSR and the Game Theory of its Implementation (Part II): Fairness and Equilibrium', in L. Sacconi, M. Blair, R.E. Freeman and A. Vercelli (eds), *Corporate Social Responsibility and Corporate Governance: The Contribution of Economic Theory and Related Disciplines*, London: Palgrave Macmillan.

L. Sacconi and G. Grimalda (2007) 'Ideals, Conformism and Reciprocity: A Model of Individual Choice with Conformist Motivations, and an Application to the Not-for-Profit Case', in P.L. Porta and L. Bruni (eds), *Handbook of Happiness in Economics*, Cheltenham: Edward Elgar.

L. Sacconi and S. Moretti (2008) 'A Fuzzy Logic and Default Reasoning Model of Social Norms and Equilibrium Selection in Games under Unforeseen Contingencies', *International Journal of Uncertainty, Fuzziness and Knowledge Based Systems*, **16** (1), pp. 59–81.

L. Sacconi and G. Degli Antoni (2009) 'A Theoretical Analysis of the Relationship between Social Capital and Corporate Social Responsibility: Concepts and Definitions', in Sacchetti S. and Sugden R. (eds), *Knowledge in the Development of Economies. Institutional Choices under Globalisation*, London: Edward Elgar Publishing Ltd.

L. Sacconi and M. Faillo (2010) 'Conformity, Reciprocity and the Sense of Justice. How Social Contract-based Preferences and Beliefs Explain Norm Compliance: the Experimental Evidence', *Constitutional Political Economy*, **21** (2), pp. 171–201.

U. Segal and J. Sobel (2007) 'Tit for Tat: Foundations of Preferences for Reciprocity in Strategic Settings', *Journal of Economic Theory*, **136**, pp. 197–216.

E. Van Damme (1987) *Stability and Perfection of Nash Equilibria*, Berlin: Springer Verlag.

3
Trustful Banking: A Psychological Game-Theoretical Model of Fiduciary Interactions in Micro-credit Programs

Vittorio Pelligra

'If we want to succeed we must rely on trust'

Mohammad Yunus[1]

1. Introduction

In many underdeveloped areas, rural villages in Asia or Africa as well as poor and segregated neighborhoods in Western cities, micro-credit initiatives have revealed to be an efficient instrument to overcome the credit-rationing problem and to promote social, economic and human development of the 'poorest of the poor'. The success of many of these programs is difficult to account for within the traditional explanatory framework, that, mainly because of the assumptions of self-interested behavior and asymmetric information, predicts adverse selection, opportunistic behavior and, as a consequence, credit rationing. In practice that means that credit will be provided only to those able to back it with collateral. However, micro-finance initiatives (MFIs) that require neither collateral nor joint liability[2] tend to experience unusually high rates of repayment. Many authors suggest that in micro-finance programs traditional material incentives to repay the loan are substituted by other forms of social and dynamic incentives (i.e. loss of reputation, the risk of ostracism, non-refinancing threats). Although such explanations stress the importance of key factors, they nevertheless neglect another, more pristine element, most notably, interpersonal trust.

The chapter presents a simple psychological Trust Game that formalizes the fiduciary bond between borrower and lender in micro-credit initiatives. It argues that this bond helps in overcoming the informational asymmetries that usually affect such relationships and renders more efficient the working of the other forms of incentives. The general idea is that the reasons why a borrower repays the loan are many and differentiated, interpersonal trust is one of them, the most basic and fundamental, and interacts with the others in complex ways. We think that focusing primarily on trust may help in understanding such complexity.

The Grameen Bank, in particular the mechanisms and practices implemented in its second phase (*Grameen Bank II*), represents the case our discussion will assume as paradigm as it presents all the key characteristics of micro-finance: small transactions, loans for entrepreneurial activity, collateral-free loans, group lending, focus on poor clients, focus on female clients and, finally, market-level interest rates (see Goldberg and Karlan 2006).

In this context, the main empirical phenomenon or stylized fact we want to shed light on is the surprisingly high rate of repayment experienced in recent years by its micro-credit program.[3] A high rate of repayment is associated with benefits both for the lender and for the borrower and it is a prerequisite for financial sustainability. Besides, in reducing the cost of credit it allows more borrowers access to it. Thus, the rate of repayment can be taken as a measure of the success of any micro-finance institution (Godquin 2004).

The model I present focuses on a trustworthiness eliciting mechanism, known as trust responsiveness (Bacharach et al. 2007; Dufwenberg and Gneezy 2000; Pelligra 2005, 2007, 2010; Pettit 1995), that explain how a borrower's reliable behavior can be induced by genuine trust on the part of the lender. In the next section (2) I shall describe the basic elements of a micro-credit program, assuming the example of Grameen Bank. Such a typology will be schematically compared with the traditional practices adopted in the formal credit sector (3). Several theories that aim at accounting for the Grameen's performance will be introduced and discussed (4). I shall propose an alternative explanation based on the idea of trust responsiveness (5–6) that will be next formalized by means of a psychological Trust Game characterized by, among the others, a 'lend-repay equilibrium' (7–9). The analysis in terms of a psychological game sheds new light on several important features of many MFIs, such as the refusal to use formal contracts, which, by framing the relationship as a cooperative one, are able to stimulate borrowers' trustworthiness. In the end, some implications for policy and institutional design are drawn (10). Conclusions close the chapter (11).

2. A Bank for the 'Un-bankable'

Bangladesh is one of the poorest countries in the world. Most of its population lives in conditions of great poverty. Forty per cent cannot even satisfy the most basic daily needs, life expectancy does not reach 40 years, and famines are endemic and regular. In the rural areas of the country especially, a system of religious and traditional norms, the so-called *purdha*, is in use, that, in its most radical version, keeps women in a condition of submission, excludes them from any opportunity of self-determination and makes their lives isolated and miserable (Cain et al. 1979; Islam and Begum 1984). The principal cause of poverty in Bangladesh's rural areas, as stressed by Yunus (1997), is the impossibility to break the vicious circle of poverty related to the impossibility of access to the formal credit market that, in turn, severely impairs the possibility of setting up productive initiatives.

To contrast such a *modus operandi* and its perverse consequences, in 1976, Muhammad Yunus established the Grameen Bank. Its explicit aim was to provide access to credit for the 'poorest of the poor' and help them to escape the poverty trap.

A fundamental requirement to enter Grameen's program is for the applicants to form a group of at least five people who, after an instructional period during which they learn the modalities of functioning of the program, will each get an individual credit of which they will be *not* jointly responsible. The average amount of the loans is about $100, repayable in one year by weekly installments. To formalize the agreement, the members of the group commit themselves to the respect of the so-called 'sixteen rules'; especially important is the commitment to provide formal instruction to the members of their families, to vegetable planting, to better the hygienic standard of their houses with the installation of sanitary latrines and to avoid giving or receiving dowries (Hossain 1993). However, they are not required to sign any formal agreement or legal document. Every week, the group meet to pay the interest to the bank's representative and to discuss the state of their projects, additional requests and suggestions for the members' economic activities. These weekly meetings represent for many of the members (especially for women) the only occasion for socialization they have in their daily life.

Since 1976, Grameen has provided credit, through its programs, to more than 4.48 million borrowers, 96 per cent of which are women. The total amount of loan disbursed, since inception, is US $6.13 billion (US $5.46 billion has been repaid). During the past 12 months (from April 2006 to March 2007) the bank disbursed US $727.85 million. The loan recovery rate is 98.28 per cent. According to a recent internal survey, 64 per cent of Grameen borrowers' families have managed to cross the poverty line.[4] These data have attracted the attention not only of development economists, but also of others more interested in the understanding of their social, organizational and financial implications (Bardhan et al. 1999; Holcombe 1995; Jain 1996; Larance 2001; Yaron 1994). One of the elements that strike most economists' imagination is the extremely high rate of repayments experienced by Grameen.[5] Contrary both to theory's advice and standard practices, Grameen's loans are not backed with collateral, nevertheless, about 98.91 per cent of them are said to be regularly repaid. Data on this point are controversial. A re-examination of the balances conducted in independent studies (Morduch 1999a) shows that the effective rate of repayment is about six points lower than that declared. Others have stressed that the Grameen

Bank was able to survive and develop only because of the constant stream of exogenous aids and donations and that the profits are principally due to the negative cost of credits.[6] However, if we consider that, although operating in the open market, the main aim of the bank is not to distribute profits to its shareholders, but to help the poor to overcome their poverty problems, such a scaling down of the financial performances does not significantly affect the puzzling features of the phenomenon that can be summarized as follows: contrary to theoretical predictions, the great majority of poor repay their loans. That is precisely what I want to explain. In next section the credit problem will be re-framed in game-theoretical terms in order to isolate the main factors that define a lender-borrower relationship.

3. Asymmetric information, opportunism and the standard solution

Asymmetric information and the assumption of narrowly self-interested behavior produce screening, incentive, auditing and enforcement problems in the credit market. In fact, first, borrowers differ in the likelihood that they will default and it is costly to determine the extent of that risk for each borrower, secondly, it is costly to ensure that borrowers take those actions which make repayment more likely, thirdly, it is difficult to know how projects have really turned out and, finally, it is difficult to compel repayment. We can describe in formal terms the simple case of a would-be borrower by means of the 'Simple Trust Game' (Figure 3.1). In this game, the lender (L) decides whether to give (G) or not to give (NG) the loan to the borrower (B). If L chooses to give, the decision passes to B. Suppose B receives a loan of f, which represents her only source of funding. The money is invested in a project that yields, at the end of the year, a total

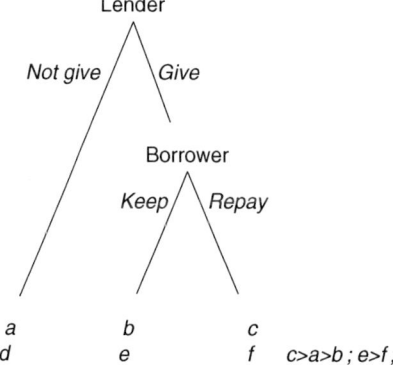

Figure 3.1 The Simple Trust Game

return of x. Suppose there is not a moral hazard problem at this stage, that is, the borrower always exerts her maximum level of effort. At the end of the period, player B has to decide whether to repay the loan and keep the profits x, or to 'take the money and run', that is, to keep both loan and profits ($e = f + x$). In order to decide whether to give (G) the money, the lender wants to know the probability that the loan will be repaid. However, since this situation is characterized by asymmetric information, this factor will be opaque to the lender. If the agents' incentive structure is similar to those described in the payoff matrix of the game, then a rational optimizing borrower (player B) would keep all the money. The lender anticipates that and decides not to give the money.

Because of the risk of opportunism and the impossibility of credibly committing to trustworthy behavior, a rational borrower and a rational lender, end up with an inefficient outcome (a, d). The inefficiency of this outcome will be even worsened if we consider that informational problems may refers not only to borrowers' actions (moral hazard), but also to their characteristics (adverse selection) and, in general, to all the future states of the world.

The traditional solution to this market failure is based on a redefinition of the agent's incentives structure aimed at reducing the advantage that B would get by not repaying the loan. Such a redefinition is generally obtained by requiring the loan be backed with collateral. This case is described in the game of Figure 3.2.

The requirement of collateral is logically equivalent to the imposition of a sanction for breaching the agreement. If this sort of sanction S can be imposed and efficiently enforced, players' incentive structure and, therefore, their predicted behavior will change. The introduction of the sanction S alters the equilibrium outcome by associating a cost to the borrower's decision to keep the money, that, in this case yields a payoff equal to ($e - S$).

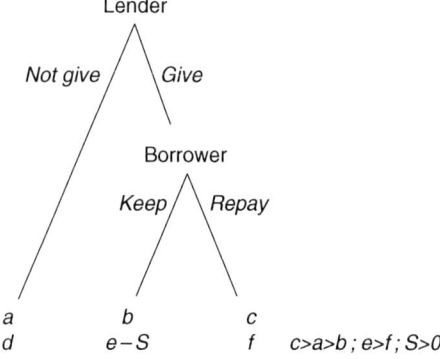

Figure 3.2   The Banking Game

Thus, if the condition $S > (e - f)$ is met, the strategy pair (G, R) is the unique equilibrium of the game. By implementing this backing practice, the lender problem could, in theory, be resolved. This solution, however, implies that only those who are able to provide collateral can have access to the formal credit market. While, on the one side, this standard solution protects the lender from the risk of insolvency, at the same time, it tends to exclude not only the untrustworthy borrowers but also those who cannot provide collateral because they are too poor. The negative consequences of this practice become more evident in those countries where the class of this latter group is larger. Thus, in these less developed economies the only available alternative for the 'unbankable' becomes, too often, usury, which, however, in the medium-term, does nothing but worsen the situation.

In this context and within this theoretical framework the success, in term of repayment rate, of financial institutions such as the Grameen Bank, appears to be at best paradoxical. First, in fact, the bank is willing to trust the would-be borrower when the *ex ante* risk of insolvency seems to be high; secondly, and most strikingly, once the borrowers have entered the program they prove that this trust is well grounded by showing a high ex-post level of trustworthiness. How can this pattern of behavior be explained?

4. Alternative explanations

In this section I shall briefly discuss some of the potential explanations that have been proposed to account for the high rate of repayment experienced by many MFIs. The first important mechanism that may affect borrowers' behavior, which is often portrayed as the key factor in MFIs, is group lending and joint liability. Many micro-credit programs, in fact, condition individual loans to the formation of groups of borrowers bound by joint liability. In case of default by one of the members the others would cover the shortfall. The group system facilitates repayment via three mechanisms: first, it produces self-selection of trustworthy members. Each member, in fact, prefers to have fellow members with low probability of default; second, the group membership provides information about others' behavior, facilitating monitoring; third, the risk of social ostracism that the opportunist incurs mitigates, to some extent, the enforcement problem. Strategic default, in fact, would imply the exclusion from the village's other economic and social activities.[7] The MFIs spring into a 'missing market' and help solving, through the group-lending mechanism, the problem of moral hazard (Stiglitz 1990) and adverse selection (Ghatak 1999) that can affect such kind of situations, so that the bank experiences a reduction in the costs for screening, monitoring and enforcing the (informal) agreements. At the same time, transaction and administrative costs are reduced as well. Such elements, together with 'extraordinary repayment rates' – lead to the conclusion that – 'group liability is a better guarantee of financial responsibility than property' (Devereux and Pares 1990: 23; see also Jaffer 1999). A related explanation stresses the fact that micro-credit programs contribute to fostering a 'credit-conducive culture', by insisting, for instance, on the attendance at weekly meetings and other occasions that help disseminating information about people's reputation (Pankaj 1996). Social ties and homogeneity among members facilitate the working of social incentive thus affecting the rate of repayment (Besley and Coate 1995).

A second mechanism that has been used to explain borrowers' trustworthy behavior is based on the idea of 'reputation'. As David Hume noticed centuries ago: 'There is nothing, which touches us more nearly than our reputation, and nothing which our reputation more depends than our conduct, with relation to the property of others. For this reason, every one, who has any regard to his character, or who intends to live on good terms with mankind, must fix an inviolable law to himself, never, by any temptation, to be induct to violate those principles' (1740: 501). If a good reputation is a prerequisite for re-financing, a borrower will be willing to forgo short-run profits in order to obtain higher profits in the long run. The prospect that the lender and the borrower have to continue, with some probability, to interact in the future drastically modifies the way they will behave. In this situation, as stressed by Yunus: 'There is no reason why [the poor] should not repay the debt, *especially if they want ask for another one*, that help them survive one more day' (1997: 76, italics added). Suppose that a borrower, while the first loan has still to be repaid, decides to apply for a second one and perhaps a third one, and so on, for any finite or indefinite number of times.[8] This situation can be formalized by modifying the original payoff matrix of the Simple Trust Game in order to incorporate the flow of the payoffs that the players may get in the future rounds. The folk theorem implies that, given a certain probability that the next round will not be the last, and given a discount factor sufficiently close to 1, there exist a set of strategies that sustain the cooperative outcome (G, R) even in situations like the Simple Trust Game. Suppose, in fact, that a borrower at a certain moment decides not to repay her debt. This will immediately prevent her from getting re-financed. If the loss she derives from being excluded from future credits is bigger than the one-shot gain from the present opportunistic behavior, then it would be rational for the borrower to repay the debt. This situation is logically equivalent to that considered in the Banking Game of Figure 3.2, where the loss of future opportunities is equal to the sanction S.

All these explicative strategies can be summarized by the game of Figure 3.3, where beside the monetary sanction, a social element (i.e. social pressure, others' approval or disapproval, the cost of ostracism) is introduced. Approbation and disapprobation, in this simplified framework, are triggered by transgressing or conforming to a social norm that, in this case, is assumed to be 'not to consciously breach others' trust'. In this case (G, R) represents the equilibrium outcome only if $W > (e - S - f)/(\alpha + \beta)$.

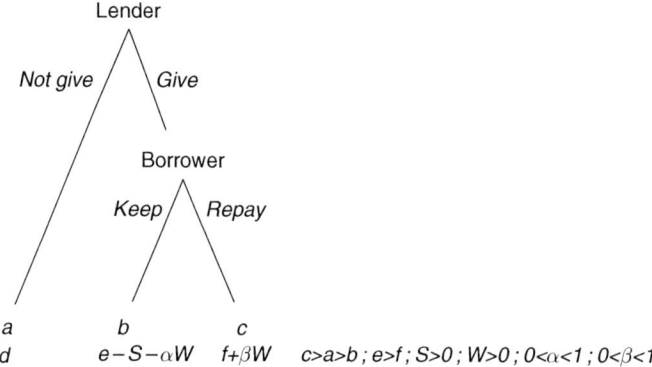

Figure 3.3 The Simple Trust Game with monetary sanction and social sentiments

The explanations I have sketched out so far all consider different factors that are important in determining the high rate of repayment experienced by micro-credit initiatives such as Grameen Bank. Nevertheless, they define a partial picture of the situation. Reputation, social collateral and joint liability are important but unable, if taken in isolation, to account for the evidence at issue. Bond and Rai (2002) convincingly argue that collateral substitutes such as social sanctions and credit denial are only imperfect substitutes. The successful imposition of social sanctions, in fact, requires the difficult solution of a delegation problem, and non re-financing threats are prone to a severe adverse selection problem. For this reason, using credit denial as a form of punishment sets up the possibility of being trapped into inefficient non-repayment equilibria.

On the other hand, Sadoulet (2000) stresses the fact that joint-liability in certain situations becomes costly and inefficient, and not a sufficient condition to assure repayment. Joint liability represents for many the flagship and the most innovative practice of MFIs and the main focus of the theoretical accounts of their success. In recent years, however, many micro-lenders, such as ASA in Bangladesh, BRI in Indonesia, BancoSol in Bolivia and Grameen Bank itself, decided to convert large shares of their portfolio into individual liability lending. In general, while retaining the group lending mechanism, they have abandoned the joint-liability clause. The rationale for such a move has to be found in the pitfalls of group liability that have become clearer after years of experience. First, joint liability tends to impose on the group members an excessive pressure that cause many voluntary dropouts and may harm their social capital. Second, the joint-liability scheme attracts bad risks who may want to free-ride at the expenses of good risks, causing an increase in the number of defaulters and discouraging the latter entering the group. Third, good risks incur higher costs because they are often required to cover others' defaults. On the empirical side, Giné and Karlan (2007) find in a filed experiment with 169 pre-existing groups in the Philippines, clear evidence that the shift from group to individual liability does not affect borrowers' rate of repayment while, at the same time, it creates conditions that attract new clients who form new groups that are 10 per cent less likely to be dissolved.

My thesis is that although reputations, social collateral and joint-liability may play an important role in explaining why people repay their loans, their effective working relies on the existence of a fiduciary relationship between lender and borrower. The idea behind the establishment of the Grameen Bank, and of many other similar initiatives, is precisely to set up an organization that does not operate according to the scheme of the 'Banking Game', but according to the rules of the 'Simple Trust Game', where the credit is given in such a way that lender's trust induces borrower's trustworthiness. Such a shift is justified once the anthropological assumption of material self-interested behavior is relaxed. Yunus himself emphasizes this point: 'Nowadays, banks tend to suspect every borrower of wanting to run with the money [...] for *Grameen*, on the contrary, the starting point is that the borrowers are honest. We can be seen as naive, nevertheless, in the 94 per cent of the cases, our trust has been repaid' (1997: 108).

5. Trust responsiveness

That trust among agents is important even for market transactions is, nowadays, popular wisdom. According to John Stuart Mill: 'the advantage of humankind of being able to trust one another, penetrates into every crevice and cranny of human life: the economical is perhaps the smallest part of it, yet even this is incalculable' (1848: 131). In the same vein, a century later, Kenneth Arrow defines trust as the lubricant of the social system and convincingly argues that, 'much of the economic backwardness in the world can be explained by a lack of mutual confidence' (1974: 357).

Trust has been variously defined as a *personality trait* (Baker 1987; Deutsch 1973; Jones 1986), or as an eminently *probabilistic phenomenon* (Baier 1986, 1994; Gambetta 1988; Luhmann 1979, 2000) or as a matter of *encapsulated interest* (Hardin 1993, 2001). Among all those conceptions, however, the one that best seems to account for the relational feature of the trust phenomenon, is the idea of trust as *responsive* behavior (Pelligra 2005, 2010; Pettit 1995).

The main feature of the responsive conception of trust refers to the fact that trust is basically a matter of interpersonal relationship and that the relational factor should play a central part in its understanding. An act of trust takes place within a (often personalized) relation between two agents. It is extremely unlikely that a theory that considers the reasons to behave trustfully and trustworthily as entirely external to the relationship itself, would be able to give a satisfactory account of what trust is. The consequentialist structure of traditional game theory implies that, for instance, whether or not player B decides to behave trustworthily at a given node of the interaction does not depend on which strategy player A has chosen in the previous nodes. On the contrary, a more satisfactory theory of trust should be able to account for the influences that A's intentions and observed choices exert on B's preferences and choices. In the trust responsiveness hypothesis, a trusting move induces trustworthiness through an endogenous modification of B's preferences structure. A single act of genuine trust may provide additional reasons to behave trustworthily. In other words, trust responsiveness is the act of conferring benefits on people who have shown that they expect you to do so, and have willingly exposed themselves to harm in the event that you act on material self-interest. In this respect trust is said to be self-fulfilling. I suggest that this mechanism could be a major factor in explaining the high rate of repayment experienced by most microcredit programs. Pelligra (2005, 2010) extendedly discusses the basic elements of the trust responsiveness hypothesis, which, moreover, has recently obtained empirical support in various experimental studies (Bacharach et al. 2007; Dufwenberg and Gneezy 2000; Pelligra 2007; Guerra and Zizzo 2004).

6. Strategies as a signal of expectations

As we have already said, the idea of trust responsiveness refers to a particular sort of subjective reaction that can be elicited by the expression of an expectation of trustworthiness. In situations like those described by the Trust Game, such an expectation is signalled by the choice of a trustful strategy (*Give*) and specifically by the trustor's conscious acceptance of the risk implied by that choice. Trust responsiveness assumes that B has a preference to fulfill L's expectations when these express a good opinion of him, even though in so doing L incurs some material cost. The basic assumption of this hypothesis is that people are sensitive to social emotions, that is, the emotions that depend on our beliefs about others' belief about our behavior (second order beliefs). While social approval is captured by the exogenous parameter W (see game in Figure 3.3), social or belief-dependent emotions are produced endogenously through a process of psychological forward induction. Suppose a lender (L) and a borrower (B) interact in a 'Simple Trust Game': L moves first and B observes her choice. It is common knowledge that both L and B prefer more material wealth than less. Suppose that out-of-equilibrium moves are allowed and that such moves are 'rationalized', that is, they are not interpreted by the observer (the player that has not done the move) as errors. Suppose that, having observed L's choice, the observer (B, in this case) engages in a process that allows him to revise his beliefs according to the fact that a trustful or a mistrustful strategy signals different expectations, and that such expectations elicit in B a consistent response. When B observes L playing *Give*, if he rules out mistakes or mere masochism, L's behavior signals that she expects a trustworthy response. From observing trustful behavior, B may extract such a signal about L's expectation upon his choice. Suppose B gets the signal correctly. Now he is aware of L's expectations. In deciding what to do, B takes into account not only the material consequences of his action, but also the psychological reward and cost associated respectively to the fulfillment or the frustration of L's expectation. These derive both from the anticipation of L's reaction to his choice and from the self-evaluation of her own choice. L's reaction, and consequently its effects on B's psychological utility will be positive (pride) if B's choice fulfills L's expectation or negative (guilt) in the case of divergence between expectations and action.[9]

Given these considerations, B's choice will come out of the net balance between the material gain and the psychological loss (in the case of opportunistic behavior) or between a material loss and a psychological gain (in the case of trustworthy behavior). The idea of trust responsiveness implies that B's psychological utility increases by responding positively to L's trustful expectations and decreases by frustrating such an expectation.

7. A simple model of psychological forward induction

To keep things simple, in the following example I shall focus only on the formalization of players' material and psychological reasons, leaving aside other incentive already discussed, like monetary sanctions and social pressure. Another crucial assumption of the model is that the emotions triggered by L's perceived or anticipated reaction to B's choice are proportional to L's degree of belief about that choice. In other words, in case of opportunism, L's frustration and, consequently, B's guilt will be proportional to L's expectation of trustworthiness. The converse is true for pride. B's pride will be positively dependent from L's expectation of opportunism. I assume also that positive and negative emotions, pride for trustworthiness and guilt for opportunism, are symmetric. Given all these assumptions, we may formalize both internal and external reasons with a single psychological factor. B's extended payoff, therefore, comes out of his objective payoff, say the amount of money, plus a psychological factor. In choosing his action, B seeks to maximize the sum of material and psychological utility. Such a motivational structure can be formalized for a class of games with the structure of the Simple Trust Game by using psychological game theory.[10] Consider now the variant of the Simple Trust Game depicted in Figure 3.4.

Denote with $p \in [0,1]$ the probability that B plays *Repay*; $1 - p$ is the probability with which B plays *Keep*. In the same way, $q \in [0,1]$ represents L's belief about p.[11] Analogously, r denotes B's belief about q, that is, B's belief about L's beliefs about B's choice. In this way we describe B's *hierarchy* of beliefs,

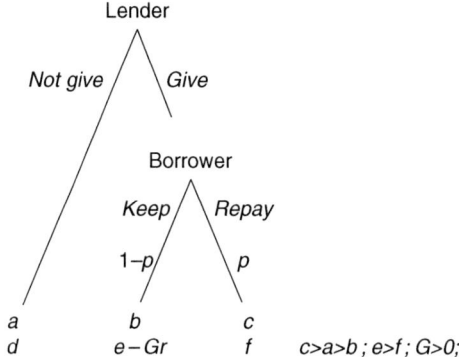

Figure 3.4 The Simple Trust Game with sentiments

in particular, his first and second order beliefs. These beliefs are crucial to transform the standard game into a psychological one. I restrict my formal discussion to the usual equilibrium analysis, leaving aside considerations of out-of-equilibrium behavior.

Suppose B observes L's trustful choice; we are now in the second node of the game, where B has to move. In this version of the Trust Game, B's payoff from being opportunist is formed by the material part and the psychological one, which in turn depends on B's guilt. The negative impact of guilt on B's overall utility is a multiple $G(G > 0)$ of L's expectation r. The intuition underlying such a formalization is that B suffers a psychological loss when he deliberately lets L down knowing that L has trusted him, and such a loss is proportional to B's belief about L's expectation of B's trustworthy behavior.

8. Trustful and trustworthy equilibria

Following Geanakoplos et al. (1989) we can solve the game by isolating its psychological equilibria. In a psychological equilibrium, players maximize their utility, and their first and second order beliefs are confirmed ($p = q = r$). This particular game shows three such equilibria. In the first, L expects B to play trustworthily; given this expectation, B's psychological cost deriving from frustrating it becomes strong enough to lead B to the expected choice. L knows that and sets q accordingly ($q = 1$): she[12] plays *Give*; B knows that as well, and sets $r = q = 1$: he plays *Repay*. In the first equilibrium, L plays *Give* and $p = q = r = 1$, that is, B plays *Repay*. This represents a trustful and trustworthy pure strategy equilibrium. Here, in fact, L's expectation about B's trustworthiness justifies L's trustful choice and such a choice strengthens B's reasons (avoiding psychological costs) to behave according to what L expected. Trust is self-fulfilling.

In the second equilibrium, L expects B to play opportunistically; that choice would not produce any psychological cost for B, L knows that and sets $q = 0$; consequently B sets $r = q = 0$. In the second equilibrium L plays *Not Give* and $p = q = r = 0$, that is, B plays *Keep*.

The third (mixed-strategy) equilibrium is obtained by setting B's payoff from opportunism and from trustworthiness equal, and imposing $p = r$. In this third equilibrium, which only exists if $pc + (1 - p)b > a$, that means that L plays *Give* provided that $p = q = r = (e - f)/G$ and $0 < (e - f)/G < 1$, the associated payoffs are equal to $pc + (1 - p)b$ for L and $(1 - p)(e - rG) + pf$ for B.

In this third case both trustworthiness and opportunism may follow L's trustful move, depending on players' beliefs. The denominator G in (3) represents the impact of social sentiments, or internal reasons, on B's utility. This factor as well as the difference $(e - f)$ directly affects the probability of B's trustworthy behavior.

The model is consistent both with (pure) trustful and trustworthy equilibrium and with (pure) mistrustful and opportunistic equilibrium. There is also a third, mixed-strategy equilibrium that shows how the likelihood of the different outcomes depend on subjective elements.

The Simple Trust Game, when analyzed as a psychological game, becomes a coordination game.[13] Which equilibrium will be selected depends, in fact, on the way players coordinate their first and second order expectations. It is natural then that the next step in the description of the fiduciary basis of this class of interactions would be the analysis of some of the elements that contribute to solve this coordination problem.

9. Fiduciary dynamics

Trust responsiveness is based on the perception of the idea that the others have of us and on its direct and indirect influence on our self-esteem. Such a perception develops and strengthens in relation to others' actions, and particularly in relation to *our interpretation* of such actions. This interpretation, in turn, is strongly affected by the context and the framework within which actions take place. In strategic environments, people's behavior is heavily influenced by the way the situations they are in are framed and described, that is, by what kind of norm they think would be appropriate to follow in a specific situation. The so-called framing effect precisely describes how the same action may induce different reactions depending on the context where it takes place. Ross and Ward (1996), Burnham et al. (2000) and Dufwenberg et al. (2006) present experimental results that show how subjects' behavior in objectively the same situation is modified by non-theoretically relevant elements, as, for instance, the mere semantic description of the situation (community game vs. Wall Street Game), or of the co-players (opponent vs. partner). The semantic framing of the situation in these examples, as well as pre-play communication in others, works as a coordinating device that helps players in aligning their first and second order beliefs by modifying their beliefs about others' expected behavior and about others' expectations on each other's behavior.

The fact that the model exhibits multiple equilibria may be interpreted as giving rise to problems of indeterminacy, as Battigalli and Dufwenberg (2009) suggest. In my interpretation, on the contrary, it constitutes an element of realism, in particular because it leaves room for the working of the framing effects just mentioned.[14]

A second factor that is important to take into account in order to isolate those elements involved in micro-credit programs that favor the working of interpersonal trust, is the so-called motivational crowding-out (Frey 1997; Frey and Jegen 2001). The crowding-out mechanism explains why, in certain cases, subjects' willingness to perform a given action is decreased (increased) by the prospect of a material incentive (disincentive). Such an effect operates when the use of monetary rewards or punishments transforms the subject's motivations from intrinsic to extrinsic. The reasons behind such a phenomenon are many;[15] among them, those concerning subject's self-determination and self-esteem are particularly relevant. Imposing an external system of material incentives may produce in the subjects the impression of being controlled and of losing control of the situation (Rotter 1966), so that the *locus* of motivation shifts from internal to external. An external intervention, in the same way, may bring the message that a subject's individual responsibility (and therefore also her potential merit) is not acknowledged and that her intrinsic motivation is rejected. In this way, as Frey suggests: 'An intrinsically motivated person is denied the chance to display his or her own interest and involvement in an activity, when someone else offers a reward' (1997: 47). As a result of an underestimated responsibility, the subject experiences an impairment of her self-esteem that, consequently, reduces her willingness to perform the given action.

Furthermore, the way the subject perceives the external intervention plays a crucial role in determining the crowding-out or crowding-in effect. In fact, such an intervention can be seen either as *controlling* or as *supporting*, subjects' behavior. In the latter case, we observe a strengthening of subjects' intrinsic motivations (crowding-in), in the former case, because of the impaired self-determination and self-esteem we observe its weakening or even destruction (crowding-out).

A third element, that favors the activation of the trust responsiveness, and that, in certain aspects is related to the other two, is the so-called 'Feeling of Freedom-Effect'. There is a research program in cognitive psychology that investigates the mechanisms that rule a class of behaviors defined as 'compliance without pressure', that is, those mechanisms that determine a positive (costly) response to a request or to an expectation in the absence of any kind of coercion (Chartrand et al. 1999; Joule et al. 1989; Kiesler 1971). One of the main findings is that when subjects perceive themselves as free to act, they are more willing to positively respond to a given request or expressed expectation. Consider the example of voluntary charitable donations. Experiments show that the level of such donations, as well as the sense of commitment, significantly increases when requests are formulated using sentences such as 'it is up to you to see', 'up to you to choose', 'but you are free of...' (Guéguen and Pascual 2000). The explanation of this phenomenon is related to the semantic characteristics of the requesting formulas. Such formulas elicit a sense of freedom in the potential donor and, at the same time, suggest that the petitioners' are trusting her, are relying on her contribution. It has been noticed that: 'The verbal evocation of the freedom [...] really activates the feeling of freedom for the subject' (p. 268). The positive relation between such a perception and the level of compliance has been investigated, obtaining support, in several studies (Cialdini 1993; Kiesler 1971) that show how the feeling of freedom acts as 'facilitator of commitment towards the expected behavior' (ibid.).

10. The risk of a counterproductive regulation

The relational basis of our motivations suggests that the kind of responsiveness to others' actions and beliefs implied by the trust responsiveness mechanism is somehow symmetrical. That means that one may be motivated to be trustworthy by being trusted (trust responsiveness) but one also may be induced to opportunism by distrust, by being treated as a potential opportunist (distrust responsiveness). Let us try now, to explicitly apply such elements to the lender-borrower relation as conceived in micro-credit initiatives. To do so, it is necessary to schematically describe the principles that underlie the usual practices of the lender. Consider, for simplicity's sake, the case of the Grameen Bank. The following sentence clearly summarizes Grameen's attitude: 'Banks tend to suspect every clients to want take the money and run. So they bind her with every kind of clauses especially designed by specialized lawyers. In the bank system there is only diffidence [...] for Grameen, on the contrary, the starting point is that debtors are honest. Since our first day we decided that our system will not had relied on police and courts [...] nowadays to recover our credits we never use lawyers [...]. Following the same logic we do not use formal contracts between clients and the bank. We establish relationships with people not with documents' (Yunus 1997: 106–108).

In the case of the micro-credit, a trustful lender is signaling to the borrowers that she believes them to be trustworthy and sets her expectations on the basis of that belief. We have already seen how such a signal may motivate agents to behave trustworthily to fulfill the principal's expectations. Consider now what happens when the principal behaves distrustfully, as in the case of the traditional credit institutions. In this case, the bank is signaling a belief that without the external intervention (collateral and monitoring) the agents would not be willing to behave according to the nature of the relation (repay her debt). According to the logic of the motivational crowding-out, this signal itself would contribute to elicit the opportunistic behavior. Moreover, it is not difficult to realize that not asking for collateral, and not evoking lawyers' interventions or other formal enforcement systems, favors the fact that the clients frame their relations with the bank as highly cooperative. Besides, such a practice elicits in the clients the 'feeling of freedom-effect' that increases their willingness to fulfill the bank's expectations.

The effects of principles such as crowding-out, social framing and feeling of freedom, have to be carefully taken into account when designing schemes of interaction and legal norms that rule collective actions. Recent studies (Blair and Stout 2000) show that considering such elements is crucial when devising and applying social norms, that even when operating in a highly competitive environment, the markets often are based on the fiduciary duty, and that they are difficult to be accounted for only in term of economic incentives. With regard to the study and the design of legal rules it has been noticed that: 'there is a danger in failing to appreciate the tremendous value to be added by incorporating the phenomenon of trust into legal scholarship [...] danger not only for academics, but for lawmakers, practicing lawyers and business folk. [...] this is so because the attempts to employ external incentives can often reduce levels of trust and trustworthiness within the firm by eroding corporate participants' *internal* motivations' (Blair and Staut 2000: 4). If that is true in a highly competitive environment, it is true *a fortiori* for micro-finance programs and in general for all development programs, where the market pressure is often attenuated. It is easy to understand then, how factors like participants' self-determination and self-esteem, as well as the framing of the situation as a cooperative one, are essential in order to reduce the risks of opportunism ingrained in such actions. It is now widely accepted (Ayres and Braithwaite 1992; Brennan and Pettit 2004; Grabowsky 1995; Sunstein 1990) that if such factors are neglected it is possible to develop codes of norms which, contributing to the creation of a competitive framing, lead to inefficient and counterproductive outcomes, that is, to a reduction in subjects' willingness to behave cooperatively, as those norms would prescribe.

The case of Grameen constitutes, in this sense, a paradigmatic example showing how it is possible to encourage agents to behave according to their fiduciary duties, not by means of pecuniary sanctions or incentives, but by *both* trusting them and attributing to the environment the distinctive traits of a cooperative relationship, that is freedom, responsibility, commitment; favoring, in this way, the development of trustworthy behaviors.

Incidentally, it is worth noticing that, *ceteris paribus*, the institutions capable of developing trustful and trustworthy relations among its members enjoy, in the long run, a competitive advantage. That fact should help in solving the problems of micro-credits initiatives' financial sustainability.

11. Conclusions

This chapter is primarily aimed at suggesting a theoretically sound and empirically well-grounded explanation for the high rate of loan repayment observed in the Grameen Bank as well as in many other micro-finance institutions. This explanation is based on the notion of trust responsiveness. Since, in micro-credit programs, loans are not usually backed with collateral, their success in terms of repayment rate cannot be fully explained within traditional rational choice theory. After having schematically described the problem of opportunism, I have delineated the essential characteristics of the Grameen program. I have, then, discussed some of the theories that can be used to account for the phenomenon, recognizing how such explanations are partial and, more importantly, tend to neglect some of the aspects that are instead considered crucial by the participants to the program themselves, that is, trust and self-esteem. For this reason we explored and formalized in a psychological game theoretical model the role of trust, and in particular of the concept of trust responsiveness. In this model, guilt-averse borrowers tend to fulfill lenders' expectations, giving rise to a multiplicity of equilibria. I have discussed some of the factors that may positively and negatively affect its functioning as equilibrium selection devices. Those factors were used to provide an explanation of the phenomenon at issue and to stress the risks implied in policy and institutional design activities that do not take into account the fiduciary dynamics that the case of Grameen so clearly illustrates.

Acknowledgements

I would like to thank Larry Blume, Luigino Bruni, Shaun Hargreaves-Heap, Tiziana Luisetti, Martin Paldam, Maurizio Pugno, Robert Sugden, Stefano Zamagni and especially Giacomo Degli Antoni and Marco Faillo for their comments on an earlier draft, as well as the audiences at the XII World Congress for Social Economy (Amsterdam) and at the workshop on 'Social Capital, CSR and Sustainable Economic Development' (Trento). The usual disclaimer applies.

Notes

1. Quotations from Yunus (1997) are translated from the original French into English by the author.
2. Many commentators, especially economists, have traditionally emphasized the role of joint liability in the succes of MFIs. However, recent studies (see Giné and Karlan 2007) have challenged this position, pointing out that individual liability not only does not affect borrowers' trustworthiness, but introduces more flexibility and favors the formation of new and more stable groups.

3. Similar results can be observed in other programs. See Amendàriz de Aghion and Murdoch (2005) for a general overview on performance.
4. Source: Yunus M., 'Grameen Bank at Glance' (March 2007), www.grameen-info.org.
5. Other micro-finance institutions obtain similar results: PRIDE Africa, which has extended more than 60,000 loans of between $50 and $1000 in East Africa, reports repayment rates of 99 percent in Tanzania and 100 percent in Uganda. The Kenya Rural Enterprise Program (KREP), which had lent to over 12,000 borrowers by the end of 1996, consistently reports repayment rates of higher than 95 percent. ACCION International (based in Cambridge, Massachusetts, but operating in Latin America) reports similar figures. The Union Regional de Apoyo Campesino (operating in Mexico), which requires that borrowers maintain a savings account balance equal to at least 20 percent of their outstanding loan, reports repayment rates of 95 percent (see Jaffer 1999).
6. See the review by Morduch (1999b) and references therein.
7. Among the recent studies that formalize the process of social enforcement, see Stiglitz (1990), Varian (1990), Prescott (1997) and Conning (1997); Ghatak and Guinnane (2000) summarize the existing literature on group lending and joint liability.
8. The folk theorem that supports such result applies when the number of repetitions is indefinite. However, Kreps and Wilson (1982) show that, given certain assumptions, a cooperative behavior can emerge even in games with finite (but large) number rounds.
9. See, for a debate on this point, Charness and Dufwenberg (2006, 2007), Ellingsen, Johannesson, Torsvik and Tjøtta (2008) and Vanberg (2008).
10. See Huang and Wu (1994), Ruffle (1999) and Dufwenberg (2002) for similar applications.
11. L's belief can be though of as the mean of B's subjective distribution over the probability p.
12. I will keep using 'she' for the 'Lender' (Player L) and 'he' for the 'Borrower' (player B).
13. Camerer and Thaler (2003) provide a similar interpretation.
14. A further point is important to notice: the degree of indeterminacy in a sequential trust game is much less determinant than in a, for example, simultaneous Prisoner's Dilemma. In the Trust Game, the coordination of players' beliefs is simplified by the fact that player B can observe L's move and infer her belief from it. Her playing G, means reasonably that L expects B to play R.
15. See Frey (1997), for a complete review.

References

B. Amendàriz de Aghion and J. Murdoch (2005) *The Economics of Microfinance* (Cambridge MA.: MIT University Press).

K. Arrow (1974) *The Limits of Organisations* (New York: W.W. Norton).

I. Ayres and J. Braithwaite (1992) *Responsive Regulation* (Oxford: Oxford University Press).

M. Bacharach, G. Guerra and D. Zizzo (2007) 'The Self-Fulfilling Property of Trust: An Experimental Study', *Theory and Decision*, 63(4), 349–388.

A. Baier (1986) 'Trust and Antitrust', *Ethics*, 96, 231–260.

A. Baier (1994) *Moral Prejudices* (Cambridge: Harvard University Press).

J. Baker (1987) 'Trust and Rationality', *Pacific Philosophical Quarterly*, 68, 1–13.

P. Bardhan (ed.) (1999) 'Special Issues on Group Lending', *Journal of Development Economics*, 60, 3–269.

P. Battigalli and M. Dufwenberg (2009) 'Dynamic Psychological Games', *Journal of Economic Theory*, 144, 1–35.

T. Besley and S. Coate (1995) 'Group Lending, Repayment Incentives and Social Collateral', *Journal of Development Economics*, 46, 1–18.

M. Blair and L. Stout (2000) 'Trust, Trustworthiness, and the Behavioural Foundations of Corporate Law' Working Paper, Georgetown University Law Center.

P. Bond and A. Rai (2002) 'Collateral Substitutes in Microfinance', Center for International Development Working Paper, Harvard University.

G. Brennan and P. Pettit (2004) *The Economy of Esteem* (Cambridge: Cambridge University Press).

T. Burnham, K. McCabe and V. Smith (2000) 'Friend- or Foe: Intentionality Priming in an Extensive Form Trust Game', *Journal of Economic Behavior and Organization*, 43, 57–74.

M. Cain, S. R. Khanam and S. Nahar (1979) 'Class, Patriarchy, and Women's Work in Bangladesh', *Population and Development Review*, 5, 405–438.

C. Camerer and R. Thaler (2003) 'In Honor of Matthew Rabin: Winner of the John Bates Clark Medal', *Journal of Economic Perspectives*, 17, 159–176.

G. Charness and M. Dufwenberg (2006) 'Promises and Partnership', *Econometrica*, 4(6), 1579–1601.

G. Charness and M. Dufwenberg (2007) 'Broken Promises: An Experiment', Working Paper, http://econ.arizona.edu/downloads/working_papers/Econ-WP-07-17.pdf.

T. Chartrand, S. Pinckert and J. Burger (1999) 'When Manipulation Backfires: The Effects of Time Delay and Requester on the Foot-in-the-Soor Technique', *Journal of Applied Social Psychology*, 29, 211–221.

R. Cialdini (1993) *Influence* (New-York: HarperCollins).

J. Conning (1997) 'Joint Liability, Peer Monitoring, and the Creation of Social Collateral', *mimeo*, Department of Economics, Williams College.

M. Deutsch (1973) *The Resolution of Conflict* (New Haven: Yale University Press).

S. Devereux and H. Pares (1990) *Credit and Savings for Development* (Oxford: Oxfam).

M. Dufwenberg (2002) 'Marital Investment, Time Consistency, and Emotions', *Journal of Economic Behavior and Organization*, 48, 57–69.

M. Dufwenberg, S.Gächter and H. Hennig-Schmidt (2006) 'The Framing of Games and the Psychology of Strategic Choice', CeDEx Discussion Paper No. 2006–20, University of Nottingham.

M. Dufwenberg and U. Gneezy (2000) 'Measuring Beliefs in an Experimental Lost Wallet Game', *Games and Economic Behavior*, 30, 163–182.

T. Ellingsen, M. Johannesson, G. Torsvik and S. Tjøtta (2008) 'Testing Guilt Aversion', Working Paper, http://www2.hhs.se/personal/Ellingsen/pdf/GuiltGEBrev.pdf.

B. S. Frey (1997) *Not Just for the Money* (Cheltenham, UK: Edward Elgar).

B. S. Frey and R. Jegen (2001) 'Motivation Crowding Theory', *Journal of Economic Surveys*, 15, 589–611.

D. Gambetta (ed.) (1988) *Trust: Making and Breaking Cooperative Relations* (Oxford: Basil Blackwell).

J. Geanakoplos, D. Pearce and E. Stacchetti (1989) 'Psychological Games and Sequential Rationality', *Games and Economic Behavior*, 1, 60–79.

M. Ghatak (1999) 'Group Lending, Local Information and Peer Selection', *Journal of Development Economics*, 60, 27–50.

M. Ghatak and W. T. Guinnane (1999) 'The Economics of Lending with Joint Liability: Theory and Practice', *Journal of Development Economics*, 60, 195–228.

X. Giné and D. Karlan (2007) 'Group Versus Individual Liability: A Field Experiment in the Philippines', *mimeo*, Yale University & Innovations for Poverty Action.

M. Godquin (2004) 'Microfinance Repayment Performance in Bangladesh: How to Improve the Allocation of Loans by MFIs', *World Development*, 32(11), 1909–1926.

N. Goldberg and D. Karlan (2006) 'The Impact of Microfinance: A Review of Methodological Issues', *mimeo*, Yale University & Innovations for Poverty Action.

P. Grabowsky (1995) 'Counterproductive Regulation', *International Journal of the Sociology Of Law*, 23.

N. Guéguen and A. Pascual (2000) 'Evocation of Freedom and Compliance', *Current Research in Social Psychology*, 5, 264–270.

G. Guerra and D. J. Zizzo (2004) 'Trust Responsiveness and Beliefs', *Journal of Economic Behavior and Organization*, 55(1), 25–30.

R. Hardin (1993) 'The Street-Level Epistemology of Trust', *Politics and Society*, 21, 505–529.

R. Hardin (2001) *Trust and Trustworthiness* (New York: Russell Sage Foundation Publications).

S. Holcombe (1995) *Managing to Empower: The Grameen Bank's Experience of Poverty Alleviation* (Wiltshire, England: Redwood Books).

M. Hossain (1993) 'The Grameen Bank: Its Origin, Organization, and Management Style', in A. N. M. Wahid (ed.), *The Grameen Bank: Poverty Relief in Bangladesh* (Boulder, CO: Westview Press).

P. Huang and H.-M. Wu. (1994) 'More Order Without More Law: A Theory of Social Norms and Organizational Cultures', *Journal of Law, Economics and Organization*, 10, 390–406.

D. Hume (1740 [1978]) *Treatise on Human Nature* (Oxford: Clarendon Press).

C. Kiesler (1971) *The Psychology of Commitment* (New-York: Academic Press).

D. Kreps and R. Wilson (1982) 'Reputation and Imperfect Information', *Journal of Economic Theory*, 27, 253–279.

S. Islam and J. Begum (1984) 'Women: Victims of Violence 1975–1984', Working paper, Centre for Women and Development, Dhaka.

J. Jaffer (1999) 'Microfinance and the Mechanism of Solidarity Lending', Working paper, Harvard Law School, John M. Olin Center for Law, Economics and Business.

P. S. Jain (1996) 'Managing Credit for the Rural Poor: Lessons from the Grameen Bank', *World Development*, 24, 79–89.

K. Jones (1996) 'Trust As an Affective Attitude', *Ethics*, 107, 4–25.

R. Joule, F. Gouilloux and F. Weber (1989) 'The Lure: A New Compliance Procedure', *The Journal of Social Psychology*, 129, 741–749.

L. Y. Larance (2001) 'Fostering social capital through NGO design: Grameen Bank membership in Bangladesh', *International Social Work*, 44, 7–18.

N. Luhmann (1979) *Trust and Power* (New York: John Wiley and Sons).

N. Luhmann (2000) 'Familiarity, Confidence, Trust: Problems and Alternatives', in D. Gambetta, (ed.), *Trust: Making and Breaking Cooperative Relations*, electronic edition, Department of Sociology, University of Oxford.

J. S. Mill (1848) *Principles of Political Economy* (London: John W. Parker).

J. Morduch (1999a) 'The Role of Subsidies in Microfinance: Evidence from the Grameen Bank', *Journal of Development Economics*, 60, 229–248.

J. Morduch (1999b) 'The Grameen Bank: A Financial Reckoning', Working Paper, Princeton University.

S. Pankaj (1996) 'Managing Credit for the Rural Poor: Lessons from the Grameen Bank', *World Development*, 24, 79–89.

V. Pelligra (2005) 'Under Trusting Eyes: the Responsive Nature of Trust', in R. Sugden and B. Gui (eds), *Economics and Social Interactions* (Cambridge: Cambridge University Press).

V. Pelligra (2007) 'The Not-so-Fragile Fragility of Goodness', in P. L. Porta and L. Bruni (eds), *Handbook of the Economics of Happiness* (Cheltenham: Edward Elgar).

V. Pelligra (2010) 'Trust Responsiveness. On the Dynamics of Fiduciary Interactions', *Journal of Socio-Economics*, 39, 653–660.

P. Pettit (1995) 'The Cunning of Trust', *Philosophy and Public Affairs*, 24, 202–225.

E. S. Prescott (1997) 'Group Lending and Financial Intermediation: An Example', *Federal Reserve Bank of Richmond Economic Quarterly*, 83, 23–48.

L. Ross and A. Ward (1996), 'Naive Realism in Everyday Life: Implications for Social Conflict and Misunderstanding', in E. S. Reed, E. S., Elliott Turiel and T. Brown (eds), *Values and Knowledge*. Lawrence Erlbaum Associates, Mahwah, N. J., 103–135.

J. Rotter (1966) 'Generalized Expectancies for Internal versus External Control and Reinforcement', *Psychological Monographs*, 80, Whole No. 609.

B. J. Ruffle, (1999) 'Gift Giving with Emotions', *Journal of Economic Behavior and Organization*, 39, 399–420.

L. Sadoulet (2000) 'The Role of Mutual Insurance in Group Lending', Working Paper, ECARES, Université Libre de Bruxelles.

J. E. Stiglitz (1990) 'Peer Monitoring and Credit Markets', *World Bank Economic Review*, 4, 351–366.

C. Sunstein (1990) 'Paradoxes of the Regulatory State', *University of Chicago Law Review*, 57, 407–441.

C. Vanberg (2008) 'Why Do People Keep Their Promises? An Experimental Test of Two Explanations', *Econometrica*, 76, 1467–1480.

H. Varian (1990) 'Monitoring Agents with Other Agents', *Journal of Institutional and Theoretical Economics*, 146, 153–174.

J. Yaron (1994) 'What Makes Rural Finance Institutions Successful?', *The World Bank Research Observer*, 1, 49–70.

M. Yunus (1997) *Vers un monde sans pauvreté* (Paris: Éditions Jean-Claude Lattès).

4

The Relationship Between Competition and Trust: An Essay in an Historical and Theoretical Perspective

Sergio Beraldo and Gilberto Turati

1. Introduction

Competition is generally claimed to be good for social welfare, even though this claim is rarely coupled with a plain account of the circumstances under which it is actually true. Both the original connotation of the verb 'to compete' and the non-technical common use of the word, are grounded on the intuition that competition is a race (Blaug 2001). The view that the by-product of such a race is good beyond any reasonable doubt, is not questioned even in presence of those situations in which an impoverishment of the quality of the good supplied is observed as an effect of the race itself (e.g. Alsberg 1931).

Without denying the value of competition, its use as a multi-purpose formula for fostering development and well-being looks more like an ideological stand than a conscious statement. This is particularly true when competition is meant as the opposite of regulation.

According to critics, regulation creates an hurdle-race; according to supporters, regulation levels the playing field. In many OECD reports, the general premise seems to be that governments have to choose between competition and regulation: as competition is good, regulation must be bad (e.g. Conway et al. 2005).

This influential view notwithstanding, it seems wiser to recognize that the virtues of competition *need* some regulation to emerge; at least that regulation *implicit* in standard microeconomic textbook models (e.g. the enforcement of contracts according to the law).

Among the virtues of competition, one recently (re)-emphasized is that it generally enhances agents' trustworthiness in market economies, thus stimulating trust[1] with obvious desirable consequences (Berggren and Jordahl

2006; Bolton et al. 2008; Fischer 2008; Hörner 2002; Huck et al. 2007). This view is at the same time ancient and new. It is ancient as it is rooted in the writings of former economic scholars such as Adam Smith (1763 [1978]), who pointed out the basic reason why agents participating at the race may have a genuine interest in behaving trustworthily:

> Whenever commerce is introduced into any country probity and punctuality always accompany it. These virtues in a rude and barbarous society are almost unknown. This is not at all to be imputed to national character, as some pretend [...]. It is far more reducible to self-interest, that general principle which regulates the actions of every man, and which leads men to act in a certain manner from views of advantage [...]. A dealer is afraid of losing his character, and is scrupulous in performing every engagement. When a person makes perhaps 20 contracts in a day, he cannot gain so much by endeavouring to impose on his neighbours, as the very appearance of a cheat would make him lose. Where people seldom deal with one another, we find that they are somewhat disposed to cheat, because they can gain more by a smart trick than they can lose by the injury which it does their character.
>
> (Smith, 1763 [1978]: 538–539)

However, the view that competition fosters trustworthiness is also new, as it comes after more than 100 years of increasing state regulation in product markets, whose rationale is obviously that self-regulation is not enough, and the discipline enforced by competition needs to be strengthened in some way.

It is noteworthy that regulation was first enacted in the United States not only to meet a demand by consumers who felt at danger by food adulteration and sophistication made possible by advances in technology, but also to meet a demand by producers, especially by those specialized in high-quality products, who realized that regulation could have allowed them to distinguish their items from those of their low-quality competitors (e.g. Law 2003; Wood 1985).

Those contributions supporting the view that competition is the main engine of trustworthiness should first clarify whether modern market economies reasonably fit their assumptions. For example, in experimental studies it is taken for granted that buyers can verify *ex post* sellers' contractual performance, rewarding trustworthiness with trust.[2] This can be certainly thought of as an acceptable approximation of real situations at the early stages of economic development (when trade was local or limited to professional merchants embedded in networks that allowed efficient information transmission, and when contractual performance was relatively easy to ascertain), but it is hard to sustain that it was a good approximation thereafter.

The present chapter takes an historical perspective, but relies also on formal analysis as a means to highlight the main stylized facts, which are worth being considered in order to deal with the issue at hand rigorously. The model sketched in section 2 is grounded on Klein and Leffler (1981) and Shapiro (1983), whose main results do not appear to have been sensibly altered by the subsequent theoretical literature (e.g. Hörner 2002). The version presented here (mainly amended with the very reasonable assumption that agents do not discount the future at the same rate, and therefore differ as far as their time horizon is concerned), finds its justification in its being more suitable to our purpose, which is that of describing how the fundamental problem of ensuring agents' trustworthiness and generalized trust in market economies was historically characterized by increasing complexity.

We emphasize that, from the 1800s onward, technological and organizational changes have progressively made it more troublesome to cope with the problem of ensuring agents' trustworthiness, thus stimulating the emergence of a plethora of institutions, both market-based and enforced by the law. As complex problems generally require multifaceted solutions, is not possible to say a priori what can be considered as the better institution. It depends on the given historical circumstances. It is noteworthy that in the late nineteenth century, public regulation seemed to have a comparative advantage on spontaneous institutions to sustain a high level of trust in market economies. One century later, when public (that is, state) regulation, has de facto assumed the nature of a *local* regulation, market-based (worldwide) institutions seem to be better equipped. This is likely to be at the root of the renewed interest in competition as an engine of trust.

A basic claim of this chapter is that the virtues of competition necessarily require an adequate institutional structure to emerge: that institutional structure that appears to underpin trustworthiness and trust, which must be better thought as *epiphenomena* of the institutional environment (Fehr 2008). In this light, viewing competition as the opposite of regulation is certainly a mistake. Needless to say, this puts at the forefront the highly controversial issue of how to enforce an appropriate set of rules in a global economy.

The remainder of this chapter is structured as follows. In section 2 we briefly describe the main characteristics of a market economy at the outset of the Industrial Revolution, and outline a model of a local trade economy in order to interpret the role of competition at that time. We define a 'trustworthy economy' as an economy in which buyers' expectations that sellers always deliver high-quality commodities are fulfilled. We emphasize the circumstances that make competition a sufficient condition for a trustworthy economy to come about. In section 3, we argue that *stimuli* to concentration and mass production, entailing a separation between consumers and producers, and advancements in technology upsetting the detection of product quality even after consumption, made the competitive mechanism alone inadequate to sustain an acceptable level of trust. This caused the emergence of a set of institutions, either stemming from the market or originated by the law, to tackle the problem, which became even more troublesome with the rise of large multinational corporations and the separation of ownership from control (section 4). In section 5 it is argued that the recent focus on corporate social responsibility (CSR) and self-regulation by firms is a consequence of the present historical circumstances. A brief section of concluding remarks follows.

2. Local trade economies at the outset of the Industrial Revolution

Before the Industrial Revolution took place, economies were still dominated by all-purpose merchants (e.g. Chandler 1977; Cipolla 1974). These individuals supplied inputs to local manufacturers (generally speaking, small artisans) and sold goods to other merchants located in distant cities. These figures were close in nature to microeconomic-textbook suppliers who wrote short-term contracts to hire inputs required for production. The greatest share of trade was made up of *local exchanges* and, in addition to consumers and suppliers knowing each other, the quality of the commodities could be generally ascertained either before or after consumption.

In a simple local economy, consumers knew where the flour, the eggs and the butter came from, so that the quality of a cake, for example, relied on the work of the (known) baker.[3] Given the absence of any chemical preservative, the detection of quality *after* consumption was relatively easy for consumers. In this sense, goods could be thought as *search* or *experience* goods according to Nelson (1970). In any case, they were not *credence goods*, whose quality cannot be determined neither by inspection (search good) nor by consumption (experience good).[4]

Why did consumers trust sellers in these simple trade economies? The answer dates back to Adam Smith – who describes markets in which the characteristics of the traded goods could be discovered by inspection or at most after consumption – and is at the core of any microeconomic-textbook explanation: competition fosters trust as it gives the opportunity to consumers to choose among different suppliers on the basis of their reputation.[5]

2.1. A simple model of a local trade economy

To gain some insights into the virtues and limits of a spontaneous trust-generating mechanism, we will sketch a simple multi-period model. It will prove useful in subsequent discussion aimed at highlighting why the conditions that are crucial for its performance have become increasingly harder to satisfy.

We consider a set of buyers $B = \{b_1, \ldots, b_N\}$, $\#B = \overline{N}$, and a finite set of sellers $S = \{s_1, \ldots, s_M\}$, $\#S = \overline{M}$, with $\overline{N} > \overline{M}$. We suppose that at the beginning of each period $t = 0, \ldots$, every buyer (b^i), chooses a subset $\Theta_t^{b^i} \in \wp(S)$ of sellers (s^j), where $\wp(S)$ is the power set of S, with which she is willing to transact; then she is randomly matched, with equal probability, with one of the sellers belonging to $\Theta_t^{b^i}$. We will refer to $\Theta_t^{b^i}$ as the *matching set* of buyer b^i at time t. The probability that at time t, b^i is matched with a given $s^j \in \Theta_t^{b^i}$, is therefore:

$$Pr\left\{\mu(b^i, t) = s^j \in \Theta_t^{b^i}\right\} = \left(1/\#\Theta_t^{b^i}\right)$$

where μ is the matching function. We suppose that $\Theta_0^{b^i} = S$, $\forall i$.

To simplify matters, we assume that there exists only one commodity in the economy (q); this assumption is not crucial for the results to follow. Commodity q can be either of low (L) or high (H) quality. Quality is not observable by buyers before consuming q, and this opens the door to opportunistic behavior by sellers. They can deliver a quality lower than the one expected at the ongoing market price, thus exploiting buyers.[6]

At each t, any buyer b^i purchases one unit of commodity from the seller s^j she is matched with, paying a price $p_t(M_t)$, which is decreasing in the number M_t of sellers that are active at time t, with $M_t \leq \#S$. A seller s^j is active if there exists a b^i such that $s^j \in \Theta_t^{b_i}$, that is if the seller belongs to at least one buyer's matching set (i.e. there exists at least one buyer willing to trade with her). The buyer then consumes the commodity and, consistently with the discussion above, finds out its quality (i.e. commodities are experience goods). If the good is revealed to be of low quality, from the next period on, $s^j \notin \Theta^{b_i}$, therefore, s^j does not belong to the set of sellers b^i is willing to be matched with (which becomes the largest set not including s^j).

Sellers decide the quality of the commodity they want to provide. We suppose that at any $t = m$, each seller s^j chooses an action $a_m^j \in \{H, L\}$ knowing the history $\Omega(m) = (\omega_t)_{t=0}^{m-1}$ of the game, where $\omega_t = \left(a_t^j\right)_{j=1}^{M_t}$ is the action profile at $t = 0, \ldots, m - 1$.

If at $t = m$, a seller s^j decides to sell a commodity of quality $v = (H, L)$, its expected profit at that time is given by:

$$\pi_m^j = E^j\left(b|\Omega(m)\right)\left(p_t\left(M_t\right) - c\left(q^v\right)\right)$$

where $E^j(b|\Omega(m))$ is the expected number of buyers faced at $t = m$ by a seller s^j given $\Omega(m)$, $c(q^v)$ is the cost of providing one unit of commodity of quality v, and $p_t(\#S) > c(q^H) > c(q^L)$.[7] Throughout the chapter we assume that $c(q^v)$ is constant, that is, it does not depend on the number of buyers served by the firm.

A seller s^j's profit, is the discounted sum of its stage profits:

$$\pi^j = \sum_t E^j\left(b|\Omega(t)\right)\left(p_t\left(M_t\right) - c\left(q^{v_t}\right)\right)\left(\delta^j\right)^t$$

where δ^j, the (subjective) discount factor, is a draw from a random variable δ distributed according to some $f(.)$ with supports (θ_1, θ_2), with $0 \leq \theta_1 < \theta_2 \leq 1$.[8]

As sellers do not discount the future at the same rate, they can be distinguished by the length of their time horizon. This hypothesis, although not considered in former literature, seems very natural, and helps in explaining differences in observed behavior by sellers.

As any repeated game, the present one also endows the agents with an infinite number of strategies. A strategy for seller s^j is simply a function $\gamma^j : \Omega(t) \to a_t^j \in \{H, L\}$. A seller s^j's best strategy, is a strategy γ^{j*} that maximizes its profit given the strategies γ^{-j} of the other sellers. A set of strategies $(\gamma^*)_{j=1}^{M_t} \equiv (\gamma^{-j*}, \gamma^{j*})$ is an equilibrium, if each seller plays their best strategy.

It should be clear that under the assumptions of the model, the expected number of buyers matched with a seller is non-decreasing over time as long as the seller supplies high-quality commodities (it is increasing as long as at least one seller supplying low-quality commodities exists). Henceforth, as $E^j(b|\Omega(t))$ is non-decreasing over time as far as at each t, $\gamma^j(\cdot) = H$, whereas it is non-increasing over time as far as at each t, $\gamma^j(\cdot) = L$: in non-discounted terms the profits every trustworthy seller makes at every stage t are non-decreasing, and the profits of sellers supplying low quality commodities are non-increasing.

Being interested in studying whether competition fosters trustworthiness we propose the following:

Trustworthy equilibrium: $(\gamma^{j*})_{j=1}^{M_t}$ is an equilibrium if, for each j, $\pi^j(\gamma^{-j*}, \gamma^{j*}) > \pi^j(\gamma^{-j*}, \gamma^j)$. A set of strategies $(\gamma^{j*})_{j=1}^{M_t}$ leads to a trustworthy equilibrium if there exists a $t = m$, such that, for any active j, $\gamma^{j*}(\Omega(t \geq m)) = H$.

In words, a set of strategies leads to a trustworthy equilibrium, if, from a certain time onward, given the strategies of the others, each seller's profit maximizing strategy (γ^{j*}) requires her to play H.

Lemma 1: Suppose that (γ^{-j}, γ^j) are the strategies being played, then $\exists \delta^{j*} \in (0, 1)$, such that, if $\delta^j > \delta^{j*}, \gamma^j$ cannot be optimal if it requires s^j to play L at some t.

Proof: See Appendix.

By the previous lemma, the way through which the strategies of the other sellers affect seller s^j's behavior is both through the probability of future interaction of seller s^j with those buyers she decides not to cheat, and through the market price, which decreases with the number of active sellers. Hence the equilibrium gains from future interactions are smaller (which implies that, given the distribution of δ, it is more likely that a player is untrustworthy) when the number of sellers is higher. Perfect competition obviously represents a limit case as it implies zero profit for trustworthy sellers, which then makes cheating always a profitable option.[9]

In the following proposition we emphasize the conditions required for a trustworthy equilibrium to come about.

Proposition: A necessary and sufficient condition for a trustworthy equilibrium to come about, is that, given the equilibrium strategies, at some $t = m$ there exists a non-empty subset of sellers playing H.

Proof: See Appendix.

Competition is a reliable mechanism to keep up trustworthiness, only if there exist some sellers with a sufficiently long time horizon, who therefore choose H from a certain period onward. Notice that the higher the number of sellers is and the lower the speed with which information about sellers' past actions is made public (a point which will be discussed below), the more the distribution of time horizons has to be shifted to the right to ensure that at least a subset of sellers have an incentive to build a reputation for trustworthiness.

Indeed, a minimal requirement on the distribution of δ for a trustworthy equilibrium to come about can be stated by considering that given γ^{-j*}, by lemma 1 and the proposition above, at each $t = m$ there exists a threshold δ_t^*, such that if $\delta^j > \delta_t^*$, $\gamma^{j*}(\Omega(t \geq m)) = H$. Therefore, for a trustworthy equilibrium to come about, it is ultimately required that at some t, $\delta_t^* < \theta_2$. For, if $\delta_t^* > \theta_2$ at any t, with certainty, no seller would ever play H.

Notice that as the number of buyers increases, under the hypotheses made of no information transmission, the model approximates markets where the conditions for high-quality provision of goods become increasingly harder to satisfy. This, to some extent, explains the current interest in online markets (e.g. Resnick and Zeckhauser 2002; Bolton et al. 2004, 2008).

2.2. Information transmission

So far we have supposed that each buyer gets the commodity from a seller and can avoid further buying from her if the seller cheats. Doing this, we have implicitly assumed that there is no information transmission among buyers (or that the information transmitted is not considered reliable). After having experienced a bad outcome, a buyer simply eliminates that particular seller from the set of sellers she is willing to trade with, and this does not have any other effect on the reputation of that seller. Indeed, each buyer is willing to trade with any seller who has never cheated her before.

If the number of sellers is high – therefore any of them serves in each period only a small fraction of the buyers – untrustworthy sellers are made inactive in an extremely slow way, with the consequence that – for a trustworthy equilibrium to come about – very forward-looking sellers are required. The same is true if the number of buyers is large.

The hypothesis of no information transmission among buyers is, however, an extreme one. Markets are, in fact, embedded in social networks, and networks are nothing but a means to allow information transmission. The crucial question is how much information travels among individuals participating in the network and what is its degree of reliability. At one extreme there is the case previously emphasized in which no information about sellers' past behavior is made public. At the other extreme is the case in which all the information about sellers' past behavior is, without cost, made available to all the buyers (as in Klein and Leffler 1981; Shapiro 1983). In terms of the notation previously used, in this latter case each buyer's *matching set* is given by the intersection of the *matching sets* of all the buyers, $\bigcap_{i=1}^{N} \Theta_t^{b_i}$. In other words, all the buyers share the available information about sellers' past behavior. Clearly, the punishment for cheating is in this case much more effective, and, everything constant, the probability that a trustworthy equilibrium takes place is much higher than before.

Apart from these two extreme cases, there is the more likely situation in which a given buyer shares her available information only with a subset $B' \subset B$ of buyers. Again, all this impacts on the speed with which sellers providing low-quality commodities are punished, and, therefore, on the probability that a trustworthy equilibrium emerges.

It is noteworthy that before the effects of the Industrial Revolution (among which urbanization is not a negligible one) became fully visible, the requirements for a trustworthy equilibrium to come about via the market mechanism were to a great extent satisfied. Quality could, in fact, be ascertained by inspection or after consumption, and markets were framed by networks of personal relationships, which made information transmission very effective.

To sum up, the model above suggests that the probability that a trustworthy equilibrium comes about strictly depends on such conditions as the possibility of verifying the quality of the traded goods, the transmission of reliable information about sellers' past performance and the market structure. These conditions determine a threshold value of the time horizon over which playing honestly is individually rational for sellers. It goes without saying that the lower the threshold with respect to the distribution of time horizons, the higher the probability that a randomly chosen seller will provide high-quality commodities. In the next sections we analyze the changes (mainly institutional and technological) that have adversely affected both the position of the threshold and the distribution of time horizons.

3. From a *local trade economy* to *family capitalism*: the separation of consumers from producers

In the previous section we have assumed that quality is not observable by buyers before consuming q, but after consumption takes place consumers are *always* able to recognize whether q was of high or low quality. While this can be a good approximation of the real world as far as small communities at the early stages of industrialization are considered, it can be a hard hypothesis to sustain thereafter.

Economic historians share the view that two driving forces were fully at work during the nineteenth century (e.g. Chandler 1977; Holtfreter et al. 2006; Law 2003), both ultimately linked to a significant development of new technology. On one hand, technological advancements both increased the minimum efficient scale of production (i.e. they made small-scale productions economically inefficient) and allowed for long-term food conservation (through refrigeration, packaging and the development of chemical preservatives); on the other hand, improvements in information transmission and in transportation of goods lowered the costs of separating consumers from producers (on this, see also Coase 1937). These two forces jointly pushed for an increase in the size of firms and a (geographical) concentration of supply (Krugman 1991), with the consequence of reshaping the organization of economic activity, whose preferred form became the corporation, the ownership of which could be easily traded and transferred. The corporation carried great advantages with respect to the partnership, that is, an organization with unlimited liability generally linked to a family, as the limited liability does not require one to put at risk one's whole wealth, and makes it easier to collect the necessary funds to organize large-scale productions.

Historical examples of these processes at work are provided by Kim (2001) for the US, who analyses the case of food producers.

Meat packing is a particularly representative example, as local communities used to have their local butchers until the late nineteenth century. With the introduction of refrigerated cars, packing was concentrated in the American midwest, because of the considerable comparative advantages in the production of meat. An immediate consequence of this concentration was the increase in the size of butchers, and the inability for consumers to assess the quality of products they were purchasing: was refrigerated meat butchered under horrible conditions? Was it detrimental to health?

As Wood (1985) reminds us: 'Upton Sinclair's description of the squalor of the American meat-packing industry in his 1906 novel, *The Jungle*, horrified the public and unsettled their stomachs.'

This asymmetric information problem, which was acute for other manufactured products (drugs and medicines) and certain types of services (e.g. banking), was even more severe for those food products for which chemistry allowed the substitution of ingredients. Indeed, as suggested by the report *Adulteration of Articles of Food* by the US Senate (1902), adulteration was a profitable and a very common strategy for food producers in the late 1800s. Examples are abundant: milk was cheapened by adding water, butter was adulterated with oleomargarine, glucose was added to honey and maple syrup to make them cheaper. As Law (2003) points out, 'techno-logical change thus gave rise to new forms of food adulteration that were *imperceptible* to consumers'.

It is clear that under such circumstances competition alone could not have ensured an acceptable level of trustworthiness, as, if consumers were not able to assess quality after consuming *q*, then *they were not able to punish dishonest sellers*, since they were simply not able to recognize them. Indeed, competition (i.e. the presence of outside options for consumers) is a *broken mechanism* for creating trust when the quality of the good cannot be accu-rately assessed even after consumption. Furthermore, in this case no rational seller would supply high-quality commodities, as stated more formally in terms of the model sketched above, by the following:

Remark 1: If the quality of the good cannot be verified *ex post*, the equilibrium strategy requires any seller to play *L* at each *t*.

Proof: *Straightforward, from discussion above.*

How could consumers' trust be sustained in this environment? How did these economies originate trust? History teaches that new institutions emerged in this period to cope with the problem (e.g. Alsberg 1931; Wood 1985; Law 2003; Holtfreter et al. 2006). Some were public institutions, some others were institutions spontaneously originating from the market. What is crucial to remark here is that markets satisfactorily approximating those described in basic microeconomic textbooks *no longer existed*.[10]

For the reasons discussed above, since the nineteenth century, technologi-cal and organizational changes made the informational problem more acute, and called for new institutions, never experimented before.

A first set of institutions created to sustain trust among consumers, stemmed from *public regulation*, broadly defined to include antitrust regula-tion and products regulation. The *Sherman Antitrust Act* dates back to 1890. The US federal government also passed the *Meat Inspection Act* (1891), the *Food and Drug Act* (1906), and other laws on product quality such as the 1938 *Food, Drug, and Cosmetic Act* (e.g. Kim 2001; Holtfreter et al. 2006). Notice that the crucial task assigned to government agencies (and not-for-profit consumers organizations, which emerged in the same period) was to discover breaches of the law. Hence, it should not be surprising that trust in a par-ticular producer (and, consequently, in similar producers) would have been lowered each time their misconduct was discovered, particularly considering that a common sanction against transgression was that of stigmatizing man-ufacturers and dealers by publishing the results of agency investigation (Law 2003). High-quality goods became those that respected the standards set by the law, whose primary focus was on products easy to adulterate (mainly food and drugs).

As far as the general function of sanctioning is considered (in particular, sanctioning by making the public aware of the misconduct of a particular seller), it is clear that the purpose was that of leaving the market to enforce trustworthiness, relying on public intervention only to provide the necessary information to consumers, information that was not obtainable by search or experience anymore.

As accurate monitoring aimed – in a sense – at switching credence in experience goods (McCluskey 2000), it contributed in pushing the economy close to a situation in which market forces could have enforced *good behavior.*

The effectiveness of public monitoring was clearly greater where adequate resources were committed to this end, allowing, for example, the creation of *regulatory agencies.* As it could be expected, the problem was not thought as one of enforcing full adherence to the law, in such a way as to drive, in brief, the economy toward what we have called a trustworthy equilibrium. Rather it was thought of as one of determining the amount of resources that would have ensured an acceptable level of trust. It is reasonable to believe that differences in the amount of resources devoted to this end across regions were driven by factors shaping beliefs about trustworthiness.

It is noteworthy that this latter hypothesis, which has recently gained empirical support (Pinotti 2008), has a straightforward interpretation in terms of the model sketched above, where the only source of difference among sellers is given by the length of their time horizon. In fact, if ρ is the probability that a seller is monitored, and to keep things as simple as possible, supposing that the sanction is that of readily informing the public of seller misconduct causing zero sales to her from that period on, the resources devoted by governments to ensure (an acceptable level of) reliability must be higher, *coeteris paribus,* the shorter the time horizon of the sellers.

Remark 2: For any given δ^j, there exists a value of ρ, such that monitoring is effective in enforcing the seller to provide the high-quality good even if the quality cannot be assessed *ex post* by buyers.

Proof: See Appendix.

Even if public regulation seemed to be essential to the well-functioning of markets, it could not be enough. To solve the problem just by relying on this would have required a huge amount of resources and the rise of a *plethora* of bureaucratic controls that could not generally meet public support. Indeed public regulation was at that time joined by market-based institutions, which met the favor of firms interested in signaling reliability. These institutions were essentially based on investments in firm-specific and non-recoverable assets: promotion of *brand names* through *advertisement.* According to scholars, advertising flourished from 1880s: Pope

(2008) estimates that total advertising volume in the US grew from about $200 million in 1880 to nearly $3 billion in 1920.

Advertising was used to signal to consumers that a particular seller was credibly committing to trading a high-quality product. Why was this signal credible? Because it was costly, as, if the firm was discovered to be producing low-quality goods, trust was gone, and with trust also consumers, devaluating the firm-specific investment in brand name.

These market-based institutions worked well in presence of public regulation, which reinforced the impact of unrecoverable investments on sellers' incentive to be trustworthy.

It is, furthermore, worth mentioning that during the period under consideration families were still directly involved in managing firms, and a likely bankruptcy (after trust was depleted) would still significantly affect their wealth. This is a non-trivial difference with respect to the following periods, when investment diversification, among other things, made the involvement of families less stringent. As anyone ruling the firm can hardly have a longer time horizon than a family, this may have contributed to the shifting of the whole distribution of time horizons to the left, making trustworthiness less profitable and thus more uncommon.

3.1. Firm specific investments and heterogeneity of sellers

Before moving further, notice that in the original model by Klein and Leffler (1981), investments in advertising are a means to dissipate profits and discourage potential competitors from entering the market. This helps sustain the hypothesis that the ongoing market price for high-quality goods can be higher than cost without encouraging potential sellers to access the market. As much of the theoretical literature on the subject is grounded on the hypothesis of perfect competition, the problem of how to prevent prices being driven to the average cost levels (which would induce any rational seller to play L) emerges.

Assuming heterogeneous time preferences for sellers, as we do, suggests that if building a reputation for honesty requires an initial investment, this could constitute a real barrier to entry in the market, so that, in equilibrium, profits could be higher than normal.

This is historically consistent with the reasons that have led honest firms to invest much of their resources (through advertising or other firm-specific investments in brand name) to try to get a publicly visible signal (a green beard,[11] or, in our context, a green brand). The main point is that trying to get a publicly visible label to signal a preference for honesty, must be *prohibitively costly* for firms that try to imitate. The classical example, in a situation in which firms can set the price, is the model by Milgrom and Roberts (1986).

With a large but finite number of sellers (which seems quite a reasonable assumption) and differences in the length of sellers' time horizon, there is a straightforward reason why these firms' specific investments – which signal a willingness to behave trustworthily – may constitute a barrier to entry in the market. In fact, *coeteris paribus*, a greater δ^j allows a firm to make *greater* non-recoverable investments, and this may prevent the entry of firms with a shorter time horizon (even if these firms could have an incentive to provide high-quality goods once entered).

To keep things simple, Remark 3 below simply shows that a trustworthy equilibrium with no entry is plausible if firm-specific investments are recognized by buyers as reliable signals of trustworthiness.

Remark 3: If the number of sellers is finite and sellers differ in the length of their time horizon, a trustworthy equilibrium with no entry is made possible by firm-specific investments.

Proof: See Appendix.

There are three points which are worth emphasizing. First, firm-specific investments, by creating a barrier to entry in the market and by allowing firms to make higher profits, reward honest firms, characterized by a longer time horizon. In a sense, these extra profits are a premium for their patience. Second, the signal, to be informative, must be too costly to imitate. This second observation will be discussed at length below, when the actual recourse to ethical codes and corporate social responsibility (CSR) by firms will be discussed. Third, the presence of such investments allow the government to save public resources on monitoring, since, as far as they increase, public resources devoted to affect ρ can be reduced without this having any adverse effect on the level of reliability. The reason for this is that non-compliance with the law becomes, of course, more costly for firms.

4. From *family capitalism* to *financial capitalism*: the separation of ownership from control

According to Chandler (1990), family (or personal) capitalism – in the Anglo-Saxon countries – underpinned the preference for small-scale businesses. The need to abandon family capitalism to increase profits, was, and still is, the orthodox view taught in the most prestigious business schools, since, it is argued, family capitalism jeopardizes investments and modernization (e.g. Gallino 2005). The organizational changes that came about after the development that occurred in late nineteenth and early twentieth centuries, find, to a large extent, an explanation of the need of going beyond family capitalism in order to expand business activity. This necessarily carried with it the use of debts and other external funds.

There are at least three consequences of this process which are worth mentioning as they still have an importance in order to interpret the present-day situation. First, an increase in market concentration challenged the ability of antitrust authorities to brave firms, and – more importantly – the ability of other government agencies to control and dispute against large-scale firms, which have since then increasingly acquired the ability to shop around for less restrictive regulation. Second, the same corporations came to own different brands of specific goods, so that their presence in a certain market was no more linked to consumers' trust in a particular brand. Third, as already mentioned, the expansion of firms' size made the recourse to external finance crucial.

This latter fact, coupled with a minor involvement of families (e.g. Gordon 2007), who began to delegate their power of managing firms, led to the by now familiar *separation of ownership from control* in large corporations (Means 1931; Berle and Means 1932). This was already clear at the end of 1929, when – considering the list of 200 largest US companies – 58 per cent of wealth was under management control (Means 1931).

The separation of ownership from control was at the basis of a misalignment between managers' and owners' goals, and, to some extent, shaped a new figure of owner, linked with those who rule the firm by a trust relationship. The problem of trusting sellers became, therefore, even more acute by the existence of this side relationship, *internal to the firm*, which, however, affected the standard market interaction between consumers and producers. It is clear that if quality cannot be accurately verified *ex post*, separating ownership from control makes the determinants of trustworthiness even more complex (even in the presence of public regulation or investment in non-recoverable assets), for it is now required to consider managers' goals. They could be affected, among other things, by a shorter time horizon, for the self-evident observation that their lives are shorter than corporation ones. We come back to this point below.

The processes mentioned above assumed increasing importance during the twentieth century, raising problems that have been made sharper by further technological and organizational developments.

Is competition enough to sustain an acceptable level of trust under these conditions? The answer seems to be negative.

The emergence of a new set of institutions to regulate relationships *internal to the firm* finds, to some extent, its justification in the changes mentioned, as in the environment shortly described, that firms' reputation must necessarily rest on the ability to control managers' behavior.

Among the mechanisms adopted to enforce good behavior, one relies on monetary incentives, designed to provide professional managers with adequate *premia* in order to realign their objectives with those of the owners (e.g. Grossman and Hart 1983).

Experience, however, suggests that this has led to widespread and perverse encouragement to maximize short-term profitability, with the consequence of making the emergence of corporate scandals more likely. In terms of our model, this seems to have adversely conditioned the distribution of δ.

A second set of mechanisms, usually referred to as 'corporate governance', relies on the ability of the board of directors, the financial markets and other stakeholders to enforce compliance with the law (e.g. Fama and Jensen 1983; Tirole 2001, 2005; Damiani 2006).

Along with these market-based institutions, the need for public control on managers' behavior has become increasingly pressing. Very recent examples for the US include the Sarbanes-Oxley Act and the Organizational Sentencing Guidelines (e.g. Hess 2006). It is common opinion, however, that acts like these were more a reaction to the growing number of corporate scandals than a well-judged means to solve the problem, as shown for instance by Parker and Atkins (1999) in relation to the Sentencing Guidelines.

There are reasons to believe that the complex structure of controls has proved ineffective mainly for the intricacy of the information watchdogs need to manage. In this case, misbehavior is not prevented even in the presence of considerable disciplinary actions, as proved, for example, by Karpoff et al. (2008) in the case of managers accountable for cooking the books. Indeed, as recently shown by Dyck et al. (2008), fraud detection does not rely, crucially, on those actors which, by virtue of law, would be formally in charge of this task (such as the shareholders, the investors or the financial market regulators), but still on non-traditional stakeholders like the employees or the media.

5. Trustworthiness in a global economy

Today's markets are really different from those originally described by Adam Smith: technology has stimulated an increase in the size of firms, separating consumers from producers; ownership has divorced from control; financial conglomerates and multinational firms are now the masters of international markets and can shop around for the national regulations that best suit their interests. Technology has also given firms the ability to produce goods whose characteristics are difficult to assess not only by consumers, but also by government agencies. One prominent example is given by genetically modified ingredients in food products. How could consumers find out that a given product is obtained from genetically modified elements (other than assessing whether they are, in fact, detrimental to health)?[12] How could consumers be sure that in a highly integrated economy, firms are able to scrutinize the quality of the inputs employed in production?

The problem of how to ensure an acceptable level of trust needs to be embedded and discussed in accordance with this situation.

As for public (state) regulation, it seems particularly unsuccessful (e.g. Galgano 2001). Global enterprises require a global level regulation (as recently witnessed by the subprime financial crisis). This kind of regulation is clearly difficult to achieve, for international treaties are required to be individually rational for every country participating in the deal.

However, leaving any state free to enforce its own regulation is both inefficient and ineffective. A clear example is provided by the recent performance of the Food and Drug Administration in the US:

> The Food and Drug Administration has known for years about contamination problems at a Georgia peanut butter plant and on California spinach farms that led to disease outbreaks that killed three people, sickened hundreds, and forced one of the biggest product recalls in U.S. history, documents and interviews show. *Overwhelmed* by huge growth in the number of *food processors* and *imports*, however, the agency took only limited steps to address the problems *and relied on producers to police themselves*, according to agency documents.
>
> (Williamson 2007; emphasis added)

Relying on producers to police themselves appears more like an unconditional surrender than a strategy consciously undertaken to tackle the problem. There is, in fact, evidence that corporations are not committed to a broad ethical obligation to comply with the law (Di Lorenzo 2007); on the contrary, as controls by government agencies seem to be targeted at specific producers, there is a strategic response aimed at minimizing the probability of regulatory enforcement. This is also what Kehoane et al. (2009) have found for the case of coal-burning electric utilities faced with the enforcement of air pollution regulation in the US.

Difficulties for governments also come from the large ineffectiveness of market-based institutions. As we made clear in the discussion of Remark 2 above, the inadequacy of public resources to identify frauds or to prosecute corporations charged of fraud, becomes more acute when market-based institutions do not work properly.

Why do market devices, which proved good in the past, seem to lose their efficacy? Here, we suggest some reasons. As the discussion of Remark 3, above, made clear, firm-specific investments may signal a genuine disposition for trustworthiness if: a) mimicking the signal is too costly for low-quality competitors characterized by a shorter time horizon; b) the initial cost can be offset by future sales, taking account that firm-specific investments may constitute a barrier to entry that allows trustworthy firms to get a price premium, thus rewarding their patience.

If firms are run by managers whose time horizon is finite, consequences arise. In fact, as is implicit in the model sketched above, differences in δ^j become increasingly significant as the number of periods increase. If managers face a finite time horizon, the incentive to issue a signal sufficiently strong so as to avoid the risk of being imitated strikingly reduces. Similar problems arise when those who run the firm are induced to discount the future more heavily.

Moreover, when what really matters is not the long-term profitability of the firm, but its stock price, which can be manipulated, among other things, by higher than optimal firm-specific investments, the competitive mechanism proves ineffective, as the future loses its importance: actions have to be assessed only in terms of their immediate consequences. It is not really important what the truth is; it is important what people believe the truth to be, as this has an immediate consequence on stock prices.

As far as market-based institutions are concerned, what many scholars seem to suggest – once the ineffectiveness of incentives and corporate governance institutions is established – is reliance on *self-regulation* by firms. The recent move toward business ethics, the adoption of ethical codes, and Corporate Social Responsibility (CSR) can be interpreted as the need to signal a good reputation when other devices prove to be ineffective.

Needless to say, corporate responsibility pretends much more than it can actually deliver. CSR can be just a *cheap talk*, in a world in which it becomes increasingly difficult to enforce the law and punish corporations responsible for frauds against consumers. It is noteworthy that most of the firms involved in recent corporate scandals made extensive use of ethical codes of conduct (e.g. Enron, Lehman Brothers, Morgan Stanley). As the discussion of Remark 3, above, highlights, the costs of adopting CSR by mimicking *ethical* firms, are minimal for enterprises that defraud consumers, *because nothing but the penalty provided by the law is what really matters*. In other words, a signal is used which is not a costly one; a signal that can be easily imitated and, therefore, become uninformative. Newspapers like the *Guardian* have recently attracted public attention on this, launching a campaign to make the public aware of the fact that there does not exist, in most of the cases, any follow-up or auditing process to control the ethical responsible claims made by companies (see The *Guardian*, 23 October 2008).

Our interpretation of CSR as a self-regulation mechanism whose use is mainly driven by the ineffectiveness of public and other market-based institutions, is, to a large extent, different from those already available in the literature. Just to remember some recent and prominent examples, Besley and Ghatak (2007) view CSR as the creation of public goods or curtailment of public bads, but they assume that consumers are able to observe the 'public good content' of a given product, which we argue is clearly untenable in today's economies. If this were possible, then it would also be possible for consumers to find out the quality of the goods supplied, and thus CSR would have no specific role. Heal (2005) suggests that CSR plays a role in reducing externalized costs or in avoiding distributional conflicts, but fails to give account of what happens when managers breach *ethical codes* (apart from some focal cases, which attract the interest of the media and stimulate a public reaction).

Some other interesting views of CSR are discussed at length in other chapters of this volume (see, e.g. Degli Antoni and Sacconi, *infra*, and Aoki, *infra*, and the references therein). Here, CSR is basically linked to the adoption of an extended model of corporate governance, according to which managers are responsible not only toward the owners, but toward society at large, in agreement with the rules set up in the constitutional contract of the firm. The adoption of CSR standards, supporting the belief that firms aim at keeping cooperative relations with the whole set of stakeholders, would contribute to the accumulation of a specific form of social capital at the *individual firm* level, thus enhancing firms' economic performance. Also in these contributions, however, the fundamental difficulty of discovering how and when firms breach the contract, and what happens after a violation occurs, remains. It is not surprising then, that some authors advocate to combine CSR with an explicit provision by law, to make the former enforceable. However, it is difficult to grasp what the difference is between this solution and the use of public regulation per se.

6. Concluding remarks

In this chapter we have emphasized that technological and organizational changes have progressively made it more troublesome to cope with the problem of ensuring an acceptable level of trust in market economies, stimulating the emergence of a plethora of institutions.

As complex problems generally require complex solutions, is not possible to say a priori what can be considered as the better institutions, whether market-based or ultimately rooted in public regulation. It depends on the given historical circumstances. It is noteworthy that in the late nineteenth century, public regulation seemed to have a comparative advantage on market-based devices to enforce contractual performance. One century later, when public (that is, state) regulation, had de facto assumed the nature of a local regulation, market-based (worldwide) solutions seem to be better equipped. This is likely to be at the root of the renewed interest in competition as an engine of trust.

We have emphasized some reasons, which argue for skepticism in assessing the role that competition can play.

What many scholars seem nowadays to suggest, given that the inadequacy of public regulation and other traditional market-based institutions has been proven, is that we should rely on *self-regulation* by firms. The recent move toward business ethics, the adoption of ethical codes and Corporate Social Responsibility (CSR) can be interpreted as the need to signal a good reputation when other devices prove to be ineffective.

As competition needs well-functioning public institutions, similarly CSR can be just 'cheap talk' in a world in which it becomes increasingly difficult to enforce the law and punish corporations responsible for frauds against consumers.

The pressing need for public regulation has found a response in many legislative acts, which were more a reaction to the increasing number of corporate scandals than a means to solve the problem. This was partially due to the fact that global problems require global-level regulation, as the recent subprime financial crisis has shown. However, this is something that is difficult to achieve, as international treaties are required to be advantageous for every country participating in the deal.

Acknowledgements

We wish to thank Roberto Cagliozzi, Michele Grillo, Carmine Ornaghi, Francesca Stroffolini and the editors of this book for their comments to previous drafts of this work. The usual disclaimers apply.

Appendix

Proof of Lemma 1: Given γ^{-j}, a seller's s^j's optimal strategy requires her to play L either never or a finite number of times $z > 0$. First consider the case in which γ^{-j} is required to play H at each t, and suppose that, according to γ^j, s^j has already played L a number $z - 1$ of times, with γ^j requiring her to play L again at $t = m \geq z - 1$. If s^j behaves accordingly, for any buyer cheated she gets $[(p(\overline{M}) - c(q^H)) + (c(q^H) - c(q^L))](\delta^j)^m$. Yet it would be possible for s^j to play an alternative strategy, $\gamma^{j\prime}$, which differs from γ^j only in the behavior it requires from $t = m$ on, that is $\gamma^{j\prime}(\cdot)_{t=m}^{\infty} = H$. Adopting $\gamma^{j\prime}$, a buyer not cheated at $t = m$ will be willing to keep on trading in subsequent periods, ensuring s^j an additional profit equal to

$$\frac{\sigma\left(p\left(\overline{M}\right) - c\left(q^H\right)\right)}{1 - \delta^j}\left(\delta^j\right)^{m+1}$$

where $\overline{M} = \#S$, and $\sigma = (1/\overline{M})$ is the probability of being matched at $t > m$ with one of those buyers that s^j could have cheated at $t = m$ and did not. For player s^j not to play L at $t = m$ it is therefore required that

$$\frac{\sigma\left(\overline{p} - c\left(q^H\right)\right)}{1 - \delta^j}\left(\delta^j\right)^{m+1} > \left(c\left(q^H\right) - c\left(q^L\right)\right)\left(\delta^j\right)^m$$

or

$$\sigma\left(\overline{p} - c\left(q^H\right)\right)g\left(\delta^j\right) > \left(c\left(q^H\right) - c\left(q^L\right)\right)$$

where $\overline{p} = p(\overline{M})$ and $g(\delta^j) = (\delta^j/1 - \delta^j)$ is continuous and increasing in δ^j, with $lim_{\delta^j \to 1}g(\delta^j) = \infty$. If δ^j is sufficiently high, that is, above a certain threshold δ_z, playing L at $t = m \geq z - 1$ cannot be optimal, therefore the optimal strategy cannot be required to play L a number z of times. Suppose therefore that γ^j requires s^j to play L a number $z - 1$ of times. With identical reasoning it is possible to show that if $\delta^j > \delta_{z-1} = \delta_z$, then γ^j cannot be optimal. The reasoning applies to any number of times γ^j requires s^j to play L. We can therefore conclude that $\exists \delta^{j*} = \delta_z = \delta_{z-1} = \ldots = \delta_0 : \forall \delta^j > \delta^{j*}$ if $\gamma^j(\Omega(.)) = L$ at some t, then $\gamma^j \neq \gamma^{j*}$: the optimal strategy can never be to play L. Suppose now that γ^{-j} is a profile of arbitrary strategies. This implies, everything equal, that σ', the probability of being matched in subsequent periods with one of those buyers s^j could have cheated at a certain t, is not smaller than before, $\sigma' \geq \sigma$, because the average number of sellers belonging to the matching sets of those buyers matched with s^j at t, cannot be greater than $\overline{M} = \#S$; by the same token, the price paid for the good, is not smaller, $p(M_t) \geq p(\overline{M})$. Therefore, the conclusion that $\exists \delta^{j*} \in (0, 1)$, such that, if $\delta^j > \delta^{j*}$, γ^j cannot be optimal if it requires s^j to play L at some t, applies.

Proof of Proposition 1: Necessity is obvious, as, if at any t, the subset $S' \subset S$ of sellers playing H is empty, a trustworthy equilibrium cannot come about. As for sufficiency, note that if $(\gamma^{-j*}, \gamma^{j*})$ are the equilibrium strategies, by lemma 1, since σ' and $p(.)$ are not decreasing over time, γ^{j*} cannot require s^j to play L at $t = m$ if it required her playing H at $t = m - 1$. Therefore, if at some $t = m$, $\exists S' \neq \emptyset \subset S : \forall s^j \in S'$, $\gamma^{j*}((\Omega(m)) = H$, for any such s^j, $\gamma^{j*}((\Omega(t > m)) = H$. As any other player in a finite number of periods either comes to belong to S' or is driven out, a trustworthy equilibrium will be achieved.

Proof of Remark 2: For simplicity, suppose that γ^{-j} requires any $s^k \neq s^j$ to play H at each t (which is the worst situation for s^j to play trustworthily). Given γ^{-j}, by proposition 1 seller s^j's optimal strategy requires either to play H or to play L forever. If s^j plays H, she gets:

$$\pi^{jH} = \frac{\left(1/\overline{M}\right)\left(\overline{p} - c\left(q^H\right)\right)}{1 - \delta^j}$$

otherwise she gets:

$$\pi^{jL} = \frac{(1 - \rho)\left(1/\overline{M}\right)\left(\overline{p} - c(q^L)\right)}{1 - \delta^j(1 - \rho)}$$

$$\pi^{jH} > \pi^{jL} \rightarrow \frac{\overline{p} - c\left(q^H\right)}{\overline{p} - c\left(q^L\right)} > \frac{\left(1 - \delta^j - \delta^j \rho\right) - \rho}{\left(1 - \delta^j - \delta^j \rho\right)} = h(\rho) \, [*]$$

As $\rho \to 0$, [*] is never satisfied. As $\rho \to 1$, [*] is always satisfied. As $h'(\rho) < 0$, given δ^j, it is possible to find a value of ρ, call it ρ^*, such that, for any $\rho > \rho^*$,

$\pi^{jH} > \pi^{jL}$. It is straightforward to note that as far as δ^j increases, the value of ρ necessary for [*] to hold, gets smaller.

Proof of Remark 3: First consider that in equilibrium profits are increasing in the length of the time horizon. This is obvious if $\gamma^{j*} = \gamma^{k*}$, for any pair of sellers s^j and s^k with $s^j \neq s^k$. Therefore, if $\gamma^{j*} \neq \gamma^{k*}$, as the only source of difference is that $\delta^j \neq \delta^k$, and supposing that $\delta^j > \delta^k$, π^j would be greater than π^k if s^j played $\gamma^{j\prime} = \gamma^{k*} \neq \gamma^{j*}$. However, as γ^{j*} is s^j's optimal strategy, it must imply an higher profit than $\gamma^{j\prime}$.

Suppose that conditions are given for a trustworthy equilibrium to come about when all the sellers participate in the game from $t = 0$. Then there exists a subset $S' \subset S$ of sellers with a typical element $s^j \in S'$, playing H from $t = m$ on.

Let S now be the set of potential sellers, however large but finite, and suppose that at $t = 0$ only sellers belonging to S' play the game. These must be the sellers with the highest time horizon. If at $t = 0$ any $s^j \in S'$ makes an investment F equal to $\underline{\pi}$, where $\underline{\pi}$ is the profit of that $s^h \in S'$ such that $\delta^h = min\Delta$, and $\Delta = \left\{ \delta^j \right\}_{j \in S'}$, then no seller with a discount factor smaller than δ^h enters the market.

Notes

1. For an analysis of the relationship between trustworthiness and trust see Fehr (2008) and Tullberg (2008).
2. Recent experimental studies (Bolton et al. 2008; Huck et al. 2007) argue that competition yields higher levels of buyer trust and seller trustworthiness, with this having obvious desirable consequences on market efficiency. The setting analyzed in these studies basically resembles the classical Trust Game, with the first mover (the buyer) deciding whether to purchase an item, and the second mover (the seller) deciding whether to cheat (by providing an item of a quality different from the one promised or by not shipping the item). The efficient outcome is supposed to be the one in which the buyer trust the seller and this in turn repays trust with trustworthiness. Both studies compare a no-competition treatment, where the buyer is constrained to play the game with a seller randomly matched with her, with a competition treatment, where the buyer has the option of choosing among different sellers on the basis of their reputation, represented by the list of actions made in previous periods. Experimental evidence then suggests that introducing competition (to be meant as the presence of different sellers among which the buyer can choose) together with some information about sellers' past choices, enhances market efficiency, given that sellers who behave dishonestly can be traced and punished (buyers can avoid dealing with them in the future), with this creating strong incentives for sellers to be trustworthy (and for buyers to trust).
3. Clearly enough, not all the required inputs were provided in a narrow local area. Just to make an example, cinnamon used in some desserts came from Sri Lanka. Also, for these exchanges – though the minority of the economic activity – one

need to explain how trust evolved. The mechanism in this case was *direct control* through a representative or a reliable captain of the ship involved in transportation (Chandler 1977). Indeed, all-purpose merchants were also responsible for financing local economic activities and for transporting and distributing goods.

4. See Darby and Karni (1973), and Dulleck and Kerschbamer (2006).

5. These insights into the formal game theory terminology were first developed by Tullock (1985).

6. Shapiro (1983) considers a set of heterogeneous buyers, each of them having a different taste for quality. In equilibrium, each buyer may get the desirable quality level (provided that this is higher than the minimum enforced quality standard) by paying a premium (defined as the difference between the price paid and the cost of production). Such a premium is increasing in the quality level. In our model we assume that all consumers have the same preferences and only prefer the good of the highest quality.

7. Notice that with positive profits new suppliers may be induced to enter the market. We will discuss this point below.

8. A better hypothesis would seem to be that of assuming each seller sets her own price on the basis of the expected number of buyers (a seller increases her own price when her expected number of buyers increases). This would imply dropping the assumption of uniform random matching, as the price would become a signal for trustworthiness. However, under the hypotheses made in this section, nothing would prevent sellers with a smaller number of expected buyers from raising the price in such a way as to mimic those with a larger number. Therefore, the price signal would become uninformative. As the hypothesis on price formation does not affect the main point we want to highlight, we choose the assumption that allows us to keep things as simple as possible.

9. As has been emphasized by the literature (e.g. Shapiro 1983), the long-run competitive equilibrium cannot imply $p_t = c(q^H) > c(q^L)$. In fact, in this case, no seller would have the incentive to provide high-quality goods. Consumers would rationally anticipate this and would prefer not to buy. Hence, the existence of *ex ante* asymmetric information about quality prevents the price being the one that gets established in competitive markets where information is perfect. The existence of a price premium is a necessary condition for firms to provide high-quality goods.

10. This is not to deny that in earlier phases of economic history, both spontaneous and enforced by the law, institutions served the purpose of ensuring trustworthiness in market transactions. Remarkable examples of the latter had their source in the *Theodosian Code* (438 AD) or the *Ordonnance du Commerce* (1673). As for the former, it is worth mentioning the set of conventions spontaneously risen for regulating relationships among merchants, generally known as *lex mercatoria* or *ius mercatorum*, whose roots can be found in the need to expand economic activity over the limited borders within which public authorities could have been effective in enforcing contractual performance (e.g. Galgano 2001). It is significant that such conventions proved effective in ensuring an acceptable level of trustworthiness (notably among the individuals belonging to the *societas mercatorum*), because they were adequate to cope with the problem of ensuring sufficient information both about product quality and merchants' behavior (e.g. Greif 1993).

11. Theoretical literature addressing the problem of cooperation among rational agents in a setting where the information is scarce, has made use of the so-called *green beard hypothesis* (Dawkins 1976), which dictates that agents are labeled with

a generally recognizable and publicly visible signal, which carries valuable information about their willingness to cooperate with others. Much discussion has arisen about the validity of such models (e.g. Fehr and Fischbacher 2005; Frank 2005; Sobel 2005; Sugden 2004). What is generally held to be the most prominent shortcoming of this hypothesis is that opportunists may mimic the signal, thus gaining an advantage. There are, however, examples (especially in biology, e.g. Keller and Ross 1998) showing that in many cases imitating the signal is too costly.

12. It is not at all surprising that, according to a survey conducted in different European countries, a limited share of people believe that common food items like burgers or canned tomatoes are very safe to eat, with British, Danes and Norwegians being the more trusting people (e.g. Poppe and Kjærnes 2003; Kjærnes 2006). On food biotechnology, see Nestle (2004).

References

C. L. Alsberg (1931) 'Aspects of Adulteration and Imitation', *The Quarterly Journal of Economics*, 46(1), 1–33.

N. Berggren and H. Jordahl (2006) 'Free to Trust: Economic Freedom and Social Capital', *Kyklos*, 59, 141–169.

A. A. Berle and G. C. Means (1932) *The Modern Corporation and Private Property* (New York: Macmillan).

M. Blaug (2001) 'Is Competition Such a Good Thing? Static Efficiency versus Dynamic Efficiency', *Review of Industrial Organization*, 19, 37–48.

G. E Bolton, E. Katok and A. Ockenfels (2004) 'Trust among Internet Traders', *Analyse & Kritik*, 26, 185–202.

G. E. Bolton, C. Loebbecke and A. Ockenfels (2008) 'Does Competition Promote Trust and Trustworthiness in Online Trading? An Experimental Study', *Journal of Management Information Systems*, 25(2), 145–170.

T. Besley and M. Ghatak (2007) 'Retailing Public Goods: The Economics of Corporate Social Responsibility', *Journal of Public Economics*, 91(9), 1645–1663.

A. D. Chandler Jr. (1977) *The Visible Hand. The Managerial Revolution in American Business* (Cambridge (MA): The Belknap Press of Harvard University Press).

A. D. Chandler Jr. (1990) *Scale and Scope* (Cambridge (MA): Harvard University Press).

C. M. Cipolla (1974) *Storia economica dell'Europa pre-industriale* (Bologna: Il Mulino).

R. H. Coase (1937) 'The Nature of the Firm', *Economica*, IV(13–16), 386–405.

P. Conway, V. Janod and G. Nicoletti (2005) 'Product Market Regulation in OECD Countries: 1998 to 2003', OECD, *Economics Department Working Papers*, 419.

M. Damiani (2006) *Impresa e Corporate Governance* (Roma: Carocci).

M. R. Darby and E. Karni (1973) 'Free Competition and the Optimal Amount of Fraud', *Journal of Law and Economics*, 16(1), 67–88.

R. Dawkins, (1976). *The Selfish Gene* (New York: Oxford University Press).

V. Di Lorenzo (2007) 'Business Ethics: Law As A Determinant of Business Conduct', *Journal of Business Ethics*, 71, 275–299.

U. Dulleck and R. Kerschbamer (2006) 'On Doctors, Mechanics, and Computer Specialists: The Economics of Credence Goods', *Journal of Economic Literature*, XLIV, 5–42.

A. Dyck, A. Morse and L. Zingales (2008) 'Who Blows the Whistle on Corporate Fraud?', The University of Chicago Booth School of Business, Working Paper No. 08–22.

E. F. Fama and M. C. Jensen (1983) 'Separation of Ownership and Control', *Journal of Law and Economics*, XXVI(2), 301–325.

E. Fehr and U. Fischbacher (2005) 'Altruists with Green Beards', *Analyse & Kritik*, 27, 73–84.

E. Fehr (2008) 'On the Economics and Biology of Trust', *IZA Discussion Paper*, No. 3895.

J. A. V. Fischer (2008), Is Competition Good for Trust? Cross-Country Evidence using Micro-Data', *Economic Letters*, 100, 56–59.

R. H. Frank (2005) 'Altruists with Green Beards: Still Kicking?', *Analyse & Kritik*, 27, 85–96.

F. Galgano (2001) *Lex Mercatoria* (Bologna: Il Mulino).

L. Gallino (2005) *L'impresa irresponsabile* (Torino: Einaudi).

S. Grossman and O. Hart (1983) 'An Analysis of the Principal-Agent Problem', *Econometrica*, 51, 7–45.

J. N. Gordon (2007) 'The Rise of Independent Directors in the United States, 1950–2005: Of Shareholder Value and Stock Market Price', *Stanford Law Review*, 59, 1465–1568.

A. Greif (1993) 'Contract Enforceability and Economic Institutions in Early Trade: The Maghribi Traders' Coalition', *American Economic Review*, 83(3), 525–548.

G. Heal (2005) 'Corporate Social Responsibility: An Economic and Financial Framework', *The Geneva Papers*, 30, 387–409.

D. Hess (2006) 'A Business Ethics Perspective on Sarbanes-Oxley and the Organizational Sentencing Guidelines', *Michigan Law Review*, 105, 1781–1816.

J. Hörner (2002) 'Reputation and Competition', *American Economic Review*, 92(3), 644–663.

K. Holtfreter, S. Van Slyke and T. G. Blomberg (2006) 'Sociolegal Change in Consumer Fraud: From Victim-Offender Interactions to Global Networks', *Crime, Law, and Social Change*, 44, 251–275.

S. Huck, G. K Lünser and J. R. Tyran (2007) 'Competition Fosters Trust', available at http://eurequa.univ-paris1.fr/S%E9minaires-GT-Eurequaecopsycho/papiers/Huck1.pdf.

N. O. Kehoane, E. T. Mansur and A. Voynov (2009) 'Averting Regulatory Enforcement: Evidence from New Source Review', *Journal of Economics and Management Strategies*, 18(1), 75–104.

J. M. Karpoff, D. S. Lee and G. S. Martin, (2008) 'The Consequences to Managers for Financial Misrepresentation', *Journal of Financial Economics*, 88, 193–215.

L. Keller and K. G. Ross (1998) 'Selfish Genes: A Green Beard in the Red Fire Ant', *Nature*, 394, 573–575.

Kim, S. (2001) 'Markets and Multiunit Firms from An American Historical Perspective', in J. A. C. Baum and H. R. Greve (eds), *Multiunit Organization and Multimarket Strategy: Advances in Strategic Management*, vol. 18 (Oxford: JAI Press).

U. Kjærnes (2006) 'Trust and Distrust: Cognitive Decisions or Social Relations?', *Journal of Risk Research*, 9(8), 911–932.

B. Klein and K. B. Leffler (1981) 'The Role of Market Forces in Assuring Contractual Performance', *The Journal of Political Economy*, 89(4), 615–641.

P. Krugman (1991) *Geography and Trade*, (Cambridge: MIT Press).

M. T. Law (2003) 'The Origins of State Pure Food Regulation', *The Journal of Economic History*, 63(4), 1103–1130.

J. J. McCluskey (2000) 'A Game Theoretic Approach to Organic Foods: AN Analysis of Asymmetric Information and Policy', *Agricultural and Resource Economics Review*, 29(1), 1–9.

G. C. Means (1931) 'The Separation of Ownership and Control in American Industry', *The Quarterly Journal of Economics*, 46(1), 68–100.

P. R. Milgrom and J. Roberts (1986) 'Pricing and Advertising Signals of Produce Quality', *Journal of Political Economy*, 94, 796–821.

P. Nelson (1970) 'Information and Consumer Behavior', *The Journal of Political Economy*, 78(2), 311–329.

M. Nestle (2004) *Safe Food. Bacteria, Biotechnology, and Bioterrorism* (Berkeley and Los Angeles: University of California Press).

J. S. Parker and R. A. Atkins (1999) 'Did the Corporate Criminal Sentencing Guidelines Matter? Some Preliminary Empirical Observations', *Journal of Law and Economics*, XLII, 423–453.

P. Pinotti (2008) 'Trust, Honesty and Regulation', Bank of Italy, *mimeo*.

D. Pope (2008) *Making Sense of Advertisements*, from the Making Sense of Evidence series on: 'History matters: The U.S. survey on the Web', http://historymatters.gmu.edu.

C. Poppe and U. Kjærnes (2003) *Trust in food in Europe. A Comparative Analysis*, Professional Report n. 5, Oslo: National Institute for Consumer Research (SIFO).

Resnick P. and R. Zeckhauser (2002) 'Trust Among Strangers in Internet Transactions: Empirical Analysis of eBay's Reputation System', in M. R. Baye (ed.), *The Economics of the Internet and E-Commerce* (Amsterdam: Elsevier Science), pp. 127–157.

C. Shapiro (1983) 'Premiums for High Quality Products as Returns to Reputations', *The Quarterly Journal of Economics*, 98(4), 659–679.

A. Smith (1763 [1978]) *Lectures on Jurisprudence* (Oxford: Clarendon Press).

J. Sobel (2005) 'Interdependent Preferences and Reciprocity', *Journal of Economic Literature*, XLIII, 392–436.

R. Sugden (2004) *The Economics of Rights, Cooperation and Welfare* (New York: Palgrave-Macmillan).

J. Tirole (2001) 'Corporate Governance', *Econometrica*, 69(1), 1–35.

J. Tirole (2005) *The Theory of Corporate Finance* (Princeton: Princeton University Press).

J. Tullberg (2001) 'Trust – The Importance of Trustfulness Versus Trustworthiness', *The Journal of Socio-Economics*, 37, 2059–2071.

G. Tullock (1985) 'Adam Smith and the Prisoners' Dilemma', *The Quarterly Journal of Economics*, 100(Suppl.), 1073–1081.

E. Williamson (2007) 'FDA was Aware of Dangers to Food', *The Washington Post*, 23 April 2007.

D. J. Wood (1985) 'The Strategic Use of Public Policy: Business Support for the 1906 Food and Drug Act', *The Business History Review*, 59(3), 403–432.

Part II

Social Capital and Corporate Social Responsibility: a Game Theoretical and Network Analysis Approach

5
Linking Economic and Social-Exchange Games: From the Community Norm to CSR

Masahiko Aoki

Why are corporations engaged in various non-economic activities to meet societal demands (such as environmental protection) beyond their legal obligations? In other words, why do corporations 'over-comply' (Heal 2005) with the social demands? Does it benefit corporations (their stockholders)? If so, how? Common-sense-wise an answer may appear obvious. However, it may not necessarily be so for the prevailing framework of economists' thinking: 'corporations do not need to do anything beyond legal obligations in order to serve stockholders interests'. The object of this chapter is to suggest an analytical framework to challenge such orthodox views without abandoning the premise of a bounded-rationality of agents concerned (various stakeholders of corporations as well as the citizens of the society). An essential idea is to endogenize the relevance of such social constructs as (individual) social capital, norms, status ascriptions and the like to economic behaviors within an expanded framework of game-theoretic thinking.

I begin with conceptualizing the social-exchange game analogous to, but distinct from, the economic-transaction game. I then link both games to endogenously explain the relevance of the said social constructs for sustaining, as well as transiting to, a certain mode of economic transactions that are not possible as stand-alone transactions. I illustrate arguments by parables drawn from a simple domain of the closed rural community to a domain of global commons where the so-called corporate social responsibility (CSR) programs can emerge as equilibrium strategies of corporations.

A third way to approach social norms

Traditionally, there have been two major social-scientific approaches to social norms in relation to economic analysis. The first approach, which may be termed as the dichotomous view, is to treat social norms simply as irrelevant, or at most as exogenous, to economic analysis. In a seminal book published in 1947, which set a conceptual and analytical framework of neoclassical economics for decades to come, Paul Samuelson haughtily claimed that 'many economists would separate economics from sociology upon the basis of rational or irrational behavior' (1947: 90), implying that economics has nothing to do with such things as social norms. Even if not dismissed as 'irrational', the social norms are regarded by some as belonging to different categories of rationality than instrumental choices prevailing in economic actions.[1] In the last two decades or so, when institutional economics has been re-emergent, social norms have started to be recognized as relevant to economic actions, but are still largely regarded as exogenous (given) to economic analysis (e.g. North 1990; Ostrom 2005). They are usually treated as exogenous constraints on economic choices or exogenous modifications of pay-off functions.[2] But their origins are regarded as explained outside economics (possibly in sociology).

Oddly, however, not only in neoclassical economics but even in some once-influential sociological theories like the Parsonian paradigm, social values were treated as a quasi-exogenous entity waiting for to be individually internalized through socialization processes such as family rearing, formal education, religious teaching and the like. However, a deeper and more meaningful approach could be to view social norms/customs and the like as endogenously generated and sustained through social interactions of people and to give the process an analytical focus (e.g. the phenomenological approach of Berger and Luckmann 1967; new Institutional sociology by DiMaggio and Powell 1991; and others). This approach, which may be called the endogenous view, has an immediate analogue in economics. Kandori (1992) characterized the social norm as a sub-game-perfect equilibrium outcome of a bundle of trading games played by multiple traders. Traders of a community are sequentially matched pair-wise randomly to play a trading game of two-person prisoners' dilemma type, but they are somehow informed of the record of past plays of successive trade partners so that they can collectively replicate the reputation mechanism as would be possible between particular two persons. Social norm is then identified with collectively shared (equilibrium) beliefs regarding the possible outcome (punishment) of 'cheating', which would deter the actual play of cheating. Note, however, that in this approach the 'social' norm is constructed within the domain of the economic trading game itself. Punishment is exclusion from further trading in that domain. Greif's work (1993, 2006) on cultural beliefs as regulating possible dishonesty in long-distance trading among the Maghreb traders is constructed on the same spirit, although his work is subtle in viewing that players' beliefs regarding the consequence of off the path of play sub-game (cheating) were formed as historical legacy (accordingly 'cultural' beliefs). This rationalist construction of norms as shared beliefs is full of meaningful implications and the present chapter will essentially follow this track. However, to regard social norms as endogenously generated within economic-transaction domains raises some questions. For example, if agents are not excludable from economic- transaction domains as in the case of commons, is it that the social norm cannot evolve to deal with its possible 'tragedy' à la Harding (i.e. over-exploitation)? Then, is it that a legal regulation is only a solution? When a group of people bound by a norm face a new mode of economic transaction, is the old social norm bound to be doomed and play no role in the transition and thereafter? More generally, when agents evolve a certain norm in economic transactions, do they do so only based on rationalistic calculations of hedonistic utilities?

In order to deal with these and other questions, this chapter adopts a third way, which is to consider explicitly both the domain of economic-transaction game and the domain of social-exchange game and then to link the two. It may be said that it de-couples the social and economic aspects of choices and then re-couples them. It assumes that the community of people repeatedly play both an economic-transaction game and a social-exchange game characterized by different instruments (action choices), different languages and different intentions (payoffs), but each player coordinates his/her own strategies across the two domains in an unified manner, that is, by considering trade-off between hedonistic payoff and social payoff. In this way, some strategies, which are not strategically viable in an economic-transaction game in isolation, may become viable with the support of a certain mode of social interaction. It may be considered as a game-theoretic restatement of the notion of 'social embeddedness' originating in the writing of the economic sociologist Granovetter (1985). But we try to go beyond his framework by considering dynamic 'overlapping social embeddedness' (Aoki 2001) of different modes of economic transaction, as well as feedback impacts of change in the mode of economic transaction on the social norm and so on.[3]

Conceptualizing the social-exchange game

Let us start out with conceptualizing the social-exchange game analogous to the economic-transaction game, but made distinct from the latter particularly in terms of the player's intention, the technical rules of the game and by physical and cognitive instruments of play. Suppose there is *a community (group) of agents who interact with (relate to) each other using symbolic messages (such as words, gestures, gift-giving and the like), physical actions (such as helping) and/or provision of non-marketable goods (such as valuable information) with the intention of affecting emotional impacts of targeted agents and with unspecified obligations of reciprocity.*[4] Let us call the set of such mutually interactive agents and the sets of their action choices the domain of social-exchange and their interactions as the play of the social-exchange game. Also, the emotional impact in the game is referred to as social payoffs (neuroscientific support for such concepts is to be provided later). A few words need to be said to distinguish this from games in the economic-exchange domain.[5]

First, although exchanges of symbolic messages (speech acts) may be involved in other types of domains as well, those in the social-exchange domain are distinct by the nature of unspecified reciprocity and their objectives. In contrast, any economic transaction is essentially a contract that cannot be implemented without specific mutual agreements, although they may be unilaterally or bilaterally defaulted. Second, the utterance of speech or dispatch of other social symbols in social exchanges may be generated by sender's own emotions (e.g. appreciation, impression, empathy, disapproval, anger and so on), but their messages are intended to have an impact on the receiver's social (emotional) payoffs, either positive (e.g. pride, satisfaction, consolation and so on) or negative (e.g. shame, regret, guilt, exclusion and so on). In that sense, they are distinct from mere speech acts or the so-called 'cheap talk' in the 'signaling game' in the economic-transaction domain that are not by themselves intended to directly affect others' payoffs. They are also not cheap in the sense that they are costly in terms of time, emotional and physical efforts, resource costs and so on. The expected reciprocity may be broadly interpreted in that the agent perform social actions as exemplified above in expectation of certain actions from others (even from unspecified members of the community) to compensate their actions in terms of social payoff (e.g. unilateral help toward some stranger in need that may be socially approved). However, I first start with a parable in which social actions are reciprocated among mutually identifiable members of the community.

Each agent can derive positive/negative payoffs from the other's actions directed toward him or her. However, in order to be able to expect continual positive actions from others, he or she must reciprocate positive actions toward them. If somebody is mean to him/her, on the other hand, he or she may wish to take revenge on the opponent to stop further malicious actions. Thus, expected social payoffs of agents over time in the social-exchange domain will be conditional on others' actions that are expected in response to their own actions. Thus, agent's social payoff becomes, in reduced form, the function of his or her own action, albeit implicitly via their own belief about the other's reaction. The unit value of social payoff of revealed actions may be theoretically considered as measurable by the marginal opportunity cost sacrificed in terms of the hedonistic payoff in economic-transaction domain. It may be noted that the tradability between monetary rewards and emotional payoffs is experimentally supported by some recent neuroscientific studies founded on the notion of 'common neuro-currency' due to Montague and Berns (2002). For example, a functional magnetic resonance imaging (fMRI) experiment by Izuma et al. (2008) found that the acquisition of one's good reputation activates rewards-related brain areas, notably the striatum, and these partially overlapped with the areas activated by the pleasure of receiving monetary rewards.[6]

Let us refer to the present value sum of an agent's expected emotional payoffs over time as his or her *social capital*. It represents agents' expected capacity to derive positive net emotional payoffs over time as well as to use it to derive benefits in other domains. Some scholars adopt the word 'social capital' referring to intangible collective assets held by society as a whole (e.g. norms, social networks, the educational level of the society) as analogous to tangible collective assets (e.g. public goods, commons). But we conceptualize social capital as owned and used by individual agents (including individual corporations).[7] As discussed shortly, it is to be conceptually distinguished from social norms and other such social categories that evolve as societal outcomes of play of the social-exchange games in which individual agents accumulate social capital to derive future social and other payoffs.

Individual agent's social capital has a double feature. One, it is the object of individual investment. It depreciates without effort. Thus, agents exchange social symbolic actions in such a way that they consider the most fit/desirable in order to increase, as well as to make the best use of, their own social capital. I will provide concrete examples later, but it may be pointed out at this point that the basic structure of social-exchanges as described indicates its strategic nature, although it is not exclusively self-regarding.

Individual agent's social capital actually depends not only on one's own actions but also on one's belief regarding others' actions, other's beliefs regarding one's beliefs and so on. In this sense, the social-exchange game shares the same problem of infinite regression as the psychological games introduced by Geanakoplos et al. (1989) (referred to as GPS below) and applied by Rabin (1998). However, the concept of the social-exchange game as a class of societal game *recursively* played within a population suggests a reasonable solution to this problem. If agents are recursively engaged in social-exchanges within an informative, homogenous community, then their actions are more easily known and others' beliefs are more easily inferred. Namely, in the small community, experiences, information and expectations may be shared. Then there may evolve some standard of social exchanges, that is, norms of reciprocity, through practices and customs. Such standards may be theoretically regarded as representing a Nash equilibrium of the psychological game as defined by GPS in summary form. It would then constitute the shared beliefs of agents about salient ways by which the social-exchange game is being recursively played and to be played.

These shared beliefs would serve as a guide for the agents to act properly socially. For, as a Nash equilibrium, it is not beneficial for agents not to follow them. The failure of compliance with the implied norm would be believed to be punished ('sanctioned' in the traditional sociological terminology) by the loss of social capital. Such loss may not necessarily be implemented only by external sanctions by others in the form of extreme ostracism. If norms are internalized, they are followed even when violation would be unobserved by others, because not doing so may create guilt, shame and other negative emotional payoff. Such moral sense need not be considered as derived from an abstract supernatural axiom or primarily imposed by an external authority, such as schools or churches. But it can be regarded as originating in practices. Aristotle (1955) noted that 'moral goodness (*etike*)...is the result of habit, from which it has actually got its name, being a slight modification of the word *ethos*' (Book II.i: 91). Arrow also noted 'internalized feelings of guilt and right are essentially unconscious equivalents of agreement that represent social decisions' (1967: 79).

Linking the commons game and the social-exchange game

Now let us link a social-exchange game thus defined with an economic-exchange game and see how something that cannot be possible in the latter alone becomes endogenously possible in this way.[8] For this purpose I adopt a simple parable. Imagine a domain in which the community of agents can use commons in an economically beneficial manner, but the maintenance of its values requires collective effort. Assume further that it is not technically feasible to exclude any individual member of the community from using the commons, so that there is a potential problem of free-riding. For example, the remarkable growth of rice production in the Edo period (from the seventeenth to the nineteenth centuries) of Japan was largely owed to the continual land reclamation and the associated development of irrigation systems in the rural community. However, rice paddies owned and cultivated by member families were scattered and mutually intermeshed due to the incremental land development by fairly homogenous member families, while the irrigation system was such that water drawn from a canal was successively supplied from one paddy field to the next using the natural slope (the gravity system).[9]

Under such conditions, the usual reputation mechanism to punish any member family who shirked in collective development and maintenance works was not just feasible. A solution for such a problem, suggested by economists, would be to integrate rice paddies under a single private property rights to internalize externalities or to subject the management of the irrigation system to a centralized public control. However, there was no political power willing and capable to grant and enforce integrated property rights or to wield the centralized control of the irrigation system in the Edo period. The political power of the load was limited to impose collective tax obligations on the rural community as a whole, of which members were rather egalitarian in paddy cultivation and decision-making rights, with no option to exit from the community. Under this situation, member families were engaged in a social-exchange game such as to reciprocate mutual help in times of emergencies (e.g. fire, illness, birth, death) as well as to participate in collective symbolic/informative activities (e.g. festivities, wedding, gossiping, outings and so on). Member families derived social pay-offs from participating in such activities with some cost in terms of time, efforts, resources, psychological burdens, and so on[10] Roughly speaking, the present value sum of net welfare for individual member families may then be conceptualized as social capital possessed by individuals. The exclusion of individuals from the said social exchanges implies the deprivation of such social capital, since they cannot be compensated elsewhere by exiting from the community.

Then, even though exclusion from the use of the commons is not techno-logically possible, shirking of collective efforts in developing and sustaining the commons may be punishable by exclusion from the benefits of social-exchange game, that is, ostracism, with the consequence of deprivation of social capital. Suppose that families follow the following strategy combina-tions, depending on specified contingencies: (1) Play 'Shirk' in the irrigation game and 'Do not participate' in the community social-exchange game if they have played 'Shirk' in any previous commons game or they have ever been ostracized in the community social-exchange game. Otherwise they cooperate in both the irrigation and community social-exchange games; and (2) Exclude any other family, and only that family, who has ever shirked in the commons game from participating in the social-exchange game in all future years. Suppose that the belief of each family is such that almost all other families have played, and will play in the future, the strategy combina-tion prescribed above.[11] It can then be proved that such beliefs can constitute a sub-game perfect equilibrium of the linked games under a mild condition[12] and, once selected at the community level, they can deter member fami-lies from actually shirking. Under normal circumstances, only cooperative behavior among village families can be observed as a standard of behavior. We refer to such *a standard of cooperative behavior, supported by the shared behavioral beliefs of collective punishment of shirking, as a community norm*.[13] It can be grasped theoretically as an endogenous outcome of linked games rather than an exogenous constraint (rules of the game) given from out-side the socio-economic system. Once it is established evolutionarily under certain historical conditions, each player may neither calculate prescribed strategies from the scratch nor be aware of its rational property, collective or individual. They may be sometimes tempted to shirk, but be just frightened at the thought of what might happen if they actually do. Or, they may fol-low the standard of behavior just as a habit or because of their disposition. Even if so, their behaviors and beliefs can be reproduced and guide their further behavior because there is neither reason nor benefit to act otherwise under unchanged conditions.

As I pointed out in Aoki (2001), various conditions are necessary for such a specific kind of community norm to evolve and become self-enforcing – such as historical, political and natural conditions for member families to have become relatively homogenous in terms of cultivation rights and internal political decision-making, the consequential unanimity of interests in sanctioning deviants in the use of the commons, the no-exit option from the community and repeated plays therein. Identifying these conditions may help to clarify the role of the norm in sustaining a certain specific economic order but not in others, as well as provide a clue for understanding why other solutions, such as the integration of ownership to internalize externalities, could emerge elsewhere or later on. In the following, I try to relax the assumptions of homogeneity, static plays and no-exits in turn.

Heterogeneity of players and ascriptions of differential social capital

The above example is built on rather simple conditions and its implications are intuitively straightforward. But essentially, similar mechanisms may be feasible under different conditions. Suppose, for example, the players' skills in collective production are of different levels, but their (marginal) contributions to collective outputs cannot be measured precisely because of the team property of production *à la* Alchian and Demsetz (1972). Under such conditions, even if the distribution of outputs is made in a rather compressed way, the more able player may be compensated by the ascription of higher social capital as represented by high esteem and respect from fellow workers. However, whether such mechanisms of status differentiation can really contribute to the incentives of the able, as well as the restraint of free-riding of the less able, may depend on the intensity of social interactions among the players, while the intensity of social interactions may in turn depend on mode of collective production. For example, ambiguous demarcation of jobs, for example, mutual help, ad hocish back-up arrangements in emergencies, on- and off-the-job teaching-learning and the like, on one hand, and the social exchanges of team-spirit-intensifying messages (e.g. praise, encouragement, togetherness), on the other, may not only be linked strategically but may also be complementary to each other in terms of productivity and emotional satisfaction.[14]

Turning to the modern civic society, we recognize that citizens are increasingly heterogeneous in wealth, occupations, educational and cultural backgrounds and so on, while becoming increasingly mobile across communities. Thus, it may appear at first that social relationships have lost regulatory power in the provision of public goods. Yet, there seem to have emerged a growing awareness that non-governmental organizations, voluntary associations, professional communities and the like can play important roles in the provision of, and suasion of needs for, public goods such as natural environments, public safety, poverty and disaster reliefs, technological innovation and transfer, and so on. For example, take open source software (OSS). They are public goods *par excellence* in the cyberspace because they provide basic infrastructure for Internet communications as well as the basis and elements for further development of programming. They are distributed free with open source codes and are continually being improved through the participation of many programmers from all over the world via e-mail communications. As a result, OSS has become a much more stable and reliable software than commercially licensed software protected by compiled object codes. As legal protection of software invention would eminently retard the development of communication technology, participating programmers may be driven to improve on the software they themselves use, but they may also derive non-pecuniary rewards for their contributions similar to those ascribed to eminent academic scholars (e.g. the recognition and esteem paid by peer engineers), and the the accumulation of such social capital can also be complementary to career opportunities (e.g. easier access to venture capital funds).

The traditional economist's view was to regard quasi-market arrangements (e.g. intellectual property rights, emission taxes) and the government as substitutes with each other in the charge of public goods. There was no recognition of the role of intermediate associations in the highly developed market economy. However, partly from the rising ease of communications facilitating the formation of cross-border communities of various interests and partly due to the increasing cognizance of citizens' responsibility, voluntary associations are becoming progressively active and influential. Thus, the generation of unique intangible social capital for members (e.g. sharing of values, professional ego/pride satisfaction, esprit de corps, etc.) bound by common concerns, interest, and causes may become instrumental in nurturing civic norms and professional values conducive to the provision of various public goods in non-governmental and diverse ways. Thus, we see the generic relevance of 'social embeddedness' of the commons domain even in contemporary context. I will come back to this point later and relate it to the discussion of the role of CSR.

Social norms may matter in institutional transition

The endogenous view of social norms by economists alluded to in the beginning of this chapter – that is, identifying social norms with reputation mechanisms in the economic domain itself – implies that norms emerge and disappear with relevant modes of economic transactions. Looking at the same thing from a different angle, one may say that the inherent inertia of the social norm is, in general, detrimental to the emergence of new mode of economic transaction. Greif's seminal historical comparative institutional analysis (1993, 2006) provided one instance for this to be true. Cultural beliefs among the Maghreb traders that dishonest trading would be punished by ostracism from their community could not be shared by outsiders, so that the Maghreb failed to expand the orbit of their trading beyond their internal reach. It is claimed that this was a major reason why they eventually lost competitiveness in long-distance trading in spite of their possible internal efficiency vis-à-vis the Genoese traders, who relied on efficiency to wage discipline on recruits of agents from market. We may then ask generally: are pre-market community norms necessarily to be destroyed prior to market transitions and replaced by entirely new market mores? How could the latter emerge? Traditional views, whether those of economists (e.g. Hicks 1969) or scholars in other social science disciplines such as economic anthropology (e.g. Geertz 1963; Polanyi 1944) have drawn a sharp line between the market economy and the pre-modern economy for entertaining such a view. However, recently a revisionist view has emerged, which contends that the rural community bound by cooperative norms could play a positive role in facilitating the gradual transition of pre-modern rural economies to market economies under certain circumstances (Aoki and Hayami 2001). The complete destruction of rural communities may be neither sufficient nor necessary for the emergence of external market relationships and their eventual integration into the market economy. In other words, under certain conditions the presence of community relationships may be complementary to, rather than a substitute for, the emergence of market relationships with outsiders without third-party involvement in contract-enforcement. What are those conditions? Let me provide again a parable drawn from the history of the latter half of the Edo period in Japan as an illustration, hoping that more general implications of the roles of norms in institutional transition may be inferred from it.

In the rural community, as discussed above, where a norm based on the homogeneity of members prevails, opportunities for mutually beneficial, intra-community material trading were severely limited. However, as the productivity of agricultural crops gradually rose through the improvement of indigenous technology, the potential for surplus products and working time beyond the subsistence level and tax obligations gradually expanded. In order to exploit gains from such potential, the community needed to open up trade with outsiders. Suppose that a merchant who resided in a (castle) town remote from the village arrived. Since village families could offer only more or less homogenous goods, they were mutually substitutes as trading partners to the merchant. Therefore, if the merchant were able to trade with them individually, he might possibly prey some families and then switch to other families to gain from further cheating. However, the merchant would be compelled to believe that such opportunities were unrealistic. This belief would be derived from the presumed ability of the village community to punish any member of the community who would defect from boycotting trade with a dishonest merchant. On the other hand, the merchant would threaten that if any commodity were not exchanged honestly he would terminate trade with them and tell his story to all his fellow merchants back in the city. If the future value of trading was assessed by the village members as better than the no-exchange option, even if individual temptation to cheat vis-à-vis a single merchant were high, peer pressure could persuade them not to jeopardize future trading opportunities. For example, if any family delivered defective products, the defector could easily be spotted by other village members and accused in a manner reminiscent of the community norm. Thus, the vesting of social capital with village families would provide a foundation for them to initiate exchange with outside merchants and enforce honest trading on both sides without third-party involvement.

As productivity differentials in cash crops or craft production widened and their products became gradually specialized, community cohesion among the villagers was bound to start eroding. Option values from outside exchange would increase for more entrepreneurial village families, while social slack from the community social exchanges would start to decline for them. By then, outside merchants would also have became more knowledgeable about the traits and capabilities of some individual families in the village. The outside merchant and village families could initiate individual putting-out contracting, for example, for the supply of craft products such as textile yarn and fabrics. Furthermore, successful entrepreneurial families could start organizing subcontracting relationships with less enterprising families. In this way, trade relationships first induced by the presence of a community norm start to destroy the relative homogeneity of the village community, thus encroaching upon the social basis of the community norm. The community norm, based on the symmetric ability of community members to punish a possible deviant in the social-exchange game, need then to be succeeded by personal trust and/or traders' community norms based on their ability to identify and punish an individual deviant in the economic-transaction domain itself. However, information networks necessary for sustaining such mechanisms would have been partially prepared within the community prior to, and in the transition to, such relationships.[15]

Another interesting case for a collective norm to help their transition to a new institutional set-up may be found in the emergence of the so-called 'industrial districts' in Italy. These emerged after highly integrated textile companies failed to survive because of high wages and labor disputes in the 1960s, and finally the highly protective Workers' Statute adopted in 1970. Skilled workers released from large companies were encouraged to establish their own enterprises, often by purchasing equipments from large companies that were closing (Barca et al. 1994). The types of transactions and coordination that quickly developed among their small firms, such as the reciprocity of subcontracting and sharing of productivity-enhancing knowledge, would not have been feasible without mutual trust as an essential governance mechanism. They became possible because the transaction domain was embedded in a pre-existing social-exchange domain in which the new owners of those small firms had invested a significant amount of social capital as the members of the civic community and/or labor organizations which confronted the old integrated companies (Dei Ottati 1994). This is an instance of overlapping social embeddedness, that is, possible replication/transplant of a norm developed in one domain onto a different domain.

Also, a claim is often made that the group norm prevailing on the shop floor and in the internal business organization of the Japanese firm most typically found in the period of high growth is a replication of the community norm from the pre-market economy as discussed above (e.g. Hayami 1998). The historical process of such transplant, if any, was neither straightforward nor consciously designed, on which I will not dwell upon here (see Aoki 2001, chapter 10), although I will touch upon one speculative point, which may be suggested by the process. In the economic-transaction domain, individual choices are relatively more easily susceptible to entrepreneurial design, conscious transplant and so on, in comparison to the social-exchange domain in which choices may be more inertial. Such design/transplant may not immediately yield a stable outcome by standing alone, however. In order for stable outcome to evolve out of it, it may need some kind of anchoring. A deep-seated, social-exchange heritage may be called for to meet this need. However, a replication of social norm may not be straightforward because equilibrium outcome ought to be generated by linked plays of the economic-transaction game of a new form (in terms of a set of players, their possible choices and so on). Norm cannot be simply imposed exogenously nor transplanted as have existed elsewhere. It needs to be recreated through everyday plays, although it may reflect a deep generic structure of the society transmitted through historical process.[16]

How do stock market assess corporate social capital and CRS?

I finally would like to apply above conceptual framework to the issue of corporate social responsibility (CSR). A relevant question may be framed as: Should corporate firms be regarded as nothing but entities solely engaged in economic transactions in product, capital and labor markets? Or is there any point to regard them as engaged, or ought to be engaged, in some kind of social exchange with the society of citizens at large beyond their own markets? By posing questions in this way I set aside from my immediate concern such matters as corporate brand names embodying accumulated reputations in relevant markets (in terms of product qualities, after-purchase services, delivery timing and the like). Costly signaling (such as advertisement), which would not directly affect utilities of buyers, may also be left outside the scope of our discussion (although advertisement may promote the so-called conspicuous consumptions). I do not mean that brand names and advertisements are not important for understanding social implications of corporate behavior. Certainly they are. The point is that the nature and roles of corporate reputation, signaling and the like operating within specific markets of relevance have been extensively analyzed and fairly well understood in economics. I am concerned with whether or not corporate firms accumulate own social capital, as distinct from market-specific reputation capital? The conceptual distinction between market-specific reputation capital and corporate social capital beyond specific markets is crucial, although the distinction is sometimes subtle and ambiguous in practice as I will discuss below.

An obvious starting point is that many corporate activities cause external diseconomies of various kinds beyond their own market relationships and reaching to wider communities and their commons. Remedies for them prescribed by economists, lawyers, governments and others include Pigouvian tax-subsidies, Coasian direct bargaining between generators and recipients of externalities, quantity and other regulations, as well as market-regulation hybrids such as the creation of emission-rights markets. However, it is increasingly recognized nowadays that these measures alone may not be perfect and may be incomplete due to various reasons, for example, capacity limits of the public authority in information processing, the lack of proper incentives of public administrators, the difficulties of setting up direct or mediated bargaining and reaching formal agreements among various interest groups, increasing assertiveness of environmental movements and so on.[17]

However, corporate firms and citizens at large can be directly and informally engaged in social-exchanges. In other words, corporate firms may be increasingly recognized as players in the global commons game embedded in the society at large, in a sense somewhat similar to the irrigation parable narrated above. If corporate firms pollute natural environments and/or generate health hazards through their economic activities, these firms may incite people to react adversely by criticisms, protests, etc., even if those economic activities are not immediately illegal within current legal framework. On the other hand, corporate firms can, if they wish, directly provide resources for social benefits such as environmental protection, poverty reduction, public health, educational and scientific progress and so on through the so-called corporate social responsibility (CSR) programs. For a while let us assume that these programs do not immediately contribute to their profits nor are legally called for.[18] In response to social contributions, which are costly, the citizens at large possibly ascribe social recognitions to provider corporations, which would constitute their corporate social capital. Corporate social capital may not be immediately cashed in, but it may be enjoyed by various corporate stakeholders in non-pecuniary manner, for example, the pride of employees working for a socially reputable corporation, the satisfaction of environmentally conscious stockholders from owning 'green' stocks, amenities of citizens living in clean local community and the like. These benefits may compensate for the pecuniary costs of CSR programs. This much is common sense. But there can be more than just that.

If stockholders try to select their portfolios only from stocks of corporate firms engaged in CSR programs, theoretically they must perform worse in terms of financial performance, because they restrict the universe from which stocks can be picked. But, interestingly enough, empirical evidences seem to suggest a possibility, if not conclusively, that expenditures for CSR and stock price performance may be correlated, contrary to the theoretical prediction (e.g. Dowell et al. 2000; Heal 2005; King and Lennox 2001). Why? One simple, but plausible reason could be that profitable corporate firms may be more willing to contribute to a costly CSR program, but the same result obtains even if profitability is statistically controlled (Siegel and Vitaliano 2001). Another possibility is that there may be complementarities between social capital investment and product-specific reputation capital. Let us consider the following possibility. The development and commercialization of environmentally friendly technology may be costly and its social value may not necessarily be fully appreciated by potential buyers of its products. For example, potential buyers of eco-cars may value the savings of gasoline costs but may not be willing to bear the full external costs in terms of higher car price. Thus, managerial calculus of market-specific reputational capital alone may not immediately warrant a corporate firm to pursue the costly technological development and commercialization. However, the failure to do so may be damaging to the accumulation of corporate social capital ascribed by the society at large, while investment in environmentally friendly technology may enhance the accumulation of corporate social capital. The attribution of such social standing may, however, amplify the value of market-specific reputation as well, because the former may enhance the beliefs of potential buyers of products regarding their user cost-efficiency, durability and the like, as well as its symbolic value to them (e.g. environmental 'conspicuous' consumption). In other words, higher social corporate capital may serve as a positive signal (analogous to advertisement) and contribute to prospects of long-term profits net of costs of CRS.[19] In other words, accumulation of social capital may be complementary to market-specific reputation capital. This is consonant with the orthodox logic of economics. However, there is still another, more subtle possibility as well.

The logic of capital pricing involving CSR, according to Baron (2007), suggests the following interesting story. Suppose that a contribution of CSR is positively but partially (say, θ per cent) reflected in the stock value of a corporation. This implies that, for citizens-cum-investors who value the corporate giving more than that proportion the stock price is virtually discounted. Namely, they can contribute to a social cause with less cost (that is, $100-\theta$ per cent less). Therefore, contrary to Friedman's assertion, they are better off by buying the stocks of CSR firms rather than making social contribution as individuals. Therefore, the presence of CSR corporations can increase aggregate social giving. Although the CSR entrepreneurs (and possibly other stakeholders) bear the remaining cost (i.e $100-\theta$) per cent of corporate giving), they can derive social satisfaction not only from their own contributions but also by expanding opportunity sets for CSR shareholders by providing an alternative to personal giving.

Corporate CSR activities, pure and complementary combined, can thus link economic, commons and social-exchange games between business corporations (and their stakeholders, such as CSR entrepreneurs and employees) and concerned citizens. Concerned citizens may be engaged in those games by attributing corporate social capital to CSR corporations, investing in CSR stocks, as well as being potential buyers of products of CSR corporations. Business corporations are engaged in these games as social-givers as well as potential developers of profit-making, environmentally friendly technology. Corporations can do, in general, cognitively more than what the mere collections of individuals can do (Aoki 2010). This is especially true with regard to the development of environmentally friendly and renewable energy technology. It requires innovative entrepreneurial initiative, organization of interdisciplinary inputs of knowledge and efforts, foresight, patience, and so on, which may be effectively provided by CSR corporations, small and large. Thus, if the linkages of games as described can indeed evolve, strategies that have not been viable in economic calculation alone may become supportable as societal equilibrium.

Summary

This chapter has presented a new way to conceptualize and analyze the relevance of social constructs, such as social norms, social capital and social status to economic analysis. Traditionally, they were treated as entirely exogenous factors to economic analysis, of which origins, sustainability and so on are to be dealt with outside economic analysis (the dichotomous approach). Recently, game-theoretic analysis sheds light on the nature of social norms as rational constructs of reputation mechanism in repeated games. However, this endogenous approach cannot explain possible roles of social norms to control externalities where the reputation mechanism fails to hold because of technological non-excludability of deviant players from game. Further, it does not provide a workable framework for understanding the dynamic role of social norms which overlap with sequentially arising economic games (such as the transition from the pre-capitalist community to the market economy; the shift of environmental property rights from the corporate sector to the civil society at large). This chapter proposed a third way between the dichotomous and endogenous approaches, which may be taken as a game-theoretic unification of economic and sociological approaches. It started with presenting a rough idea of social-exchange game in which the community of people interact with each other by using social messages for the purpose of affecting others' emotional pay-offs with unspecified obligations of reciprocity. Then this game is linked to economic-transaction games of various kinds. Norms are then understood as the standards of economic behaviors supported by self-sustaining behavioral and normative beliefs linking the two. An example was drawn from a simple parable of irrigation in the closed, homogenous community, as it was able to provide generic logics most clearly and succinctly. However, the ultimate goal of the chapter was to apply the logic to the contemporary issue of possible tragedy of global commons. It discussed why corporations are engaged in costly Corporate Social Responsibility programs to cope with it beyond legal obligations and why stock market appears to value it. The chapter suggested that the accumulation of corporate social capital may be becoming an important asset for corporations to survive economic competition at a time of gradual transition in environmental property rights arrangements.

Acknowledgements

This paper was originally read as an invited speech at the EconomEtica conference on 'Social Capital, Corporate Social Responsibility and Sustainable Economic Development' held at the University of Trento in July 2007. I benefitted from conversations with Elinoir Ostrom, Geoffrey Heal and Lorenzo Sacconi to prepare this paper, but needless to say I am solely responsible for the contents and views expressed. The idea expressed in this paper was later incorporated into *Corporations in Evolving Diversity: Cognition, Governance, and Institutions* (Oxford University Press 2010) in a broader context.

Notes

1. For example, Kant distinguished two reasons for rational action: hypothetical and categorical imperatives. The former is said to be induced by one's inclination, while the latter by the sense of one's duties. It is well known that Max Weber (1978) also distinguished two categories of rational action: Zweckrationalität (object-rationality) and Wertrationalität (value-rationality). The former is instrumental, while the latter is prescribed by some transcendental system of values.

2. Such exogenous view is echoed by some philosophers like Searle (2005) who argued that 'deontic power' prescribing peoples' duties, rights, obligations and the like precedes an individual's desire-oriented choices. See also Heath (2001) on 'deontic constraints', of which I will comment later.

3. Ostrom (2005, 2007) and Heath (2001) may be referred to as recent works dealing with relationships between the social norm and economic choices (instrumental choices) in an integrated, quasi-game-theoretic manner. In Ostrom's Institutional Analysis and Development (IAD) framework (2005), the so-called 'social dilemma' (equivalent to the Harding's tragedy of commons problem) is considered to be resolvable by, among others, individual internalization of norm. The norms are treated as exogenous parameters of preference functions of agents in the social-dilemma game. However, recently, they have been interpreted as evolving as a response to the lawless 'state of nature' (Ostrom 2007), although game-theoretic language is not explicitly used. The philosopher Heath (2001:

135–145) well-versed in game theory, also introduces the individual utility function composed of desired-based ranking of actions and categorical preferences (normative reason) of actions. Norms are then explained essentially as compromised solutions of non-strategic moral discourses among people (the axiomatic approach to Nash bargaining solution is alluded to). Thus, both instrumental choice and 'deontic constraints' are regarded as involved in individual action, but they are treated as mutually distinctly determined. We will instead treat both conjointly.

4. I do not exclude cases where the delivery of symbols and non-marketable goods generate material satisfaction, together with emotional impact, on the side of recipients.

5. For a more elaborated classification of domains of games, including those of political-exchanges and organizational exchanges, see Aoki (2001, 2010).

6. See Fehr and Camerer (2007) for other similar evidence.

7. A similar individualistic notion of social capital is discussed and measured by Glaeser et al. (2002).

8. For a more detailed discussion of linked games and their applications to institutional issues, see Aoki (2001), particularly chapters 2.2, 8.1–2, 10.1–2.

9. See Aoki (2001) chapter 2.2 for detailed descriptions regarding environmental and political conditions surrounding the rural management of irrigation system in Edo period and its game-theoretic analysis.

10. The value of social pay-offs may be revealed and measured by the opportunity costs in margin at equilibrium choice.

11. Indeed, in the Edo period severe ostracism known as *Mura-hachibu* (80 percent exclusion from village collective actions except for funeral services and fire fighting to prevent spread of disease and fire) was practised against serious deviants. The exclusion of individuals from the said social exchanges implied the wholesale deprivation of social capital, since they cannot be compensated elsewhere by exiting from the community.

12. It is important to prove that it is beneficial for the member families to socially ostracize anyone who shirks in the commons domain. It requires that the marginal contribution of any single individual member to social capital accumulations of other members is small.

13. Bicchieri (2006) provides a similar 'rational reconstruction' of social norms although not in terms of linked games.

14. An interesting comparative study of fishery villages by Platteau and Seki (2001) may be referred to on this theme.

15. Although the parable above was constructed as a sequel to the preceding irrigation story and thus is meant to reflect some historical reality in the late Edo period, similar parables can be narrated with respect to other communities as well. For example, Hayami and Kawagoe (1993) challenged a famous anthropological thesis by Geertz (1963) that entrepreneurship for modernizing non-farm business activities cannot emerge endogenously from within the village. They looked at emerging Indonesian vegetable markets in which village-based traders acted as intermediaries, delivering the produce to towns. In order for this operation to be effective, credits must have been advanced by the traders in exchange for the promised amount of daily supplies of crops by villagers, which potentially created moral hazard problems. However, community norms – not a legal system – enforced these contracts and countervailed against the temptation of farmers to cheat. Conversely, traders were compelled to give farmers a fair price, since

there would be symmetric information access to market prices in village. Thus, community norm facilitated the transition of the rural community to external market relationships.

16. The theory of common knowledge suggests that in order for shared beliefs to exist at all among the players of a game regarding the internal state of the game, it is sufficient and 'almost' necessary that there is a *common prior* among the players about the social distribution of types of the players as distinguished, for example, by pay-off function, beliefs, the set of feasible action choices (Aumann and Brandenburger 1995). The presumption of a common prior in a context of bounded rationality may imply that the actual beliefs of the players could be differentiate in details by their positions (kinds of players) and actual types (presumably conditioned by their experiences, traits, actual circumstances in each position, etc.), as well as by their information-processing capacities, but be identical in essential, summary characteristics regardless of their positions and actual types.

17. See Ostrom (2005) for a decent discussion of the limits of centralized control of 'social dilemma'.

18. What is recognized as corporate social responsibility by different societies seems to hinge on ways in which social exchanges have been structured historically in each economy. For example, American corporate executives tend to think of their ethical accountabilities as the most important corporate values, while Japanese and European corporate executives tend to place higher values on environmental responsibility. See 'Study on Corporate Values' by the Aspen Institute and Booze Allen and Hamilton reported in http://www.boozallen.com/publications/article/659548.

19. The reverse may not necessarily be the case. For example, tobacco companies may have less social capital, but some of them may have high reputations among smokers.

References

A. Alchian and H. Demsetz (1972) 'Production, Information Costs, and Economic Organization', *American Economic Review*, 62, 777–795.

M. Aoki (2001) *Toward a Comparative Institutional Analysis* (Cambridge, Mass.: MIT Press).

M. Aoki (2010) *Corporations in Evolving Diversity: Cognition, Governance, and Institutions* (Oxford UK: Oxford University Press).

M. Aoki and Y. Hayami (eds) (2001) *Communities and Markets in Economic Development* (Oxford and N.Y.: Oxford University Press).

Aristotle (1955) *Ethics*, trans. By J. A. K. Thompson (rev. trans. by H. Tredennick) (London: Penguin Classics).

Arrow K. J. (1967) 'The Place of Moral Obligation in Preference Systems', in S. Hook (ed.) *Human Values and Economic Policy* (NY: New York University Press). Reprinted in *Collected Papers of Kenneth J. Arrow*, Vol. 1 (Cambridge, MA: Harvard University Press), pp. 78–80.

R. Aumann and A. Brandenburger (1995) 'Epistemic Conditions for Nash Equilibrium', *Econometrica*, 63, 1161–80.

F. Barca, M. Bianchi, F. Brioschi, L. Buzzacchi, P. Casavola, L. Filippa and M. Paganini (1994) *I Modelli di Controllo e la Concentrazione Proprietaria Messi a Confronto Empiricamente* III vols. Vol. II, *Assetti, Proprietà e Controllo nelle Imprese Italiane Medio-Grandi* (Bologna: Il Mulino).

D. P. Baron (2007) 'Corporate Social Responsibility and Social Entrepreneurship', *Journal of Economics & Management Strategy*, 16, 683–713.

P. Berger and T. Luckmann (1967) *The Social Construction of Reality: A Treatise in the Sociology of Knowledge* (N.Y.: Doubleday Anchor).

C. Bicchieri (2006) *The Grammar of Society: The Nature and Dynamics of Social Norms* (Cambridge: Cambridge University Press).

G. Dei Ottati (1994) 'Trust, Interlinking Transactions and Credit in the Industrial District', *Cambridge Journal of Economics*, 18, 529–546.

P. DiMaggio and W. Powell (eds) (1991) *The New Institutionalism in Organizational Analysis* (Chicago: University of Chicago Press).

G. Dowell, S. Hart and B. Yeung (2000) 'Do Corporate Global Environmental Standards Create or Destroy Market Value?', *Management Science*, 46, 1059–74.

E. Fehr and C. F. Camerer (2007) 'Social Neuroeconomics: The Neural Circuitry of Social Preferences', *Trends in Cognitive Sciences*, 11, 419–27.

J. Geanakoplos, D. Pearce and E. Stacchetti (1989) 'Psychological Games and Sequential Rationality', *Games and Economic Behavior*, 1, 60–79.

E. Glaeser, D. Laibson and B. Sacerdote (2002) 'An Economic Approach to Social Capital', *Economic Journal*, 112, 437–458.

C. Geertz (1963) *Peddlers and Princes* (Chicago: University of Chicago Press).

M. Granovetter (1985) 'Economic Action and Social Structure: The Problem of Embeddedness', *American Journal of Sociology*, 91, 480–510.

A. Greif (1993) 'Contract Enforceability and Economic Institutions in Early Trade: The Maghribi Traders' Coalition', *American Economic Review*, 83, 525–548.

A. Greif (2006) *Institutions and the Path to the Modern Economy: Lessons from Medieval Trade* (New York: Cambridge University Press).

Hayami, Y. (1998) 'Toward an East Asian Model of Economic Development', in Y. Hayami and M. Aoki (eds) *The Institutional Foundations of East Asian Economic Development* (Basingstoke: Macmillan), pp. 3–35.

G. Heal (2005) 'Corporate Social Responsibility: An Economic and Financial Framework', *The Geneva Papers*.

J. Heath (2001) *Communicative Action and Rational Choice* (Cambridge, Mass.: MIT Press).

J. Hicks (1969) *A Theory of Economic History* (Oxford: Oxford University Press).

K. Izuma, D. N. Saito and N. Sadato (2008) 'Processing of Social and Monetary Rewards in the Human Striatum', *Neuron*, 58, 284–294.

M. Kandori (1992) 'Social Norms and Community Enforcement', *Review of Economic Studies*, 59, 63–80.

A. A. King and M. J. Lennox (2001) 'Does It Really Pay To Be Green? An Empirical Study of Firm Environmental and Financial Performance', *Journal of Industrial Ecology*, 5(1), 105–116.

P. R. Montague and G. S. Berns (2002) 'Neural Economics and the Biological Substrates of Valuation', *Neuron*, 36, 265–284.

D. North (1990) *Institutions, Institutional Change and Economic Performance* (Cambridge, U.K. and New York: Cambridge University Press).

E. Ostrom (2005) *Understanding Institutional Diversity* (Princeton, NJ: Princeton University Press).

E. Ostrom (2007) 'Developing A Method for Analyzing Institutional Change', draft.

Platteau, J-P. and E. Seki (2001) 'Community Arrangements to Overcome Market Failures: Pooling Groups in Japanese Fisheries', in M. Aoki and Y. Hayami (eds) *Communities and Markets in Economic Development* (Oxford:Oxford University Press), p. 344–402.

K. Polanyi (1944) *The Great Transformation* (New York: Farrar Rinehart, Inc.).

M. Rabin (1998) 'Psychology and Economics', *Journal of Economic Literature*, 36, 11–46.

P. Samuelson (1947) *Foundations of Economic Analysis* (Cambridge, Mass.: Harvard University Press).

J. Searle (2005) 'What is an Institution?' *Journal of Institutional Economics*, 1, 1–22.

D. S. Siegel and D. F. Vitaliano (2007) 'An Empirical Analysis of the Strategic Use of Corporate Social Responsibility', *Journal of Economics & Management Strategy*, 16, 773–792.

M. Weber (1978) *Economy and Society*, eds. G. Roth and C. Wittich (Berkeley, CA: University of California Press).

6
Social Capital in Networks of Relations

Steffen Lippert

1. Introduction

The idea of *social capital* is increasingly used in various fields of social science, but rigorous definitions of this concept are rare. According to Narayan and Pritchett (1999), social capital 'is many things to many people'. This confusion does not contribute to the growth of knowledge in these fields.

The World Bank identifies five 'key dimensions' along which useful proxies for social capital can be generated: *groups and networks*, for example, used in Putnam et al. (1993), Putnam (1995, 1996), Massey and Espinosa (1997); *trust*, for example, used in Narayan and Pritchett (1999), Knack and Keefer (1997), La Porta et al. (1997), Zak and Knack (2001); *collective action*, for example, used in Portes and Sensenbrenner (1993), Fernandez-Kelley (1995); *social inclusion*, for example, used in Portes (1995), Light and Karageorgis (1994); and *information and communication*, for example, used in Massey and Espinosa (1997). These five dimensions are clearly interrelated. However, despite their commonly interchangeable use in the literature, they are conceptually very different. For example, while trust refers to the expectation that cooperative behavior will not be met with opportunism, collective action and social inclusion often refer to the choice of cooperative behavior, groups and networks to the source for cooperation and trust, and information and communication can even refer to either cooperative behavior or the source for cooperation.

This chapter summarizes the findings of the theory of networks of relations by Lippert and Spagnolo (2010), from here on, LS (2010), and applies them to define *individual social capital* in the spirit of Bourdieu (1986) and Coleman (1990) and *aggregate social capital* in the spirit of Putnam (1995). These conceptualizations of social capital build on the idea of linked games as put forward in Spagnolo (1999) and Aoki (2010). The chapter gives an interpretation of the features of networks of relations that unify the different concepts of social capital used in the empirical literature. It finally shows how network properties relate to individual social capital in the spirit of Bourdieu (1986) and Coleman (1990). In particular, it shows that denser social networks do not necessarily provide higher social capital.

2. Social capital in networks of relations with public information

Aiming at providing a model of social capital based on social networks, this section first reviews some theoretical results of the theory of networks of relations by LS (2010). This review concentrates on an environment in which every actor in the social network observes the actions chosen by all other actors in his network. These results are then applied to shed light on the modeling of social capital within networks of relations.

2.1. Pooling asymmetries in the theory of relational networks with public information

LS (2010) show that if actors each repeatedly interact in several bilateral Prisoners' Dilemmas with other actors, and if in each bilateral interaction they have generic payoffs, then they can cooperate for a larger set of discount factors if they are able to pool payoff asymmetries within a network of such cooperative long-term relationships by means of a multilateral punishment mechanism than if they are not able to do so.

More precisely, they consider n economic agents who are able to inter-act in pairs determined by an underlying geography. Time is discrete and the agents share a common discount factor δ. Within the geography, agents repeatedly interact in bilateral social dilemmas with the features of Prisoners' Dilemma games. In each interaction, in every period t, each agent chooses from two available actions: cooperate, C, or do not cooperate, D. The pay-offs from the action profiles in the Prisoners' Dilemmas are assumed to be idiosyncratic according to the payoff matrix below.

In this payoff matrix, c^{ij} stands for the cooperation payoff of agent i in his interaction with agent j, d^{ij} for his payoff if both defect, b^{ij} is the payoff of agent i if he betrays agent j while agent j cooperates, and l^{ij} stands for his payoff if he suffers a loss because agent j betrayed him while he cooperated. These payoffs satisfy the usual assumptions for a Prisoner's Dilemma: $l^{ij} < d^{ij} < c^{ij} < b^{ij}$ and $l^{ij} + b^{ji} < c^{ij} + c^{ji}$, $\forall i, j, \ i \neq j$. Within the bilateral interactions,

agent j

		C	D
	C	c^{ij}, c^{ji}	l^{ij}, b^{ji}
agent i	D	b^{ij}, l^{ji}	d^{ij}, d^{ji}

players are said to share a relationship if and only if both choose to play C in every period on the realization path of a given strategy profile in the n – player supergame.

It is well-known that in the two-player supergame, cooperation is an equilibrium outcome as long as

$$\frac{c^{ij}}{1-\delta} \geq w^{ij} + \frac{\delta d^{ij}}{1-\delta}, \forall i, j. \tag{1}$$

If, in a bilateral interaction, for example, due to asymmetric idiosyncratic payoffs, this inequality does not hold for both players, these players cannot share a relationship.

LS (2010) find that in this case, pooling payoff asymmetries within a social network by making actions in one interaction of a player depend on the actions chosen in another interaction can overcome the players' inability to cooperate. Take the example of three agents, agent 1, agent 2 and agent 3. Assume the underlying geography to be such that each of the three agents can interact with each other. Suppose further that in the bilateral interaction between agent 1 and agent 2, inequality (1) does not hold for each of them. Then, making agent 3's actions in his interactions with actors 1 and 2 depend on the actions, which agents 1 and 2 choose in their interaction, could provide incentives for 1 and 2 to cooperate with each other. Such a multilateral punishment mechanism essentially implements third-party or community enforcement.

In particular, LS (2010) show that if every agent observes every action chosen within the network, and if for every agent the sum of the net gains from cooperating is positive, then by means of a multilateral mechanism the agents can sustain cooperation within each bilateral interaction in the network, even though they could not have done so had they viewed each interaction in isolation. LS (2010) show that agents can pool payoff asymmetries, for example, by playing a multilateral grim trigger strategy. In such a strategy, there are two phases: a cooperation phase and a punishment phase. The game starts in the cooperation phase, in which every player plays C with all neighbors. The game stays in the cooperation phase as long as every player continues to play C with all neighbors. It switches to and stays in the punishment phase if not all players chose C with all neighbors. In the punishment phase, every player chooses D with all neighbors.

In a graphical representation, let an incoming arrow to a player denote that inequality (1) holds and no incoming arrow denote that inequality (1) does not hold. Then in Figure 6.1, none of the relations in the bilateral interactions would be sustainable if strategies did not take into account actions chosen in other relations. If they do, then, for example, agent 1 can be disciplined to cooperate with agent 2 not only by a threat of punishment by agent 2, but also by a threat of punishment by player 6, and as long

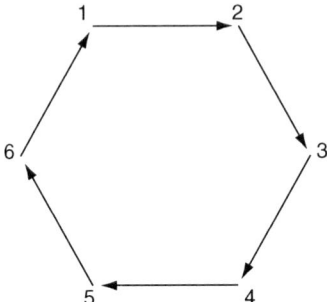

Figure 6.1   Circular network with six players. An incoming arrow signifies positive net gains from cooperation; no incoming arrow signifies (strictly) negative net gains from cooperation. No pair of actors in the network could sustain cooperation without third-party punishment. As all actors have an incoming arrow, they can use slack enforcement power from one interaction to enforce cooperation in their other interaction

as what 1 has to gain from cooperating with both 2 and 6 is larger than what he has to gain from cheating on both 2 and 6 and then entering the punishment phase, he prefers to cooperate with both.

Note that asymmetric payoffs are the generic case in interactions in social dilemmas. The idiosyncratic payoffs in the payoff matrix capture this property. Note further that it is the *circularity* of the network that enables players to pool their payoff asymmetries across different relations. Coleman calls this circularity *closure*. For closure to effectively enable agents to cooperate where they could not otherwise, however, it is necessary that each agent benefits more from cooperating than from cheating with at least some neighbors. In Figure 6.2(b), agent 1 does not have neighbors with whom cooperating is better than cheating. Thus, there is neither bilateral nor multilateral enforcement of cooperation for agent 1 available. In Figure 6.2(a), on the other hand, agent 1 benefits more from cooperating with than from cheating on agent 5. If the benefit from cooperation is sufficiently much larger than that from cheating, with public information, agent 5 can make

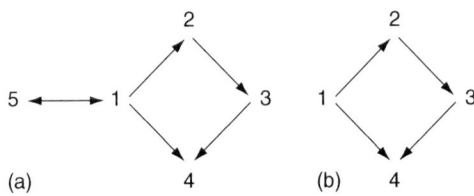

Figure 6.2   With public information, community enforcement can make agent 1 cooperate with agents 2 and 4 in (a), but not in (b)

his cooperation with agent 1 depend on what agent 1 does in his interactions with agents 2 and 4 and, thus, community enforcement of cooperation of agent 1 with agents 2 and 4 is possible.

2.2. Social capital with public information

In a formal model of networks of relations, which generate 'slack enforcement power' for some agents, LS (2010) have shown how these agents may be enabled to sustain cooperation in additional deficient relations, even in *one-shot* Prisoner's Dilemma interactions. This section offers an interpretation of this use of networks of relations as cooperation-enforcement/governance devices for new social dilemmas in terms of social capital.

Micro-level social capital

Networks of social relations generate slack enforcement power, which can be used to sustain cooperation in other than the social interactions. These other interactions can even be one-off dilemmas, such as an *occasional business transaction*, in which each agent can 'hold up' the other one, and which can be represented by a *one-shot Prisoner's Dilemma*. In such a one-off business transaction, inequality (1) does not hold for either of the two agents involved.

Consider the cycle in Figure 6.1, and let this cycle represent a *network of social relations*. Consider that agents 3 and 6 are contemplating whether they can cooperate in a *business interaction* or a *series of business interactions*. Clearly, if the business interaction(s) between agents 3 and 6 fulfills inequality (1) for both of them, as in Figure 6.3(a), they can cooperate without having to draw from the resources of the social network. However, already if the interaction is such that inequality (1) does not hold for one of the two agents, for example, for agent 3 as in Figure 6.3(b), they will have to draw on the social network's resources to enforce cooperation in their business interaction. LS (2010) show that agents 3 and 6's membership in the network of relations may help them sustain cooperation in their bilateral interactions

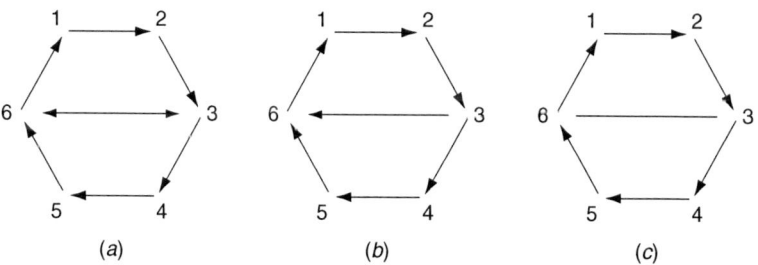

Figure 6.3 Social capital in networks of relations

even if inequality (1) does not hold for either of them. This case is given in Figure 6.3(c).

Agents 3 and 6 can enforce cooperation in such an interaction if what they have to lose in their social relations is sufficiently valuable, that is, if they dispose of sufficient slack enforcement power to enforce cooperation in the additional business interaction. They would draw on the social network's slack enforcement power by means of a multilateral punishment mechanism that threatens agent 3 with non-cooperation in the social sphere by agents 2 and 4, and agent 6 with non-cooperation in the social sphere by agents 1 and 5.

The slack enforcement power from a social network, used to govern this one-shot business interaction, is very close to what Bourdieu (1986) and Coleman (1990) define as *social capital*. Bourdieu (1986) writes:

> Social capital is the aggregate of the actual or potential resources which are linked to possession of a durable network of more or less institution-alized relationships of mutual acquaintance and recognition – or in other words, to membership in a group – which provides each of its members with the backing of the collectivity-owned capital, a 'credential' which entitles them to credit, in the various senses of the word. [...] The volume of the social capital possessed by a given agent thus depends on the size of the network of connections he can effectively mobilize and on the volume of the capital (economic, cultural or symbolic) possessed in his own right by each of those to whom he is connected.

Coleman's definition is less precise but, in a similar way to Bourdieu's, characterizes social capital as an attribute of individuals:

> Social capital is defined by its function. It is not a single entity, but a variety of different entities having two characteristics in common: They all consist of some aspect of social structures, and they facilitate certain actions of individuals who are within that structure. [...] Unlike other forms of capital, social capital inheres the structure of relations between persons and among persons. It is lodged neither in individuals nor in physical implements of production.

Both definitions characterize social capital at the micro level. They describe *individuals* who can make use of the capital lodged in their connections within the social network in order to facilitate certain actions of individuals who are within that network. Bourdieu's definition suggests quantifying social capital in terms of the volume of capital that can be mobilized from a network of connections in order to affect the governance of other interactions. Coleman's perspective suggests quantifying it in terms of the extent to which one can affect the governance of other interactions by using the capital that can be mobilized from a network of connections. Neither of them specifies that social capital can *only* be mobilized from *direct* contacts. For example, in Figure 6.3(c), agent 3 relies on third-party punishment by agents 1, 2, 4, and 5; yet agent 3 is connected to agents 1 and 5 only *indirectly*.

Clearly, the *extent* to which an individual agent can affect the governance of other than social interactions by means of the capital he can mobilize from his network of social connections depends on the *volume* of such capital available to the agent from each network member he is directly and indirectly connected to. Both characterizations are, thus, two sides of the same coin. Using this insight, LS (2010) allows for a game-theoretic definition for this micro-level social capital.

Definition 1 (*Micro-level social capital*) *The social capital two agents can draw on by being part of a social network equals to the slack enforcement power of the network usable to enforce cooperation-compliance in other interactions in need of governance through a multilateral punishment mechanism involving a social network.*

With public information, this is an *agent-pair specific* definition. Whether agents 3 and 6 in Figure 6.3(c) can enforce cooperation in a one-off business transaction depends: (i) on the slack enforcement power in the social relations of agent 3, (ii) on the slack enforcement power in the social relations of agent 6, and (iii) on whether this slack enforcement power is larger than the deficit of enforcement power in their business transaction. The slack enforcement power from agent 3's social relations equals to the sum of his net gains from cooperation in all his social relations. More formally, define $g^{ij} = \dfrac{c^{ij}}{1-\delta} \geq w^{ij} + \dfrac{\delta d^{ij}}{1-\delta}$ and let R_i denote the set of neighbors that agent i has social relations with. Then, for a one-off business interaction with symmetric payoffs between i and k,

$$\mathrm{sc}_{ik} = \min\left\{ \sum_{j \in R_i} g^{ij}, \sum_{j \in R_k} g^{kj} \right\}. \tag{2}$$

Bourdieu's definition explicitly contains the elements of the formalization in definition 1: the number of connections a player has in a social network or a group, that is, 'the size of the network of connections [an agent] can effectively mobilize', and the slack enforcement power an agent can draw on for enforcing cooperation in other interactions, that is, 'the volume of the capital [...] possessed in his own right by each of those to whom he is connected'.

Also Coleman's (1990) definition contains the main elements of the formalization in definition 1. Coleman insists on the role of social structure, that is, 'social capital inheres the structure of relations between persons

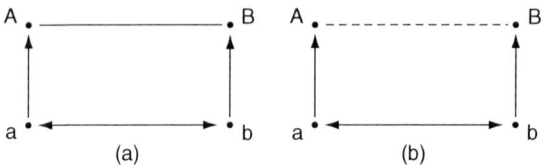

Figure 6.4   Representation of two communities: (a) with and (b) without intergenerational closure (adapted from Coleman 1990)

and among persons', and the function of social capital to 'facilitate certain actions of individuals who are within that structure'.

Even though Coleman's social capital definition is not necessarily networks-based, he explicitly insists on the importance of the 'closure' (circularity) of social networks for the provision of some sorts of social capital. Giving a graphical representation as in Figure 6.4, he suggests that if parents (A and B), whose children (a and b) are friends, share a relation also, as shown in panel (a), they have more 'power' over their children – thanks to what Coleman calls 'intergenerational closure' – than if they do not, as shown in panel (b). Lack of relations among parents makes it more difficult for them to successfully impose/enforce norms on/upon their children. Coleman does not provide a game-theoretical foundation for his claim, but this chapter's model fits his story precisely.

Reviewing '(game-)theoretical questions stimulated by a reflection on social capital', Sobel (2002) identifies two ways in which Coleman's (1990) network closure or – put differently – 'dense social networks make enforcement of group cooperative behavior more effective'. This is accomplished first by creating 'common knowledge of information', and second by increasing 'the quality and reliability of third-party monitoring needed to enforce cooperative dynamic equilibria'. This chapter's adaptation of LS (2010) offers an additional explanation of why closure might be important for social capital, namely the pooling of payoff asymmetries.

Macro-level social capital

Empirical studies that use cross-country or cross-regional data to evaluate the impact of social capital on economic performance use aggregate measures of social capital. Using our micro-level definition, it is straightforward to justify the use of such macro-level measures.

Definition 2 *(**Macro-level social capital**) In a sustainable social network, a macro-measure of social capital corresponds to the average pair-specific micro-level social capital of agents within the social network.*

This definition captures Robert Putnam's (1995) macro-level perspective on social capital. For him, the concept 'refers to the *collective* value of all "social networks" and the inclinations that arise from these networks to do things for each other'.

2.3. Discussion

Spagnolo (1999) describes how players can draw on slack enforcement power from a cooperative bilateral social interaction to sustain otherwise not enforceable cooperation in a business interaction by linking these two games. Similarly, Aoki (2010) describes how a group of players link cooperation in a commons game to cooperation in a game of social interaction. Cooperation in the commons game is enforced by the threat of ostracizing cheaters in the commons game from social interaction.

Building on idea of linking two games and using the theory of networks of relations from LS (2010), this chapter takes one step further and shows that the amount of social capital depends on the structure of the underlying social network. In the model with public information, social capital is interaction or agent pair-specific. It depends on the sum of the net gains from cooperation in the social network of *each* of the two players who are trying to enforce cooperation in their bilateral business interaction. Furthermore, denser social networks will only lead to higher social capital of an individual if higher density comes about by means of more slack enforcement power – the extra relations have to increase the sum of the net gains from cooperation for the pair of agents which is trying to enforce cooperation in their bilateral business interaction.

The formalization of social capital based on LS (2010) highlights how the two main measures of social capital used in empirical studies, the expectation of cooperative outcomes in (one-shot) collective actions problems, *Trust*[1] and the social structure that may lead to it, *Social Networks*[2] are linked. This formalization also highlights that it is the collective norm to enforce business cooperation in the social sphere, which distinguishes trust as a form of social capital from trust generated elsewhere and which allows social networks to proxy for social capital and to measure the return to social networks in the business sphere (compare Lin 2001).

3. Extension: Social capital in networks of relations without public information

This section first reviews some theoretical results of LS (2010), now in an environment in which every player only directly observes the actions chosen in his own bilateral interactions. It considers two cases, the one where players can pass on soft information about these actions and the case where they cannot. These results are then applied to shed light on the modeling of social capital within networks of relations.

3.1. Pooling asymmetries in the theory of relational networks without public information

LS (2010) study sustainability conditions for cooperation in relational networks without public information. In particular, they study an environment in which players only observe the history in their own bilateral interactions without being able to talk about it. In this environment, players can make use of contagious strategies for community enforcement of bilateral cooperation. They find that gatekeepers, players who connect two components of the network, need an incentive to cooperate with each component separately for the network to be sustainable. In a graphical representation, let an incoming arrow to a player denote that inequality (1) holds. Then agent 1 in Figure 6.5(a) cannot be punished by player 5 for his choices in the interaction with agents 2 and 4. Thus, agent 1 does not have an incentive to cooperate with agents 2 and 4; and neither in panel (a) nor in the one in panel (b) of Figure 6.5, will any of the agents cooperate.

LS (2010) go on to show that with contagious strategies, if in networks with closure for each player the sum of the net gains from cooperating with their neighbors, discounted appropriately for the delay in punishment by contagion, is positive, they can sustain cooperation within each bilateral interaction in the network, even though they could not do so if they viewed each interaction in isolation. The result from the environment with public information is generalized to the environment without public information.

LS (2010) then show that if, in the case without public information, players are able to transmit non-verifiable information about their histories and about third-hand information they possess, they can sustain more cooperation as long as information transmission is sufficiently fast. Players have an incentive to pass on truthful information if they use multilateral repentance strategies, according to which players cooperate with all neighbors during a cooperation phase and, if a deviation occurred, they enter a time-limited punishment phase. During the punishment phase, non-cheating players (1) transmit information of the occurrence of cheating to their neighbors, (2) continue to cooperate with non-cheating neighbors and (3) play non-cooperatively with the original cheater(s) for a cheater-specific number of periods. During a punishment phase, cheaters have to repent toward all their neighbors for that number of periods. After the punishment period

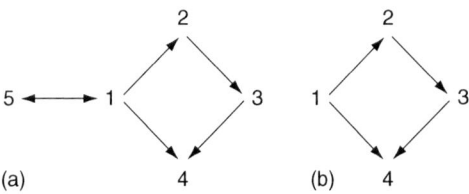

Figure 6.5   Player 1 is a gatekeeper: without public information, community enforcement cannot make him cooperate with players 2 and 4

is over, all agents return to the cooperation phase. LS (2010) show that multilateral repentance strategies are an optimal punishment scheme in this environment whereas contagion is not.

Closure facilitates contagion and information transmission within the network, and is therefore necessary for pooling payoff asymmetries. It enables the formation of slack enforcement power that, together with the norm to enforce cooperation in the business sphere by means of punishment in the social sphere, forms social capital.

3.2. Social capital without public information

For environments without public information about the actions every player chose in the network, the extent to which existing relations in a social network can facilitate 'the achievement of certain ends' for an agent does not depend only on his net gains from cooperation, that is, how much he has to lose in his social relations. Since the delay with which an eventual punishment sets in matters, it also depends on partners' locations in the network.

Network density affects social capital in two different ways. First, the denser the networks the shorter the paths, and the earlier punishment of non-cooperative actions sets in. This increases social capital. Second, if higher density means that more relations have to be sustained for which at least one player has negative net gains from cooperation, then slack enforcement power is weakened as social relations have to be sustained by indirect enforcement. This reduces social capital. This, once more, implies that denser networks do not necessarily lead to higher social capital.

4. Conclusion

This chapter used the theory of networks of relations to provide game-theoretically founded definitions of micro-level social capital in the spirit of Bourdieu (1986) and Coleman (1990) and of macro-level social capital in the spirit of Putnam (1995). These definitions unify the different concepts of social capital used in the empirical literature, such as trust, properties of groups and social networks, collective action, social inclusion, and information and communication. The chapter used the game-theoretic interpretation of the concept of closure as the ability of players to pool payoff asymmetries within social networks, due to LS (2010), and showed how closure is related to social capital. Finally, it showed that denser social networks do not necessarily provide higher social capital.

Notes

1. See Knack and Keefer (1997), La Porta et al. (1997) or Zak and Knack (2001).
2. See Narayan and Pritchett (1999), Massey and Espinosa (1997) or Temple and Johnson (1998).

References

M. Aoki (2010) 'Linking economic and social-exchange games: from the community norm to CSR', Paper given at the EconomEtica conference on Social Capital, Corporate Social Responsibility and Sustainable Economic Development in Trento, 2007.

P. Bourdieu (1986) 'Forms of capital', in J. G. Richardson (ed.) *Handbook of Theory and Research for the Sociology of Education* (Westport CT: Greenwood Press), pp. 241–260.

J. Coleman (1990) *Foundations of Social Theory* (Cambridge MA: Harvard University Press).

M. P. Fernandez-Kelley (1995) 'Social and cultural capital in the urban ghetto: implications for the economic sociology of immigration', in A. Portes (ed.), *The Economic Sociology of Immigration* (New York: Russell Sage Foundation).

S. Knack and P. Keefer (1997) 'Does social capital have an economic payoff? A cross-country investigation', *Quarterly Journal of Economics*, 112, 1251–1288.

R. La Porta, F. Lopez-de-Silanes, A. Shleifer and R. W. Vishny (1997) 'Trust in large organizations', *American Economic Review Papers and Proceedings*, 87, 333–338.

I. Light and S. Karageorgis (1994) 'The ethnic economy', in N. Smelser and R. Swedberg (eds), *The Handbook of Economic Sociology* (Princeton, NJ: Princeton University Press).

N. Lin (2001) *Social Capital* (Cambridge: Cambridge University Press).

S. Lippert and G. Spagnolo (2010) 'Networks of relations and word-of-mouth communication', Games and Economic Behavior (forthcoming). doi:10.1016/j.geb.2010.08.010.

D. S. Massey and K. E. Espinosa (1997) 'What's driving Mexico-U.S. migration? A theoretical, empirical, and policy analysis', *American Journal of Sociology*, 102, 939–999.

D. Narayan and L. Pritchett (1999) 'Cents and sociability: household income and social capital in rural Tanzania', *Economic Development and Cultural Change*, 47, 871–897.

A. Portes (1995) 'Economic sociology and the sociology of immigration: a conceptual overview', in A. Portes (ed.) *The Economic Sociology of Immigration* (New York: Russell Sage Foundation), pp. 1–41.

A. Portes and J. Sensenbrenner (1993) 'Embeddedness and immigration: notes on the social determinants of economic action', *American Journal of Sociology*, 98, 1320–1350.

R. Putnam (1995) 'Bowling alone: Americas declining social capital', *Journal of Democracy*, 6, 65–78.

R. Putnam (1996) 'The strange disappearance of civic America', *The American Prospect*, 24, 34–43.

R. D. Putnam, R. Leonardi and R.Y. Nanetti (1993) *Making Democracy Work: Civic Traditions in Modern Italy* (Princeton: Princeton University Press).

J. Sobel (2002) 'Can we trust social capital?', *Journal of Economic Literature*, 40, 139–154.

G. Spagnolo (1999) 'Social relations and cooperation in organizations', *Journal of Economic Behavior and Organization*, 38, 1–25.

J. Temple and P.A. Johnson (1998) 'Social capability and economic growth', *Quarterly Journal of Economics*, 113, 965–990.

P. J. Zak and S. Knack (2001) 'Trust and growth', *Economic Journal*, 111, 295–321.

7
Modeling Cognitive Social Capital and Corporate Social Responsibility as Preconditions for Sustainable Networks of Relations

Giacomo Degli Antoni and Lorenzo Sacconi

1. Introduction

1.1. Subject and aim

In recent years, increasing attention has been paid to trust, trustworthiness and social norms of reciprocity and cooperation as key factors in socioeconomic development. Even though from different perspectives, both the concept of social capital and the notion of corporate social responsibility refer to these elements.

Since the seminal work by Putnam et al. (1993) focusing on the effects of social capital (hereafter also SC) on economic and government performance, the concept of SC has been widely used to analyze how interpersonal relations affect economic activity by favoring cooperation. Many definitions of social capital have been proposed, and two principal approaches to this concept may be identified. On the one hand, social capital is defined in terms of generalized trust, civic norms, beliefs and dispositions which affect the propensity to cooperate (e.g. Knack and Keefer 1997; Putnam et al. 1993). On the other hand, social capital is defined in terms of cooperative networks among agents (e.g. Burt 2002; Coleman 1988; Lin 2001). Many approaches are also taken to the notion of corporate social responsibility (hereafter also CSR). In particular, if we consider the stakeholder approach (Freeman 1984, 2000; Freeman and Evan 1990) or the contractarian approach to CSR (Sacconi 2004, 2006, 2007a, 2007b), relational aspects in terms of trust, trustworthiness, beliefs and dispositions to cooperate seem to be fundamental in promoting the coordination processes between the firm and its stakeholders that are essential to implement CSR practices.[1] Even though SC and CSR seem to share several features, their relationship has not yet been analyzed in depth.

In this paper we model the relationship between the firm and its stakeholders and show analytically how (cognitive) social capital and corporate social responsibility generate (structural) social capital.

1.2. Social capital

Taking into account the multidimensional character of SC (e.g. Paldam 2000), and starting from the distinction drawn by Uphoff (1999), we consider a cognitive and a structural dimension of the concept. In our approach, the former dimension essentially refers to the dispositional characters of agents that affect their propensity to behave in different ways. The latter refers to social networks that connect agents. More specifically, we approach the idea of cognitive social capital by focusing on trustworthy attitudes grounded on preferences for social norm compliance, which in turn is based on reciprocal beliefs and more basic dispositions to conformity. Reciprocal beliefs (in the behavior of others) depend on the behavior that others have already exhibited in the past but can be generated (or reinforced) by ethical commitments undertaken by them (for example, if agents subscribe to an agreement on an ideal principle). Dispositions stem principally from more basic cultural traits in the community where agents live, but they also depend on micro elements (e.g. genetic and psychological factors). Both beliefs and dispositions can promote (or, obviously, reduce) trust and the propensity to cooperate. Structural social capital is constituted by cooperative linkages among agents. We consider four main factors able to promote the creation of structural social capital (three pertaining to the cognitive dimension of social capital, the fourth to the structure of interaction): (i) reciprocal belief that others will cooperate, (ii) disposition to cooperate, (iii) agreements on social norms and principles that may activate reciprocal beliefs and dispositions and translate them into motives to act (this is the point where the logical connection with CSR will become stringent) and (iv) the existence of credible sanctions against the agents that decide not to cooperate.[2] Our definitions of structural and cognitive social capital differ from those proposed by Uphoff. However, they share some essential characteristics with them. In regard to the structural definition, both our approach and that adopted by Uphoff include in this dimension the networks that contribute to cooperation. In regard to the cognitive dimension, Uphoff's approach states that this category 'derives from mental processes and resulting ideas, reinforced by culture and ideology, specifically norms, values, attitudes, and beliefs that contribute cooperative behavior' (Uphoff 1999: 218). We refer to cognitive social capital by focusing on beliefs and dispositions, and we show how they affect the propensity of agents to share ethical principles of cooperation.

1.3. Corporate social responsibility

We take a contractarian approach to corporate social responsibility and define it as a 'model of extended corporate governance whereby those who run a firm (entrepreneurs, directors and managers) have responsibilities that range from fulfilment of their fiduciary duties[3] toward the owners to fulfilment of analogous fiduciary duties toward all the firm's stakeholders' (Sacconi 2006). The definition of CSR in terms of extended responsibility toward all the stakeholders of the firm is rooted in neo-institutional theory (Grossman and Hart 1986; Hansmann 1996; Hart 1995; Hart and Moore 1990; Williamson 1975, 1986). According to this approach, the firm is an institutional form of 'unified transactions governance' aimed at remedying imperfections in the contracts that regulate exchange relations among subjects endowed with diverse assets (capital, labor, instrumental goods, and so on) that may generate a surplus if put together. The incompleteness of contracts that should regulate the agreements on the investment to be made by each agent, and on how the surplus is to be divided among them, reduces the incentive of subjects to invest at an optimal level. The firm responds to this problem by bringing the various transactions under the control of a hierarchical authority, which owns the firm and is entitled by its ownership to make decisions on the contingencies that were not *ex ante* contractible.[4] This party is thus safeguarded against opportunism by the other stakeholders. Nevertheless, this configuration generates a risk for the other parties, which are vulnerable to an abuse of authority (Sacconi 1999, 2000, 2006). Many non-controling stakeholders will *ex ante* be discouraged from investing at an optimal level, while *ex post* they will resort to conflicting or disloyal behavior (typically possible when information asymmetry is inherent in the execution of some subordinate activity), in the belief that they are being subjected to the abuse of authority. Therefore, the optimal level of investment cannot be achieved and a second-best solution arises. This result, which approximates social efficiency, is always connected with governance solutions based on the allocation of property rights to a single party.

According to the contractarian approach, this problem can be overcome if CSR is viewed as 'extended governance' (Sacconi 2000, 2006). The firm's legitimacy deficit is remedied if the residual control right is associated with further fiduciary duties of the controling stakeholder toward the non-controling ones faced with the risk of abuse of authority. The firm must be grounded on a rational agreement (the constitutional contract of the firm) between those who run it (entrepreneurs, directors and managers) and the non-controling parts (Sacconi 2006). It is the constitutional contract of the firm which determines

- that authority is delegated to the stakeholder most efficient in performing governance functions;
- the fiduciary duties of this party toward the non-controling stakeholders.

Once the social contract of the firm has been defined, the firm must develop a reputation in order to convince all the non-controling stakeholders that it will respect the duties stipulated in the contract. The problem with creating reputation is that the firm and its stakeholders are characterized by settings in which information or knowledge about the action of the firm is incomplete or highly asymmetric.[5] Because of incomplete information, the stakeholders cannot verify whether the firm has actually behaved according to the fiduciary duties defined in the social contract and, consequently, the firm cannot develop a reputation. In order to do so, it must adopt an explicitly announced standard (a CSR standard) that sets out general principles and whose contents are such to elicit stakeholder consensus, as well as explicit commitments to comply with principles and rules known *ex ante* by stakeholders.[6]

1.4. Weak and strong stakeholder

Finally, with respect to the term 'stakeholder', which denotes individuals or groups with a major stake in the running of the firm and who are able to influence it significantly (Freeman and McVea 2002), we accept the distinction between stakeholders in the strict or in the broad sense. The former are stakeholders who have an interest at stake because they have made specific investments in the firm (i.e. investments that may significantly increase the total value generated by the firm and that are made in relation to a specific firm and not any other). Stakeholders in the broad sense are stakeholders connected to the firm because they *undergo* the 'external effects' of the transactions performed by it, even if they do not directly participate in those transactions. With respect to this classification we introduce, within the category of stakeholders in a strict sense, the original distinction between strong and weak stakeholders. Strong and weak stakeholders are distinguished by the consequences that the breaking-off of the relationship with the firm produces both on the stakeholder and on the firm.

a) *Strong stakeholder*. The difference between the discounted payoff that strong stakeholders and firms obtain by cooperating forever and by defecting at the first stage (and never cooperating again) is positive. Strong stakeholders are stakeholders in the strict sense who bring strategic assets into the firm. They are, for example, highly skilled workers or institutional investors.

b) *Weak stakeholder*. Weak stakeholders would like to cooperate forever with the firm, but the discounted payoff that the firm obtains by cooperating forever with them is lower than the payoff it obtains by defecting at the first stage and never cooperating again. Weak stakeholders are stakeholders in the strict sense who do not bring strategic assets into the firm. They are, for example, ordinary investors, unskilled workers or unskilled contractors.

1.5. Main results and outline of the chapter

Considering the notions of cognitive and structural SC, a contractarian approach to CSR and the distinction between strong and weak stakeholders, we develop a model that yields three main results.

1. The level of cognitive SC, in terms of the generic community or society-wide disposition to comply with fair social norms, plays a key role in providing opportunities for the firm to agree (with strong stakeholders) on CSR principles of fairness and hence to induce incentives to comply with them with respect to all the stakeholders, especially the weak ones.
2. The explicit agreement on CSR principles and norms engenders cognitive social capital on its own. It does so by creating room for conformist preferences that exploit beliefs of mutual conformity and dispositions to conform by converting them into specific reasons to comply with an agreed principle of CSR. Moreover, the agreement on CSR principles of fairness by itself (through framing effects and default reasoning) positively affects beliefs about reciprocal conformity on the part of the firm and its strong stakeholders.
3. The level of cognitive social capital (both beliefs and dispositions) and the decision to adopt CSR principles and norms (that translates the former into conformist preferences) generate structural social capital understood as long-term cooperative relationships between the firm and its stakeholders, even though, on considering the material payoffs characterizing the single relationships, the firm would have no incentive to cooperate with weak stakeholders. We show that strong stakeholders endowed with high cognitive social capital, which start cooperating with a firm that adopts a CSR standard, have an interest in punishing the firm if it is not cooperative with weak stakeholders. The sanction may induce the firm to cooperate with weak stakeholders as well, and it generates cooperative networks that would not be sustainable without the power of the sanction.

The second section presents the analytical framework used to study the networks of relations between firms and stakeholders. It analyzes these relations by considering Prisoners' Dilemmas (with respect to the relationship between the firm and weak stakeholders) and an enlarged version of the Trust Game (the relationship between the firm and strong stakeholders), and also illustrates a basic flaw in this literature on social capital. The third section considers the possibility that agents are not motivated exclusively by material payoffs (the idea of conformist preferences is introduced) and reinterprets the relationship between the firm and its strong stakeholders by introducing a psychological game with its psychological payoffs and equilibria. This section illustrates the role of cognitive social capital in affecting the psychological payoff of the firm and of strong stakeholders.

Section four shows how cognitive social capital (in terms of disposition), agreed CSR principles and learning from iterated games played in the network affect the strong stakeholder's strategy in interacting with the firm. Discussed in particular is the effect of CSR and of the firm's behavior in repeated games with its weak stakeholders on strong stakeholders' belief formation and strategy. It is argued that cooperation in the network is supported by cognitive social capital. The fifth section analytically presents the mechanism behind the formation of the firm's and strong stakeholders' beliefs and the strategies determined by how iterated games involving the firm and all its stakeholders in the network are played. Thus, repeated strategies are defined that induce cooperation and the endogenous sanctioning of 'defection' and 'unfair behavior'. Section six verifies that the strategies inducing cooperation in all the games the firm plays with its stakeholders satisfy a condition of sustainability and stability in the psychological game played by the firm and its strong stakeholders, this being seen as a stage sub-game in the entire iterated interaction among all the participants in the network. Herein resides the chapter's main result: the demonstration that, due to conformist preference and psychological payoffs (i.e. the way in which the model depicts the players' cognitive social capital) cooperative behavior throughout the entire network (namely the emergence of structural social capital) is a sub-game perfect equilibrium due to the stage-game equilibria of the psychological game, wherein strong stakeholders have the proper incentive to punish the firm's deviations from a strategy of multilateral cooperation. Section seven identifies and verifies the conditions guaranteeing that the multilateral cooperative strategy played by the firm in the repeated games with each of its stakeholders satisfies the condition for the existence of repeated games' Nash equilibria. In accordance with standard treatments of repeated games, it is shown that, when cognitive social capital is sufficiently high and beliefs are coherent with the cooperative equilibrium in the psychological game, for reasonable values of the firm's discount factors δ, the firm will cooperate also with weak stakeholders in order to continue its cooperation with strong stakeholders. Section eight concludes.

2. A relational network involving the firm and its (strong and weak) stakeholders

2.1. The analytical framework

We will analyze the relational networks between firms and stakeholders by using the analytical framework suggested by Lippert and Spagnolo (2010) (hereafter L&S), which is summarized here for the reader's convenience (see also Lippert 2010, *infra*). L&S study relational networks in order to investigate the power of sanctions and networks' equilibrium conditions under different configurations and information transmission technologies.

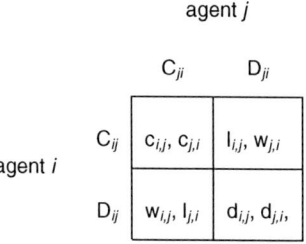

Figure 7.1 Generalized form of the PDs played by pairs of players located at any adjacent node of the network

Consider a set $N = \{1, \ldots, n\}$ of infinitely lived agents $i \in N$. The agents can interact in pairs according to a connection structure C of two element subsets of N. C_i is the set of connections that characterizes agent i. In each period t, the agents that are connected play a Prisoner's Dilemma (PD) with payoffs given by the matrix of Figure 7.1. The payoff structure is: $l_{i,j} < d_{i,j} < c_{i,j} < w_{i,j}$ and $l_{i,j} + w_{i,j} < 2c_{i,j}$, $\forall i,j \in N$, $i \neq j$ and the stage-game is assumed to be constant over time. The payoffs imply the static Nash equilibrium $(D_{i,j}, D_{j,i})$. Agents are assumed to interact repeatedly, time is discrete, all agents are assumed to have a discount factor $\delta < 1$,[7] agents are assumed to aim at maximizing their discounted utility.

According to L&S's definition, two agents share a relation (R) if they repeatedly play (C_{ij}, C_{ji}). Individual gains are defined by means of the following notation: g_{ij} is the net expected discounted gain of agent i from the relation with player j and it is the difference between the discounted payoff that agent i gets by playing $(C_{i,j}, C_{j,i})$ forever and defecting and starting to play the static Nash equilibrium $(D_{i,j}, D_{j,i})$ thereafter:

$$g_{ij} \equiv c_{i,j} - (1 - \delta)w_{i,j} - \delta d_{i,j}$$

A relation of player i with player j in which $g_{ij} < 0$ is called a 'deficient relation' for player i; a relation of player i with player j in which $g_{ij} \geq 0$ is called 'non-deficient' for player i; a relation between i and j is called 'mutual' *iff* $g_{ij} \geq 0$ and $g_{ji} \geq 0$; it is called 'unilateral' *iff* either $g_{ij} < 0$ and $g_{ji} \geq 0$ or $g_{ij} \geq 0$ and $g_{ji} < 0$; and it is called 'bilaterally deficient' *iff* $g_{ij} < 0$ and $g_{ji} < 0$.

A graphical representation of the possible kinds of relations between i and j according to the value of g_{ij} is as follows:

- an incoming arrow to player i represents a non-deficient relation for player i (i.e. $g_{ij} \geq 0$)
- an outgoing arrow from player i represents a deficient relation for player i (i.e. $g_{ij} < 0$).

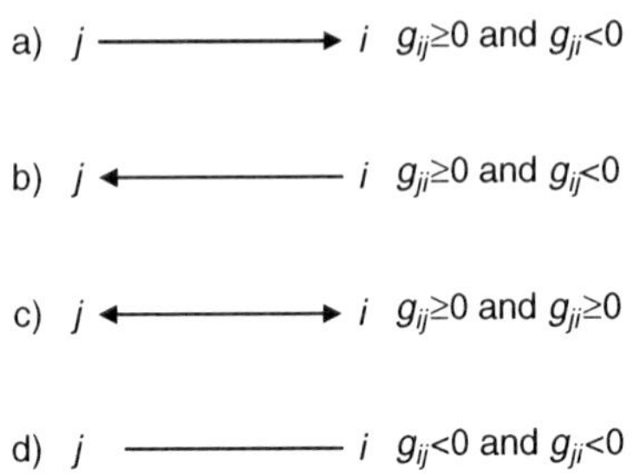

a) j $\longrightarrow$ i $g_{ij} \geq 0$ and $g_{ji} < 0$

b) j $\longleftarrow$ i $g_{ji} \geq 0$ and $g_{ij} < 0$

c) j $\longleftrightarrow$ i $g_{ij} \geq 0$ and $g_{ji} \geq 0$

d) j $\longrightarrow$ i $g_{ij} < 0$ and $g_{ji} < 0$

Figure 7.2   Graphical representation of relations

According to the above definition, Figures 7.2a) and b) depict unilateral relations. Figure 7.2c) depicts a mutual relation and Figure 7.2d) depicts a bilaterally deficient relation.

Lippert and Spagnolo (2010) start from this framework to analyze the sustainability of different network configurations under three information transmission mechanisms (Perfect Information Transmission, No Information Transmission, Network Information Transmission) and considering two types of multilateral strategy: multilateral grim trigger strategies and multilateral repentance strategies.

We focus our analysis on the situation under perfect information transmission considered by L&S. Under Perfect Information Transmission every player observes the actions taken by any other player in the network.[8] It can be shown that a sustainable strategy profile for the network is the adoption by every agent of the MG trigger strategy:

Every player $i \in N^s$

1. starts playing $C_{ij} \ \forall j \in R_i$,
2. continues playing $C_{ij} \ \forall j \in R_i$ as long as s/he observes $C_{mn} \ \forall m, n \in N^s$ and
3. reverts to $D_{ij} \ \forall j \in R_i$ forever otherwise.

The resulting relational network is sustainable if each player prefers to cooperate with all his/her neighbors rather than deviating from playing cooperatively with regard to any subgroup of them and facing retaliation from all neighbors. If a player decides to deviate from his/her relations with any subgroup of his/her neighbors, s/he faces retaliation from all neighbors and can thus just as well (and should optimally) deviate from all his/her relations. In terms of net gains from cooperation this result can be expressed as follows:

Under Perfect Information Transmission (I1), a relational network is sustainable if and only if $\sum_{j \in R_i} g_{ij} \geq 0 \ \forall i \in N^s$

The following Table 7.1 summarizes the basic notation used throughout the chapter.

Table 7.1 Basic notation used throughout the chapter

E	Firm – Enterprise	e; ¬e	Enter, non-enter strategy in the PG (strategy which may be played by S_S)
S_S	Firm's strong stakeholders	PD_{Ej}	Prisoner's Dilemma(s) played in the network connecting the firm E with its weak stakeholder S_{Wj} where $j = 1, 2$
S_{Wj}	Firm's weak stakeholder j	C_{Ej}	E's Cooperative strategy in the PDs
PG	Psychological Game involving the firm and its strong stakeholders	D_{Ej}	E's Non-Cooperative strategy in the PDs
U	Collusive strategy of S_S in the PG inducing an Unfair treatment	T	CSR ideal principle with which agents endowed with conformist preferences want to conform
F	The S_S's Fair strategy in the PG	λ	Exogenous parameter representing the disposition to conform with the ideal principle T
F_E	The E's Fair strategy in the PG		
U_E	The E's collusive Unfair strategy in the PG		

2.2. Modeling the network linking the firm and its stakeholders

The above analytical framework is used in this section to model the relationship of the firm with its weak and strong stakeholders. Consider the relational network of Figure 7.3.[9]

A strong stakeholder (S_S), locked by mutually dependent specific investments into the transaction carried out in cooperation with the firm, and the firm ('enterprise' E) are connected by a mutual not deficient relation, while the firm E has also unilaterally deficient relations with two categories of weak stakeholders (S_{W1}; S_{W2}) that, in turn, have relations with other members of the social network. To give a specific example of the network, we may imagine that: S_{W2} are employees in a plant owned by the Multinational

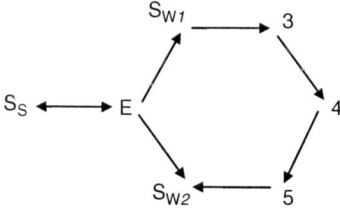

Figure 7.3 A relational network including the firm and its stakeholders

Enterprise E in a poor developing country, where E has relocated mature productive processes for some of the items that it traditionally supplies to the global market, whereas S_{W1} is the first firm in the international supply chain furnishing components that E continues to assemble in the old plant at its headquarters located in a rich developed country. S_S may consist of high-skilled core employees at the headquarters belonging to the same local community as E's managers, well unionized and endowed with some threat power, or pension funds holding a significant share in E. Agent 3 is a second-order supplier firm (located in a developing country) within E's supply-chain (i.e. a supplier firm to E's direct supplier), agent 4 represents firm 3's employees (assumed to be better paid than S_{W2}), and agent 5 represents the developing country's retailers whose best customers are the workers belonging to 3 (whereas they are less interested in satisfying demand by S_{W2}, who are too poor to be commercially attractive).

The games involving the firm and its weak stakeholders

We start the analysis of the network by focusing on the relationship between the firm and the two weak stakeholders. According to our definition of weak stakeholders, we suppose that each S_{Wj} (for $j = 1, 2$) makes an effort to become unique to E by investing idiosyncratically in their human capital and dedicated technologies and processes, in order to increase their value to E. However, E still considers each S_{Wj} replaceable, because its main reason for relocating and having this foreign supply chain is to cut labor costs, wages etc. Each S_{Wj} wants to maintain the cooperative relation with E, while E is not symmetrically interested in continuous cooperative relations with any of them, and seriously considers the short-term convenience of breaching, at any time, labor and supply chain contracts in order to relocate its plants elsewhere (where wages are even lower), or recruiting new suppliers offering components at even lower prices. Note that not cooperating does not imply for the firm the complete severing of any connection with S_{Wj}. It may merely take the form of maintaining a network of not truly cooperative relations within which E tries to expropriate opportunistically all the surplus that S_{W1} and S_{W2} may expect as the equitable remuneration of their investments. Hence, in our model, E taking all the surplus amounts to a continuing network in which E acts uncooperatively toward S_{Wj}.

To put the relation between the firm and each weak stakeholder in formal terms, we assume that they play iterated Prisoner's Dilemma Games (hereafter also PDs). The firm may cooperate or not cooperate in the PDs with weak stakeholders where:

A. cooperating means E underwriting a long-term contract including guarantees reassuring each S_{Wj} about his/her appropriation of a reasonably equitable part of the surplus generated;

B. not cooperating means E threatening to breach short-term supply chain contracts or incomplete labor contracts in order to extract all the surplus from S_{wj}.

We assume that the discount rate δ_E that allows E to appreciate the long-term mutual benefits produced by S_{wj} specific investments in term of increasing returns is not high enough to counterbalance the short-term incentive to appropriate all the surplus, which depends on the strategic possibility of keeping salaries and prices paid to the developing country's workers and supply-chain firms very low (note that in any repeated Prisoners' Dilemma there are many possible equilibria and some of them allow substantial exploitation of one player over the other).

Finally, according to our approach, even though each S_{wj} would like to cooperate with the firm in the PDs, they also have some defection capability (it is for this reason that we model the relationship using PDs). Weak stakeholders, S_{wj}, are assumed to be able to defect (and retaliate against the firm) by using the only weapon available to them: maintaining low effort and poor quality of the goods and services provided as long as E has imperfect monitoring ability on their actions.

The game involving the firm and its strong stakeholder

The relationship established by E with S_S comprises various elements which, as we shall see, make a modified version of the Trust Game suitable for its formalization. Specific investments are assumed to be symmetrical and mutually dependent between the firm and strong stakeholders. E (S_S) specific investment depends for realization of its value on maintenance of the cooperative relation with S_S (E). Essentially, strong stakeholders depend for their welfare on the continuity of the cooperative relation with E but, vice versa, E depends on their cooperation for its continuing existence. This does not mean that they lack an exit strategy that interrupts or reduces the rate of cooperation, or a strategy that enables free riding on the other party's cooperative effort. In fact, a key feature of the game is that S_S may choose to stay out of the interaction with E if s/he does not trust E enough to play a cooperative strategy with it. Nevertheless, continuing cooperation in this case far outweighs the discounted value of resorting to these defect strategies.

On this interpretation it is quite natural to suppose that S_S, as far as his/her material payoff is concerned, may collude with enterprise E in order to appropriate all the surplus generated by the set of specific investments made in relation to the firm. Interpretatively, we may assume that these are made by both strong and weak stakeholders, although continuous cooperation with the latter is less essential to the firm than with the former (so that expropriation of weak stakeholders may be preferred by the firm). On the other hand, both types of stakeholder depend on the firm in order to realize their investments.

In order to capture this key point of our analysis, we modeled the relationship between strong stakeholders and the firm by considering a game with two active players, S_S and E, and a dummy player that ideally represents the category of weak stakeholders (S_W) affected by interaction involving the two active players. This entails that S_S and E may decide either to collude so that no resources are invested (or reserved) in order to improve the cooperation with weak stakeholders in the games that the firm will play with them in the remaining part of the network, or to treat them according to equitable terms. This means allocating part of an existing surplus for the purpose of increasing weak stakeholders' payoffs to an equitable distribution in the games that they will play with the firm in further parts of the network. We will see that the effective implementation of this decision – if it has been taken at this stage – can be interpreted as depending on a cooperative decision by the firm in the ensuing games. For the moment, however, we maintain that if this decision is taken by S_S and E, it generates payoffs also for weak stakeholders (the best interpretation is that S_{Wj} payoffs are *saved* to be given to them in the ensuing games). Here, therefore, weak stakeholders are taken as dummy players because at this stage they can only be subject to the effects of the firm and strong stakeholder's interaction, without having any voice in it. They will become active players only later, when they participate in games where they interact directly with the firm at further nodes of the relational network. Technically, this means that – with reference to the network of games in Figure 7.3 – the game played by E and S_S is different in form from games played by E and any S_{Wj} later in the network. Figure 7.4 illustrates this game in extensive form. The normal form corresponding to the extensive Trust Game is given by Figure 7.5.

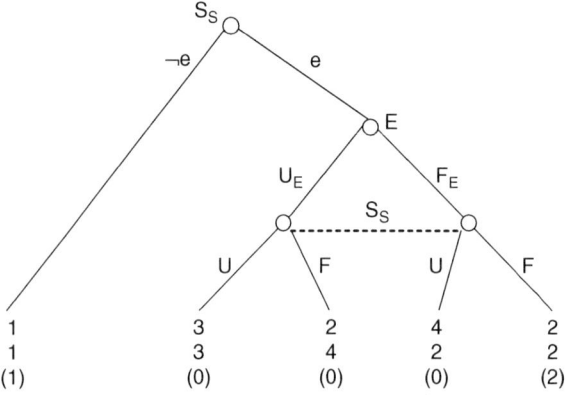

Figure 7.4 The stage-game played by the firm E and its strong stakeholder S_S – Extensive form

E

		F_E	U_E
	e, F	2, 2, (2)	2, 4, (0)
S_S	e, U	4, 2, (0)	3, 3, (0)
	¬e	1, 1, (1)	1, 1, (1)

Figure 7.5 The stage-game played by the firm E and its strong stakeholder S_S – Normal form

In both figures, the dummy player's payoffs are reported within brackets and represent the share of a total surplus that active players refrain from appropriating so that they can pay equitable wages or prices to S_{Wj}. Thus, the dummy player's payoffs are only stakes that weak stakeholders hold in the firm's operation (payoffs are reported within brackets and the dummy player has no strategy in the game), whereas strong stakeholders not only hold stakes in the firm but also exercise influencing power.

As said, the game considered is a modified version of the Trust Game. Before S_S plays the interaction with the firm, s/he has a move where s/he may choose to enter (e) or stay out of (¬e) the relation with E. Entering means trusting E and making a specific investment in relation to it. If S_S decides to enter into a relation with the firm, E has two possible strategies available. It may implement a collusive strategy (U_E) that allows itself and S_S to appropriate all the surplus if S_S enters and plays U as well (see payoffs (3,3,0)), or it may implement a fair division rule, F_E, that allocates a fair share to the dummy player only if S_S enters and plays F as well. This entails *saving* a share of the surplus (equal to 2) to which the weak stakeholders are entitled (see the extensive form of the game in Figure 7.4 and its normal form in Figure 7.5, where this occurs with the payoffs (2,2,2)). One-sided opportunistic behavior against S_S occurs when S_S enters and plays 'fair' (strategy F) by restraining his/her claim, but E cheats and appropriates all the residual so that nothing is left for the dummy player. In this case we say that E is abusing S_S's trust, in so far as we understand S_S's entrance, if s/he plays (e, F), as expressing his/her intention to behave equitably toward weak stakeholders. However, one-sided opportunistic behavior may also occur the other way round: S_S may claim the larger portion of the surplus while E moderates its pretensions. Without effective coordination on the pair of strategies F, we assume that the party which claims more by playing U is in fact able to reap the larger part of the surplus (consider payoffs (2,4,0) and (4,2,0)).

An important feature of this game is that by entering a collusive agreement (e, U; U_E), or acquiescing with the firm's opportunistic behavior, U_E, S_S puts the dummy player in a situation even worse than when S_S refuses to enter by ¬e. In other words, because of S_S's essential role in generating the firm's surplus and in allowing the firm's activity (for example, the key role of institutional investors), egoistic collusion involving both S_S and E, or at least S_S's acquiescence with E's opportunism, is strictly necessary for the complete expropriation of the dummy player. Hence a S_S that cares also for the dummy's welfare and is aware of E's devious strategy for getting around its candid self-restraint move, has an alternative for the pursuit of full fairness. This consists in boycotting E on behalf of the dummy's (second-best) stakes in the transaction. To exemplify a possible weak stakeholder situation, imagine a small firm which converts its productive plant so as to become a specialized supplier to a multinational enterprise. After the specific investment has been made, the multinational enterprise demands that the supply contract is changed, threatening that otherwise it will find a different supplier. This generates a situation which is worse for the supplier than the situation antecedent to the specific investment. The idea is that staying out of a relation with the firm may prevent the strong stakeholder from inducing weak stakeholders to make specific investments that will be expropriated.

The S_S-E game's equilibrium solution and the instability of GM trigger strategies

The only Nash equilibrium solution of this game is (e, U; U_E), which, moreover, is in dominant strategies. This entails that the solution of this simple two-person division game is such that both players play the collusive and egoistic strategy U. Because it is the unique equilibrium point in dominant strategies of the one-shot game, it will also be one equilibrium point of the repeated game that has this game as a stage-game. Hence, one obvious equilibrium profile of the repeated game is for S_S (after having entered) and the firm E to adopt the iterated strategy 'play U at the first stage and thereafter, no matter what the other player does'. In the interpretive context adopted here, this solution amounts to socially irresponsible conduct by the firm with respect to weak stakeholders, while a collusive agreement is reached with the strong one (for example, unions or pension funds).

The unique equilibrium in dominant strategies clarifies the extent to which this modified version of the Trust Game (TG) differs from the original TG, where the unique Nash equilibrium would be 'not entering' for the stakeholder. In this case, staying out is not the S_S's best response, because 'abuse' is at the expense of a third party, the weak stakeholder. In the original TG, staying out is a credible threat that the trustor may implement by means of a repeated game equilibrium strategy, if s/he believes that the trustee will play the dominant strategy of the one-shot game, since it is also part of the unique Nash equilibrium of the stage-game. This is not the case here, because staying out is the worst payoff to S_S, and would not be a credible move that a S_S motivated to care also about S_{Wj}'s well-being could make in order to deter adoption of a collusive unfair strategy by E.

Note that on this point our analysis significantly differs from that conducted by L&S (see Lippert and Spagnolo 2010). But it also highlights a problem inherent to the analytical framework of relational networks. L&S consider a network like the one described in Figure 7.3 but in which all the players' relations (including the relation between S_S and E) are modeled as iterated PDs. They state that, under perfect information and assuming that all players adopt the MG trigger strategy, a network of this kind would be sustainable (in the sense that all the players would cooperate with each other) because of the threat of endogenous sanction against defectors implicit in the structure of MG trigger strategies. We raise a basic objection against this approach: why should player S_S implement the sanction (by stopping his/her cooperation with E) if s/he learns that the E has defected against other players in the network? Since the cooperative relation between S_S and E is mutual, and given that no other player can sanction S_S if s/he deviates from his/her MG trigger strategy, there are no endogenous material incentives for S_S to sanction E if E defects with the weak stakeholders. It seems that the MG trigger strategy would require player S_S to behave contrary to rationality, so that the sanctioning behavior implicit in player S_S's MG trigger strategy is an ineffectual threat to player E, and would be unable to prevent it from 'defecting' with its weak stakeholders.

The game we have introduced to model the S_S – E relationship is explicitly intended to show even more clearly the instability of the MG trigger strategy in the case of a deviation from cooperation. This problem, in fact, would entail elimination of the equilibrium based on the MG trigger strategies played by all the network participants as a sub-game imperfect equilibrium (specifically, imperfection would result within the overall dynamic game constituted by the repeated games that any pair of adjacent agents plays in the network, from the irrationality of the behavior required in the sub-game played by E and S_S in Figure 7.3).

We shall discuss this point by showing how the game specified in the previous subsection enables us to introduce a psychological game PG, which in its turn will make it possible to formalize player S_S's and E's MG trigger strategy in a way that evades this instability (equilibrium imperfection) problem. This amounts to showing that cognitive social capital and the adoption of CSR principles – which we will characterize in terms of the elements of the PG game – generate endogenous incentives for S_S to punish the firm if it defects against the weak stakeholders.

3. A psychological game

3.1. Conformist preferences

Our assumption is that the game played by the E and S_S described in the previous section (see Figure 7.4 and Figure 7.5) is only the basis, in terms of *game form* and *material* payoffs, for introducing the psychological game PG played by active players (the firm E and its strong stakeholder S_S) endowed with the cognitive social capital that we associate with the concept of conformist preferences (Grimalda and Sacconi 2005, 2007; Sacconi 2007a; Sacconi and Faillo 2010). A psychological game results directly from the former simply by adding the assumption that the players' payoffs are defined in terms of psychological utility functions (see Geanakoplos et al. 1989; Rabin 1993). Our specification of the psychological game is based on the idea of conformist preferences.

According to the conformist preferences model, agents have preferences that are defined over states of affairs described as sets of interdependent actions characterized in terms of their degree of consistency with a given abstract principle or ideal. Essentially, the model of conformist preferences is based on the idea that agents are motivated not only by material incentives, but also by the desire to conform with some ideal principle, which in the original model (proposed by Grimalda and Sacconi 2005, 2007) is a normative principle of welfare distribution, given the players' belief in others players' conformity.

The utility function of a generic agent i characterized by conformist preferences is

$$V_i = U_i(\sigma) + \lambda_i F[T(\sigma)]$$

where the first term $U_i(\sigma)$ is the material utility obtained by agent i in state σ. The second term, $\lambda_i F[T(\sigma)]$ is the agent's ideal utility and represents conformist preferences reflecting the agent's concern for reasons to act different from the traditional consequentialist ones. Essentially, these reasons amount to a desire to conform with a normative principle T, which is believed to be reciprocally conformed with – up to some level – by the agent itself and by the other agents participating in the same interaction through the production (by means of the agents' behaviors) of the social state of affairs σ.

First, the ideal principle T represents the principle on which agents agree in a pre-play communication stage under the 'veil of ignorance'. In our analysis it represents the CSR principle on which the firm and stakeholders agree from a position of impartiality and which makes explicit the firm's commitments in terms of fiduciary duties toward all its stakeholders. In general, the formal specification of T, intended to express the agreed criterion of fair distribution among all the players (irrespectively of their strong or weak positions), is given by the Nash bargaining solution (Nash 1950), also called the Nash social welfare function N:

$$T(\sigma) = N(U_{1,\ldots,}U_n) = \prod_{i=1}^{n}(U_i - d_i)$$

where d_i stands for the reservation utility that player i can obtain when the bargaining process collapses. Note that the status quo payoffs reflect the hypothesis that the agreement is signed under the symmetric position engendered by a 'veil of ignorance'.

Second, the weight λ_i (a positive number), is an exogenous parameter representing the maximum possible magnitude of the disposition to conform with the ideal principle T. The intensity of the motivation to conform with the principle T for agent i is then related to the value of λ_i. The higher λ_i is, the more agent i will be disposed to conform with the principle T, granted that it has been agreed and that agent i believes that the others will conform with the same principle. The parameter λ_i represents a component of cognitive social capital defined in terms of a generic disposition to conform with shared or agreed social norms, and is taken to be an endowment of cognitive social capital (meaning disposition) that agent i inherits from his/her social environment (it can also be considered a biological trait fixed through evolution).

Third, the function F captures the effects on ideal utility of beliefs about the degree of reciprocal conformity with the ideal exhibited by the agent him/herself and other agents. F therefore expresses the component of our idea of cognitive social capital understood as a system of mutual beliefs on the degree of norm compliance exhibited by a given state of affairs (strategy combination) of the game. Following Grimalda and Sacconi (2005), we adopt a specification for F based on the hypothesis that each agent has a measure of his/her own conformity with the principle T, given what s/he believes about other agents, and that at the same time the agent has a measure of how much other agents' are believed to reciprocate conformity, given their own beliefs.

Let us consider a two-person game. In this case, F can be specified by considering two elements:[10]

1. $1 + f_i$: the index of player's i conditional conformity. The value of f_i depends on the extent to which player i contributes to fulfilling the ideal T with his/her actions (i.e. by conforming with or deviating from the ideal), given what s/he believes about the other player's choice.
2. $1 + \tilde{f}_j$: the index of player's j expected reciprocity in conformity, or the esteem that player i forms concerning j's compliance with the ideal T. The value of $\tilde{f}_j$ depends on the extent to which the other player contributes to fulfilling the ideal T with his/her actions (i.e. by conforming

with or deviating from the ideal T), given what the second player believes (and the first player believes that the second player believes) that the first player will do.

Both f_i and $\tilde{f}_j$ assume values from 0 to -1, so that they represent degrees of deviation from the best possible conformity with the principle T given the other player's (believed) action. Hence the overall utility function of agent i characterized by conformist preferences may be written thus (for more details see Appendix I):

$$V_i(\sigma_i, b_i^1, b_i^2) = U_i(\sigma_i, b_i^1) + \lambda_i[1 + \tilde{f}_j(b_i^1, b_i^2)][1 + f_i(\sigma_i, b_i^1)]$$

where b_i^1 is the first-order belief that player i has in the action of player j; b_i^2 is the second-order belief about player j's belief in the action adopted by player i.

It is clear that both conditional conformity and beliefs on reciprocal conformity as captured by the function F, and disposition to conform as represented by λ, play a key role in generating the (ideal) utility of player i. The ideal component of the utility function works as follows.

a) If i fully conforms with the principle T and believes that j will fully conform as well, then i's ideal utility will be:

$$\lambda_i \times 1 \times 1 = \lambda_i$$

that is, the maximum possible value of ideal utility.

b) If i does not fully conform and believes that neither will j fully conform, the value of the ideal utility will be lower than λ_i:

$$(1 - x)(1 - y)\lambda_i < \lambda_i$$

c) Finally, if the conformity of at least one of the two agents is believed to be zero, then the ideal utility obtained by agent i goes to zero:

$$(1 - 1)(1 - y)\lambda_i = 0$$

The ideal principle T, mutual beliefs with regard to reciprocal conformity with the ideal principle T, and the disposition (λ) to conform with T, given such beliefs, are the components of our notion of cognitive social capital and they collapse into the value of ideal utility that the conformist agent may obtain for each give state of affairs. Hence conformist preferences equate to our definition of cognitive social capital.

As we have already noted, the disposition λ is generated by both micro and macro factors. It is connected with psychological and genetic factors that affect the disposition of each individual, and it is affected by basic social norms and cultural traits shared in the community where the agents live in a broad sense. These social norms are more general than the principle T, which is a principle on which agents may agree with reference to a definite domain of interactions or an organization. Thus, while T is an endogenous variable determined by the players' interaction, normally engendered by their pre-play communication (agreement), λ is a contextual variable that affects the magnitude or motivational force of conformist reasons to act as they are represented by the functional F of the principle T.

3.2. A CSR principle at the basis of conformist preferences

We assume that players with conformist preferences are involved in a psychological game PG based on the modified version of the Trust Game described in Figure 7.4. Hence, they will evaluate strategy combinations in terms of a fairness (CSR) principle T to which they have agreed in a pre-play communication stage of the game and whereby they make an impartial distributive justice-based assessment of the division problem that they have to solve in the game. The distributive (CSR) principle T is modeled as the Nash bargaining solution (NBS) of a three-person bargaining situation involving players E, S_S and a representative agent S_{Wj} – that is, simply maximizing the product of players' payoffs net of the status quo. The NBS is a natural result of the assumption that E, S_S and S_{Wj} reach agreement on a distributive principle relative to the division of the surplus at stake in PG. It is not necessary that this bargaining game be taken as a game actually played. What is required is that in a pre-play communication stage the players reason 'as if' they could carry out such an agreement under the hypothesis that they cannot (or do not want to) identify with any particular player's role in the subsequent PG effectively played. Thus, in this 'counterfactual stage', they may take all the roles in the game PG to be symmetrically interchangeable.[11] For this reason, we set the status quo at (0,0,0), so that all the players consider the not-fair agreement option from the point of view of the worst-off player, who would get nil if there was no impartial agreement on the surplus division. We thus express the idea that a fair agreement on the principle T *must* include all the players, and if one player gains nil from the agreement, 'behind the veil of ignorance' this amounts to not agreeing at all. Hence the two-side egoistic collusive strategy pair (U; U_E), or the one-side egoistic strategy U played against a fair cooperator, both signal absence of reference to any three-person equitable agreement in playing the game. This also enables the strategy ¬e to play a role in the solution, since with respect to the worst case of no distribution at all the stay-out option with payoffs (1,1,1) could also be considered a possible improvement reachable by agreement. Considering the payoff matrix reported in Figure 7.5, the decreasing ordering of the game states assessed according to the principle T – namely, by taking the Nash bargaining product of the payoffs corresponding to the relevant states of the game – is

1. $T(e, F; F_E) = 8$,
2. $T(\neg e; U_E) = 1$, as well as $T(\neg e; F_E) = 1$,
3. $T(e, U; U_E) = 0$, $T(e, F; U_E) = 0$, $T(e, U; F_E) = 0$.

where the last line identifies states of non-equitable agreement that are no better than the status quo. Note that this ordering states, as previously discussed, that S_S's staying out entails a higher level of distributive fairness in terms of Nash product than if s/he enters and acquiesces with E's collusive offer or its opportunistic endeavor to exploit S_S's fairness in order to appropriate the entire surplus.

The two active players' agreement on a principle of fair treatment including both strong and weak stakeholders amounts, in this context, to subscription by the firm to a social contract on their fair treatment – which is the core idea of CSR as we understand it. Moreover, for both the firm E and the S_S the 'fairness' strategy corresponds to 'walk the talk' behavior with respect to the commitment announced in the CSR norm (i.e. a code of ethics), while the 'stay out' strategy is similar to a boycotting strategy that the active strong stakeholder may (and in real life in fact does) carry out to punish companies that do not comply with the CSR commitments that they have *ex ante* enunciated. These intuitions are reflected by the maximum T value assigned to the pair of strategies (e, F; F_E), and the intermediate T value associated with the states where S_S decides to stay out, i.e. (¬e; U), (¬e; F).

However, it might be asked why the firm E and the strong stakeholder S_S should enter an agreement on the CSR principle T; and in particular what incentive E would have to do so. This question is important because – as we shall see in the next sections – in the psychological game PG that takes place after players agree on the CSR principle T, the player E will be induced not to abuse S_{Wj} and, consequently, to give up part of its material payoff. One could simply assume that the firm E has a value system and a corporate culture whose principles are shared by strong stakeholders and are summarized by T. Yet in the economic theory of the firm, 'corporate culture' is a solution for the need to acquire reputation in a context of incompleteness of contracts and unforeseen contingencies structured as a TG (Kreps 1990). In a context of this kind, the very existence of definite commitments and types functional to reputation accumulation cannot be assumed without the introduction of general and abstract principles of ethics which define, albeit with a margin of vagueness, what has to be done under unforeseen contingencies (Sacconi 2000, 2010a). In this case, the firm E must at least convince the strong stakeholders to enter the relation with it. Hence, the firm must reach an agreement with strong stakeholders on general principles of fair treatment that may be employed to accumulate a reputation at least in the relation with S_S. Of course, one may say that in the one-shot modified TG the firm E knows that there is a unique Nash equilibrium which entails collusion with S_S, so that E does not need any particular reputation to be able to reach such a collusive agreement with S_S. But this is not the case in the repeated game, where equilibria are necessarily multiple, and where, moreover, the commitments attached to any equilibrium strategy cannot be specified in a situation of unforeseen contingencies without recourse to general, abstract, albeit vague, principles of corporate culture. Our hypothesis is that when the firm E endeavors to devise an acceptable agreement on general and abstract principles that must concern the division of a sum among all the three payers, the very nature of the logical exercise of formulating such principles requires it to universalize the principle of fair treatment, and hence to have exercise of the agreement cover also the weak stakeholders (who, in fact, have no real power in the game). This amounts to saying that the agreement is reached under the veil of ignorance by active players considering the equally probable possibility of their also being in the position of the weak stakeholder. Under this hypothesis we know that the resulting agreement falls on the egalitarian solution or symmetrical NBS, as a direct consequence of impartiality when the outcome space is restricted to the equilibrium set of the repeated game (Binmore 2005, Sacconi 2010b). Besides, in the theoretical literature, this result is also supported by empirical evidence on the collective choices reached by active players involved in a division problem similar to the one considered here. It has been shown that, when active players are asked to agree on a rule of division behind a veil of ignorance concerning the role that they may assume in playing the game effectively – that is, they are faced with the possibility of occupying the dummy player's position as well – they quite directly agree on the egalitarian rule of division.

To conclude, the assumption concerning λ may also play a role, albeit an indirect one, in explaining how E or S_S can agree on the CSR principle *T*. In a context of social norms and culture wherein the presence of a high disposition to conformity (i.e. λ is high) is common knowledge, even agreeing on non-binding CSR principles with stakeholders through pre-play communication can be considered anything but 'cheap talk'. In fact, this parameter makes it possible for conformist preferences to be formed that impinge on the players' payoff function to an extent sufficient to change the possible results of the game (of course, this could also be considered a good strategic reason for a self-interested firm not to agree at all, one to be traded off against the signal that this decision would send to stakeholders about its lack of intention to develop a reputation).

3.3. The psychological game (PG) and the ideal payoffs of players E and S_S

The previous section linked the game played by E and S_S to a basic component of the conformist preferences model: agreement on the principle T. However, a full description of the relevant PG game requires specification of the psychological payoffs associated with any pair of strategies. The overall utility function given in section 3.1 shows that players attach a motivational force (able to drive their practical behavior) to something akin to 'conformity with the principle concern' – intuitively a 'deontological' motive to act – which amounts at most to a utility weight λ. This represents the maximal force of the disposition to act in conformity with the fairness principle that can counteract self-referred motives to act represented by material payoffs.

Moreover, the strength of this disposition to act in conformity with a given principle (in our case the CSR principle that implies fair behavior by the firm toward all its stakeholders) is conditional upon beliefs that the players entertain about their reciprocal conformity with the principle. The functional F represents what a player deems to be the overall degree of conformity as based on the combination of the two personal indexes of conformity attached to players' decisions in relation to the principle. Taking S_S's perspective, these indexes state:

(i) the extent to which S_S conceives him/herself to be conforming by choosing any particular strategy, given his/her belief about E's strategy choice, and

(ii) the extent to which S_S thinks player E conforms by means of any particular strategy that s/he believes E may choose, given S_S's second-order beliefs about E's belief in S_S's choice.

Recall that the values of the two conformity indexes result from the subtraction of a deviation measure ranging between 0 (no deviation at all from the principle) and -1 (complete deviation) from the unit (i.e. 1 means maximal conformity), and consider in turn the different possible belief systems (i.e. first- and second-order beliefs) justifying the prediction of any given outcome of the game. Then the conformity indexes attached to how players carry out each state of the game (and consequently their ideal utility) may be computed with reference to the basic game form given in Figures 7.4 and 7.5, keeping track of the T values computed for each strategy combination given in section 3.2.[12] Let us start by considering the ideal utility to be added to the material payoff of player S_S because of his/her conditional conformity index and the expected reciprocal conformity index of the firm, namely $1 + f_{SS}\left(\sigma_{SS}, b_{SS}^1\right)$ and $1 + \tilde{f}_E\left(b_{SS}^1, b_{SS}^2\right)$, as they are specified at each possible state of the game. Consider first the strategy $\sigma_{SS} = (e, F)$ of player S_S, given his/her first-order belief that E plays F, $(b_{S_S}^1 = F_E)$, and his/her second-order belief that E believes that S_S plays (e, F), $(b_{S_S}^2 = (e, F))$. The index of conditional deviation of player S_S (note that symbol | means 'given') is

$$\frac{T(e, F|F_E) - T^{\text{MAX}}(F_E)}{T^{\text{MAX}}(F_E) - T^{\text{MIN}}(F_E)} = \frac{T(e, F|F_E) - T(e, F|F_E)}{T(e, F|F_E) - T(e, U|F_E)} = 0,$$

In fact, given that E plays 'fair' F_E, for S_S by responding with (e, F) the best T value is attainable, which entails a conditional conformity index $1 + f_{S_S}(e, F; F_E) = 1$. For the same strategy pair, by symmetrical reasons, the expected reciprocal deviation of player E is

$$\frac{T(F_E|e, F) - T^{\text{MAX}}(e, F)}{T^{\text{MAX}}(e, F) - T^{\text{MIN}}(e, F)} = \frac{T(F_E|e, F) - T(F_E|e, F)}{T(F_E|e, F) - T(U_E|e, F)} = 0$$

which entails that the expected reciprocal conformity index of player E is $1 + f_E(F_E; e, F) = 1$. Thus the ideal utility of player S_S for this strategy combination is the full weight λ (namely, $1 \times 1 \times \lambda$).

By the same method, S_S's conditional conformity indexes and E's expected reciprocal conformity indexes can be computed for each strategy pair, and the ideal utility of player S_S can be derived (see the appendix to this chapter for calculations). The results are the following:

- Player S_S's strategy (e, F), given his/her first-order belief that E will play U_E and his/her second-order belief that E believes that s/he will play (e, F), obtains ideal utility 0 for S_S. In fact, against a player E who unfairly plays U_E, entering and playing 'fair' by (e, F) gives the worst T value, which is equal to 0 with respect the best possible alternative of 'staying out' by ¬e, which gives a T value equal to 1. Recall that a single conformity index equal to 0 entails that ideal utility is nil.

- Player S_S's strategy (e, U), given his/her first-order belief that E will play F_E, and his/her second-order belief that E believes that s/he will play (e, U), obtains ideal utility 0 for S_S. In fact, against a player E who plays 'fair' by F_E, responding with (e, U) means selecting the worst T value, which is equal to 0, with respect to the better alternative of responding fairly by (e, F), with T value 8.

- Player S_S's strategy (e, U), given his/her first-order belief that E will play U_E and his/her second-order belief that E believes s/he will play (e, U), gives ideal utility 0 to S_S. In fact this choice entails 'collusion' with the worst T value, equal to 0, whereas responding by 'staying out' would give a better T of value 1, which is also the best, given player E's choice.

- Player S_S's strategy (¬e), given his/her first-order belief that E will play U_E and his/her second-order belief that E believes that s/he will play (¬e), gives S_S ideal utility λ. In fact, responding by (¬e) to E who plays U maximizes the T value, so that player S_S's deviation is 0. At the same time, given that player S_S 'stays out', player E cannot do any better in order to maximize T than choose one or other (indifferently) of its two strategies U_E or F_E, since both of them give a T value equal to 1, and both of them have a deviation index 0. However, if E chooses F_E, choosing ($\neg$e) would no longer induce a conformity index 1, because S_S in this case could maximize T by choosing (e, F).

- Player S_S's strategy ($\neg$e), given his/her first-order belief that E will play F_E and his/her second-order belief that E believes that s/he will play ($\neg$e), obtains ideal utility $1/8\lambda$. In this case, given that E plays 'fairly' by F_E, player S_S does not maximize the T value by 'staying out'. However, nor does s/he minimize it, since the worst T value equal to 0 would be reached if s/he played unfairly (e, U). Player S_S thus scores a high deviation index $-7/8$, and hence his/her complementary conditional conformity index is low, that is, $1/8$. On the other hand, player E, who believes that player S_S stays out, cannot do any better in order to enhance the T value than playing one or other (indifferently) of its strategies, F_E or U_E. Thus, by playing F, it obtains its maximum T value conditional on the ($\neg$e) choice by S_S. So the E's expected reciprocal conformity index is 1, which combined with $1/8$ allows only an ideal utility $1/8\lambda$ to enter player S_S's overall payoff for this state.

To sum up, the only way for S_S to be fully conformist is to 'enter' and choose 'fair' if s/he predicts that also E plays 'fair', but to stay out otherwise. This latter behavior is an important consequence of the conformist preference model: staying out of an unfair cooperative relation can induce the relative best level of conformity if the other player's 'cooperative' choice is such that acceding to such a proposal of unfair cooperation or collusion would induce a lower level of implementation of the principle T. Thus, accepting whatever level of cooperation or collusion, if it is unfair in terms of the principle T, is not supported by conformist preferences. On the contrary, a 'principled' refusal to interact can be supported by conformist preferences, which translates into an endogenous psychological incentive to punish the other party's unfair choices. On the other hand, by 'staying out' when E chooses 'fair', the strong stakeholder S_S permits only poor implementation of the principle. Finally, compliance would be nil not only if S_S colludes, but also if s/he acquiesces with E's opportunism by candidly choosing 'fair' when E is getting around its 'pure' intention by playing U_E to appropriate the entire surplus.

Thus far, things have been considered from S_S's perspective. Note, however, that player E's index of conformity and its index of expected reciprocal conformity about player S_S are derived by combining the same strategies described above. For example, E's index of conditional conformity $1+f_E\left(\sigma_E, b_E^1\right)$ is based on the identical strategic combinations taken into account by player E's expected reciprocal conformity index $1 + \tilde{f}_E\left(b_{S_S}^1, b_{S_S}^2\right)$ as seen in the eyes of player S_S – since the first-order beliefs of player S_S

consist of player E's strategies, and his/her second-order beliefs about player E's beliefs equal player E's beliefs about player S_S's strategies. Therefore, the two indexes must have the same values. Situations and payoffs, considered according to player E's or player S_S's beliefs of first and second order predicting such combinations, are perfectly symmetrical for the strategies pairs (e, F; F_E), (e, F; U_E), (e, U; F_E) and (e, U; U_E). Of course, player E does not have move e, but it is ineffectual with respect to the symmetry of the situation that occurs after player S_S's 'entrance'. Then E's indexes of conditional conformity and expected reciprocal conformity must be respectively identical to those just considered for S_S; hence the ideal payoffs must also be the same. The only situations left to consider are those that cannot be symmetrical between players E and S_S, namely ($\neg$e, F), ($\neg$e, U) – i.e. situations where E's first-order belief predicts that player S_S will choose ($\neg$e) while E's second-order belief is that S_S believes that it will choose either F or U. In these cases

- Player E's strategy F_E, given his/her first-order belief that S_S will play $\neg$e and its second-order beliefs that S_S believes that E will play F_E, obtains ideal utility equal to $1/8\lambda$. In fact, when E predicts that S_S will stay out, it cannot do any better to maximize the T value than choose either of its strategies F_E or U_E. However, what reduces overall conformity in this case is the expected reciprocal conformity of S_S, which is at the poor level of 1/8 (consider that his/her best conformity index would be associated with playing (e, F), while the worst one would be given by playing (e, U)). The result is $1 \times 1/8 \times \lambda$, which is the ideal utility that enters E's payoff for this outcome.
- Player E's strategy U_E, given his/her the first-order belief that S_S will play $\neg$e and his/her second-order belief that S_S believes that E will choose U_E, obtains the highest ideal utility λ. In fact, also in this case player E is doing as much as possible to maximize the T value, given the $\neg$e choice by S_S (since by staying out S_S frustrates any attempt by E to affect the result). But in this case this also applies to S_S, who predicts that E will in fact choose U_E, and hence rightly chooses to stay out, which makes the T value equal to 1, whereas if s/he had 'entered', that value would have been only 0 (in the case of both bilateral or unilateral collusion).

To be noted in regard to these last two points is that, symmetrically with what we said concerning the motivational force of S_S's decision to 'stay out', when S_S is commonly predicted to play $\neg$e, the individual responsibility of player E concerning the level of principle attainment is nullified. E cannot do anything about the level of T, which cannot deviate from the one determined by player S_S's decision. Since E cannot be responsible for any deviation from the level of T, conformity is intact and maximal whatever the choice of E (U_E included). This may also be understood in the sense that, by staying out, S_S prevents any deviation from conformity that might be attributable to a choice by player E, whose intentions cannot be relevant in terms of responsibility, as far as they are at all fanciful (E knows that, whatever its virtual choice, the game is over due to ¬e) and ineffective with respect to the game's outcome. In any modified TG, such as the one under consideration, ¬e entails that the game ends before E's decision node has even been reached. However, the conformity index is not a measure of a player's counterfactual intentions, but only a measure of the factual deviation due to his/her decision from the best reachable level in terms of a given standard, conditional on the other players' behavior. It takes the dictum 'ought implies can' quite seriously, and in this case player E cannot be considered responsible for any deviation from the given level of conformity with the principle T set by player S_S. A different conclusion would be admissible if E assigned a positive probability to S_S not being truly playing ¬e. But this hypothesis is not admitted under the psychological games assumption that beliefs are internally consistent with their psychological equilibria and are common knowledge among the players. Hence it is admissible for conformity indexes in these cases to assign a zero deviation to any choice by player E and hence full conformity with player E's choices. However, the case of player S_S is quite different. When player S_S predicts that player E will choose U_E at his/her decision node either because it plans to collude or because it already knows that S_S will stay out and hence feels relieved of any decisional responsibility toward T, then s/he is fully responsible for prevention of the possible effect of the predicted decision by E on T attainment. Hence, in order to conform with the principle, s/he must play ¬e. This is reflected in the best S_S conditional conformity index (or in the best expected reciprocal conformity index, as seen in the eyes of player E), which is equal to 1 for that choice by player S_S.

To sum up, in correspondence to each combination of strategies (states of the game) conditioned on a system of consistent first- and second-order beliefs (i.e. beliefs predicting exactly the state of the game under consideration), for every player we can single out the values of the conformist component of his/her utility function by computing the relevant combination of both the conformity indexes of a player.

Before continuing with discussion of the psychological equilibria resulting from integration of material payoffs with ideal utilities deriving from conformist preferences, we give some intuitive substance as to why we consider the possibility that a firm may have a positive psychological payoff from applying an ethical principle of cooperation with all its stakeholders. Here our approach is closely linked with Aoki's notion of corporate social capital (Aoki 2010, *infra*): 'Corporate social capital may not be immediately cashed in, but it may be enjoyed by various corporate stakeholders in non-pecuniary manner, e.g. the pride of employees working for a socially reputable corporation, satisfactions of environmentally-conscious stockholders from owning "green" stocks, amenities of citizens living in clean local community and the like.' λ_E may be interpreted as the psychological payoff obtained by those with residual control rights (the owner or the top management in case of public companies), who may have conformist preferences and may obtain a positive psychological payoff from adopting corporate responsible behavior.

3.4. Psychological equilibria in the PG

Given the different values of ideal utility deriving from conformist preferences, the normal form of the psychological game with conformist preferences is shown in Figure 7.6.

The generalized form of this game under the assumption that payoffs satisfy the conditions d > c > b > a, is depicted in Figure 7.7.

		E	
		F_E	U_E
	e, F	$2 + \lambda_{Ss}, 2 + \lambda_E, (2)$	2, 4, (0)
S_S	e, U	4, 2, (0)	3, 3, (0)
	¬e	$1 + 1/8\lambda_{Ss}, 1 + 1/8\lambda_E, (1)$	$1 + \lambda_{Ss}, 1 + \lambda_E, (1)$

Figure 7.6 Normal form of the PG played by S_S and E

		E	
		F_E	U_E
	e, F	$b + \lambda_{Ss}, b + \lambda_E, (b)$	b, d, (0)
S_S	e, U	d, b, (0)	c, c, (0)
	¬e	$a + k\lambda_{Ss}, a + k\lambda_E, (a)$	$a + \lambda_{Ss}, a + \lambda_E, (a)$

Figure 7.7 Normal form of the PG played by S_S and E – generalized form (where $0 \leq k \leq 1$)

It is evident from inspection of the psychological payoffs that, in general, if λ_E and λ_{Ss} are both $> d - b$ and $\lambda_{Ss} > c - a$ (with the particular specification of payoffs' parameters with which we have worked thus far, however, both conditions collapse to $\lambda > 2$), there are three Nash psychological equilibria under conformist preferences: (e, U; U$_E$), (e, F; F$_E$) and (¬e; U$_E$). Most interesting are the equilibrium strategy profiles (e, F; F$_E$) and (¬e; U$_E$). Each of these must be understood as being contingent on the respectively appropriate system of mutually consistent beliefs of first and higher order. In regard to the former, player S$_S$ must be believed to be playing (e, F) and player E must be believed to be playing F$_E$, while both of them must believe that the other has exactly these beliefs (and the consistent beliefs about beliefs). When these conditions are satisfied, the conformist payoffs reported in the upper left cell of the normal form game in Figure 7.6 are effective (because they depend on indexes of conformity contingent on exactly these beliefs), so that if λ_E and λ_{Ss} are both $> d - b$, the players' mutual best responses are (e, F) and F. This means that both players have a desire to conform with their ideal principle of justice sufficient for them to prefer forgoing a material self-interested benefit achievable through a collusive agreement in order to ensure fair treatment of the dummy player.

Because of the existence of the second equilibrium, S$_S$ must be believed to stay out and E must be believed to play U$_E$, while both of them must believe that these beliefs are also held by the counterparty and that they know what the other believes. When these beliefs are satisfied, the psychological conformist payoffs reported in the bottom right cell of Figure 7.6 are effective, so that ¬e is S$_S$'s best response to E's strategy U$_E$ (which in turn is its best response to ¬e). Note that the condition for the existence of this second equilibrium is $\lambda_{Ss} > c - a$, which is not required for λ_E. This is required only of player S$_S$ since the decision to stay out of the cooperative relation with E is his or hers alone. Intuitively, this implies that, by trading-off conformist utility with material payoffs, S$_S$ prefers to boycott E more than collude with it. Essentially, the 'sanction strategy' of strong stakeholders, which have a key role in inducing the firm to be 'fair' with weak stakeholders by respecting the CSR principles, does not require any condition on the firm's psychological payoffs, which may be 0. Consequently, even firms which are not intrinsically motivated by cognitive social capital, if they agree on CSR principles in order to induce their stakeholders to undertake optimal investments, may suffer sanctions by strong stakeholders (if the value of λ_{Ss} is high enough) and may be induced to cooperate with weak stakeholders.

Finally, a further psychological equilibrium is the old Nash equilibrium (e, U; U$_E$), which materializes when the previous conditions on beliefs systems are not fulfiled even if the conditions on λ_E and λ_{Ss} are satisfied. That is, notwithstanding the absolute potential of the disposition to act in accordance with the principle of justice, this equilibrium emerges when mutual confidence in reciprocal effective conformity breaks down. This amounts to a beliefs system such that player E neither believes that S_S is effectively compliant with the principle, so that s/he would really play strategy (e, F) if E were to choose strategy F_E, nor is confident that S_S would really play strategy ¬e if it offered collusion by strategy U_E. At the same time, S_S neither believes that E will play F_E when s/he plays (e, F) nor believes that player E is confident that s/he will really play ¬e if E plays U_E. Under these conditions of mistrust, an S_S playing ¬e would act against the systems of mutually consistent beliefs that predict (e, U; U_E) as the result, which is not admissible in terms of psychological equilibrium. In the absence of beliefs systems that justify playing one of the other two psychological equilibria, (e, U; U_E) emerges as the only psychological equilibrium, even though it is based on just material payoff.

4. Cognitive social capital and the endogenous sustainability of cooperative networks of relations

The psychological game PG played by E and S_S reveals the importance of both cognitive social capital and of CSR principles in allowing the endogenous sustainability of cooperative relations between the firm and all its stakeholders that were considered as mere possibilities – far from being effective – in networks like the one reported in Figure 7.3. In this section we set out the main result. A rigorous proof must wait for the next sections.

4.1. Cognitive social capital as conformity disposition

A high level of cognitive social capital in terms of disposition (λ) is a necessary, even if not sufficient, condition for obtaining structural social capital between the firm and all the stakeholders. If the conditions on the parameter λ are not satisfied, only the unfair or collusive equilibrium (e, U; U_E) can emerge. Referring to the distinction between bridging and bonding social capital – 'There may be high social capital within a group ("bonding" social capital) which helps members, but they may be excluded from other groups (they lack "bridging" social capital')' (Narayan 1999: 3) – we may say that the collusive equilibrium is an example of bonding social capital (between the firm and the strong stakeholders), while the fair cooperative equilibrium between the firm and its strong stakeholders is an example of bridging social capital. Sufficiency conditions for bridging social capital include both dispositions and beliefs systems. Bonding social capital obtains whenever the disposition to conform with impartial norms is insufficiently strong or when, owing to contingent conditions, expectations of mutual distrust emerge concerning reciprocity in conforming with fair and impartial norms, whereas players have consistent beliefs systems that allow them to predict collusion (which, moreover, must be a Nash equilibrium). This characterization of bridging social capital in terms of equilibrium conditions shows that, even though some of its components may be objectively determined at the level of the biological or cultural heritage of a given category of individuals, most of it is nevertheless relative and contingent on fragile conditions of social interaction among rational individuals. Beliefs systems, in particular, exhibit this contingency, for there is no absolute reason for some of them to be completely discarded so as to ensure that only the 'desired' beliefs systems emerge to support good equilibria. In fact, how could we exclude a priori that a situation of mistrust may emerge even among people with the highest disposition to conform with social norms and ethical principles?

4.2. What affects beliefs in the PG? The role of agreement

As usual, multiple equilibria (especially multiple psychological equilibria) make any prediction about the effective solution of the game depend on the availability of an equilibrium selection mechanism able to explain the formation of any given system of mutually consistent beliefs whereon equilibria are contingent. This is not a matter of brutally biological or traditionally determined cultural inheritance. On the contrary, equilibrium selection depends on fragile cognitive mechanisms of belief formation, such as how individuals reasonably react to different choice contexts and how they learn from past interactions. Far from being able to uniquely answer this problem, conformist preference theory is not completely mute about it. Recourse to the 'cognitive role' of ethical norms and distributive justice principles helps give partial predictability to the emergence of the system of beliefs required for bridging social capital to be created and the corresponding fairness equilibrium to be implemented (see Sacconi 2010c, *infra*).

Modeling the game in terms of conformist preferences entails some implicit assumptions. In particular, as already said, it amounts to assuming that, before this game is played, there must be a phase of pre-play communication (traditional game theory would rule it out as 'cheap talk', but we shall see that it is quite important in affecting the players' preferences). In this phase, players adopt the cognitive perspective of an ideal game 'under a veil of ignorance' such that they are able to agree impartially on a norm or a principle of fairness which they deem relevant to the distribution of surpluses generated in interactions like the one involving E and its stakeholders. The 'impartiality' of this point of view consists in the fact that, with ignorance of who will take *ex post* whatever role in the game (be it the role of E or the role of whichever category of stakeholders), a (CSR) principle of fair division is *ex ante* agreed upon by anonymous players in order to establish how the real life division game will be played *ex post*. This may be seen as reasoning 'as if' the players were involved in a fictitious bargaining game 'under the veil of ignorance'. But alternatively it may also be seen as simply a cognitive process of reasoning whereby players are detached from the personal perspective and their interests in the concrete situation, and simply recognize that the situation (the game) they are going to play has to be categorized as one element pertaining to a more general class of situations where a given principle or social norm of fairness is normally applied. Put differently, the situation exhibits to a significant degree the pattern or the silhouette of a category – or fuzzy membership of a set – which is normally understood as the domain of application of a given principle or norm of justice.[13]

What is distinctive in this pre-play communication stage is that in one way or another it operates as a *framing effect* on both players' motivations and beliefs. According to the motivational point of view, framing a situation as one involving a fair agreement on a principle of justice activates a motivational drive (what we may call a disposition to act in conformity with a mutually agreed principle) able to produce a specific behavior or the 'desire' to be just. The intensity of this 'desire', or the causal force of this disposition seen as a preference (which is a sort of *passe-partout* for intending whatever motive to act) is what the model captures with the parameter λ. Hence, it is because in a pre-play communication phase the situation has been assessed in terms of an impartial agreement or according to a commonly shared principle that in the 'real life' game players may frame the situation so that they feel the motivational force to act in accordance with it 'up to level' λ.

From the cognitive point of view, framing the situation as one of impartial agreement, or simply as an exemplar of a wider category to which a general abstract principle of impartial treatment applies, affects the players' beliefs. When a situation is recognized as belonging to an abstract category requiring impartial treatment, the individual reasoner proceeds *by default* to the position that there is no reason or evidence for not believing that both him/herself and the counterparts will envisage the situation in the same way. The abstract norm or principle (in our case the agreed CSR principle) defines a mental model of *the* rational agent as a typical agent that agrees on a principle and hence is (until proof to the contrary) committed to it, or as an agent who behaves as normally observed within a category of cases subsumed within the domain of a norm or principle. 'People that voluntarily agree on a principle or who understand this situation as belonging to a category identified by the validity of a norm, normally behave like that ...' – this defines a normative mental model of agent that the individual reasoner endorses under the framing effect of what we called the pre-play communication phase (see Sacconi and Faillo 2010).

There is no definitive proof that all agents will actually act according to this model. Rather, it is the simplest model of agent that follows from the fact that the situation has been framed as a situation of impartial agreement or a case belonging to a general class identified by a norm of justice. It might be said that if one freely agrees to a principle, one expresses the plan or the intention of acting according to the provisos of the agreement itself. Hence, until proof to the contrary, one may expect the rational agent to act 'normally' according to his/her free agreement. If one categorizes a situation as a case in a class subsumed under the domain of an abstract norm, the norm defines how people *normally* act within the category (or must act to stay in it) until proof to the contrary. Hence, one has a mental model of how people normally behave (or normally *should* behave to satisfy the premise of an impartial agreement or consistency with the normative statement of a norm) under the current categorization, until proof to the contrary.

Admittedly, all these are just *default* inferences, valid under *caveats* such as 'normally', 'until proof to the contrary', 'not contrary to what we already know' etc. But they are nevertheless perfectly legitimate within their limits. If these are the stereotypes of a rational agent under the current framing of the situation, they are also the mental models that 'come to the agent's mind' when s/he tries to decide rationally those that s/he takes for granted or as provisionally valid to plan his/her action. There is no conclusive reason for doing this except that these constitute the model of the rational agent that comes to his/her mind under the current framing effect.

Now imagine that the same agent is asked to forecast the behavior of other agents (for example, the second player in the real life game). In the absence of contradictory information or evidence to the contrary, by default s/he will simulate the other agents' reasoning and behavior by applying the same mental model used to provisionally define his/her own plan or conduct. The rational basis for this replication has the same fragile but nonetheless intelligible basis as before: the simplest way to forecast other agents' behavior, as long as there is no evidence or proof to the contrary, is to deduce their behavior from the best mental model of an agent inferred from the frame of the situation. '*Assuming that the situation has been understood as one of impartial and generally acceptable agreement, or one normally categorised as the domain of application of a neutral norm, given that I need to work out a forecast of other agents, I do not find any reason not to apply to these other agents the same mental model that seems valid for myself as it is consistent with a norm which is independent of any characteristics that make me different from any other*'. As long as there is no evidence that other players do not participate in the same impartial agreement or do not categorize the current situation in like manner, by default we conclude that the same model of agent that came to our mind to define our action is also valid for symmetrically forecasting other agent's decisions and behaviors.

Given the mental model just described, if players participate in the pre-play communication stage (the agreement on CSR principles) their first-order beliefs in the psychological game consist of the mutual prediction that strategy choices are (e, F) and (F), and their mutual second-order beliefs are hence consistent with these predictions about choices.

4.3. Cognitive social capital and 'modified' MG trigger strategies

The analysis of belief formation resulting from the pre-play communication phase provides a sound and workable starting point for our model, but no more than that. In fact, it works only in a one-shot game, where there is no previous experience and no evidence can be uncovered that contradicts the mental model derived from the ideal choice or the abstraction and categorization process carried out at the pre-play communication stage. However, when the game is repeatedly played, observations of previous effective behaviors necessarily influence beliefs about what strategy the counterpart is effectively playing.

Here we make our first basic assumption about the dependence of player S_S's beliefs and behaviors in our psychological game (the PG) on what s/he learns from the behaviors of player E in the other games in which it participates through the relational network considered in Figure 7.3. We call all of them PD_{Ej} in order to indicate that they are Prisoner's Dilemmas played by E in relation to player $S_{Wj} = j$. We assume that

A1) If S_S learns that player E defects at time t in a PD_{Ej}, s/he understands that E is not 'really' playing the strategy F in the PG from that stage onward.

In fact, what has been *saved* and entitled to S_{Wj} in the solution of the component game of division of the surplus PG has not been used to remunerate players S_{Wj} equitably by cooperating with them. Thus, at stage $t + 1$, S_S will predict that player E is not playing 'fair' in the current repetition of PG. This signifies that the condition for the emergence of the 'no entry' psychological equilibrium has been activated (obviously, the 'no entry' decision depends also on the value of λ). Of course, this point is particularly important in relation to the strategy ¬e, that is, what in our model takes the place of the punishment stage strategy discussed in section 3.4; the psychological equilibrium involving ¬e seems to be what we need to show that implementing the punishment phase in player S_S's strategy is compatible with S_S's (conformist) incentives. To guarantee this result, however, we need not only to show that, when s/he learns about a defection against weak stakeholders, S_S believes that E will choose U_E in PG at $t + 1$. We also need to show that E predicts that S_S will not enter at time $t + 1$. The 'no entry' equilibrium is contingent on this reciprocal beliefs system.

Assumption *A1* requires a *caveat*: S_S does not understand that E is not really playing the Fair strategy F_E in the PG when it defects for the first time in the PDs with weak stakeholders, in case this is required by implementation of E's MG trigger strategy. It seems, in fact, likely that E does not lose his/her trustworthiness in the eyes of S_S if s/he knows that E is required to defect by compliance with a MG trigger strategy, which is itself intended to support cooperation throughout the network. Nevertheless, this forgiveness cannot last for more than one period because player S_S's sanctions based on how s/he assesses player E's behavior are also needed in order to provide player E with the appropriate incentive not to take advantage of its relation with S_S to exploit weak stakeholders.

It is quite intuitive to suppose that, in a context where players have first agreed on a fairness norm and have also conformed with it, E realizes that S_S will not enter at $t + 1$ after it has defected against weak stakeholders, so that player E knows that S_S has effective conformist preferences encapsulating a desire to be consistent with a shared norm of fairness. However, having a strong disposition to conformity is not enough if the relevant beliefs do not exist as well. This hypothesis must be rigorously justified, for the emergence of a psychological equilibrium in a given stage-game depends strictly on the players' reciprocally consistent beliefs. Here we introduce our second assumption concerning the link between the equilibria of the game PG and how other games are played by different players throughout the network. We assume that S_S plays each PG stage-game by following a version of the multilateral grim ($=$ MG) trigger strategy.

> A2) S_S at first plays (e, F), but after some stage t s/he plays $\neg e$ if s/he learns from a defection occurring at stage t-1 in a PD_{Ej} – which E plays with any S_{Wj} – that E is not going to play Fair in the current PG (under the same caveat valid for assumption A1).

The strategy adopted by S_S to play his/her repeated game as a function of E's past behavior is common knowledge in the network. This entails that once, at whatever stage t in a repeated game PD_{Ej}, player E chooses to defect, it also obtains the information that player S_S will play $\neg e$ in the following stage $t + 1$ of the PG. But this is exactly the basis for the E's belief that at $t + 1$ S_S will play $\neg e$, and for S_S's second-order beliefs that E predicts that s/he will stay out at stage $t + 1$ – that is, the condition for the emergence of the 'no entry' psychological equilibrium at $t + 1$.

The *caveat* to *A1* is again relevant. Also E's strategy is common knowledge, so that S_S knows whether E will adopt a MG trigger strategy, such that if at $t - 1$ a defection occurs in the network, then player E will play 'defection' in the PD_{Ej} at the stage t. But it is *not* required by assumption *A1* that player S_S immediately anticipates that player E is not going to play consistently with the fair strategy at stage t. This understanding can be delayed until after E's defection effectively occurs, so that player S_S, given his/her state of information and repeated strategy, must start to play $\neg e$ at stage $t + 1$. Player S_S believes that E predicts that s/he will change her choice at $t + 1$ and also that s/he realizes that E defected at t. At the same time, E predicts that S_S will change his/her strategy at $t + 1$ and also believes that s/he realizes that E's change of strategy occurred at t. Mutually, consistency of beliefs is satisfied in order to allow the emergence of the 'no entry' equilibrium profile at $t + 1$.

As a consequence, we are not assuming that S_S should implement the MG trigger strategy as a rule follower without having the proper psychological incentive to do so (as noted in subsection 2.2). On the contrary, the sanctioning strategy adopted at the $t + 1$ stage in game PG has a perfectly endogenous explanation. The adoption of the multilateral grim trigger strategy is perfectly consistent with the equilibrium behavior that S_S implements in the stage-game in which the strategy requires him/her to sanction E. We may say that player S_S plays $\neg$e *because* s/he is believed to follow the multilateral grim trigger strategy as a function of E's behavior, but the content of this belief is now perfectly consistent with the psychological equilibrium behavior that s/he implements in the game.

In conclusion, although we have not still precisely worked out the relation between what happens in a single PG stage-game and the strategies played in the repeated games that take place throughout the network, we have laid the bases for answering the central question: why should S_S carry out his/her threat to punish E if the latter had failed to cooperate with some S_{Wj}? Our answer is that, under the proper beliefs about S_S, s/he is ready to act as a conformist agent also if E continues not to conform with the agreed norms. Hence, punishing player E by 'staying out' in the current stage-game PG, is perfectly in line with player S_S's psychological incentive (when λ is high enough to counterbalance the material payoff). By anticipating S_S's behavior, given our assumption (on belief formation and value of λ[14]), the firm E will also have the incentive to avoid opportunistic behavior against weak stakeholders so as to prevent S_S's retaliation.

This suggests (even if a rigorous proof must wait until the next two sections) that cognitive social capital, as understood here in terms of conformist preferences and the related systems of consistent beliefs, is at the very root of the possibility to make cooperation sustainable in a relational network of repeated games, which is what we typically mean by the term 'structural social capital' seen as a set of effective cooperative relations based on trust.

5. Strategies and beliefs formation in the psychological game as a function of repeated playing of games in the relational network

The aim of this section is to provide a clear link between the one-shot psychological game (PG) played by E (the firm) and S_S, discussed in section 3, and the framework of network analysis reported at the beginning of section 2. Hence, here we consider the PG as a stage-game within the repeated playing of the games (not only repeated PG but also other games) in which players are involved throughout the network. Our aim is to adapt the MG trigger strategy to the roles performed by E and S_S in the repeated playing of games in the network: that is, its specification in consideration of the peculiar game in which players S_S and E are involved – the repeated PG. We use the analytical framework introduced in section 2.1 and we refer to the notion of sustainability of a relational non-mutual network as set out in L&S (2010). We introduce a variation of the MG trigger strategy that will account for how this strategy is specified with reference to the manner in which the repeated PG must be played in function of behaviors maintained in games nested in each other throughout the network so that it can support cooperation in all these repeated games.

To this end, we first need to identify the strategy profile of a player i involved in the network described in Figure 7.3, which comprises players E, S_S, S_{W1}, S_{W2} and agents 3, 4 and 5, that at each stage participate in playing the repeated games (normally, with the exception of S_S and E, two adjacent games) in the network. It should be borne in mind that S_S plays only an iterated PG with E, while all the other agents play two iterated Prisoners' Dilemmas with adjacent agents belonging to the network. As a consequence, only player E is involved in three games (the PG and two PDs) at each stage.

We define h^t as a history of all the repeated games played by the agents belonging to the network. h^t is one of the possible sequences of moves available to players until the period t. The set of all the possible histories h^t is termed H^t. Player i's strategy is defined as a function that, at any time t, associates with each history $h^t \in H^t$ the moves that will be selected by player i from $t + 1$ onward: $s_i : f(H^t) \rightarrow A_i^{t+1} \forall t$.

Note that the strategies of an agent i who plays a repeated Prisoner's Dilemma in our network do not only depend on the decisions made by i and the players who play the game with him/her. They are also determined by the moves made by the other agents in the network, even though they are not directly connected with i. In fact, the MG trigger strategy, which we assume to characterize the way in which these games are played, implies that every player $i \in N$ starts cooperating with his/her neighbors, and continues to cooperate as long as s/he observes that all the other players cooperate. But s/he stops cooperating if s/he observes that someone, somewhere in the network, defects. Moreover, the strategies of the firm E and of the S_S also depend on the history that characterizes the psychological game in which they are involved and which is different from the PDs played in the rest of the network. This amounts to saying that both the enterprise's and the strong stakeholder's strategies in the psychological game are a function of the Cartesian product of the histories, which come about both in the psychological game and in all the repeated Prisoner's Dilemmas:

$$s_i : f(H_{PG}^t \times H_{PD1}^t \times H_{PD2}^t \times \ldots \times H_{PDn}^t) \rightarrow A_i^{t+1} \forall t \ (i = E, S_S)$$

where: H_{PD1}^t is the set of all the possible histories till the period t which may hypothetically characterize the PD_1 – that is, the repeated Prisoner's Dilemma between the firm and the first agent connected with it in the network. In regard to the network depicted in Figure 7.3, for example, PD_1 is the game between E and S_{W1} (more specifically, we will call this game PD_{E1}) and PD_2 is the game between E and S_{W2}(PD_{E2}). To simplify the notation, hereafter E's strategies in these PD_{Ej} will be C_{Ej} and D_{Ej} respectively for 'cooperation' and 'defection' where $j = S_{Wj}$.

To understand the effect of all the network's relationships on the PG played by E and S_S we start from the strategies of E and S_S in particular by investigating the process that drives the belief formation of these two agents in the PG. S_S's and E's beliefs in the PG are a function of the histories characterizing both the psychological game PG and all the PDs.

5.1. The strong stakeholder's beliefs and strategy

Player S_S's beliefs about the firm E's behavior in the PG at time t depend both on the past behavior of E in the repeated PG and on the behavior of E in the repeated Prisoner's Dilemmas in which it is involved (in our example: PD_{E1} and PD_{E2}). The latter, because of the MG trigger strategy, is also related to all the other Prisoner's Dilemmas played in the network. Essentially, S_S forms his/her belief about E's behavior in the PG by looking at the moves made by E in the previous periods, both in the PG and in the PD_{Ej}. In particular, before giving more technical formalization, we assume that the belief formation of S_S is based on the following considerations:

1. the initial belief of S_S is that the firm will play F_E in the PG, in consideration of the rational agreement on the CSR principle T subscribed to by the firm (section 4.2);
2. if at any time E does not play F in the PG, thereafter the trust of S_S in the 'fair' behavior of E goes to zero (sufficient condition);
3. S_S's belief also depends on the moves made by E in the repeated Prisoner's Dilemmas that it plays with weak stakeholders. If the firm E always cooperates with all its weak stakeholders (i.e. it plays C_{Ej} $\forall j$), then the trust of S_S in the fair behavior F_E of E remains unchanged. If at any time E defects in one repetition of a Prisoner's Dilemma that it plays with a S_{Wj}, his/her belief changes.
4. However S_S's trust in E does not change in consideration of the fact that somewhere in the network a player different from E has defected and that, owing to player's E adoption of the MG trigger strategy, E must start punishing the S_{Wj} (i.e. E's defection is aimed at punishing some other defections occurring in the network). The simple fact that E adopts its MG trigger strategy keeps it trustworthy, because it complies with a commitment intended to prevent opportunistic behavior in the network.

The idea is that E is not trustworthy as a fair player in the PG in two cases (besides the fact that it has evidently started to play unfairly in the PG):

a) Either if E is the first player that defects against a weak stakeholder in a repetition of the Prisoner's Dilemmas it plays with weak stakeholders – *in fact cooperation in PG is aimed at producing positive output for weak stakeholders, for this reason the defection against them in the following PDs can be reasonably associated with a 'not fair' behavior in the psychological game.*
b) Or if it does not punish the defection of other agents by avoiding implementing the MG trigger strategy – *which is exactly aimed at guarantee the cooperation in the network by resort to its implicit treat of punishment.*

For this reason, S_S's belief at time t depends (a) on E's move at time $t-1$ in the PG; (b) on E's moves in the PD_{Ej} at time $t-1$ (in particular if it defects or not); (c) on the moves of all the players involved in the PDs at time $t-1$ and $t-2$. In fact: (c.1) if some agent other than E defects at time $t-1$, E keeps its trustworthiness at time t; (c.2) if some agent defects at time $t-2$, and if at $t-1$ E does not implement its part in the MG trigger strategy, this move will be considered not consistent with E's fairness, and thus will turn E into an untrustworthy player thereafter.

To give a formal description, S_S's beliefs concerning E's behavior in the PG are settled according to the following rules (where for the purposes of this section B_{SS}^t means 'belief at time t of player S_S'):

$$B_{SS}^t = f(H_{PG}^{t-1} \times H_{PDE1}^{t-1} \times H_{PDE2}^{t-1})$$

In particular, the probabilities that E is going to play F_E or U_E in the PG according to player S_S's first-order belief are:

- b_{SS} (F_E) = 1 at time t *if* at time $t-1$ E plays (F_E, C_{Ej}) *and* S_S plays (e, F) in the PG
  and if

  a) at time $t-2$ $\forall k$, $\forall i \in R_k$: C_{ki}
  or
  b) at time $t-1$ $\exists k \neq E$, $\exists i \in R_k$: D_{ki}

- b_{SS} (F_E) = 0 at time t, *if* at time $t-1$ in the PG E plays U_E *or* S_S plays (¬e);
  and if

  a) at time $t-2$ $\exists k \neq E$, $\exists i \in R_k$ s.t. D_{ki} *and* at time $t-1$ E plays (F_E, C_{Ej}) *or*
  b) at time $t-1$ $\exists k = E$, $\exists i \in R_k$ s.t. D_{ki}

Note that $b_{SS}(F_E) = 1$ is compatible with the case that having learnt that at time $t-1$ $\exists k \neq E$, $\exists i \in R_k$: D_{ki}, the player E at time t is reacting to such information by playing (F_E, D_{Ej}). That is, S_S does not infer from condition 1 b) that player E will play (F_E, D_{Ej}) at *t*.

Given these hypotheses, the following repeated strategy by player S_S is consistent, and we assume that it is played by S_S

1. S_S starts by playing (e, F) at time $t = 1$
2. $\forall t > 1$, S_S continues playing (e, F) *if*

   a) at time $t - 1$ in PG E plays F_E *and* S_S plays (e, F)
      and if
   b) at time $t - 1$ E plays C_{Ej} in PD_{Ej} $\forall j \in R_E$ and at time $t - 2$ $\forall k$ and $\forall i \in R_k$: C_{ki}
      or
   c) at $t - 1$ E plays C_{Ej} in PD_{Ej} and at the *same time* $t - 1$, $\exists k \neq E$, $\exists i \in R_k$, s.t. D_{ki}

3. reverts to ¬e forever otherwise

where $j = 1, 2$ are the weak stakeholders S_{Wj} linked to E; $i = 1, \ldots, m$ are agents that may have relations with a generic agent in the network (normally different from E), $I \in R_k$ are the agents included in agent k's set of relations, $k = 1, \ldots, s$ are agents in the network that have a set of relations, and R_k is the set of relations that characterizes agent k.

Note again that the strategy of player S_S is compatible with the hypothesis that at time t, when s/he continues to play (e, F), player E reverts to (F_E, D_{Ej}) if and only if at time $t - 1$, $\exists k \neq E$, $\exists i \in R_k$, s.t. D_{ki}. In other words, player S_S does not react to the information that at $t - 1$, $\exists k \neq E$, $\exists i \in R_k$, s.t. D_{ki} by immediately reverting to a sectioning strategy ¬e. In order to do so, s/he waits for at least one period, wherein player E will revert to a sanctioning strategy D_{Ej} because of the defection that occurred in some other part of the network at the time immediately before.

According to this strategy, at any t S_S punishes E (which means that s/he does not enter into a relation with E and plays ¬e) if (a) E defects in the PG; (b) E fails to contribute to maintaining cooperation in the network by implementing the MG trigger strategy if someone anywhere in the network defects at an immediately previous time; (c) E defects in one of the PD_{Ej} at $t - 1$. However, the player S_S's reported game strategy shows more forgiveness than the standard MG trigger strategy, which if information is received about a player defecting somewhere in the network immediately requires each player to punish its adjacent network agent as it is involved in a repeated game wherein s/he is also involved. On the contrary, in the case of player S_S, his/her modified MG trigger strategy waits for one period before the punishment starts, giving player E the chance to show whether it is consistent with its MG trigger strategy (that is to start its punishment continuation strategy with respect to the S_{Wj} as a consequence of a breach of cooperation somewhere in the network). Thus player S_S is ready to accept one-stage defection by player E, which plays (F_E, D_{Ej}), before starting the sanctioning part of his/her repeated strategy. In fact, if E defects at time t as a consequence of someone's else defection at time $t-1$, S_S does not anticipate its defection and continues to play (e, F) at time t (i.e. s/he does not punish E at time t), but at time $t+1$ cooperation in the PG will have stopped anyway and S_S will play ¬e. This happens even though E does not have any primitive responsibility for the occurrence of defections in the Prisoner's Dilemmas. In fact, were S_S not punishing E at time $t+1$ the sanction power implicit in the MG trigger strategy could not be effective. To sum up, in order to have a sanction power against E, the S_S's MG trigger strategy does not allow playing (e, F) when E effectively defects with its weak stakeholders in the Prisoner's Dilemmas, even though E's defection is the consequence of implementation of its MG trigger strategy. But it is not so harsh as to start punishing E just because someone else in the network has defected against any other agent.

5.2. The firm's beliefs and strategy

Player E's beliefs are defined according to the following rules (where, for the purposes of this section, B_E^t means 'belief at time t of player E'):

$$B_E^t = f(H_{PG}^{t-1} \times H_{PDE1}^{t-1} \times H_{PDE2}^{t-1})$$

In particular, the probability that S_S is going to play any of his/her PG strategy according to player's E first-order beliefs is

- b_E (e, F) = 1 at time t, *if* at time $t-1$ in the PG S_S plays (e, F) *and* E plays (F_E)
  and if

  a) at time $t-1$ $\forall k$, $\forall i \in R_k$: C_{ki};
     or
  b) at time $t-1$ $\exists k \neq E$, $\exists i \in R_k$ s.t. D_{ki}

- b_E (¬e) = 1 at time t *if* at time $t-1$ in the PG S_S plays ¬e *or* E plays (U_E)
  or

  a) at time $t-1$ $\exists k = E$, $\exists i \in R_k$ s.t. D_{ki}
     or
  b) E plays C_{Ej} at time $t-1$ and at time $t-2$ $\exists k \neq E$, $\exists i \in R_k$ s.t. D_{ki}

- b_E (U) = 1 at time t *iff* S_S plays U at time $t-1$.

Note that b_E (e, F) = 1 does not exclude the possibility that having learnt at time $t-1$ that $\exists k \neq E$, $\exists i \in R_k$ s.t. D_{ki} at time t player E is in fact playing

(F_E, D_{Ej}), and hence S_S according to E may fail to predict that E is changing its strategy. Given these hypotheses on E's beliefs, the definition of the E's relevant strategy considers the role of E both in the PG and in PD_{Ej}. Hence we state that player E acts as follows:

1. E starts by playing (F_E, C_{Ej}) at time $t = 1$
2. $\forall t > 1$, E continues playing (F_E, C_{Ej}), *iff*

   a) at time $t - 1$ in PG S_S plays (e, F) *and* E plays F_E
      and
   b) at time $t - 1$ $\forall k$, $\forall i \in R_k$: C_{ki}

3. E reverts to (U_E, D_{Ej}) *if* at time $t - 1$ in PG S_S plays $(\neg e)$ *or* E plays U_E
4. E reverts to (F_E, D_{Ej}) *if* at time $t - 1$ $\exists k \neq E$, $\exists i \in R_k$, s.t. D_{ki}
5. At $t > 2$, E reverts to (U_E, D_{Ej}) *if* at time $t - 2$ $\exists k \neq E$, $\exists i \in R_k$, s.t. D_{ki}.

We assume that E follows the MG trigger strategy with regard to all the players involved in the repeated PDs, that is, it defects at time t if it knows that a defection has occurred anywhere in the network at time $t - 1$. If E does not learn about defections, it continues to cooperate in the PD_{Ej}. With regard to the PG, E plays F_E as long as S_S plays (e, F), and no defection has occurred in the network, and until itself has played D_{Ej} in the PD_{Ej} at least once in order to start the sanctioning part of its strategy when someone defects in some of the PDs, but it reverts at any time $t > 1$ to (U_E, D_{Ej}) if it learns about S_S playing $\neg e$ or U – because it has no incentive to play cooperatively in the PD_{Ej} in the absence of the psychological payoff associated with high mutual compliance with the principle T in PG. It also reverts to (U_E, D_{Ej}) when it is sanctioning any deviation from cooperation occurring in the network for at least two periods – since in the first period E starts sanctioning by playing (F_E, D_{Ej}).

Thus, if E starts to defect at time t in PD_{Ej} in order to punish agents who started to defect at time $t - 1$, given the S_S strategy already described, it knows that S_S will still play (e, F) at time t because s/he does not want to prevent the firm's defection aimed at implementing the MG trigger strategy. Hence, at this stage, player E plays (F_E, D_{Ej}) and S_S does not anticipate this defection. Nevertheless, at time $t + 1$, according to his/her strategy (see section 5.1), S_S will play $\neg e$ and E – having already defected at least once – will play (U_E, D_{Ej}) on its own. Thereafter, E will continue to play (U_E, D_{Ej}) given that S_S plays $\neg e$.

Note that if S_S learns at time $t - 1$ about a defection in the network by one or more agents other than E, s/he starts to play $\neg e$ only at time $t + 1$ even if E implements its MG trigger strategy already at time t by using (F_E, D_{Ej}). But s/he also punishes E at time $t + 1$ if it does not play the MG trigger strategy at time t when a breach of cooperation has occurred at time $t - 1$, so that at time t it has played (F_E, C_{Ej}). On the other hand, player E's modified MG trigger strategy is so conceived that it will start defecting after any information about an agent, other than itself, defecting in whatever part of the network, by playing F in the PG but D_{Ej} in the consequent PDs. Given the delay in reaction to the same information by player S_S – or, to put it somewhat differently, given that S_S does not react immediately to such information but only to vis-à-vis defection by E in their interaction, or in the subsequent PD_{Ej} after having played F in PG – player E may profit from one period of forgiveness in which it can reap a higher payoff than would be allowed in the case of immediate sanction by S_S.

5.3. How E and the S_S play the repeated PG according to the modified MG trigger strategies

The strategies and the beliefs discussed in sections 5.1 and 5.2 define two modified versions of the MG trigger strategy by specifying how players E and S_S will act according to such a multilateral harshly sanctioning strategy, with respect to the repeated play of their particular interaction, as a result of what happens in the network. This identifies a repeated strategy profile with respect to the particular subset of players constituted by S_S and E, and hence induces the following strategy combination, whereby the psychological game PG will be solved through its repeated play.

At time $t = 1$, the strategy profile in the stage-games including the move of just S_S and E is (e, F_{Ss}; F_{Ej}, C_{Ej}) – that is, S_S enters and plays F in the PG and the firm plays F_E in the PG and cooperates in the two PDs that it plays with its S_{Wj} (because we are considering only the strategy profile characterizing how repeated games are played by S_S and E, here we disregard S_{Wj}'s choices). This state holds through all the repetitions of the PG and $DP_{E,SWj}$ stage-games until someone in the network decides to 'defect' at some time t. In this case, there are two possible deviations from the just-defined stage-games strategy profile.

1. E carries out the sanction entailed by its MG trigger strategy at time $t + 1$, that is, E plays D_{Ej} in the PD_{Ej} from $t + 1$ onward. S_S's belief in the 'fair' behavior of E remains unchanged only for the first period t, and the stage-games strategy profile involving both S_S and E at time $t + 1$ becomes (e, F; F_E, D_{Ej}). However, from time $t + 2$ onward, the stage-games strategy profile becomes ($\neg$e; U_E, D_{Ej}) because the MG trigger strategy of player S_S implies not preventing the defection of E for just one period if it is the consequence of E's MG trigger strategy execution, but requires punishment of E for all the periods after it has defected once against weak stakeholders. According to its MG trigger strategy, E will continue to sanction its weak stakeholders from time $t + 1$ onward, so that from time $t + 2$ the continuation strategy profile within this players' subset becomes ($\neg$e; U_E, D_{Ej}).

2. For some reason, Player E does not implement the MG trigger strategy at time $t+1$. In this case, S_S at time $t+2$ punishes player E for not behaving so as to render effective the sanction required for implementation of the MG trigger strategies in the network. Since player E reverts to (U_E, D_{Ej}) when it learns that S_S plays $\neg e$, the resulting strategy profile from time $t+2$ onward, relative to the stage-game played by S_S and E, is $(\neg e; U_E, D_{Ej})$ as well.

Note that E cannot avoid the decision of S_S to play $\neg e$ when someone else starts to defect in the network. Let us suppose that after someone has defected in a PD at time t, the firm E decides to implement its MG trigger strategy at time $t+1$ in order to avoid player S_S's sanction at $t+2$, but it also tries to avoid the S_S sanction at $t+3$ by cooperating by playing C_{Ej} in the PDs that it plays at time $t+2$. Under the hypothesis that the strong stakeholder S_S is adopting his/her version of the MG trigger strategy just defined in section 5.1, this attempt will be unsuccessful. In fact, once S_S learns that the firm does not contribute to punishing other agents who are continuing defection from $t+1$ onward, s/he will in any case punish E.

6. 'Sub-game perfection' and endogenous sustainability of cooperation

The aim of the previous section was to define a modified version of MG trigger strategies by players E and S_S able to support cooperation in all games played in the network, because player E is sanctioned by S_S if it defects in any PD_{Ej}. According to the analytical framework set out in section 2.1, these strategies, played simultaneously with standard MG trigger strategies adopted in each repeated game by each pair of adjacent agents in the network, define a repeated game Nash equilibrium (verification of the conditions for existence of this equilibrium is delayed until section 7). Our aim here is to verify whether the execution of player S_S's modified MG trigger strategy is really compatible with player S_S's incentives in the iterated PG: that is, is sanctioning player E player S_S's best response if E defects in some PD_{Ej}? The relevant game theoretical concept here is the S_S strategy's 'sub-game perfection'. In other words, if the repeated play of games according to the players' MG trigger strategies (modified or otherwise) were to reach branches or sub-games out of the equilibrium path, then in that contingency the sanctions implicit in player S_S's strategy could be rationally carried out in accordance with player S_S's incentives. In this regard, we first present an intuitive analysis of sub-game perfection with reference to the stage-game PG psychological equilibrium taken as a game on its own. We will make informal use of the idea of 'trembling hand': that is, the possibility that, owing to random mistakes occurring when a given equilibrium strategy profile is played, any part of the relevant game tree out of the equilibrium path can be reached, even though with low probability. By considering the possible deviations due to random mistakes, we will verify that, in any situation, player S_S's MG trigger strategy requires only playing a stage-game psychological equilibrium. In other words, even in sub-games out of the equilibrium path the strategy profile is always compatible with the principle of a player's best response.

6.1. Sub-game perfection in the psychological stage-game

Before considering the sub-game perfection of the entire MG trigger strategy of players S_S and E, let us determine whether some instability (equilibrium imperfection) may be found in the psychological equilibria of the PG stage-game – considered on its own – based on player S_S's and E's conformist preferences. Figure 7.8 illustrates the PG in extensive form under the hypotheses of mutually consistency and common knowledge of (at least) first- and second-degree beliefs – which are typical of psychological games. Payoff vectors reported on the edge of each game tree branch show that both players have iteratively predicted that they would play the moves belonging to the path reaching a particular edge. Hence, they include the ideal component of players' payoffs that materialize when mutual beliefs are reciprocally consistent and conformist preferences are activated. To satisfy the conditions on parameters given in section 3.4 ($\lambda > d - b$ and $\lambda > c - a$) we here assume $\lambda = 2.5$. An explanation is required for the two payoff vectors reported at the branch edge ¬e. Each vector assigns the players' overall payoffs (included ideal utilities) based respectively on a different beliefs system concerning how the game would have been played in the remaining part of the game

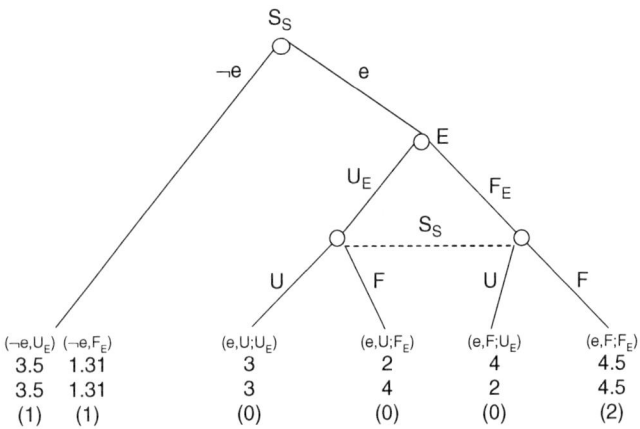

Figure 7.8 Extensive form of the PG stage-game with consistent belief systems and conformist preferences

tree. On the left side is the psychological payoffs vector under the hypothesis that reciprocally consistent first- and second-order beliefs predict that players would choose ($\neg$e, U_E), while on the right side is the psychological payoffs vector under the hypothesis that reciprocally consistent first- and second-order beliefs predict that players would choose ($\neg$e, F_E). We use intuitively the notion of sub-game perfection to analyze this game.

Hence, for each psychological equilibrium we will consider what would happen if, under the hypothesis that players are playing a particular equilibrium strategy profile, some sub-game or branch is reached out of the equilibrium path, and whether in this case playing according to the equilibrium strategies would be irrational for the relevant player. In order to conduct this analysis we use an intuitive application of the 'trembling hand' argument. Reinard Selten (1967, 1975) suggested this idea in order to introduce a random perturbation into games by means of uncorrelated small probabilities of deviation, so that, with some probability, each sub-game or branch of the game tree – also out of the equilibrium path – can be reached when players are in fact playing a given equilibrium. Equilibrium perfection consists in robustness of the equilibrium behavior under the game perturbation induced by such small probabilities of uncorrelated random deviation 'by mistake'. Note that the extensive-form game of Figure 7.8 includes two sub-games: one starting from the second information set attributed to player E, and one starting from the individual choice attributed to player S_S at the first information set, beyond the entire game itself.

To begin with, consider that players S_S and E are playing the psychological equilibrium (e, F; F_E) and are hence endowed with the relevant mutually consistent beliefs that predict such a state and consequently induce their conformist preferences. Then introduce with small probability a random mistake that when player S_S is playing e, s/he is in fact playing $\neg$e, so that s/he ends the game. Assuming that player E knows this random mistake probability, at the second decision node should it play differently with regard its equilibrium strategy? Consider that the players' beliefs are consistent with (e, F; F_E). Then the selection of $\neg$e under the belief that player E chooses F_E will entail, with small probability, a psychological payoff 1.31 for player E, which would be enhanced if, in the case of mistake, player S_S entertained the belief that player E is playing U_E. On the other hand, if player E changes its choice to U_E at the second information set, it can fool player S_S, who – believing that E has played F_E – continues to play Γ, so that E reaches a payoff 4 less than 4.5. Nevertheless, consider that player S_S must know that player E has changed its behavior at the second information set because of the probability of a mistake; otherwise s/he would not believe that player E has chosen U_E when s/he mistakenly plays $\neg$e (enhancing its payoff to 4 instead of 1.31). Because of this prediction, however, s/he would play U at the third information set. As a result, in order to obtain a tiny improvement in its payoff in the case of a mistaken $\neg$e choice, which occurs with very small probability, with high probability E forgoes a payoff 4.5 to obtain a payoff 3 instead, which is clearly irrational. Hence, under the 'trembling hand' hypothesis, player E must not change its behavior with respect to what is required by its strategy in the equilibrium (e, F; F_E).

Now consider the hypothesis that players are playing the psychological equilibrium ($\neg$e; U_E) with reciprocally consistent beliefs. Then introduce the small probability of mistake that, when playing $\neg$e, player S_S is in fact playing e. They are thus allowed to reach the sub-game that starts from the second information set, which is out of the equilibrium path. Should this perturbation of the game tree induce player E to change its strategy, which requires it to implement the move U_E? Certainly not. Consider that, since they are playing according to the equilibrium ($\neg$e; U_E), player S_S believes that player E plays U_E if its information set is reached by a random mistake occurring at the first node. Consistently with this belief, player S_S's best response is to choose U if the third information set is reached (by a random mistake). Moreover, in order to be predicted as playing U_E (according to the rationality assumption), player E must believe that player S_S, if his/her second decision node has been reached, would play U. Thus player E's best response is to play U_E at its information set if, by mistake with small probability, it is reached. This incentive-compatible behavior in the sub-game gives player E a payoff 3 that adds with small (mistake) probability to the high probability payoff 3.5. What, on the contrary, is the case if player E decides to change its move at the second decision node? Because player S_S's beliefs are still consistent with the equilibrium ($\neg$e; U_E), s/he will nevertheless play U, so that E obtains a poor payoff 2 instead of 3, which is clearly irrational.

Finally, consider the case that players are playing the equilibrium (e, U; U_E) and have beliefs consistent with this psychological equilibrium – that is, they are both predicted to play U after S_S has entered. But again introduce the small random mistake probability that when S_S is playing e, s/he is in fact playing $\neg$e. What is player E's reaction to this probability of mistake? Consider that, under the current beliefs of the players – that is, in the sub-game they will both play (U; U_E) in the case of mistake (with small probability) – they will get a payoff 4 higher than 3. In fact, if player S_S chooses $\neg$e when believing that player E will play U_E (which is nevertheless required by the psychological equilibrium under consideration), then the psychological payoff is 4. Could player E enhance its payoff further by changing its behavior to F_E? Certainly not in the case of a mistake, for if S_S chooses $\neg$e while believing that player E is playing F_E the psychological payoff for both decreases to 1.31. Why, therefore, should player S_S believe that player E in the case of mistake is changing its behavior so that its own payoff is reduced? But if player S_S has no reason to believe that player E is changing its behavior, s/he will play U when his/her decision node is reached (s/he, in fact, continues to believe that E is playing U_E); hence, by changing its move, player E would worsen its payoff from 3 to 2 with high probability. Thus there is no basis for saying that incentive compatibility and the logic of best response under the perturbation hypothesis would induce the players to change their moves in the game.

To sum up, under the intuitive 'trembling hand' hypothesis that allows players to reach any branch of the game tree out of the equilibrium path, nothing authorizes them, as long as they are rational, to make any significant modifications with respect to what is required by each of the three psychological equilibria.

6.2. Definition of the relevant sub-game

Each adjacent pair of agents in the relational network are players involved in two subsequent repeated games, except for player E, that plays three repeated games with its adjacent stakeholders, and S_s, who plays just one repeated game with E. The strategies whereby all players make their choices in each stage-game at any time are conditional on choices made by all other players in the network through the assumption that each player adopts a MG trigger strategy (including the modified version defined in section 5). These are rules for deciding how to play any stage-game at any time in relation to the past history of the game. However, MG trigger strategies have the peculiarity that how each player chooses at any time t in a given stage-game depends on the decisions made at a time $t - 1$ by any other player participating in the network, also playing a different and remote repeated game. In fact, if a defection occurs somewhere in the network, any player, according to his/her MG trigger strategy, starts to punish the players s/he is related with, thereby changing any player's incentive to continue cooperation in the immediately subsequent game that s/he plays with his/her successor in the network. This construction makes it possible to consider all the stage-games played at time t as if they were sub-games of a unique dynamic game played at any time t by all the network's agents. Moreover, the dynamic game is repeated ad infinitum, and the way in which each repetition is played – under our current assumptions – is dictated at any time by the players' MG trigger strategies.

Within this context, we must define the proper sub-game to be analyzed. It is necessary to select a sub-game that may convey not just the information that E has abandoned its stage-game equilibrium strategy F_E, shifting to the other stage-game strategy U_E, but also the information that, in some subsequent PD games with S_{Wj}, it has played D_{Ej} instead of C_{Ej} after having played the strategy F_E in PG. Put differently, it is necessary that the stage-game – taken as the relevant sub-game of the overall dynamic game played by all the network's players – allows player S_s to entertain correct beliefs not only on the choices F_E or U_E that player E makes in the PG, but also on choices that it makes in the subsequent PD_{Ej}. Of course, player S_s needs to understand whether player E is consistent with a 'fair' mode of playing the PG (strategy F_E of the stage-game) and must also take into consideration how it plays the following PD_{Ej} game, because it is only in these games that the amount of surplus saved on behalf of players S_{Wj} will be effectively allocated to pay them fairly for their cooperation with E. Recall that this was our first assumption in section 4.3 and that it was also incorporated in the assumption that player S_S believes that player E is playing F_E with probability zero if s/he learns about its defection in the subsequent PD_{Ej}.

The underlying intuitive idea is that if in the PG stage-game one or both of the players choose the collusive and egoist strategy U, no part of the surplus is saved or entitled to S_{Wj}, so that the result of PG has no effect on the payoffs accruing to the S_{Wj} in the subsequent PD_{Ej} games. This is clear when S_S plays U unilaterally, since s/he simply takes away from the game for his/her personal consumption the extra rent that could be allocated to the S_{Wj} for his/her personal consumption. But this is also true if E chooses U_E because, for instance, E thus allocates to the private earnings of E's shareholders or managers any extra rent that otherwise could be an endowment available to the firm in order to improve its cooperation with S_{Wj}. Thus, if the players choose U or U_E in PG there is no information that can arise from the subsequent games concerning player E's consistency with the adopted strategy or the effective payoffs engendered in PG. In these cases, player S_S will obtain directly from the equilibrium solution of PG all the information necessary to establish that E plays unfairly, so that s/he will anyway not trust E for 'Fair play'. Choices like C_{Ej} and D_{Ej} in these cases may only give information about how player E responds to 'external' incentives (with respect to PG) deriving from the subsequent stage-games or the MG trigger strategies that players adopt to play these repeated games and are indifferent with respect to the PG game payoffs. If these choices are reported in the sub-game under consideration it is only for completeness of the formal representation, and without giving any information about their outcome in the subsequent games. Their attached payoffs are only relative to the PG, with respect to which they are indifferent. To be sure, nor does the information concerning the choice of PD_{Ej} strategies by player E if the PG was played according the equilibrium $(e, F; F_E)$ give any information about the payoffs' distribution depending on the solution of subsequent PD_{Ej} games. What it does provide, however, is very relevant information concerning whether the PG payoffs really correspond to what is expected from playing the equilibrium $(e, F; F_E)$.

In fact, when the PG is played according to the equilibrium $(e, F; F_E)$ a part of the surplus is saved and entitled to the S_{Wj} (according to Figure 7.5 it amounts to 2 utils). The interpretation is that player E is committed to using it in order to pay the S_{Wj} a fairer payoff for mutual cooperation in the PD_{Ej} games. This will not change – as we shall soon see – the basic strategic structure of the PD_{Ej} game. It can be considered as only an addition to the payoff that S_{Wj} gets conditionally on how player E will play these games. In particular, if player E chooses to cooperate by C_{Ej} with the S_{Wj}, the amount of 2 utils saved on behalf of S_{Wj} is effectively used to pay him/her more than

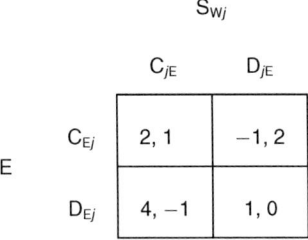

Figure 7.9 The basic PD_{Ej} in normal form

the standard PD_{Ej} payoffs that otherwise characterize E's relations with weak stakeholders.

To illustrate how the PG game equilibrium solution $(e, F; F_E)$ may affect the subsequent PD_{Wj}'s payoff levels, see Figure 7.9 and Figure 7.10. The first figure is a numerical example of the basic PD game played by any two adjacent players in the network. It also represents the interaction between E and S_{Wj} seen as independent from the conclusion of the antecedent game played by E and S_S. The figure reports the PD_{Ej} game as it will typically unfold if the antecedent PG game had an unfair solution such as $(e, U; U_E)$ or $(\neg e; U_E)$. The second figure illustrates how the former payoff matrix is changed by the additional payoffs 2 provided to S_{Wj} by the solution $(e, F; F_E)$ reached by E and S_S in the antecedent PG, granted that E plays cooperation C_{Ej} in the PD_{Ej}. Note, however, that in PD_{Ej} player E is not constrained to do so by the solution of the antecedent game PG, since it can choose its strategy freely, and also appropriate the extra rent by playing D_{Ej} in the game.

The payoff transformation in 7.10 can be explained as follows. The endowment of 2 utils saved on behalf of player S_{Wj} through the fair solution of the antecedent PG game, is managed by player E in PD_{Ej} so that it can be mutually advantageous in the case of full cooperation between them. E allocates the endowment to paying player S_{Wj} a higher wage in exchange for a player's S_{Wj} extra effort with respect to what was already incorporated in payoffs of

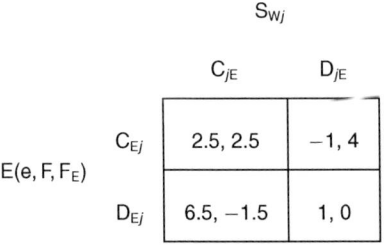

Figure 7.10 The PD_{Ej} if the antecedent PG has been solved by $(e, F; F_E)$

Figure 7.9. Effort enters S_{Wj} payoffs negatively (-0.5) but produces an advantage ($+0.5$) for E. The result is an effectively fairer (equal) payoff in the case of mutual cooperation (C_{Ej}, C_{jE}) = (2.5, 2.5) in the DP_{Ej} (with a significant improvement of S_{Wj} payoffs with respect to the basic game). However, the game has not changed its basic Prisoner's Dilemma structure. By playing 'defection', S_{Wj} can take the entire payment (the basic wage 2 plus the additional payoff 2) without incurring any production cost. On the other hand, if S_{Wj} agrees to increase his/her investment by 0.5, player E may appropriate the entire surplus engendered both player S_{Wj}'s basic and additional investments ($4 + 0.5$) plus the additional 2 utils that were saved on behalf of S_{Wj}, but in this case were in fact simply 'robbed' by E.

It can also be verified that the payoff transformation by means of the additional 2 utils does not change the players' incentive to cooperate in the *repeated* PD. In particular, it does not eliminate the basic asymmetry that characterizes the PD_{Ej}. That is to say, whereas each S_{Wj} considers continuous cooperation with E worth carrying out by repeated plays of the game, player E (the firm) does not find it sufficiently profitable to play iterated cooperation with the S_{Wi}, and prefers to defect even in the repeated game. This can be seen by comparing the critical discount rates δ^* that make repeated cooperation for the two players profitable under the two cases with their actual discount rate δ. In the basic and modified case respectively, the player's E critical discount rates are

$$\delta_E^* = (4-2)/(4-1) = 0.666, \quad \delta_E^{**} = (6.5-2.5)/(6.5-1) = 0.7272$$

Since by assumption player E's actual discount rate (or level of myopia) is $\delta < \delta^*$, it is necessarily also $\delta < \delta^{**}$ (since $0.666 < 0.7272$), so that in the modified PD_{Ej} game E has an even more intense incentive to defect from repeated cooperation. On the other hand, the respective critical discount rates that make repeated cooperation profitable for players S_{Wj} in the two cases are

$$\delta_{S_{Wj}}^* = (4-1)/2 = 1.5, \quad \delta_{S_{Wj}}^{**} = (4-2.5)/4 = 0.375$$

In this case, by assumption player S_{Wj}'s actual discount rate (or myopia level) is $\delta > \delta^*$ and hence necessarily $\delta > \delta^{**}$ (since $1.5 > 0.375$). Whereas the payoff-transformed PD_{Ej} game – due to the antecedent PG game's fair solution – makes players S_{Wj} even more willing to engage in mutually profitable cooperation with E, nonetheless the transformed PD_{Ej} reinforces game player E's preference for defection. Therefore, the external support for cooperation deriving from the 'Fair play' psychological payoff in the PG is even more important in order to sustain cooperation in the PD_{Ej}.

There is consequently a very compelling sense in which player S_S needs to assess player E's behavior in the subsequent PD_{Ej} in order to ascertain whether the fair strategy F_E has been effectively played in PG. To understand whether player E has effectively implemented the strategy F_E chosen in PG, s/he must check E's behavior until the subsequent stage-game is reached, wherein the allocation of the endowment to improve S_{Wj} conditions is carried out through C_{Ej}. Otherwise, the F_E choice in PG would be ineffectual or simply apparent, since what in fact results is the same outcome that E could have determined by choosing U_E when S_S chose F (i.e. E appropriates the residual of 2 utils set aside by S_S). In this case, player S_S considers player E's pair of subsequent moves (F_E, D_{Ej}) as essentially identical to playing U_E in the PG (recall S_S's learning rule in section 5.1).

Consequently, the relevant sub-game must include the following information: has the strategy adopted by E in the subsequent PD_{Ej} effectively allocated the payoff 2 to the dummy player according to the saving decisions (F; F_E)? If E plays C_{Ej} it has effectively implemented the strategy F understood as consistent with the *T* principle agreed in the pre-play stage of PG. If E plays D_{Ej} it has simply betrayed player S_S. The proper sub-game is given in Figure 7.11.

Note again that, in order to convey the relevant information, the sub-game includes the choices C_{Ej} and D_{Ej} in the subsequent PD_{Ej} but does not anticipate the description of the following stage-game payoffs. However, if player E adopts the strategy (F_E, D_{Ej}), against S_S playing (e, F), the material payoff vector becomes (2,4,0). The psychological payoffs change accordingly. Only if player E plays the pair (F_E, C_{Ej}) when S_S plays (e, F) are the

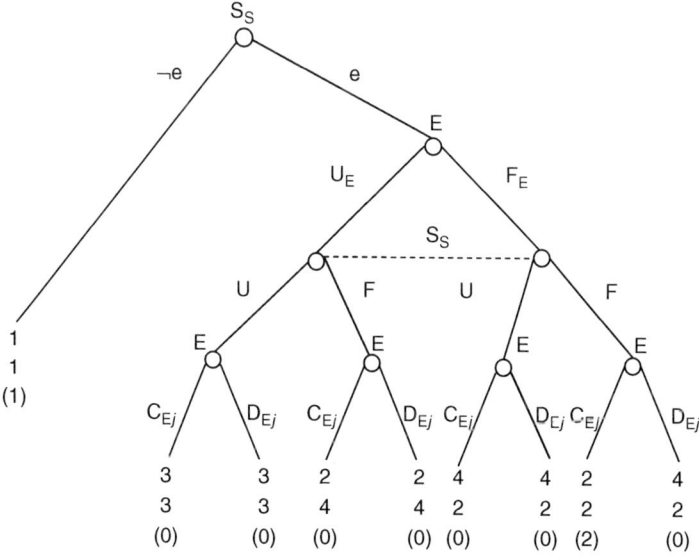

Figure 7.11 The relevant sub-game in extensive form, illustrated only in terms of material payoffs

E

	(F_E, C_{Ej})	(F_E, D_{Ej})	(U_E, C_{Ej})	(U_E, D_{Ej})
(e, F)	4.5, 4.5, (2)	2, 4, (0)	2, 4, (0)	2, 4, (0)
S_S (e, U)	4, 2, (0)	4, 2, (0)	3, 3, (0)	3, 3, (0)
¬e	1.31, 1.31, (1)	3.5, 3.5, (1)	3.5, 3.5, (1)	3.5, 3.5, (1)

Figure 7.12   Normal form of the relevant psychological sub-game

material payoffs of the PG (2,2,2), which may give rise to a psychological equilibrium of the game.

As in section 6.1, the psychological payoffs can be computed under the assumption of mutually consistent and common knowledge of reciprocal first- and second-order beliefs that activate conformist preferences (once again it is assumed that $\lambda = 2.5$). Figure 7.12 illustrates the corresponding sub-game in normal form, where the psychological payoffs are computed to represent conformist preferences.

Player E's strategies are labeled C_{Ej} and D_{Ej} only in order to account for what may happen in the stage-game PG because of these components of player E's strategies as well. Again, no consideration is given here to the payoffs that these strategies will accrue to player E when the proper PD_{Ej} is played. Recall also that only when they are associated with F_E are the strategies C_{Ej} and D_{Ej} material to this sub-game. Inspection of the psychological payoff matrix shows that the three psychological equilibria present in the game of Figure 7.6 and discussed in sections 3.3 and 3.4 also exist in the just defined sub-game.

Consider first the stage-game strategy profile (e, F; F_E, C_{Ej}). This is the sub-game psychological equilibrium inducing 'Fair play' in the PG and 'cooperation' by player E in the subsequent PD_{Ej}. In fact, the chosen value of λ and mutually consistent first- and second-order reciprocal beliefs predicting that player S_S will use (e, F) and player E will use (F_E, C_{Ej}), respectively, induce the psychological payoffs vector (4.5,4.5) for the two active players, which makes such strategies clearly mutual best responses. The distinctive feature of this sub-game representation is that, in order to give rise to such a 'Fair play' psychological equilibrium, player E's consistency in the consequent PD_{Ej} game must be included in the strategy description. This consists in using the cooperative strategy C_{Ej} that entails no appropriation by E of the surplus share saved for S_{Wj} by choosing the Fair strategies F and F_E in PG.

Also the strategy profile ($\neg e; U_E, D_{Ej}$) is a sub-game psychological equilibrium. If both the players reciprocally believe that E will play U_E in the sub-game if S_S enters, whereas player S_S will 'stay out' by playing $\neg e$, given the chosen value of λ the payoff vector in the sub-game for the two active player becomes (3.5,3.5), and $\neg e$, (U_E D_{Ej}) are the mutual best responses. This equilibrium is apparently weak because E has two further strategies, (F_E, D_{Ej}) and (U_E, C_{Ej}), that give the same psychological payoffs when player S_S chooses $\neg e$ and beliefs are aligned with the relevant strategy profiles. But this is not the case. To see why, consider the third strategy profile (e, U; U_E, D_{Ej}). If the beliefs of players E and S_S are such that each thinks that they will play collusively and that they believe that s/he/it will play collusively, then the value of λ goes to 0 and the payoff vector for active players is (3, 3), which entails that (U; U_E) is a pair of mutual best responses in the sub-game. Clearly, this is a strategy profile that defines a psychological equilibrium in the sub-game under consideration, and also in all the subsequent PD_{Ej} – where it coincides with the unique equilibrium point of one-shot Prisoners' Dilemmas. Recall in fact that player E's strategy (U_E, D_{Ej}) means that it will defect in its relationship with weak stakeholders in the PD_{Ej}, which is in line with E's incentives internal to the subsequent Prisoners' Dilemma Games seen as sub-games (so that there is no difficulty in maintaining that any strategy profile of the current sub-game that prescribes that this player E strategy choice will be incentive-compatible in the following sub-games for E).

Note the importance of the foregoing argument in regard to the apparent weakness of the sub-game equilibrium ($\neg e; U_E, D_{Ej}$). The strategy (U_E, D_{Ej}) is compatible with both the last two equilibria, and for whatever mutually consistent belief system, in at least one case (U_E, D_{Ej}) gives player E an higher psychological payoff than (F_E, D_{Ej}). Therefore, it is weakly dominant on the strategy (F_E, D_{Ej}). Since weakly dominated strategies like (F_E, D_{Ej}) can be eliminated, there is no reason for E to be consistently believed to have chosen (F_E, D_{Ej}). Thus the strategy profile ($\neg e; F_E, D_{Ej}$) is not a reasonable psychological equilibrium of the sub-game (the mutually consistent belief system that could justify it is not consistent with common knowledge of rationality). But what about E's strategy (U_E, C_{Ej})? Under the proper beliefs systems this allows strategy profiles (e, U; U_E, C_{Ej}) and ($\neg e; U_E, C_{Ej}$) that correspond to payoff vectors (3, 3) and (3.5, 3.5). These are psychological equilibria of the sub-game, so that (e, U; U_E, D_{Ej}) also seems to be a weak equilibrium, while ($\neg e; U_E, D_{Ej}$) remains weak owing to this indifferent alternative. But consider that (U_E, C_{Ej}) entails that player E will cooperate in the subsequent PD_{Ej} games, under the conditions that in the antecedent PG game the equilibrium solutions are either (e, U; U_E, C_{Ej}) or ($\neg e$; U_E, C_{Ej}). Both such profiles exclude 'Fair play' in the PG and do not provide E with any conditional incentive for cooperation in the PD_{Ej} (recall that player E's MG trigger strategy requires it to play 'defect' in the subsequent DP_{Wj} if the antecedent PG game player S_S's strategy has been either (e, U) or $\neg e$). Thus the strategy (U_E, C_{Ej}) is clearly dominated by the alternative (U_E, D_{Ej}) in the sub-games that follow the one considered here, and hence cannot be considered as part of reasonable psychological equilibria of the sub-game under consideration (there is no basis for a mutually consistent system of beliefs that predicts player E will cooperate in the PD_{Ej} when S_S does not resort to a strategy that benefits E with the psychological payoffs associated with Fair play conditional on the prosecution of cooperation). Not only can player E's strategy (F_E, D_{Ej}) be eliminated in the current sub-game, but also the strategy (U_E, C_{Ej}), because it is dominated in the subsequent PD_{Ej} sub-games – being not superior to (U_E, D_{Ej}) in the current one. Consequently, there are only three strategy profiles that are reasonable psychological equilibria in the sub-game.

6.3. Sub-game perfection of players' S_S and E MG trigger strategies

In this section we finally show that the combination of player S_S's and E's modified MG trigger strategies as defined in sections 5.1, 5.2 and 5.3 is a sub-game perfect equilibrium. The task is accomplished by considering various cases in which one can observe a deviation from the equilibrium path that would be traced in the current sub-game under the hypothesis that the two players follow their MG trigger strategies. We will verify the equilibrium property of choices that the players should make according to this pair of repeated strategies out-of-the-equilibrium-path in the relevant sub-game. This again employs an intuitive version of the 'trembling hand' argument used in section 6.1.

To begin with, recall that execution of S_S's and E's pair of MG trigger strategies, adopted to play repeated games, entails in the sub-game currently under consideration that the strategy profile (e, F; F_E, C_{Ej}) will be implemented. Thus, as long as neither player deviates from his/her equilibrium strategy, this strategy profile induces 'Fair play' in each repetition of the PG and player E's 'cooperation' in each repetition of any PD_{Ej}. The learning rules whereby the players adapt their beliefs to the past behavior of players in the network work are as stated in sections 5.1 and 5.2, respectively. Finally, if player S_S understands that player E is de facto playing U_E in the PG, his/her MG trigger strategy dictates reverting to ¬e. At the same time, when player E learns that player S_S will not keep playing (e, F) but from the forgoing period has changed to U or ¬e, according to its MG trigger strategy, it must also change to U in the PG and also to D_{Ej} in the subsequent PD_{Ej}.

Hence, assume that, when players E and S_S are adopting the modified MG trigger strategies, there is a small probability of the occurrence of a random mistake such that at time t they find themselves out-of-the-equilibrium-path. According to the sanctioning part of their grim trigger strategy, actions would produce a strategy profile different from (e, F; F_E, C_{Ej}) in the current sub-game (see Figures 7.11 and 7.12). The random deviation is imputable to player E because of one of three possible mistakes: (a) at time $t-1$, contrary to expectations, E has stopped playing F_E and started to play U_E in the

PG; (b) at time $t-1$, after playing F_E as expected, E has been the first in the network to play D_{Ej} (without any justification); (c) at time $t-1$, after the information was transmitted throughout the network that one member had played uncooperatively at time $t-2$, E continued playing C_{Ej}.

According to his/her learning rules, after having observed at time $t-1$ U_E or (F_E, D_{Ej}) or also (F_E, C_{Ej}) (in the special case that information circulated that someone else had played D in some PD in the network), at time t, S_S realizes that player E is de facto playing the PG unfairly, that is, the probability of F_E is 0. Thus, his/her MG trigger strategy requires that S_S play ¬e at time t in the PG (which is coherent with these beliefs).

On the other hand, player E's MG trigger strategy requires it to play (U_E, D_{Ej}) because the condition for continuing to play (F_E, C_{Ej}) that nobody in any PD at time $t-1$ deviated from C_{ki} has been violated either by E itself (case b) or by another player in the network (case c). In fact, for these cases, E's learning rules state that the probability of S_S playing ¬e is 1. Moreover, player E's MG trigger strategy requires it to start playing (U_E, D_{Ej}) if E itself at time $t-1$ played U_E (coherently with its learning rule that predicts in this case that the probability of S_S playing (e, F) is 0).

Do these strategies induce any irrational choice in the relevant sub-game out-of-the-equilibrium-path? Note that if E plays (F_E, D_{Ej}) at $t-1$ (case b), it would not be rational for E to continue playing in this way, because this is a weakly dominated strategy. If E thinks that S_S is going to play ¬e at t, (F_E, D_{Ej}) would not be a better response than (U_E, D_{Ej}). But if E realizes that S_S thinks that it believes s/he is going to play U, so that s/he chooses U, then playing (F_E, D_{Ej}) at t would be inferior to playing (U_E, D_{Ej}). There is no reason for E to play a strategy that can only give it less than the alternative. This is consistent with player S_S's learning rule that induces him/her, after observing at $t-1$, to believe that E will play U_E. Thus the profile (e, F; F_E, D_{Ej}) can be only a transitory state from the initial profile to a different continuation strategy profile. It cannot stabilize. Neither could player E respond to the deviation by playing in the sub-game (even though this was its deviation at $t-1$). In fact, player S_S's learning rule induces him/her to play ¬e and it must be believed by E. Moreover, there is no incentive for E's repeated cooperation in the subsequent PD_{Ej} without a psychological payoff deriving from PG. Finally, in the cases of both mistakes b) and c), E must know that throughout the network players have started the sanction stage of their MG trigger strategies, so that there will no longer be cooperation in the PD(s). Thus, replying to the deviation by (U_E, C_{Ej}) would be irrational. By contrast, the profile (¬e; U_E, D_{Ej}) is a psychological equilibrium of the sub-game, and under the appropriate mutually consistent reciprocal beliefs system it could emerge as a completely rational combination of mutually best responses. Indeed, player S_S's rules of belief adaptation predict that E will play U_E, while player E's rules of belief adaptation predict that player S_S will play (¬e). These beliefs are common knowledge. Thus, each player has a second-order belief predicting exactly the change of beliefs which is occurring to the other player. Given the first- and second-order beliefs that they will play the pair ($\neg$e; U_E) in the PG at t, player S_S must also believe that E will play D_{Ej} in the subsequent games, and this is also player E's only second-order belief about S_S's beliefs that is consistent with E's choice. Under our assumption of the value of λ, conformist preferences are activated in the PG, and the psychological equilibrium ($\neg$e; U_E, D_{Ej}) arises at time t in the sub-game. The deviation from the equilibrium path – after one stage – induces the transition from one psychological equilibrium of the sub-game to another. The strategy profile in which S_S sanctions the deviation coincides with the emergence of a sub-game psychological equilibrium, so that there is no instability in the required behavior, and the carrying out of the threat is perfectly credible.

But now assume that the relevant deviation in E's behavior occurs at time $t - 1$ because of a choice by a S_{Wj} player who – in contrast with the execution of his/her MG trigger strategy – during the cooperative stage $t - 2$ mistakenly deviates to D_{Wj}. According to its MG trigger strategy at $t - 1$, player E must play (F_E, D_{Ej}), and, at the subsequent time t, it must play (U_E, D_{Ej}). The deviation at time $t - 2$ does not immediately affect S_S's behavior in the sub-game at time $t - 1$, because his/her beliefs about E change only conditionally on learning of its effective choice in a stage sub-game. Thus, in the transition stage $t - 1$, S_S still chooses (e, F), while player E chooses (F_E, D_{Ej}), giving rise to (e, F; F_E, D_{Ej}). This is clearly an unstable strategy profile that may last only the time necessary for player S_S to realize that E is de facto playing the sub-game unfairly. From time t onward, the players will revert to the sub-game psychological equilibrium ($\neg$e; U_E, D_{Ej}) through a line of reasoning completely analogous to the one given for deviations directly due to player E's mistakes. Essentially, at time $t - 1$, E correctly does not changes its beliefs about S_S since it knows that his/her learning rules and strategy forgives a single period in which E may play (F_E, D_{Ej}) in order to start punishing S_{Wj}. From t onward, however, player S_S's first-order beliefs will be aligned with player E's behavior, while player E's beliefs about S_S's choice $\neg$e and their mutual second-order beliefs are also aligned. The sub-game psychological equilibrium ($\neg$e; U_E, D_{Ej}) again emerges – which is consistent with the sanctioning stages dictated by the players' MG trigger strategies.

Finally, a deviation may also arise from a mistake by player S_S. At time $t - 2$, player S_S chooses U, in contrast with his/her MG trigger strategy, while player E still chooses (F_E, C_{Ej}). The result in the sub-game at time $t - 2$ is a disequilibrium transition state (U; F_E, C_{Ej}). Players do not have mutually consistent beliefs, since – to exemplify – E fails to predict S_S's choice, believing mistakenly that s/he is still choosing (e, F), and S_S believes that E fails to predict his/her behavior because E' belief is still (e, F) when s/he is choosing U instead.

At time $t - 1$, because of the rule of beliefs adaptation, player E comes to believe that S_S chooses U with probability 1, and in the relevant sub-game, owing to its MG trigger strategy, E starts playing (U_E, D_{Ej}). At the same time, S_S correctly believes that E is playing (U_E, D_{Ej}), because of the learning rule whereby s/he no longer believes at t that E will play F_E if some player deviated at time $t - 2$ from its component of the strategy profile $(e, F; F_E, C_{Ej})$. Moreover, because S_S knows that it is unprofitable for player E to cooperate in the iterated PD_{Ej} when there is no Fair play in the PG, S_S also predicts D_{Ej}. Because of common knowledge of the players' beliefs adaptation rules, it is likely that, at $t - 1$, players entertain the following second-order beliefs: player E predicts that S_S believes it is playing (U_E, D_{Ej}); player S_S predicts that E believes s/he is choosing U.

Thus, if S_S were effectively choosing U at time $t - 1$, the result would be $(e, U; U_E, D_{Ej})$. Given the aforesaid first- and second-order beliefs – $b_E = U$, $b_{SS} = (U_E, D_{Ej})$; $b_E^2 = (U_E, D_{Ej})$, $b_{SS}^2 = U$ – that strategy combination would be a psychological equilibrium of the sub-game: to be sure, a psychological equilibrium wherein the players' ideal payoffs are nil, because of the unfair distribution, but nevertheless a psychological equilibrium that would stabilize and replicate at time t and thereafter. This would entail that, when a random deviation is caused by S_S, a collusion equilibrium is reached in the sub-game at time $t - 1$, contrary to the requirements of the MG trigger strategies of both players, which command that any deviation be sanctioned by the stay-out strategy of player S_S.

However, this is not the case. It is true that player S_S's adaptation rule states that if s/he at $t - 2$ has not chosen (e, F), then s/he believes with probability 1 that at time $t - 1$ E will do U, but his/her modified MG trigger strategy also states that if at $t - 2$ any whatever player has deviated from his/her component of the strategy profile $(e, F; F_E, C_{Ej})$ then at $t - 1$ S_S will move to $\neg e$. Thus, at $t - 1$, the result is in fact $(\neg e; U_E, D_{Ej})$, which contradicts player E's first-order belief that S_S does (e, U) and entails that player S_S's second-order belief that E believes that s/he does (e, U) mistakenly predicts his/her own behavior so that s/he knows that the beliefs system is inconsistent. At time $t - 1$ the players' reciprocal beliefs system does not exhibit the typical mutual consistency and alignment with the actual behavior required for psychological equilibria. Therefore, at $t - 1$, neither the psychological equilibrium (e, U, U_E, D_{Ej}) – which is what player E mistakenly predicts will happen – nor the psychological equilibrium $(\neg e; U_E, D_{Ej})$ – which is what actually occurs, even though it is not consistently represented through the players' beliefs – emerge. In the actual state of affairs $(\neg e; U_E, D_{Ej})$, in fact, the players cannot profit from any psychological payoff, given their mutually inconsistent beliefs system (E does not believe what S_S really does, and S_S predicts that E does not believe what s/he really does), so that they obtain only the material payoffs $(1,1)$.

But, at time t, E's beliefs are finally aligned with S_S's actual behavior. Because of what has been observed at $t - 1$, E believes that S_S does $\neg e$, while S_S continues to believe that E chooses (U_E, D_{Ej}). Since they know the reciprocal rules of adaptation, they also correctly believe what they believe, and all these beliefs converging on the state $(\neg e; U_E, D_{Ej})$ are aligned with their actual choices. This is, therefore, a psychological equilibrium of the sub-game, which may stabilize and can be replicated thereafter. Moreover, it is completely consistent with the dictates of the repeated-games MG trigger strategies of the two players.

To sum up, if a player S_S random mistake occurs, two transition periods are needed before a psychological equilibrium of the sub-game is reached. At $t - 2$ the outcome is (e, U; F_E, C_{Ej}), with a worse material payoff for E, and a material advantage for S_S, no payoff to the dummy S_{Wj} and no ideal utilities at all. At $t - 1$ the outcome is ($\neg$e; U_E, D_{Ej}), which is not even a psychological equilibrium because of the still inconsistent players' beliefs, so that they merely obtain the 'stay-out' material payoff (1,1,1). But at t the psychological equilibrium ($\neg$e; U_E, D_{Ej}) is finally reached because it is supported by the appropriate reciprocal and consistent beliefs and provides psychological motivations for implementation of player S_S's sanction and support for the 'would-be-ready-to-cooperate' preference by E.

The conclusion is that, for whatever random mistake that takes the sub-game play out of the equilibrium path established by the pair of modified repeated MG trigger strategies of player S_S and E, there is no reason to think that the out-of-the-equilibrium-path choices will stabilize on a sub-game psychological equilibrium that would induce stable deviation from what the pair of modified grim trigger strategies would require the players to do. In particular, there is no reason to think that the logic and incentives faced in the sub-game will prevent player S_S from carrying out the punishment stages of his/her repeated MG trigger strategy, which is at the basis of the sustainability of fair cooperation throughout the network, when player E has no direct material incentive to play cooperatively with both its S_{Wj}. By contrast, after a maximum of two transition stages, a sub-game psychological equilibrium is reached which guarantees that the punishment stages of player S_S's MG trigger strategy will be implemented in accordance with his/her psychological 'incentives' and the sub-game best response logic. Assuming that the pair of modified MG trigger strategies, together with the standard ones played by any other player in the network, constitutes a repeated games Nash equilibrium, this result ensures that cooperation in the firm-stakeholders-other-agents bilaterally deficient relational network is endogenously stable (*Quod Erat Demostrandum*).

7. Conditions for a fair cooperative equilibrium in the firm-stakeholders network

This section is concerned with the precise conditions whereby the repeated games strategies of players S_S and E studied so far are a Nash equilibrium of the games that they repeatedly play between themselves and (in the case of E) in relation to weak stakeholders S_{Wj}. This has been presumed thus far in accordance with intuition and standard results concerning the MG

E

		F_E	U_E
	e, F	$b + \lambda_{Ss},\ b + \lambda_E,\ (b)$	$b,\ d,\ (0)$
S_S	e, U	$d,\ b,\ (0)$	$c,\ c,\ (0)$
	$\neg e$	$a + 1/x\,\lambda_{Ss},\ a + 1/x\,\lambda_E,\ (a)$	$a + \lambda_{Ss},\ a + \lambda_E,\ (a)$

Figure 7.13   Again the PG in normal form (where $d > c > b > a$ and where the conditions for the existence of the psychological equilibria are: $b + \lambda_E > d$, $a + \lambda_E < b + \lambda_E$, $a + \lambda_{Ss} > c$)

trigger strategies used in this kind of bilaterally deficient relational network, wherein adjacent players are involved in repeated PD(s) (see section 2). We have concentrated largely on the effective sustainability of the cooperation induced by these equilibrium repeated game strategies, because the main challenge was their sub-game perfection in the stage-game wherein S_S must back all the sanctioning mechanisms without apparently having any incentive to do so in the event that the need to implement the threat of his/her strategy arises. But we must now show that the modified MG trigger strategies that players S_S and E use in their repeated games (the PG and PD_{Ej}) satisfy the conditions for the existence of a repeated game Nash equilibrium.

We must verify the following (the payoffs reported for the reader's convenience in Figure 7.13 are the same as in the PG of Figure 7.7):

1. S_S prefers to continue:

    - to play (e, F) instead of playing ($\neg e$) as long as E plays (F_E) in the PG and
    - to play (e, F) instead of playing (e, U) as long as E plays (F_E) in the PG.

2. E does not have an incentive to defect either in the PG or in the PD_{Ej} as long as:

    - all the players involved in the PDs are cooperating and
    - S_S is playing (e, F)

Let us start with point 1 and consider the payoff that S_S may obtain in the repeated PG. In order to verify whether S_S has any incentive to defect and stop playing (e, F) as long as E plays (F_E), we have to compare the repeated payoff obtained by S_S when s/he plays (e, F) and E plays (F_E) with:

a) the payoff obtained by S_S when s/he plays ($\neg e$) and consequently in the continuation of the game E plays (U_E)

b) the payoff obtained by S_S when s/he plays (e, U) and consequently the continuation of the game E plays (U_E).

If S_S and E play F and F_E respectively, S_S obtains a payoff (hereafter also the 'cooperative payoff') equal to $\sum_{n=0}^{\infty}(b+\lambda_{Stks})\delta^n/(1-\delta)$

The payoff obtained by S_S in case (a) is obviously lower than the 'cooperative payoff' because it is equal to $[a+(1/x)\lambda]\delta$ (the payoff obtained at the first stage when S_S defects ($\neg e$) and E plays F_E) plus $\sum_{n=0}^{\infty}(a+\lambda_{Stks})\delta^n/(1-\delta)$, which is the payoff obtained by S_S from the second stage, after his/her defection, onward (recall that $b > a$).

The payoff obtained by S_S in case (b) is:

i. d in the 'first' period of deviation, when S_S defects and plays (e, U) while E plays F_E;
ii. c from the 'second' period after the deviation onward when the continuation profile becomes (e, U; U_E).

Obviously, this strategy is not convenient for S_S either, at least if we assume that the players are endowed with high environmental cognitive social capital so that $\lambda >(d - b)$, the 'cooperative payoff', is higher than the payoff obtained by playing (e, U):

$$\sum_{i=1}^{\infty}(b+\lambda) > d+\sum_{i=2}^{\infty}c.$$

With respect to point 2 – the firm's incentive to depart from the 'fair-cooperative equilibrium' amounts to choosing 'Fair play' in the repeated PG and 'cooperation' in the repeated PD_{Ej} – we shall consider the sub-network of relations involving E (see Figure 7.14).

With regard to the relation in which E is involved, note that $\Sigma_{j\in RE}\, g_{Ej} \geq 0$ is a necessary condition in order for E to continue to play F in the PG. It amounts to saying that $g_{ESs} - (g_{ESw1}+g_{ESw2}) \geq 0$.[15]

We want to show that E has no incentive to defect when it, S_S, and all the other players in the network are cooperating. E may defect by adopting two strategies.

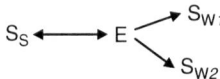

Figure 7.14   The restricted firm-stakeholders network

A) E stops cooperating with S_{Wj} at time t and, at the same time, it continues to play F_E in the PG. Given player S_S's belief formation rule, since E is the first to defect in PD_{Ej}, S_S believes that E will defect also in PG at time $t+1$. For this reason (following his/her MG trigger strategy), S_S will punish E at time $t+1$ by playing $\neg e$. Likewise, E anticipates S_S's decision and, at time $t+1$, will revert to U_E in the PG. From the period $t+1$ onward, the payoffs of the game are determined by ($\neg e$; U_E, D_{Ej}). This case applies if $a+\lambda_E \geq d$.[16]

B) E defects at time t both in the PG (where it starts to play U_E) and in PD_{Ej} (where it plays D_{Ej}). In this case, the payoffs obtained by E and S_S in the PG at time t, are respectively b and d, which are determined by the strategy (e, F; U_E). At time $t+1$, S_S will play $\neg e$ because s/he believes that E will play U_E also at $t+1$. E anticipates that S_S will not enter the PG at time $t+1$ and continues to play U_E. For these reasons, from $t+1$ onward, we will observe in the repeated PG the strategies ($\neg e$; U_E) that generate the payoffs ($a+\lambda_{Ss}$, $a+\lambda_E$). This case applies if $a+\lambda_E < d$.

The discounted payoff obtained by E in the repeated PG when it and S_S repeatedly play fair by (e, F; F_E) is

$$(b+\lambda_E)/(1-\delta), \text{ with } 0 \leq \delta \leq 1.$$

The discounted payoff obtained by E if it adopts the strategy described in case A is

$$(b+\lambda_E) + (a+\lambda_E)\delta/(1-\delta)$$

Given that $a+\lambda_E < b+\lambda_E$, it follows that

$$[(b+\lambda_E)/(1-\delta)] - [(b+\lambda_E) + (a+\lambda_E)\delta/(1-\delta)] > 0$$

Hence, E prefers to play (F_E, C_{Ej}) instead of adopting the strategy described in case A.

With regard to case B, the discounted payoff obtained by E is

$$(b+\lambda_E) + d\delta + (a+\lambda_E)\delta^2/(1-\delta).$$

Also in this case, given the assumption $b+\lambda_E > d$, it follows that

$$[(b+\lambda_E)/(1-\delta)] - [(b+\lambda_E) + d\delta + (a+\lambda_E)\delta^2/(1-\delta) > 0.$$

We conclude that, if E and S_S start to play (e, F; F_E), and if they reason as if S_S were endowed with high environmental cognitive social capital, and if E announces CSR principles that allow for the formation of reciprocal beliefs

	$C_{Swj,E}$	$D_{Swj,E}$
$C_{E,Swj}$	b, b	0, c
$D_{E,Swj}$	c, 0	a, a

Figure 7.15 The normal form PD_{Ej} stage-game involving E and S_{Wj} (where $c > b > a > 0$)

and conformist preferences (section 4), there are no incentives for E to stop playing F_E. This is true independently of the value of the discount factor δ.[17]

Since E does not have incentives to defect in the PG, the decision to deviate can only be the consequence of the strategy adopted in the PD_{Ej} played by the firm E with its weak stakeholders. This could be possible, and we will verify whether it is the case that E decides to defect in the two PD_{Ej} in which it is involved with weak stakeholders, even though it knows that this decision terminates cooperation also in the repeated PG.[18] For this reason, it is necessary to investigate the incentives that characterize E in the repeated PD_{Ej} with weak stakeholders. The stage-game normal form of the PD_{Ej} is shown in Figure 7.15.

The assumption is that, in repeated PD_{Ej}, player E's myopic value of δ does not make repeated cooperation sufficiently desirable for it. In other words, at any time t, the firm prefers to defect when the weak stakeholders play C_{SwjE} instead of continuing to cooperate, even though after the defection, the payoff that E obtains from the period $t + 1$ onward is equal to $a\delta^{t-1}/(1 - \delta)$. The deviation of E at the first stage represents the first opportunity for it to obtain the maximum advantage by defecting when S_{Wj} plays C_{SwjE}. In fact, given δ so that $g_{ESwj} < 0$, it follows that

$$[b/(1-\delta)] < \ldots < [b + b\delta + \ldots + b\delta^t + c\delta^{t+1} + a\delta^{t+2}/(1-\delta)]$$
$$< [(b + c\delta + a\delta^2/(1-\delta)] < [c + a\delta/(1-\delta)]$$

According to this payoff structure, if we consider only the PD_{Ej}, material incentives induce E to defect at the first stage in PD_{Ej} because at this first stage the incentive for E to defect (i.e. the difference $g_{ESwj} < 0$) is the greatest. The payoff which E obtains by defecting at the first stage is

$$[c + a\delta/(1 - \delta)]$$

and

$$g_{ESwj} = [b/(1-\delta)] - [c + a\delta/(1-\delta)] < 0.$$

However, in order to explain E's behavior, we must consider that E's decision to defect at the first stage in PD_{Ej} implies the sanction by S_S in the subsequent repeated PG games. In particular, according to the previous considerations, S_S will play $\neg e$ in the PG the stage after E has defected in PD_{Ej}. By anticipating S_S's intention, E will stop playing F_E in the PG as well. For this reason, in order to understand the optimality of player E's strategy, we should simultaneously consider the payoff structure in the repeated PD_{Ej} and PG.

In particular, if

$$\sum\nolimits_{j\in RE} g_{Ej} = g_{ESs} - (g_{ESw1} + g_{ESw2}) \geq 0$$

then we can demonstrate that if E, S_S and S_{Wj} start their relationship in a fair-cooperative way, there are no incentives for the firm to defect.

Consider the numerical example introduced in Figure 7.6 (section 3.4) and fix the following parameters $b=2, d=4, a=1, c=3, \lambda=3$ and $\delta_E=0.41$. When E defects at the first stage in the PD_{Ej} and at the second stage in the PG, we obtain: $g_{ESs}=0.695$, $g_{ESwj}=-0.305$ and $g_{ESs}-2(g_{ESwj})=0.085$. This result holds independently of the stage when the firm may decide to defect.

For example, if E defects at the third stage in PD_{Ej} (and consequently, at the fourth stage in PG, the outcome is $(\neg e, U_E)$), we obtain $g_{ESs}=0.107$, $g_{ESwj}=-0.053$ and $g_{ESs}-2\left(g'_{ESwj}\right)=0.001$. For this reason, given these values of parameters and $\delta=0.41$, the sub-network of E's cooperative relations is sustainable when players implement their MG trigger strategies. It is finally important to identify for which values of δ this result holds and when E, consequently, prefers playing fairly and cooperatively in the repeated PG and PD_{Ei} respectively, instead of defecting.

First of all note that, when S_S and E are endowed by cognitive social capital (i.e. λ_E and λ_{Ss} are both $> d-b$ and only $\lambda_{Ss} > c-a$), the repeated Fair F_E strategy in the PG is more profitable than the repeated unfair U_E one, independently of δ. In fact, every strategy of deviation induces the PG stage-game equilibrium $(\neg e; U_E)$ and generates the repeated PG payoff $(a+\lambda_E)\delta^{t-1}/(1-\delta)$. This payoff is strictly lower than the psychological payoff of the repeated Fair strategies (consistent with playing the modified MG trigger strategies defined in the preceding sections) inducing the PG stage-game equilibrium $(e, F; F_E)$ and the repeated PG payoff $(b+\lambda_E)\delta^{t-1}/(1-\delta)$. Thus, E will always cooperate in the PG.

Nevertheless, Fair play in the repeated PG becomes less and less profitable in comparison with defection when δ decreases while defection in PD_{Ej} becomes more and more profitable when δ decreases. For this reason, there will be a value δ^* which indicates the lowest value of player E's personal discount factor δ_E, in correspondence to which it is still convenient for E to play fairly and cooperate (i.e. the stage-game strategy (F_E, C_{Ej})), while when δ_E is lower than δ^* E has incentives to defect in all three adjacent games. Thus, when $\delta_E < \delta^*$, E will defect in both the repeated PG and the two subsequent PD_{Ej} and the cooperative equilibrium will not be sustainable.

Using the previous numerical parameters $(b = 2, d = 4, a = 1, c = 3, \lambda = 3)$, we obtain δ^* equal to 0.4. In fact, when $\delta_E = 0.4$, given the other values of parameters, it holds that $\delta^*_{ESs} - 2(g^*_{ESwj}) = 0$. For any value $\delta_E < \delta^*$ we have, the fair-cooperative repeated equilibrium fails. For example, if $\delta_E = 0.39$, $g_{ESs} = 0.6394$, $g_{ESw} = -0.3607$, and $g_{ESs} - 2(g_{ESwfj}) = -0.082$.

The critical value δ^* can be calculated in general as a function of the parameters b, d, a, c and λ_E of player E's payoff function when it compares the fair-cooperative iterated payoff and the payoff from the best deviation strategy. The relevant gains are respectively $g_{ESs} = [(b + \lambda_E)/(1 - \delta)] - [(b + \lambda_E) + (a + \lambda_E)\delta/(1 - \delta)]$ as far as the repeated PG is concerned, and $g_{ESwj} = [b/(1 - \delta)] - [c + a\delta/(1 - \delta)]$ in relation to the repeated PD_{Ej}.

Note that the gain g_{ESs} can be simplified by $(b - a)\delta/(1 - \delta)$, which, given the game's PG parameters, is in general a positive gain. Moreover, the gain g_{ESwj} can be simplified by $(b - c) + (b - a)\delta/(1 - \delta)$, which due to the negative value of $(b - c)$ and the assumptions of the other parameters in this game is in general a negative gain. Thus, in order to find δ^*, it must be established (recall that the negative gain from cooperation are doubled given that E plays two PD_{Wj}) that

$$(b - a)\delta^*/(1 - \delta^*) = -2[(b - c) + (b - a)\delta^*/(1 - \delta^*)]$$

and that, given the negative value of the difference $(b - c)$ entails

$$(b - c) = -1/2[(b - a)\delta^*/(1 - \delta^*)] - (b - a)\delta^*/(1 - \delta^*) = 1.5[(b - a)\delta^*/(1 - \delta^*)]$$

that is

$$\frac{(b - c)}{(b - a)}(-2/3) = \delta^*/(1 - \delta^*)$$

In fact, according to our parameter $\delta^* = 0.40$, which is the solution for

$$(b - c)/(b - a) = -1 \text{ (as it is in our case) and for } \delta^*/(1 - \delta^*) = 0.666.$$

We may conclude that the introduction of psychological payoffs into the game played between E and S_S – payoffs which stem from the agreement on the principle $T(= CSR)$ of fairness in the pre-play communication phase of the game – makes the network among the firm and all its stakeholders sustainable for values of player E's discount factor δ_E such that $\delta_E \leq \delta^*$, even though the firm has no material incentive to cooperating with weak stakeholders.

8. Conclusions

The aim of this chapter has been to investigate the theoretical relationship between social capital and corporate social responsibility. Our principal purpose has been to highlight the importance of cognitive social capital and CSR principles in generating cooperative networks between the firm and all its stakeholders (structural social capital).

Cognitive social capital consists of dispositions and beliefs functional to the development of conformist motivations that affect the agents' propensity to behave in different ways. Beliefs focus on reciprocal behaviors among agents and are affected by agreements on general principles and default reasoning stemming from agreements, but they also depend on the behavior that other agents have exhibited in the past. Dispositions spring principally from the cultural environment of the most general social norms and values shared in society at large, so that they have a component independent of specific agreements on small-scale social norms and principles of behavior, such as the CSR principle that a firm may agree with its stakeholders. But they also depend on micro elements (e.g. genetic and psychological factors) and cannot be activated without the other components of cognitive social capital that we have seen are related to more intentional elements like agreements on CSR norms. Conformist motivations are reasons to act in compliance with agreed principles of justice, such as CSR principles, and they are proportional to the level of conformity that an agent may reach through his/her action contingently on his/her beliefs about other agents' behaviors; they also depend on the expected reciprocity of other agents in obtaining high levels of conformity contingent on their own expectations about other agents. Conformist motivations operate as weights that determine the extent to which the exogenous and primitive cooperative dispositions can affect actual behaviors.

Structural social capital is understood as a global (multilateral) property of a relational network linking agents (for example, firms and stakeholders) so that, independently of the deficiency of the specific bilateral relations, linkages in the network are nevertheless characterized by cooperation among agents. The sustainability of such linkages, and hence the possibility of observing a network structurally characterized by social capital, depends on four factors: a) reciprocal beliefs that others will cooperate, b) a generic disposition to cooperate, c) conformist motivations contingent on agreed norms and beliefs, d) the existence of sanctions against agents that decide not to cooperate. While the first three elements are cognitive components of social capital, the fourth is a structural characteristic of the game forms whereby interaction among agents takes place.

In this context, CSR is an essential part of the cognitive social capital that agents characterized as firms and stakeholders may possess in order to make cooperation in a relational network sustainable. In particular, CSR principles are the basis for impartial agreements among agents (firms and stakeholders) on which depend mutual beliefs concerning the level of principle compliance and conformist motivations (preferences) related to each of the solutions that agents can give to their interaction.

In regard to the firm's stakeholders, we have introduced a distinction between strong and weak stakeholders. The firm is interested in cooperating in the long term with strong stakeholders, and it is not interested in doing so with weak ones.

We have based our analytical framework on the relational network literature, with particular regard to Lippert and Spagnolo (2010). But we have made an important innovation to this framework by introducing the idea of modeling at least some relations by means of psychological games. Thanks to this analytical model, we have been able to show that the agreement between the firms and its strong stakeholders on CSR fairness principles, which in their turn activate the other components of the firm's and stakeholders' cognitive social capital, generates endogenous incentives for the firm to cooperate with weak stakeholders and creates cooperative relations that would otherwise not exist.

Our argument has consisted of the six following points:

1. In a context characterized by strong dispositions to conform with norms of fair cooperation (high levels of λ), and by the decision of the firm to agree with its strong stakeholders – belonging to the same context – on a contractarian principle of fair treatment addressed to whatever stakeholder (a principle of CSR), the effective implementation of such a social norm may stem from the fact that effective conformist preferences can be formed which activate the motivational force of cooperative dispositions. Thus individuals (both members of the organization in a position of authority – the firm – or internal and external key stakeholders) will be induced by the motivational force of those dispositions to maintain fair and cooperative conduct with respect to weak stakeholders. In other words, a CSR principle will be complied with even if there is no direct advantage in terms of material payoffs accruing to the powerful members of the organization or to their strong stakeholders.
2. Dispositions do not operate in a vacuum. The agreement on a CSR principle may also favor the appropriate reciprocal beliefs concerning mutual conformity that by themselves furnish reasons to comply with the principle. The implementation of a CSR standard contributes to generating the belief in the firm's stakeholders that the firm will share cooperative relations with them. It is only with reference to explicit agreements on CSR principles that stakeholders can form their beliefs about the type of firm to which they are related.
3. This is a sort of moral reputation that reinforces cooperation which is not based only on the pursuit of material advantages. It therefore

supplements the reasons for combining a good reputation with more intrinsic reasons to act.

4. The beliefs and dispositions related to cognitive social capital induce the strong stakeholders to cooperate with the firm if and only if it is also cooperative with weak stakeholders.

5. The possibility that strong stakeholders decide not to cooperate with the firm if it defects with weak stakeholders is a reliable threat for the firm, which may decide (it depends on the payoff structure) to cooperate with weak stakeholders in order to avoid the sanction from strong stakeholders.

6. This produces structural social capital (in terms of a sustainable network of cooperative relations involving the firm, the strong and the weak stakeholders) that would not be feasible without the threat of sanction by the strong stakeholders. This sanction is not due to exogenous reasons; rather, it is determined by endogenous incentives that we have explained by considering the effect of cognitive social capital on stakeholders' behavior.

Our analysis has shown that there exists a Nash equilibrium which implies cooperation between the firm and all its stakeholders, both the strong and the weak ones. This cooperative equilibrium is sub-game perfect and it applies, for a reasonable value of the firm's discount factors δ, when the firm generates the appropriate belief in strong stakeholders – characterized by cognitive social capital in terms of disposition – by declaring a CSR standard.

Our findings raise numerous questions and ideas for further research.

First, they open the way to studies aimed at empirical verification of the effect of cognitive social capital and CSR declaration on cooperative behaviors by firms toward weak stakeholders.

Second, by shedding light on a new, important role of social capital, they encourage further theoretical and empirical analysis of the factors and the policies which may be able to increase cognitive social capital in terms of disposition to cooperate, which is a key element in fostering CSR adoption and cooperative relations between firms and weak stakeholders.

Acknowledgements

We would like to thank Luciano Andreozzi, Simone de Colle, Gianluca Grimalda, Marco Faillo, Stefania Ottone, Ugo Pagano for useful comments and suggestions, as well as the audiences at the 23rd EBEN (European Business Ethics Network) annual conference (Trento), at the eighth international conference in commemoration of Prof. Marco Biagi 'Rethinking Corporate Governance: from Shareholder Value to Stakeholder Value' (Modena), at the 2nd EMES international conference on social enterprise (Trento), at the international conference 'Happiness and Relational Goods: Well-Being and

Interpersonal Relations in the Economic Sphere' (Venezia) and at the international workshop 'Experts' Meeting: Measuring Social Capital' (Vienna). The usual disclaimers apply.

Appendix I

We report the formal representation of the function F which captures, for agents endowed by conformist preferences, the effects on ideal utility of beliefs in the degree of conformity with the ideal by other agents (see also Grimalda and Sacconi 2002, 2005; Sacconi 2010c *infra*; Sacconi and Grimalda 2007). We calculate the agents' ideal utility for each strategy pair of player S_S and the agents' ideal utility for E' strategies when it believes that S_S is going to play $\neg e$ (in this respect note that E's ideal utility associated with its strategies – F_E and U_E – when E believes that S_S is going to play F or U may be easily computed by symmetrically considering the ideal utility of S_S when his/her strategies are (e, F) and (e, U) and his/her first-order beliefs are F_E or U_E).

A1   The utility function of agents endowed with conformist preferences

The utility function of an agent i characterized by conformist preferences is:

$$V_i = U_i(\sigma) + \lambda_i F[T(\sigma)].$$

F is a function, shared by all the agents, of the normative fairness principle T. In abstract, F could be specified in different ways in order to consider various possible forms of the morality-grounded motive to behave, and it determines the weight of λ_i in the agents' gain. We follow Grimalda and Sacconi (2005) and Sacconi (2006) in adopting a particular specification for F based on an idea of expected mutuality in conforming with a contractarian principle of justice (T), captured by the Nash bargaining solution, which seems particularly coherent with the idea of an agreement involving the firm and its stakeholders (also called the Nash social welfare function N):

$$T(\sigma) = N(U_{1,\dots,}U_n) = \prod_{i=1}^{n} (U_i - d_i)$$

where d_i stands for the reservation utility that player i can obtain when the bargaining process collapses. In the present context, we consider it appropriate to set all of these reservation utilities to zero.[19] To give an example related to the calculation of the value of T, consider the payoff matrix reported in Figures 7.4 and 7.5 (section 2.2), where the payoffs obtained by the three players – the firm, the strong and the weak stakeholder (that is, the dummy player), are (2, 2, (2)). In this case, the principle T assumes the value $T = 2 \times 2 \times 2 = 8$. By contrast, when at least one player obtains a payoff equal to 0 (for example when the active players' strategies are (e, U; U_E), it is $T = 3 \times 3 \times 0$).

Now, if we consider a two-person game, it is possible to define the two indices that contribute to determining F as follows:

1. $1 + f_i$: the index of player's i conditional conformity based on the degree of deviation from pure conditional conformity with T, that is, $f_i(\sigma_i, b_i^1)$:

$$f_i(\sigma_i,\ b_i^1) = \frac{T(\sigma_i,\ b_i^1) - T^{MAX}(b_i^1)}{T^{MAX}(b_i^1) - T^{MIN}(b_i^1)}$$

where $T^{MAX}(b_i^1)$ and $T^{MIN}(b_i^1)$ are the maximum and minimum values that the welfare distribution function (which represents the normative principle or ideology T) can assume, depending on i's action, given i's first-order belief, b_i^1, about the action that j is going to perform. $T(\sigma_i, b_i^1)$ is the actual level of T when player i carries out strategy σ_i given what s/he expects from player j. f_i varies from 0 (no deviation at all from the principle T) to -1 (maximal deviation).

2. $1 + \tilde{f}_j$: the index of player j's expected reciprocity in conformity based on the evaluation that player i forms about j's deviation from full conformity with the principle T, that is, $\tilde{f}_j(b_i^1,\ b_i^2)$:

$$\tilde{f}_j(b_i^1\ b_i^2) = \frac{T(b_i^1,\ b_i^2) - T^{MAX}(b_i^2)}{T^{MAX}(b_i^2) - T^{MIN}(b_i^2)}$$

where b_i^1 is the first-order belief of player 1 about the action of player j. b_i^2 is the second-order belief about player j's belief in the action adopted by player i. $T^{MAX}(b_i^2)$ and $T^{MIN}(b_i^2)$ are the values that the welfare function takes when player j respectively maximizes or minimizes it, given the second-order belief of player i. In other words, $T^{MAX}(b_i^2)$ and $T^{MIN}(b_i^2)$ indicate the maximum and minimum value that player j can contribute to the welfare function, given his/her belief about i's action as perceived by i him/herself. $T(b_i^1,\ b_i^2)$ is the actual value that i expects the welfare function to take according to his/her beliefs. Also $\tilde{f}_j$ varies between 0 and -1, which respectively indicate the maximum and minimum degree of conformity by player j with the ideology embodied in the welfare function T.

Implementing these definitions, the utility function of agent i can be written as:

$$V_i(\sigma_i, b_i^1, b_i^2) = U_i(\sigma_i, b_i^1) + \lambda_i[1 + \tilde{f}_j(b_i^1, b_i^2)][1 + f_i(\sigma_i, b_i^1)]$$

A2   Method for calculation of the agents' ideal utility

In this part we provide a detailed illustration of the method for calculation of the ideal utility component of the players' payoffs. The reference game and the parameters of the material part of the utility functions are those given in Figure 7.4 and Figure 7.5 (section 2.2) of the main text. The calculation complements the qualitative discussion conducted in section 3.3.

First, we must remember that the values of the agents' conformity indexes $\left[1 + f_i\left(\sigma_i,\ b_i^1\right)\right]$ and $\left[1 + \tilde{f}_j\left(b_i^1,\ b_i^2\right)\right]$ result from the subtraction of a deviation measure ranging between 0 (no deviation at all from the principle) and -1 (complete deviation) from the unit (i.e. 1 means maximal conformity).

Taking account of different possible belief systems (i.e. first- and second-order beliefs justifying the prediction of any given outcome of the game), the conformity indexes attached to how players carry out each state of the game may be computed (Note: the notation (F|F) should be read as 'player *i* using strategy F *given* that player *j*'s strategy is F'. The strategy after the symbol | should be read as a first-order belief or a second-order belief about that strategy, according to the context).

- Strategy (e, F) of S_S given the first-order belief (b_{Ss}^1) that E plays F_E and given the second-order belief b_{Ss}^2 that E believes that S_S plays (e, F).

The deviation of player S_S from full conformity for strategy (e, F) is in this case:

$$f_{Ss}(e, F; F_E) = \frac{T(e, F|F_E) - T^{\mathrm{MAX}}(F_E)}{T^{\mathrm{MAX}}(F_E) - T^{\mathrm{MIN}}(F_E)} = \frac{T(e, F|F_E) - T(e, F|F_E)}{T(e, F|F_E) - T(e, U|F_E)} = 0$$

which entails a player S_S index of conditional conformity $[1 + f_{Ss}(e, F|F_E)] = 1$

Player E's expected deviation from full conformity for strategy F_E is in this case

$$\tilde{f}_E(F_E; e, F) = \frac{T(F_E|e, F) - T^{\mathrm{MAX}}(e, F)}{T^{\mathrm{MAX}}(e, F) - T^{\mathrm{MIN}}(e, F)} = \frac{T(F_E|e, F) - T(F|e, F)}{T(F|e, F) - T(U|e, F)} = 0$$

so the *index* of expected reciprocal conformity is $[1 + \tilde{f}_E(F_E; e, F)] = 1$. Thus, in this case, player S_S's strategy (e,F) obtaining ideal utility is λ (recall that the ideal utility stems from $\lambda_i\left[1 + \tilde{f}_j\left(b_i^1,\ b_i^2\right)\right]\left[1 + f_i\left(\sigma_i,\ b_i^1\right)\right]$)

- Strategy (e, F) of S_S, given the first-order belief (b_{Ss}^1) that E plays U_E and given the second-order belief b_{Ss}^2 that E believes that S_S plays (e, F).

The deviation of player S_S from full conformity for strategy (e, F) is, in this case,

$$f_{Ss}(e,F;U_E) = \frac{T(e,F|U_E) - T^{\text{MAX}}(U_E)}{T^{\text{MAX}}(U_E) - T^{\text{MIN}}(U_E)} = \frac{T(e,F|U_E) - T(\neg e,|U_E)}{T(\neg e,|U_E) - T(e,U|U_E)} = -1$$

which entails a player S_S index of conditional conformity $[1 + f_{Ss}(e,F|U_E)] = 0$

Player E's expected deviation from full conformity for strategy U_E is, in this case,

$$\tilde{f}_E(U_E;e,F) = \frac{T(U_E|e,F) - T^{\text{MAX}}(e,F)}{T^{\text{MAX}}(e,F) - T^{\text{MIN}}(e,F)} = \frac{T(U_E|e,F) - T(F_E|e,F)}{T(F_E|e,F) - T(U_E|e,F)} = -1$$

the index of expected reciprocal conformity is $[1 + \tilde{f}_E(U_E;e,F)] = 0$. Thus, in this case, the ideal utility for player S_S's strategy (e, F) is 0.

- Strategy (e, U) of S_S, given the first-order belief (b_{Ss}^1) that E plays F_E and given the second-order belief b_{Ss}^2 that E believes that S_S plays (e, U).

The deviation of player S_S from full conformity for strategy (e, U) is, in this case,

$$f_{Ss}(e,U;F_E) = \frac{T(e,U\backslash F_E) - T^{\text{MAX}}(F_E)}{T^{\text{MAX}}(F_E) - T^{\text{MIN}}(F_E)} = \frac{T(e,U|F_E) - T(e,F|F_E)}{T(e,F|F_E) - T(e,U|F_E)} = -1$$

player S_S's index of conditional conformity is therefore $[1 + f_{Ss}(e,U|F_E)] = 0$

Player E's expected deviation from full conformity for strategy F_E is in this case

$$\tilde{f}_E(F_E;e,U) = T(F_E|e,U) - T^{\text{MAX}}(e,U) = 0$$

which entails an index of expected reciprocal conformity $[1 + \tilde{f}_E(F_E;e,U)] = 1$. Thus, the ideal utility in this case for player S_S's strategy (e, U) is 0.

The calculation of the expected reciprocal conformity index $1 + \tilde{f}_E(F_E;e,U)$ highlights a distinctive feature of conformity indexes in games such as the one considered in this chapter. When the strong stakeholder S_S believes that the other player E believes that s/he is going to play U, the maximum and the minimum value of the function T (that may be generated by whatever response of player E to the strategy U) coincide. In these cases, the welfare distribution function, which represents the normative principle T, always takes value 0. This means that when the second-order belief of player S_S is U (that is, S_S believes that E believes that s/he is choosing U), s/he also believes that E cannot do any better by its choice than accept that the weak stakeholder will get 0. Thus, in these cases, a player – for example, E – has no role in affecting the implementation of the principle T.

Note that if the maximum and minimum values of T are the same, the two differences at the numerator and the denominator in the deviation index are both 0, and the index is indefinite (you cannot divide by 0). However, since the only value admitted for T at the numerator is constant (so that also the difference at numerator is 0) it does not make sense to normalize the deviation from conformity in the interval from a maximum and a minimum value. In fact no deviation at all is allowed. Consequently, we will assume that in all cases like this (in particular, note that the same reasoning applies when the second-order belief of Ss is ($\neg$e)) the value of the expected reciprocal conformity index is the difference between the value of T determined by considering simply *the absolute value* of the difference between the (expected) choice F_E given the second-order belief that (e, U) is chosen (i.e. $T(F_E|e, U)$) and the maximum value that T can take, again given the second-order belief that (e, U) is chosen (i.e. T^{MAX} (e,U)) (that is, what would be the numerator of the fraction normally representing the expected deviation from full reciprocal conformity).

- Strategy (e, U) of S_S, given the first-order belief (b_{Ss}^1) that E plays U_E and given the second-order belief b_{Ss}^2 that E believes that S_S plays (e, U).

The deviation of player S_S from full conformity for strategy (e, U) is, in this case,

$$f_{Ss}(e, U; U_E) = \frac{T(e, U|U_E) - T^{MAX}(U_E)}{T^{MAX}(U_E) - T^{MIN}(U_E)} = \frac{T(e, U|U_E) - T(\neg e|U_E)}{T(\neg e|U_E) - T(e, U|U_E)} = -1,$$

which means that player S_S's index of conditional conformity is $[1 + f_{Ss} (e, U; U_E)] = 0$.

Player E's expected deviation from full conformity for strategy U_E in this case is similar to the previous case, and hence the same method of calculation applies.

$$\tilde{f}_E(U_E; e, U) = T(U_E|e, U) - T^{MAX}(e, U) = 0$$

so that the index of expected reciprocal conformity is $[1 + \tilde{f}_E (U_E; e, U)] = 1$. Again, the ideal utility of player SS for the strategy (e, U) under these contingencies is 0

- Strategy ($\neg$e) of S_S, given the first-order belief (b_{Ss}^1) that E plays U_E and given the second-order belief b_{Ss}^2 that E believes that S_S plays ($\neg$e).

The deviation of player S_S from full conformity for strategy ($\neg$e) is in this case

$$f_{Ss}(\neg e; U_E) = \frac{T(\neg e|U_E) - T^{MAX}(U_E)}{T^{MAX}(U_E) - T^{MIN}(U_E)} = \frac{T(\neg e|U_E) - T(\neg e|U_E)}{T(\neg e|U_E) - T(e, U|U_E)} = 0,$$

which entails an index of conditional conformity of player $S_S[1+ f_{ss}(\neg e|U_E)] = 1$

Player E's expected deviation from full conformity for strategy U_E in this case is similar to the previous case and hence the same method of calculation applies

$$\tilde{f}_E(U_E; \neg e) = T(U_E; \neg e) - T^{MAX}(\neg e) = 0$$

which entails $[1 + \tilde{f}_E(U_E; \neg e)] = 1$.

These two indexes of conditional and expected conformity jointly imply an ideal utility λ for the strategy $(\neg e)$ of player S_S under this case.

- Strategy $(\neg e)$ of S_S, given the first-order belief (b_{Ss}^1) that E plays F_E and given the second-order belief b_{Ss}^2 that E believes that S_S plays $(\neg e)$.

The deviation of player S_S from full conformity for strategy $(\neg e)$ in this case is

$$f_{ss}(\neg e; F) = \frac{T(\neg e|F_E) - T^{MAX}(F_E)}{T^{MAX}(F_E) - T^{MIN}(F_E)} = \frac{T(\neg e|F) - T(e, F|F)}{T(e, F|F_E) - T(e, U|F_E)} = -\frac{7}{8}$$

the index of conditional conformity of player S_S in this case is $[1 + f_{ss}(\neg e|F_E)] = 1/8$

The expected deviation of player E from full conformity belongs to the class of cases (see also the discussion of the following case) that allow simple use of the absolute difference between the T value for the expected choice of player E given the second-order belief about player S_S's choice $\neg e$ and the maximum value of T given $\neg e$

$$\tilde{f}_E(F_E; \neg e) = T(F_E|\neg e) - T^{MAX}(\neg e) = 0$$

so that the expected index of player E's expected reciprocal conformity is $[1 + \tilde{f}_E(F_E; \neg e)] = 1$. Thus, the two indexes jointly imply an ideal utility equal to $1/8\lambda$.

Let us consider E's strategies when it believes that S_S is going to play $\neg e$.

- Strategy (F_E) of E, given the first-order belief (b_E^1) that S_S plays $\neg e$ and given the second-order belief b_E^2 that S_S believes that E plays (F_E).

The deviation of player E from full conformity with the strategy (F_E) given $\neg e$ cannot be but nil since this is a case where the maximum and minimum values of T, given player S_S's choice $\neg e$, are identical. Thus

$$f_E(F_E|\neg e) = T(F|\neg e) - T^{MAX}(\neg e) = 0$$

so the conditional conformity index of player E in this case is $[1+ f_E(F_E|\neg e)] = 1$.

The strategy $\neg e$ (and the first-order belief that Ss is going to implement that strategy) highlights the second distinctive feature of conformity indexes in the type of game we are considering. In this case, the peculiarity depends on the fact that player Ss's strategy $\neg e$ assigns the game the same result regardless of the other player's behavior, since it amounts to simply preventing interaction from occurring by a unilateral decision to stay out of it. When the strong stakeholder plays $\neg e$, it always generates the payoffs (1,1,1). Thus, in this case, the firm has no role in affecting implementation of the principle T (the value of the welfare distribution function, which represents the normative principle T, is always 1 no matter what player E's choice is).

In other words, given the strong stakeholder's strategy $\neg e$, the firm E cannot do any better than accept the T value equal to 1 determined by player Ss's choice, which is the only one possible, and hence also the one with null deviation from the maximum value T possible when player Ss does $\neg e$. Also in this case, given that the E's first-order belief about player Ss's behavior is $\neg e$, as in the case discussed above, the general form of the conformity indexes would be indeterminate (the denominator of the fraction is 0), and again there can be only one constant value of T (at the numerator). Therefore, in this case too, it does not make sense to normalize the deviation from conformity with respect to the interval between maximum and minimum values of T, since no deviation is allowed at all. As we assume in all the cases like the one considered here, the deviation measure from the maximum possible value of T will be taken to be the simple absolute difference between the value of T determined as a consequence of player E's choice (given the $\neg e$ choice of player Ss) and the maximum value of T possible under that choice (that is, the numerator of the fraction would typically represent the deviation from full conditional conformity).

Player Ss's expected deviation from full reciprocal conformity for strategy $\neg e$ is in this case an intermediate value

$$\tilde{f}_{Ss}(\neg e; F_E) = \frac{T(\neg e|F_E) - T^{MAX}(F_E)}{T^{MAX}(F_E) - T^{MIN}(F_E)} = \frac{T(\neg e|F_E) - T(F|F_E)}{T(F|F_E) - T(U|F_E)} = -\frac{7}{8}$$

so that the index of expected reciprocity in conformity for the strategy $\neg e$ of player Ss is $[1 + \tilde{f}_{Ss}(\neg e|F_E)] = 1/8$, which together with the aforementioned index of player E's conditional conformity gives to player E's strategy F given $\neg e$ the ideal utility $1/8\lambda$

- Strategy (U_E) of E given the first-order belief (b_E^1) that Ss plays $\neg e$ and given the second-order belief b_E^2 that Ss believes that E plays (U_E).

The deviation of player E from full conformity by using strategy (U_E) given that S_S does $\neg e$ cannot be positive. Once again we have a case where, given the strategy choice of S_S player E cannot do any better than simply observe that the decision of player S_S prevents the interaction from occurring and assigns a unique T value to the game, which, whatever player E's choice may be, cannot be different from $T = 1$,

$$f_E(U_E|\neg e) = T(U_E|\neg e) - T^{\text{MAX}}(\neg e) = 0$$

which entails for player E a conditional conformity index $[1 + f_E(U_E|\neg e)] = 1$

Finally, consider the expected deviation of player S_S from full reciprocity in conformity when s/he is believed to choose $\neg e$ given U_E.

$$\tilde{f}_{Ss}(\neg e; U_E) = \frac{T(\neg e|U_E) - T^{\text{MAX}}(U_E)}{T^{\text{MAX}}(U_E) - T^{\text{MIN}}(U_E)} = \frac{T(\neg e|U_E) - T(\neg e|U_E)}{T(\neg e|U_E) - T(U|U_E)} = 0$$

the index of conditional conformity of player S_S is thus $[1 + \tilde{f}_{Ss}(\neg e; U_E)] = 1$. Therefore, when player E chooses F_E given S_S staying out, and E predicts that S_S does $\neg e$ jointly the two indexes of conformity are fully positive and thus the ideal utility for player E is λ.

This concludes the calculation of the ideal utilities of players E and S_S for the different states of the PG game under the hypothesis that the players have mutually consistent beliefs systems about the game's outcomes.

Notes

1. Relational elements concerning the relationship between the firm and its stake-holders are indubitably less important if we look at other CSR approaches. Neither Friedman (1977) nor Jensen (2001), for example, give much space to explicit consideration of the stakeholder's interests by the owners of firms. The idea of Friedman is that the only social responsibility of a firm is to make profits while respecting the rules, which means without breaking the law. Jensen's contention is that in the long term maximization of the shareholder value is the best way to satisfy the stakeholders' interests that the multi-stakeholder approach to CSR wants to protect.
2. See Sacconi and Degli Antoni (2009) for a deeper discussion of these notions of cognitive and structural social capital.
3. On the concept of fiduciary duty see Flannigan (1989) and Sacconi (2006).
4. The decision about the party that must have the residual right of control may depend on various factors – e.g. a comparative analysis of the control costs of the various stakeholders: see Sacconi (2006) for a deeper explanation.
5. For a deeper explanation of this theory of reputation under unforeseen contingencies see Sacconi (2000, 2004).
6. For the design of a CSR management standard that corresponds to the features now defined: Sacconi, DeColle and Baldin (2003) and Clarkson Centre for Business Ethics (2002).

7. Additive separability of agents' payoffs across interactions and across time is assumed for simplicity.

8. We will slightly modify this assumption in our model.

9. This network configuration allows us to consider all the characteristics of the relationship between strong stakeholders, weak stakeholders and firms we are interested in for the aim of this chapter. We will not study either other possible network configurations or the density of the relationship characterizing this network (this may be a further extension of the present analysis).

10. See Appendix I for a formal representation of F.

11. Interchangeability is the obvious implication of the 'veil of ignorance' hypothesis, and allows putting aside the strategic distinction between strong and weak stakeholders and the firm.

12. See Appendix I for a complete application of the calculation method.

13. These are just two different ways to approach the same point, however. In fact, players could not categorize the situation as one whereon an impartial principle of justice normally applies if in some sense they would not envision it as if they were 'under a veil of ignorance'. A situation wherein an individual performs a format of reasoning such that independently of the consideration of his/her individual identity s/he is capable of agreeing on a principle of equitable distribution with other individuals supposedly similarly detached from the urgency of their material claims, is quite similar to the cognitive process whereby s/he performs the task of subsuming the concrete distributive case under a more general and abstract principle of justice such that the case will be treated according to the impartiality criteria inherent to the principle.

14. When we move from the one-shot game to the iterated interactions between the firm and its stakeholders, the possibility that λ could endogenously change with the games' result may be taken into account. It could be assumed, for example, that λ of S_S and E increases at each stage when they experience conformity indices equal to 1 or 1-ε. Our analysis does not consider this possibility, which could represent an extension of our model.

15. Even though the structure of the PG is different from the PDs with regard to which we have defined the concepts of deficient and mutual relationship (section 2), by g_{EStkS} we mean the difference between the payoff obtained by E when it and Stk_S play F and the payoff that E obtains by defecting in the relation with Stk_S.

16. If $a + \lambda_E < d$ it would be better for E to defect simultaneously in the PG and in the PD_{Ej}. See the following case B.

17. In respect to the sub-game perfection of the 'fair equilibrium' in the PG, an alternative argument may be based on the demonstration (section 3) that (if λ is high enough as we assume in this case) S_S's threat of punishing the enterprise if it defects is a credible threat (see on this point Geanakoplos et al. 1989).

18. According to our definition, E prefers to defect with weak stakeholders in PDs instead of cooperating with them.

19. This decision should be properly justified. Some authors argue that the proper choice for the 'exit option' would be the Nash solution of the material game played in a non-cooperative way. However, this choice could be criticized because a possible situation of prevarication of one party over the other in the status quo would generate the final 'moral' solution. For this reason, other authors have proposed the concept of a 'moralized' status quo, where some minimal form of reciprocal respect is already in place. Therefore, our choice (which follows

Grimalda and Sacconi (2005) and Sacconi (2006)) may be considered equivalent to a notion of moralization of the status quo from which the 'bargaining' starts.

References

M. Aoki (2010) *infra* 'Linking Economic and Social-Exchange Games: From the Community Norm to CSR', in L. Sacconi and G. Degli Antoni (eds) *Social Capital, Corporate Social Responsibility, Economic Behaviour and Performance* (Basingstoke: Palgrave MacMillan).

K. Binmore (2005) *Natural Justice* (Oxford: Oxford University Press).

R. Burt (2002) 'The Social Capital of Structural Holes', in M.F. Guillen, R. Collins, P. England and M. Meyer (eds) *The New Economic Sociology* (New York: Russell Sage Foundation).

Clarkson Centre for Business Ethics (2002) 'Principles of Stakeholder Management', *Business Ethics Quarterly*, 12(2), 257–264.

J.S. Coleman (1988) 'Social Capital in the Creation of Human Capital', *American Journal of Sociology*, 94, 95–120.

R. Flannigan (1989) 'The Fiduciary Obligation', *Oxford Journal of Legal Studies 9*, 285–294.

R.E. Freeman (1984) *Strategic Management, A Stakeholder Approach* (Boston: Pitman).

R.E. Freeman (2000), 'Business Ethics at the Millennium', *Business Ethics Quarterly*, 10(1), 169–180.

T. Freeman and W.M. Evan (1990) 'Corporate Governance: A Stakeholder Interpretation', *The Journal of Behavioral Economics*, 19(4), 337–359.

R.E. Freeman and J. McVea (2002) 'A Stakeholder Approach to Strategic Management', Working paper n. 01-02, Darden Graduate School of Business Administration.

M. Friedman (1977) 'The Social Responsibility of Business Is to Make Profits', in G.A. Steiner and J.F. Steiner, *Issues in Business and Society* (New York: Random House).

J. Geanakoplos, D. Pearce and E. Stacchetti (1989) 'Psychological Games and Sequential Rationality', *Games and Economic Behavior*, 1, 60–79.

G. Grimalda and L. Sacconi (2002) 'The Constitution of the Nonprofit Enterprise: Ideals, Conformism and Reciprocity', Liuc Papers n. 115, Serie Etica, Diritto ed Economia.

G. Grimalda and L. Sacconi (2005) 'The Constitution of the Not-For Profit Organization: Reciprocal Conformity', *Constitutional Political Economy*, 16(3), 249–276.

G. Grimalda and L. Sacconi (2007) 'Ideals, Conformism and Reciprocity: A Model of Individual Choice with Conformist Motivations, and an Application to the Not-for-Profit Case', in P.L. Porta and L. Bruni (eds) *Handbook of Happiness in Economics* (Cheltenham Northampton, Mass.: Elgar).

S. Grossman and O. Hart (1986), 'The Costs and Benefit of Ownership: A Theory of Vertical and Lateral Integration', *Journal of Political Economy*, 94, 691–719.

H. Hansmann (1996) *The Ownership of Enterprise* (Cambridge, Mass.: Harvard University Press).

O. Hart (1995) *Firms, Contract and Financial Structure* (Oxford: Clarendon Press).

O. Hart and J. Moore (1990) 'Property Rights and the Nature of the Firm', *Journal of Political Economy*, 98, 1119–1158.

M.C. Jensen (2001) 'Value Maximization, Stakeholder Theory, and the Corporate Objective Function', *Journal of Applied Corporate Finance*, 14(3), 8–21.

S. Knack and P. Keefer (1997) 'Does Social Capital Have An Economic Payoff? A Cross Country Investigation', *The Quarterly Journal of Economics*, CXII, 1251–1287.

D. Kreps (1990) *Game Theory and Economic Modeling* (Oxford: Oxford University Press).

N. Lin (2001) *Social Capital* (Cambridge: Cambridge University Press).

S. Lippert, and G. Spagnolo (2010) 'Networks of Relations and Word-of-Mouth Communication', Games and Economic Behavior (forthcoming). doi:10.1016/j.geb.2010.08.010

S. Lippert (2010) *infra.* 'Social Capital in Networks of Relations', in L. Sacconi and G. Degli Antoni (eds) *Social Capital, Corporate Social Responsibility, Economic Behaviour and Performance* (Basingstoke: Palgrave MacMillan).

D. Narayan (1999) 'Bonds and Bridges: Social Capital and Poverty', *Poverty Group* PREM, The World Bank.

J. Nash (1950) 'The Bargaining Problem', *Econometrica*, 18, 155–162.

M. Paldam (2000), 'Social Capital: One or Many? Definition and Measurament', *Journal of Economic Surveys*, 14(5), 629–653.

R.D. Putnam, R. Leonardi and R.Y. Nanetti (1993) *Making Democracy Work: Civic Traditions in Modern Italy* (Princeton: Princeton University Press).

M. Rabin (1993) 'Incorporating Fairness into Game Theory', *American Economic Review*, 83(5), 1281–1302.

L. Sacconi (1999) 'Codes of Ethics As Contractarian Constraint on Abuse of Authority: A Perspective from the Theory of the Firm', *Journal of Business Ethics*, 21, 189–202.

L. Sacconi (2000) *The Social Contract of the Firm, Economics, Ethics and Organisations* (Berlin: Springer Verlag).

L. Sacconi (2004) 'Incomplete Contracts and Corporate Ethics: A Game Theoretical Model under Fuzzy Information', in F. Cafaggi, A. Nicita and U. Pagano (eds) *Legal Orderings and Economic Institutions* (London: Routledge).

L. Sacconi (2006) 'A Social Contract Account For CSR as Extended Model of Corporate Governance (I): Rational Bargaining and Justification', *Journal of Business Ethics*, Special Issue on Social Contract Theories in Business Ethics, 259–281.

L. Sacconi (2007a), 'A Social Contract Account for CSR as Extended Model of Corporate Governance (II): Compliance, Reputation and Reciprocity', *Journal of Business Ethics*, 75(1), 77–96.

Sacconi, L. (2007b), 'CSR as a model of extended corporate governance, an explanation based on the economic theories of social contract, reputation and reciprocal conformism', in F. Cafaggi (ed.) *Profiles of Self-Regulation* (Boston, Mass: Kluwer Academic Press).

Sacconi, L. (2010a) 'A Rawlsian view of CSR and the Game Theory of its Implementation (Part I): The Multistakeholder Model of Corporate Governance', in L. Sacconi, M. Blair, R.E. Freeman and A. Vercelli (eds) *Corporate Social Responsibility and Corporate Governance: The Contribution of Economic Theory and Related Disciplines* (London: Palgrave Macmillan).

Sacconi L. (2010b) 'A Rawlsian view of CSR and the Game Theory of its Implementation (Part II): Fairness and Equilibrium', in L. Sacconi, M. Blair, E. LFreeman and A. Vercelli (eds) *Corporate Social Responsibility and Corporate Governance: The Contribution of Economic Theory and Related Disciplines* (London: Palgrave Macmillan).

Sacconi L. (2010c) *infra* A Rawlsian View of CSR and the Game Theory of its Implementation (III): Conformism and Equilibrium Selection in L. Sacconi and G. Degli Antoni (eds) *Social Capital, Corporate Social Responsibility, Economic Behaviour and Performance* (Basingstoke: Palgrave MacMillan).

L. Sacconi and G. Degli Antoni (2009) 'A Theoretical Analysis of the Relationship between Social Capital and Corporate Social Responsibility: Concepts and

Definitions', in S. Sacchetti and R. Sugden (eds) *Knowledge in the Development of Economies. Institutional Choices under Globalisation* (Cheltenham: Edward Elgar), pp. 134–157.

L. Sacconi and M. Faillo (2010) 'Conformity, reciprocity and the sense of justice. How social contract-based preferences and beliefs explain norm compliance: the experimental evidence', *Constitutional Political Economy*, 21(2), 171–201.

L. Sacconi, S. DeColle and E. Baldin (2003) 'The Q-RES Project: the Quality of Social and Ethical Responsibility of Corporations', in J. Wieland (ed.) *Standards and Audits for Ethics Management Systems, The European Perspective* (Berlin: Springer Verlag), pp. 60–117.

R. Selten (1967) Die Strategiemethode zur Erforschung des eingeschriinkt rationalen Verhaltens im Rahmen eines Oligopolexperiments' in H. Sauermann (ed.) *Beiträge zur Experimentellen Wirtschaftsforschung*, Vol.1 (Tübingen: J.C.B. Mohr (siebeck)), pp. 136–168.

R. Selten (1975) 'Reexamination of the Perfectness Concept for Equilibrium Points in Extensive Games', *International Journal of Game Theory*, 4, 25–55.

N. Uphoff (1999) 'Understanding Social Capital: Learning from the Analysis and Experience of Participation', in P. Dasgupta and I. Serageldin (eds) *Social Capital: A Multifaceted Perspective* (Washington, DC: The World Bank), pp. 215–249.

O. Williamson (1975) *Market and Hierarchies* (New York: The Free Press).

O. Williamson (1986) *The Economic Institution of Capitalism* (New York: The Free Press).

Part III

The Economic Effect of Social Capital and Other-regarding Preferences: Experimental and Empirical Evidence

8

Social Distance, Cooperation and Other-regarding Preferences: A New Approach Based on the Theory of Relational Goods

Leonardo Becchetti, Giacomo Degli Antoni and Marco Faillo

1. Introduction

The last few years have witnessed a dramatic growth of experimental and behavioral economics research on deviations from purely selfish behavior. Several new theoretical models have been developed, which are based on a more complex view of economic agents' motivations. At the empirical level, many studies have been focused on the context-dependent nature of other-regarding behavior. From a socio-economic point of view, particularly interesting is the experimental evidence on the relation between the reduction of the social distance among the subjects and the probability of observing deviation from purely selfish choices. Social distance has been manipulated by introducing impersonal communication (Frohlich and Oppenheimer 1998), face to face interaction (Bohnet and Frey 1999b; Rankin 2006), silent identification (Bohnet and Frey 1999a, 1999b; Scharlemann et al. 2001), information about personal characteristics (Bohnet and Frey 1999b; Charness et al. 2007) and by varying the degree of anonymity (Hoffman et al. 1996) between subjects.[1] What emerges from these studies is a positive and significant correlation between the reduction of social distance and the frequency of non-selfish and cooperative choices. Two explanations have been offered to account for this evidence. According to some authors, the reduction of the social distance promotes the emergence of a feeling of empathy among subjects, which results in higher levels of cooperation (Bohnet and Frey 1999a). A second explanation is based on the idea that 'the "framing" of the decision can influence expectations by associating a subject's decision with past experience' (Hoffman et al. 1996: 655) and, more in general, with her everyday social life. In particular, the reduction of social distance would increase the subjects' concern for the social consequences of their decisions, and this would result in a higher probability of adopting in the laboratory the same rules that drive their everyday social interactions.

Becchetti et al. (2007, 2009) proposed a different approach to the study of the effects of the reduction of the social distance in which the removal of anonymity is not decided by the experimenters, but is the consequence of a voluntary choice made by the subjects themselves. They ran two experiments based on two well-known games: the Investment Game (Becchetti et al. 2007) and the Traveler's Dilemma (Becchetti et al. 2009). The results of these experiments turned out to be very interesting, particularly because they could not be accounted for by appealing either to Bohnet and Frey's (1999a) nor to Hoffman et al.'s (1996) explanations discussed above. In this chapter we go back to Becchetti et al.'s (2007, 2009) results, and we show that it is possible to give an interpretation of this kind of evidence by referring to the concept of relational goods (Gui 2000, 2002; Uhlaner 1989).

The chapter is divided into six sections. In the second section we provide a short survey of the literature on relational goods. In the third section we describe the experimental design of the two experiments presented in Becchetti et al. (2007, 2009) (hereafter B2007 and B2009). In the fourth section we discuss the hypotheses on the effect of relational goods on players' behavior in the two experiments. In the fifth section we discuss the main findings. The sixth section concludes this chapter.

2. The concept of relational goods

Over the last few years, economic analysis has devoted more and more attention to the role of factors connected with interpersonal relations. One of the main attempts that economists have made in order to improve their understanding of them is linked to the concept of relational goods (Gui 1987; Uhlaner 1989). Relational goods 'depend upon interactions among persons' (Uhlaner 1989: 253) and are peculiar *intangible outputs of an affective and communicative nature* (Gui 2000) that are produced through social interactions. In particular, Gui (2002) proposes to consider every form of interaction as a particular productive process that the author calls 'encounter'. Relational goods may be generated in an encounter, but they are not the encounter in itself, which can generate many other different outputs[2] (Gui 2000: 155). Examples of relational goods are: social approval, friendship and its benefit, the desire to be recognized or accepted by others, but also 'the "atmosphere" that is created among waiting customers in a hair dresser's shop, or a conversation concerning non-professional matters occurring during breaks in a business meeting' Gui (2000: 152). By looking at these examples, it is clear that relational goods can be either an asset, like a friendship, or else a one-shot consumer good like the 'atmosphere' that is created among waiting customers in a hair dresser's shop or, more in general, the relational goods associated with the 'well-being' (or 'bad-being') produced by a conversation with other people (Bruni and Stanca 2008).

Relational goods have three main characteristics. *First*, they are a subset of local public goods, since they are non-rival and non-exclusive but only with regard to the people who participate in their production. According to Uhlaner, 'Relational goods can only be enjoyed with some others. They are thus unlike private goods, which are enjoyed alone, and standard public goods, which can be enjoyed by any number' (Uhlaner 1989: 254). The consumption of relational goods is contextual and simultaneous to their production, since they can not be enjoyed alone, but only through interpersonal relations with other people (Bruni and Stanca 2008; Sacco and Vanin 2000). They can be actually considered anti-rival since the joint fruition is essential to their value. *Second*, contributions to their production depend on mutual agreement (Uhlaner 1989). Goodwill is important for their production, they cannot be imposed. Even though relational goods may be generated through encounters that happen in different environments, some circumstances seem more convenient than others. In particular, relations that are not constrained but that people voluntarily decide to start, such as relations inside volunteering associations, are more likely to generate relational goods (Ben-Ner 2002: 12; Prouteau and Wolff 2004). Relational goods also 'acquire value through sincerity or genuineness – which is impossible to buy, so they can be generated as a by product of some instrumental activity but not by making contracts for their supply' (Becchetti et al. 2008: 346). *Third*, their value depends on the characteristics of people sharing the goods (Sacco and Vanin 2000) and is increased by fellow feeling.[3] In this respect, someone could prefer to share time with people she trusts or she finds friendly. For this reason, the expected value of relational goods' consumption depends on the disposition that agents have regarding the personal characteristics of people they are going to meet. A good disposition increases the probability that agents enjoy the encounter and, consequently, the quality of the relational good produced (and consumed) by it. On the contrary, feelings such as rancour or envy can interfere with their production (and, consequently, with their consumption). Therefore, it is clear that some circumstances can promote better relational goods than others.

Until now, relational goods have been mostly considered to explain social behavior such as political participation (Uhlaner 1989) or associational membership (Prouteau and Wolff 2004). Our analysis opens a new interesting field by experimentally testing whether the possibility of consuming relational goods also has a direct impact on variables such as trust and trustworthiness that are key elements for socio-economic development. In the next pages we will report the results of two experiments aimed at studying the impact of voluntary reduction of social distance on trust, trustworthiness and cooperation and we will present an interpretation of the evidence in terms of relational goods.

3. Two experiments on the voluntary reduction of social distance

The experiment run by Becchetti et al. (2007) (B2007 henceforth) is based on a two-player Investment Game (Berg et al. 1995) in which both players are endowed with ten tokens (one token = 0,50 Euros). The first mover, the Trustor, must decide how much of her endowment to send to the second mover, the Trustee. The amount sent is tripled and delivered to the Trustee, who must decide how much of the tripled sum to send back to the Trustor. Note that assuming rational and selfish individuals, the sub-game perfect Nash equilibrium of this game is the strategy vector in which the Trustee sends zero whatever the Trustor's transfer and the Trustor sends zero anticipating the Trustee's choice.

The Investment Game is particularly useful for detecting the willingness to cooperate. In this context, we say that an agent behaves in a cooperative way if she does not play only in order to maximize her monetary pay-off. A Trustor plays in a cooperative way if she is interested in the total pay-off, which may be generated in the game and exposes itself to the risk of other opportunism. A Trustee is cooperative as far as she decides not to keep all the amount sent by the Trustor and send back a positive amount.[4]

The experimental literature on the Investment Game shows that Trustors send, on average, about 50 per cent of their endowment, and Trustees repay by sending back between 95 and 110 per cent of the amount sent by Trustors. Hence, the return to a 'trustful behaviour' tends to be zero (Berg et al. 1995; Camerer 2003; Camerer and Fehr 2004).

In the B2007 experiment, subjects played the Investment Game under two different treatments: the Baseline Treatment and the Encounter Treatment. In the Baseline Treatment subjects played a standard Investment Game under full anonymity, while subjects participating in the Encounter Treatment had the possibility to decide whether to remove anonymity by encountering, at the end of the experiment, their counterpart. In particular, in this second treatment, subjects were first instructed about the rules of the Investment Game, then they decided whether to opt or not for the encounter: they signed in, they discovered their role and they played the game. Before playing the game they were aware of the fact that the meeting would take place only if both players decided to opt for the encounter and they were informed about their opponents' choice about the encounter only at the end of the experiment. The subjects expressed their willingness to opt for the encounter by replying with a 'Yes' to the following written question: 'Do you want to meet, at the end of the experiment, the person you are paired with?' At the end of the experiment, and before leaving the room, members of the pairs in which both the subjects opted for the encounter were introduced to each other. The meeting did not involve any post-play activity.

In both the treatments, the game was one-shot, and the experiment finished just after the subjects' choice. Each subject participated only in one of the two treatments. Sixteen sessions have been conducted in three Italian universities (Trento, Milano-Bicocca and Forlì) and a total of 368 subjects participated in the experiment.

The primary objective of the authors was to assess whether the introduction of the choice to remove anonymity had a significant impact on the level of cooperation (in terms of reciprocal contributions). As we will see in the fifth section, the results seem to confirm the existence of this kind of effect.

In order to check for the robustness of this result, Becchetti et al. (2009) (B2009 henceforth) ran a second experiment, with a design similar to that of B2007, but based on a Traveler's Dilemma (Basu 1994). The game owes its name to the example used to illustrate it. Two travelers returning from a remote island lose their luggage because of the airline company. In order to be reimbursed for the same souvenir contained in the luggage, they have to write down on a piece of paper the value of the souvenir, which may range between 2 units of money and 100 units. (in the original Basu 1994 paper). If the travelers write a different number, they are reimbursed with the minimum amount declared. Moreover, a penalty equal to two is paid to the traveler who declares the higher value, while a reward of the same amount is paid by the traveler who writes the lower value. If the two claims are the same, the two travelers receive the declared value without reward or penalty. Considering the characteristics of the game, if both the travelers want to maximize their monetary payoffs, the (2,2) outcome is the only Nash equilibrium of the game, independently of the size of the penalty or reward (hereafter P/R).

The Traveler's Dilemma has been introduced as an example of strategic interaction in which the Nash solution appears as far less plausible than the strategy profile in which each player declares a large number, believing that the other does the same (Basu 1994). It has been observed that the size of the punishment (reward) has a key role in emergence of Nash equilibrium, both in the one-shot and in the repeated version of the game (Capra et al. 1999; Goeree and Holt 2001). In particular, an important conclusion in the literature is that 'the Nash equilibrium provides good predictions for high incentives ($R = 80$ and $R = 50$, when the possible choice ranges between 80 and 200) but behavior is quite different from the Nash prediction under the treatments with low and intermediate values of R' (Capra et al. 1999: 680). The scarce predictive capacity of the Nash equilibrium is confirmed by Rubinstein (2007), showing that around 50 per cent of more than 4,500 subjects who played the Traveler's Dilemma online opted for the maximum choice (the minimum and maximum choice allowed were \$180 and \$300 respectively and P/R was \$5).[5] Rubinstein, by using response time data, concludes that in his experiment declaring \$300 (the largest number) can be interpreted as an instinctive (emotional) choice, while choices in the range 255–299 appear as the ones which imply the strongest cognitive effort.

The B2009 study was based on a one-shot Traveler's Dilemma with a minimum choice of 20 and a maximum choice of 200, and punishment/ reward equal to 20. The experiment consisted of three treatments: Baseline Treatment (BT), Compulsory Encounter Treatment (CET) and Voluntary Encounter Treatment (VET), with subjects participating only in one treatment. In the BT, subjects played the basic Traveler's Dilemma. In the CET, before playing the game, subjects were informed that they would meet their counterpart at the end of the experiment. The VET differs from the CET because (as in the B2007 experiment) in the former the meeting is a voluntary choice of the players (the willingness to meet their counterparts was collected by means of the same procedure adopted in the B2007 experiment). The introduction of the treatment with the compulsory meeting allowed the authors to distinguish between the effects of social distance associated with empathy and framing discussed in the introduction (which can be observed in the CET) and the preferences for the production and the consumption of a relational good (which can be observed only in the VET).

In all the treatments, at the end of the game, beliefs about the opponent's choice were elicited by asking each subject to guess the number chosen by her opponent and paying her 1 euro if the distance between her guess and their opponent's actual choice was less then 10.[6] In both the B2007 and the B2009 experiments, some socio-demographic and attitudinal data have been collected by means of a questionnaire. As we will show in the following pages, some of these data turned out to be very helpful for the interpretation of the evidence.

The experiment was conducted in two Italian universities (Milano and Forlì) with two sessions for the BT, two sessions for the CET and three sessions for the VET. A total of 140 undergraduate students participated in the experiment.

4. The role of relational goods in increasing cooperation when the reduction of social distance is a voluntary choice of players

The novelty of B2007 and B2009 experiments is the introduction of a voluntary option to meet the counterpart after having played an Investment Game and a Traveler's Dilemma, respectively. This generates the possibility to consume relational goods through a personal encounter that agents will share after having interacted in the laboratory.

Even if experimental results on Ultimatum Games (Camerer and Thaler 1995; Güth et al. 1982), Dictator Games (Andreoni and Miller 2002), Gift Exchange Games (Fehr et al. 1993, 1998), Investment Games (Ben-Ner and Putterman 2006; Berg et al. 1995) and Public Good Games (Fehr and Gächter 2000; Fischbacher et al. 2001; Sonnemans et al. 1999;) have widely stressed that human behavior is also strongly motivated by the consideration of others (i.e. for example, by fairness, reciprocity and inequity aversion), we are not aware of previous experimental studies that introduce the possibility of consuming relational goods in order to analyze their impact on cooperation.

According to our interpretation (see also the original papers for a more detailed explanation related to the two single experiments), agents who took part in the experiments carried out by Becchetti et al. (2007, 2009) may opt for the encounter in the two games for three main reasons: 1) curiosity; 2) desire to meet the counterpart in order to negatively reciprocate if she behaves opportunistically in the game; 3) desire to have a good time with the counterpart (i.e. desire to consume relational goods). Note that, if we assume non-zero opportunity cost of time, the decision to meet the counterpart at the end of the game reveals a positive utility, which players may associate to one (or more) of these three different motivations for the meeting.

By focusing on these three motivations, B2009 show that it is only when the third motivation is present that a significant difference between the behavior of players who voluntarily opt for the meeting and other agents emerges. In fact, B2009 present an empirical test (see next section), which disentangles between the first two motivations (curiosity and negative reciprocity) and the third one (relational goods) and show that the desire to consume relational goods is a necessary condition to observe departure from individual rationality in the strategies of players who opt for the meeting.

Moreover, the more cooperative attitude of players who opt for the meeting both in the Investment Game and in the Traveler's Dilemma may be interpreted as the willingness to increase the probability to consume relational goods during the meeting. Since the production and the consumption of relational goods depends on the disposition of people who meet (section 2), players who opt for the meeting are more cooperative because of the effect that game's result has on the counterpart's disposition. Trustors, Trustees and the two 'Travelers' of the Traveler's Dilemma know that the disposition of their counterpart toward them is affected by their behavior in the game. A trustful contribution by the Trustor reveals the willingness to create a cooperative relation with the Trustee and creates positive conditions for the production of relational goods after the game. On the social and economic point of view such a contribution entails a monetary risk for the Trustor, which may be traded off by non-material benefits generated by the relational good consumed during the encounter. The Trustee can, in turn, affect the disposition of the Trustor by showing herself trustworthy (i.e. by sending back to the Trustor a 'fair' amount). The trade-off between giving away monetary benefits to 'pay' non-material gains applies also to her. Disposition of the two players in the Traveler's Dilemma will be affected by the payment (or by the win) of the penalty (of the reward).

Trustors, Trustees and players in the Traveler's Dilemma who voluntarily decide to meet the counterpart after the game could decide to be relatively more cooperative in the game in order to increase the expected value of the relational goods they have the possibility to produce through the encounter.

An important qualification, relevant to the experiments used in B2007 and B2009, is that the concept of relational good may vary from a minimum to a maximum content. The minimum content is just the desire to avoid the hostility of the counterpart. The maximum content may be, for example, the hope to begin a cooperative relation with the other player starting from the small joint experience lived during the game. We may just observe in the experiment whether contributions grow when the opportunity of the encounter is chosen, but we cannot discriminate whether the players do it by having in mind the minimum or the maximum content of the relational good.

Finally, note that, if a subject decides not to meet her counterpart, she will play a standard anonymous game. According to the role of goodwill in the creation of relational goods (section 2), the voluntary character of the encounter should create (if supported by the suitable dispositions) a favorable environment for the relational goods to arise in the meeting.

5. Social distance, relational goods and cooperation: evidence from the investment game and the traveler's dilemma

This section resumes the main results reported in B2007 and B2009 and proposes a discussion of these results in the light of the concept of relational goods. The hypothesis behind this analysis is that the possibility to create and consume relational goods through the meeting increases cooperative behavior by players who have preferences for relational goods.

Evidence seems to indicate a significant difference in agent's behavior when the meeting option is introduced and chosen. In this respect, three points must be stressed.

1. In the investment game:

> *a) Trustors who opt for the meeting follow a behavior consistent with the Nash equilibrium when players have standard self-interested preferences based only on monetary arguments (that is, sending no money to the Trustee, which we define from now on as standard [textbook] behavior) significantly less than Trustors who do not opt for the meeting;*
> *b) the average contribution of Trustors is significantly larger when the meeting option is available than when it is not available. Moreover, when we restrict the analysis to the sample of the 93 Trustors who are given the opportunity to opt for the encounter, the average contribution of those who opt is significantly higher than that of those who do not opt.*

The share of Trustors who send no money to the Trustee is 11.41 on the overall sample of 184 observations. It rises to 19.78 per cent in the 91 cases in which the opportunity of the encounter is not available and falls sharply to 3.22 per cent when the opportunity is offered (93 observations). Within this subsample the share is slightly higher for Trustors who do not opt (4.17 per cent on 48 cases) and slightly smaller for those who opt for the encounter (2.22 per cent with 45 cases).[7]

Hence, the opportunity of consuming a relational good has significant effects on the deviation from the *standard behavior*. This finding shows that, with a slight departure from an aseptic context with no possibility of creating relational goods, benchmark concepts, such as the Nash equilibria, under the assumption of self-interested players, become less and less adequate to describe agents' choices. On another perspective we may as well interpret this finding by arguing that the absence of relational opportunities reduces the capacity to create trust and trustworthiness and the productivity gains that may arise from cooperation.

The comparison of the average Trustor's contribution under the two different treatments (when the option of meeting the Trustee is available or not) yields results consistent with those commented above. The average contribution is significantly larger when the option is available (5.16 tokens) than when it is not (3.78 tokens) and the difference in means is significant at 95 per cent.[8] This implies that the simple availability of the opportunity of the encounter raises on average the Trustor contribution, independently from her decision to meet the counterpart. It may be argued that the result is determined by the expected larger contribution of those who actually opt for the possibility of the encounter when the option is available. However, this does not seem to explain the entire story since the mean contribution of those who have the opportunity but do not opt for the encounter is still higher (4.37 tokens) than that of those who are devoid of such opportunity (3.78 tokens). An interpretation for this finding may be that part of the higher contribution of the sender in the presence of the opportunity to opt for the encounter is independent from the Trustor's decision to opt for it and has a *strategic component*, represented by the anticipation that the Trustee may be willing to pay back more if she opts for the encounter. Consider, however, that the difference between those who have the possibility to opt and do not and those who are not given such opportunity is only weakly significant both with parametric and non-parametric tests (77 per cent significance). When we restrict our descriptive analysis within the sample of the 93 Trustors who are given the opportunity to opt for the encounter, we observe that the average contribution of those who opt (6.82 tokens) is significantly higher than that of those who do not opt (4.37 tokens).[9] It seems that the opportunity to meet the counterpart generates a significant effect on the decision to send by Trustors, which cannot be simply explained by a selection bias effect.

Given the standard assumption that the amount given by the Trustor is tripled, our finding implies that, on average, the 'aggregate gain' generated by the option of the encounter – that is, the extra amount of tokens generated by it – is 15.48 – 11.40 = 4.08 tokens or a 42.1 per cent increase with respect to the benchmark in which the relational good is not available.

2. *In the investment game, the amount sent back by Trustees and the number of Trustees who do not behave according to the standard economic behavior is significantly higher when the option of the meeting is selected.*

The dependent variable chosen to study Trustees' behavior is the share of the amount paid back on the total amount received. The share of Trustees behaving consistently with the *standard behavior* is higher for Trustees than for Trustors (26.38 per cent on the overall sample against 11.41 among Trustors) (Table 8.1).

This is reasonable if we assume that the Trustee, differently from the Trustor, has no strategic reasons (such as the hope to stimulate the contribution of the Trustee) to deviate from the standard behavior. Another striking difference is that most of the variability is not explained just by the opportunity of the encounter (conformity to the 'standard behavior' is even higher for those who are given the opportunity of the encounter but do not opt [33.33 per cent] than for those who are not given the opportunity) but by the actual choice of opting for the encounter (in such case the share of individuals which follows 'standard behavior' drops to 16.67 per cent). Our interpretation is that the receiver has no expected additional gains from the possibility that, even though she does not opt for the encounter, the other player does. Hence there is no point to her in giving more when the option is available but she does not want to meet the Trustor. This interpretation

Table 8.1 Descriptive statistics on the Trustee's contribution under different experimental designs

Sharerest (Amount paid back/Total amount received)	All experiments (163 obs.)	Encounter option not available (73 obs.)	Encounter option available		
			Trustee's decision to opt for the encounter		
			YES and NO (90 obs.)	YES (36 obs.)	NO (54 obs.)
0	26.38	26.02	26.67	16.67	33.33
0 < sharerest ≤ 0.2	24.54	28.77	21.11	16.66	24.08
0.2 < sharerest ≤ 0.4	24.54	24.66	24.44	25.00	24.07
0.4 < sharerest ≤ 0.6	12.27	9.59	14.45	22.22	9.26
0.6 < sharerest ≤ 0.8	9.82	5.48	13.33	19.45	9.26
0.8 < sharerest ≤ 1	2.45	5.48	0.00	0.00	0
Total	100	100	100	100	100

Percent values. Authors' calculation on data from Becchetti et al. 2007.

is also supported by the fact that the opportunity of the encounter has no significant effects on the average share paid back.[10]

When we restrict the analysis to the subsample of the 90[11] individuals who have the opportunity to opt for the encounter we find that the amount sent back is significantly higher (it almost doubles) when the Trustee opts for the encounter (around 35 per cent for those who opt against around 21 per cent of those who don't). Since the distribution of the dependent variable is definitely not normal, we use non-parametric test to evaluate whether this difference is significant and find that it is.[12]

3. *In the Traveler's Dilemma, agents who voluntarily decide to meet the counter-part are more likely to have a choice that is higher or equal than their belief (in this way trying to avoid a sanction against the other player arising).*

The comparison between choice and belief in the Traveler's Dilemma gives us important insights into the effect of preferences for relational goods and agents' behavior. If we look at the distribution of the difference between choice and belief we find that only 18 per cent of players choose one unit below the belief, while around 11 per cent of them are such that $C > B + 10$.

Notice that if players' belief is correctly expressed (and we do not have reason to doubt it) agents who chose a number higher than their belief $+10$, voluntarily decide to incur, in the Traveler's Game, a penalty. With this respect, we find that the percentage of agents who declare a number higher than their belief $+10$ is equal to 17 per cent in the Voluntary Encounter Treatment, 7.5 per cent in the Baseline Treatment and 7.5 per cent in the Compulsory Encounter Treatment. More specifically, 21 per cent of subjects who opted for the meeting declared a number higher than their belief $+10$ while this percentage drops to 12.5 per cent among people who did not opt for the meeting. If we look at the difference between choice and belief, we find that agents who wanted to meet their counterpart in the Voluntary Meeting Treatment have on average a choice that is 6.89 points higher than their belief. This is a remarkable result considering that, as we expect, all the other subgroup means are negative (the choice is below the belief). More specifically, all the rest of the sample has a -5.40 average, the baseline group -5.85 and the compulsory treatment group -2.77. Differences between choice and belief are not statistically significant with respect to the different subsamples.

However, this does not undermine the idea that the willingness to consume relational goods reduces opportunistic behavior. In fact, Becchetti et al. (2009) consider a dummy variable, which takes the value of one, if players choose a number higher than their belief minus one. We may consider these agents as cooperative (or non-opportunistic) agents in the sense that they want to reduce the probability that the counterpart has to pay the penalty in the game. Becchetti et al. (2009) show that the probability to observe this kind of behavior is significantly higher when players opt for the meeting and, at the same time, they declare a level of generalized trust above median.[13] The role of generalized trust is very important for the interpretation of the increase of cooperative behavior in terms of willingness to consume relational goods (and to rule out the alternative hypotheses, which are usually considered by the literature on social distance reduction). In fact, the authors' interpretation is that generalized trust incorporates players' expectations on the counterpart in terms of social orientation. In particular, generalized trust in others would approximate players' trust that the counterpart is a social-oriented subject. Only agents who trust that their counterpart will be socially oriented (i.e. disposed to produce and consume relational goods) will avoid opportunistic behavior in order to generate an agreeable atmosphere in the meeting. In other words, it is only when players who opt for the meeting have a high level of generalized trust that we may reasonably assume that their meeting decision is due to the desire to consume relational goods.[14] In case players opt for the meeting without having high generalized trust we assume that their decision to meet the counterpart is driven by the other two motivations (curiosity or negative reciprocity).

These different hypotheses on the reason behind the decision to opt for the meeting (i.e. willingness to consume relational goods, curiosity and negative reciprocity) are tested in B2009 by verifying if the probability to observe choices ≥ beliefs is more likely to happen:

- in the compulsory encounter treatment for players who declare or who do not declare a level of generalized trust higher than the median with respect to the baseline treatment
- in the voluntary encounter treatment for players who opt for the meeting and who declare or who do not declare a level of generalized trust higher than the median with respect to the baseline treatment.

Since the difference is statistically significant only for players who opt for the meeting in the Voluntary Encounter Treatment and who, at the same time, declare a high level of generalized trust, B2009 conclude that the explanation based on the idea of relational goods seems to be appropriate to account for the non-standard behavior emerging in their Traveler's Dilemma experiment. Moreover, since the mere reduction of social distance due to the removal of anonymity after the experiment does not generate an effect (in the Compulsory Encounter Treatment or in the Voluntary Encounter Treatment for players who do not have high level of generalized trust) on players' behavior in terms of willingness to reduce opportunistic behavior, authors conclude that the usual explanation connected with the reduction of social distance (i.e. the promotion of empathy among subjects and the possibility of emergence of social norm of cooperation or fairness) do not seem to be effective in this case.[15]

6. Conclusions

Two recent papers contributed to the literature on the effects of the manipulation of social distance by making its reduction a voluntary choice of players. This original element was introduced both in an Investment Game (Becchetti et al. 2007) and in a Traveler's Dilemma (Becchetti et al. 2009) by giving players the opportunity to declare if they wanted to meet the counterpart at the end of the experiment.

The present chapter aimed at summarizing the main results of these two contributions in the conviction that they take a significant step forward in the behavioral literature by creating for the first time an experimental design in order to study the effect relational goods have on cooperation. In particular, a result which also opens interesting insights for further research has been considered in this chapter: the willingness to consume relational goods with another player (i.e. the desire to share a pleasant time with her/him) increase the probability to observe cooperative or non-opportunistic behavior among players involved in economic interactions even though it entails a monetary risk or a sure material sacrifice. In this chapter, we showed that:

- Trustors who opt for meeting the counterpart are more likely to depart from individual rationality (i.e. to send positive amount to the Trustees) and send on average higher amounts than Trustors who do not opt for the meeting;
- The amount sent back by Trustees and the number of Trustees who did not behave according to the standard economic behavior (i.e. who did not send back anything) is significantly higher when the option of the meeting is selected;
- In the Traveler's Dilemma, agents who voluntarily decide to meet the counterpart (and who trust others) are more likely to have a choice that is higher or equal than their belief (in this way trying to avoid a sanction against the other player arising).

We showed that these results may be interpreted as the willingness to positively affect (through decisions in the game) the disposition of the other players in preparation for the meeting, which is a crucial factor to create and consume relational goods during the encounter.

Acknowledgements

We would like to thank Lorenzo Sacconi for useful comments and suggestions. We also thank the Experimental Economics Lab of the University of

Milano-Bicocca (EELAB), Laboratorio di Economia Sperimentale (LES) of the University of Forlì and the Computable and Experimental Economics Laboratory (CEEL) of the University of Trento where the experiments considered in the chapter have been conducted. Our thanks go also to EconomEtica, Aiccon, and Department of Economics, University of Trento, for financial support in the research project. The usual disclaimer applies.

Notes

1. The reduction of social distance was considered, for example, in Public Good Games (Bohnet and Frey 1999a), Dictator Games (Bohnet and Frey 1999a, 1999b; Hoffman et al. 1996), Prisoner's Dilemmas (Frohlich and Oppenheimer 1998) and Trust Games (Scharlemann et al. 2001).
2. Examples of outputs that are accounted for by standard economic concepts and that are produced during an encounter are: the reallocation of goods of people involved in the interaction (e.g. a buyer and a seller) and the provision of a service (e.g. in case of a legal advice) (Gui 2000).
3. The *fellow feeling* hypothesis of Adam Smith has been recently re-elaborated by Sugden (2002) arguing that the intensity of common consent (and 'the consequent removal of unease and dissonance caused by perception of disparities in sentiments') is a source of pleasure in relational activities.
4. With respect to the Traveler's Dilemma, which will be introduced later, a cooperative behavior entails that players do not try to obtain the reward (and consequently try to avoid that the sanction against the other player arises).
5. Note that subjects who participated in the online experiment were not paid. Rubinstein stresses that the distribution of answers of his experiment is similar to that of Goeree and Holt (2001) when they use the low P/R.
6. The author decided to adopt this rule because, in this kind of experiment, a prize exclusively given to the correct guess could be considered too difficult to achieve, and can discourage players and increase the likelihood of casual answers. At the same time, eliciting procedures based on quadratic scoring rules (Davis and Holt 1993) are useless for a game – like our version of the Traveller's Dilemma – which is characterized by a large number of possible strategies. The use of tolerance thresholds for subjects' guesses is used in the literature as a valid method for eliciting beliefs (see, for example, Charness and Dufwemberg 2006; Croson 2000).
7. In relation to the Trustors' decision, when the meeting is available in the Investment Game, we observed that 45 out of 93 subjects opted for the meeting.
8. Since the distribution of Trustor's contributions departs from normality we also consider non-parametric diagnostics and find that the significance is confirmed by Wilcoxon rank-sum (Mann-Whitney) test $= -2.940$ Prob $> |z| = 0.003$.
9. The significance is confirmed by the non-parametric Wilcoxon rank-sum (Mann-Whitney) test: test $= -2.451$ Prob $> |z| = 0.014$).
10. Two-sample Wilcoxon rank-sum (Mann-Whitney) test $z = -0.802$ Prob $> |z| = 0.422$.
11. The sample is slightly smaller than the corresponding one among Trustors since Trustees receiving zero amounts are obviously dropped from the sample.
12. Two-sample Wilcoxon rank-sum (Mann-Whitney) test $z = -2.703$ Prob $> |z| = 0.007$.

13. The question that measures the level of generalized trust is the usual one: 'Generally speaking do you believe that others should be trusted?' Answers range from 10 (highest level of trust) to 0.
14. Notice that, without considering generalized trust, there is no a significant difference between the percentage of players who chose a number higher than their belief minus 1 in the three treatments. As a whole, 63 per cent of players declared a number higher than belief −1. Both in the baseline and in the compulsory encounter treatment this percentage is 65 per cent. In the voluntary encounter treatment it is 62 per cent (the percentage increases to 64 per cent among players who choose to meet the counterpart).
15. At a theoretical level, the possibility of consuming relational goods could affect the behavior of players with a high level of generalized trust also in the CET. However, this effect, which does not arise in the game, may be excluded for a simple reason connected with the characteristic of the production of relational goods. In fact, the literature on relational goods stresses that, even though relational goods may be generated through meetings which happen in different environments, some circumstances seem more convenient than others (section 2). In particular, relations that are constrained (such as the meeting in the CET) are less likely to generate relational goods (Ben Ner 2002: 12; Prouteau and Wolff 2004). For this reason, we may assume that players in the CET may think that the 'forced' encounter after the game is not a good occasion to generate relational goods. This interpretation is confirmed by experimental data.

References

J. Andreoni and J. Miller (2002) 'Giving According to GARP: An Experimental Test of the Rationality of Altruism', *Econometrica*, 70(2): 737–753.

K. Basu (1994) 'The Traveler's Dilemma: Paradoxes of Rationality in Game Theory', *American Economic Review*, 84(2), 391–395.

L. Becchetti, G. Degli Antoni, M. Faillo and L. Mittone (2007) 'The Glue of the Economic System: The Effect of Relational Goods on Trust and Trustworthiness', CEIS Working Paper No. 256.

L. Becchetti, G. Degli Antoni and M. Faillo (2009) 'Shedding Light into Preference Heterogeneity: Why Players of Traveler's Dilemma Depart from Individual Rationality?', *Econometica Working Papers n. 09*, http://www.econometica.it/wp/index.htm.

L. Becchetti, A. Pelloni and F. Rossetti (2008) 'Relational Goods, Sociability, and Happiness', *Kyklos*, 343–363.

A. Ben-Ner (2002) 'The Shifting Boundaries of the Mixed Economy and the Future of the Nonprofit Sector, *Annals of Public and Cooperative Economics*, 73, 5–40.

A. Ben-Ner and L. Putterman (2006) 'Trusting e Trustworthiness: An Experiment With Communication and Contracts', paper presented at the International Economic Association workshop on 'Corporate social responsibility (CSR) and corporate governance, the contribution of economic theory and related disciplines' (Trento, Italy, July 2006).

J. Berg, J. Dickhaut and K. McCabe (1995) 'Trust, Reciprocity and Social History', *Games and Economic Behaviour*, 10, 122–142.

I. Bohnet and B. S. Frey (1999a) 'Social Distance and Other-Regarding Behavior in Dictator Games: Comment', *American Economic Review*, 89, 335–339.

I. Bohnet and B. S. Frey (1999b) 'The Sound of Silence in Prisoners Dilemma and Dictator Games', *Journal of Economic Behavior and Organization*, 38, 47–57.

L. Bruni and L. Stanca (2008) 'Watching Alone: Relational Good, Television and Happiness', *Journal of Economic Behavior and Organization*, 65, 506–528.

C. F. Camerer (2003) *Behavioral Game Theory: Experiments in Strategic Interaction* (Princeton: Princeton University Press).

C. F. Camerer and E. Fehr (2004) 'Measuring Social Norms and Preferences Using Experimental Games: A Guide for Social Scientists', in J. Henrich, R. Boyd, S. Bowles, C. Camerer, E. Fehr, H. Gintis and R. McElreath (eds), *Foundations of Human Sociality* (Oxford: Oxford University Press).

C. F. Camerer and R. H. Thaler (1995) 'Ultimatums, Dictators and Manners', *Journal of Economic Perspectives*, 9, 209–219.

M. C. Capra, J. K. Goeree, R. Gomez and A. Holt (1999) 'Anomalous Behavior in a Traveler's Dilemma?', *American Economic Review*, 89(3), 678–690.

G. Charness and M. Dufwenberg (2006) 'Promises and Partnership', *Econometrica*, 74(6), 1579–1601.

G. Charness, E. Haruvy and D. Sonsino (2007) 'Social Distance and Reciprocity: The Internet vs. the Laboratory', *Journal of Economic Behavior and Organization*, 63, May, 88–103.

R. Croson (2000) 'Thinking Like a Game Theorist: Factors Affecting the Frequency of Equilibrium Play', *Journal of Economic Behavior and Organization*, 41(3), 299–314.

D. D. Davis and C. A. Holt (1993) *Experimental Economics* (Princeton, New Jersey: Princeton University Press).

E. Fehr and S. Gächter (2000) 'Cooperation and Punishment in Public Goods Experiments', *American Economic Review*, 90, 980–994.

E. Fehr, G. Kirchsteiger and A. Riedl (1993) 'Does Fairness Prevent Market Clearing? An Experimental Investigation', *Quarterly Journal of Economics*, 108, 437–459.

E. Fehr, E. Kirchler, A. Weichbold and S. Gächter (1998) 'When Social Forces Overpower Competition: Gift Exchange in Experimental Labor Markets', *Journal of Labor Economics*, 16, 324–351.

U. Fischbacher, S. Gächter and E. Fehr (2001) 'Are People Conditionally Cooperative? Evidence from a Public Goods Experiment', *Economics Letters*, 71, 397–404.

N. Frohlich and J. Oppenheimer (1998) 'Some Consequences of e-mail vs. Face-to-face Communication in Experiment', *Journal of Economic Behavior and Organization*, 35, 389–403.

J. K. Goeree and C. A. Holt (2001) 'Ten Little Treasures of Game Theory and Ten Intuitive Contradictions', *American Economic Review*, 91(5), 1402–1422.

B. Gui (1987) E' le'ments pour une Définition d'Economie Communautaire, Notes et Documents de l'Institut International Jacques Maritain 19/20.

B. Gui (2000) 'Beyond Transactions: on the Interpersonal Dimension of Economic Reality', *Annals of Public and Cooperative Economics*, 71(2), 139–169.

Gui B. (2002) 'Più che scambi, incontri. La teoria economica alle prese con i fenomeni interpersonali', in P. L. Sacco and S. Zamagni (eds), *Complessità relazionale e comportamento economico* (Bologna: Il Mulino).

W. Güth, R. Schmittberger and B. Schwarze (1982) 'An Experimental Analysis of Ultimatum Bargaining', *Journal of Economic Behavior and Organization*, 3, 367–388.

E. Hoffman, K. McCabe and V. Smith (1996) 'Social Distance and Other-Regarding Behavior in Dictator Games', *American Economic Review*, 86(3), 653–660.

L. Prouteau and F. C. Wolff (2004) 'Relational Goods and Associational Participation', *Annals of Public and Cooperative Economics*, 75(3), 431–463.

F. W. Rankin (2006) 'Requests and Social Distance in Dictator Games', *Journal of Economic Behavior and Organization*, 60(1), 27–36.

A. Rubinstein (2007) 'Instinctive and Cognitive Reasoning: A Study of Response Times', *Economic Journal*, 117(523), 1243–1259.

P. L. Sacco and P. Vanin (2000) 'Network Interaction with Material and Relational Goods: An Exploratory Simulation', *Annals of Publics and Cooperative Economics*, 72(2), 229–259.

J. P. W. Scharlemann, C. C. Eckel, A. Kacelnick and R. W. Wilson (2001) 'The Value of a Smile: Game Theory With a Human Face', *Journal of Economic Psychology*, 22, 617–640.

J. Sonnemans, A. Schram and T. Offerman (1999) 'Strategic Behavior in Public Good Games – When Partners drift apart', *Economics Letters*, 62, 35–41.

R. Sugden (2002) 'Beyond Sympathy and Empathy: Adam Smith's Concept of Fellow-Feeling', *Economics and Philosophy*, 18(1), 63–87.

C. J. Uhlaner (1989) 'Relational Goods and Participation: Incorporating Sociability into a Theory of Rational Action', *Public Choice*, 62, 253–285.

9
Generalized Trust: An Experimental Perspective

Gianluca Grimalda and Luigi Mittone

1. Introduction

Trust in other people is widely regarded as a key determinant for a society's economic performance. The reason lies in that trust in an 'unknown other' (Delhey and Newton 2005) is functional to solving the myriad cooperation problems that affect our relations with other people. As Arrow (1974) puts it, lack of trust – and more generally of moral values – may create inefficiencies so serious as to cause markets to be aborted. At the empirical level, a vast body of evidence has been brought in support of the relevance of trust for a country's economic development (Knack and Keefer 1997; Putnam et al. 1993), as well as institutional efficiency (La Porta et al. 1999; Rothstein and Uslaner 2005; Sampson et al. 1997). Paldam (2010 *infra*) examines the relevance of trust at the macro level. In this chapter we focus on the micro level, studying the relationship between individual trust in others and other individual-level variables, and how these are reflected into propensity to cooperate with others in controlled experiments.

We first examine the role of possible determinants of trust. In addition to standard demographic characteristics, we examine the role of membership in associations, which several observers have pinpointed as one of the main determinants of interpersonal trust (Coleman 1990; Lahno 1995; Putnam 2000; Zucker 1986). The mechanism that has been suggested is that, first, people learn norms of trust and reciprocal cooperation within an association, thanks to frequent interactions with other members backed by the possibility of sanctions. After having 'learned' the virtues of cooperation, association members would then be prepared to carry these patterns of behavior *outside* the association networks, thus shifting their trust in others from being 'personal' to being 'generalized' (Yamagishi and Yamagishi 1994; Yuki et al. 2005). We refer to this as the Association-Membership-Breeds-Trust (AMBT) hypothesis. Some observers have pointed out how such a shift still lacks theoretical and empirical support (Stolle 2001), and only few theoretical mechanisms have been put forward to account for this link (e.g. Paxton 2007). Our study will assess the existence of a relationship between the two variables, although we are not able to ascertain the direction of causation.[1]

We also examine the linkages of individual trust with other sets of factors. These are the aversion to racial or ethnic mixing, which other studies have shown to be relevant in affecting trust (Alesina and La Ferrara 2000; Alesina and La Ferrara 2002; Luttmer 2001), and measures of individual globalization and global social identity. It has been shown that an index of individual-level large-scale connectedness is significantly related to cooperation at the world level (Buchan et al. 2009a), and it has been suggested that global social identity acts as a mediating factor in this relationship (Buchan et al. 2009b). It is thus interesting to ascertain whether a significant relationship also holds with respect to trust.

The second question concerns the actual impact of individual trust on an economy. The literature reviewed above argues that the direction of causation is from higher trust to higher economic performance, for instance because of increased institutional capability in producing public goods (Putnam et al. 1993), or because trust helps solving market failures, especially within financial markets (Guiso et al. 2007; Knack and Keefer 1997). We shall refer to this claim as the Trust-Breeds-Economic-Returns (TBER) hypothesis. However, the supposed direction of causality at the macro level has been questioned (Durlauf 2002; Solow 1999).[2] More fundamentally, even at the micro level the TBER is far from having been ascertained. Is being more trusting really conducive to economic gains both for the individual and for the group with which the individual interacts? Experimental studies have thus far given contradictory results. It has been shown that survey respondents declaring to be more trusting also showed higher cooperation rates in cooperation problems (Yamagishi 1988; Anderson et al. 2004) and trusted more in Trust Games (Fehr et al. 2002), whereas Glaeser et al. (2000), and Farina et al. (2008) find different patterns within experimental Trust Games.[3]

We thus rely on experimental evidence in our possession to examine the TBER hypothesis within small groups. We can also test the parallel hypothesis that association membership breeds economic returns (AMBER), and study the interaction with TBER. We also test the incidence on cooperation of aversion to racial/ethnic integration.

In addition to providing fresh survey and experimental evidence on topics that are far from being settled, this chapter also contributes to the debate in three different respects. First, the nature of our dataset enables us to examine not only the correlation between an individual's self-reported level of trust and cooperation, but also the extent to which an individual extends her propensity to cooperate beyond the local level to the national and world level. This is made possible by the fact that participants in our research participated in three different cooperation problems at the local, national and world level. Second, our sample comprises residents of the metropolitan area of Milan, Italy, and other surrounding areas. Since much of the research carried out thus far has focused on the US, it is interesting to investigate whether similar patterns of behavior hold within a country that is far more homogenous from the racial and ethnic point of view. Third, in addition to analyzing the most commonly used question to measure interpersonal trust, we also examine two other attitudinal measures, which inquire about a subject's expectation on others' fair and helpful behavior in general situations of interaction.

The chapter is organized as follows. Section 2 illustrates the research design. Section 3 reports the results. Section 4 concludes.

2. Research design

2.1. Selection of research environments, sampling techniques and procedures

A sample of around 200 participants stratified according to age, gender and socio-economic status was recruited from the general population of Milan and other surrounding locations. Around 60 per cent of the sample was made up of Milan residents. The other locations were Pavia and Busto Arsizio, two medium-sized towns counting, respectively 70,000 and 90,000 inhabitants, and three villages – Motta Visconti, Cilavegna and Olgiate Olona – counting less than 15,000 inhabitants. This dataset is part of a larger research project on globalization and cooperation that involved five more countries (see Buchan et al. 2009a for further details).

The purpose of involving people from differently sized urban environments was to test the impact of urbanization on the main variables of interest in our study. All these locations are situated in a relatively circumscribed area – within a 200 km radius from Milan in the Italian region of Lombardy. This was motivated mainly by our willingness to keep cultural variability at its minimum to pinpoint as much as possible the influence of urbanization. Italy is well-known for its cultural diversity, which is, at least to some extent, territorially specific. Thus, sampling locations widely distant from each other would have likely introduced cultural differences in addition to the urban dimension.

We followed a quota sampling method for the recruitment, with quotas pertaining to three dimensions: age (three categories: 19–30, 31–50, 51–70), gender (two categories: male, female) and socio-economic status (three categories: high, intermediate and low). These dimensions determine an 18-cell grid. The target was to reach equal numbers of participants in each cell – namely, around 11 subjects per cell. We allowed for a tolerance factor $0 + 4/-4$ from the target. Recruitment was carried out by DEMOSCOPEA, a company specialized in survey polls and market research. The administration of the experiment was oral, in order to allow as large as possible an inclusion of participants, including illiterate people.

The experiment session was structured as follows. First, participants completed three experimental decisions. They were then asked to complete a questionnaire. In the meantime, research assistants computed subjects' payoffs, using an algorithm for sequential matching procedures provided by the experiments coordinator. Subjects then received their payments. The experiment sessions were conducted in groups of no less than six and no more than 16 participants for a total of 16 sessions. Each research session lasted around 75 minutes. The average payment was 27 Euros, with 10 Euros guaranteed as a show-up fee. Subjects failing a basic comprehension test have been expunged from the dataset.

2.2. Experimental design

Participants were involved in three Multi-level Sequential Contribution (MSC) interactions (see Buchan et al. 2009a, for details on matching procedures, experiment protocol and methodology). Incentives were similar to those in the standard Public Goods Game (PGG). In each decision, people were endowed with ten tokens, each worth half a Euro. An option was to allocate their tokens to a personal account, where the individual Marginal Per Capita Return (MPCR) was exactly one. That is, every token put into the personal account kept its monetary value unchanged for the individual. The other available options consisted in allocating tokens to some collective accounts, whose composition and rate of returns varied across the three decisions. As standard in PGGs, the MPCR from collective accounts is *less* than one for an individual, whereas the Marginal *Social* Return (MSR) – that is the sum of the per capita returns accruing to each individual – is both *greater* than one and smaller than N, the number of group members. This is obtained through the researcher multiplying by a factor greater than one and smaller than N every token allocated to the collective account, so as to create a 'positive externality' from individual contributions to the collective accounts. Consequently, this experimental MSC reproduces the tension between individual rationality – which calls for *not* contributing to the collective accounts – and group rationality – which calls for the contrary.

The three decisions differed both in their structure and in the provenance of the people involved. In the first decision (Decision L) subjects interacted with three other people coming from their local community. They were told that people in their groups were from the same locality as them, but their identity was kept secret. In the second decision (Decision N), two four-person groups from other parts of their country were added to the interaction in a *nested* PGG (Blackwell and McKee 2003; Wit and Kerr 2002). People now had the options of contributing to a local, and to a national account – in addition to their personal account. People were informed that their partners lived in their same locality or in other parts of their country. Finally, in the third decision (Decision W), two four-person groups from

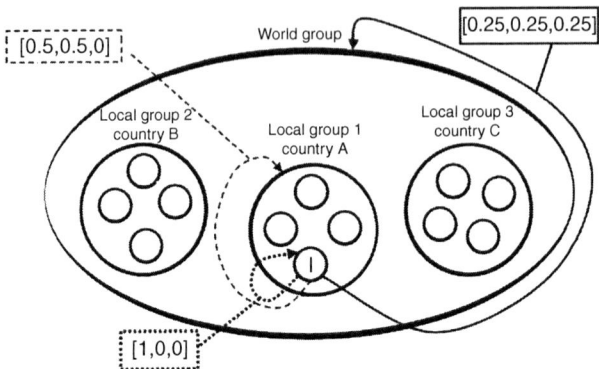

Figure 9.1   Individual incentives to cooperate at the local and world levels in Decision W.
Individual 'I' may allot the money to their 'Personal' account and/or to their 'Local'
group account, and/or to their 'World' group account. The three numbers in brackets
[x, y, z] represent the returns to I (x), to another person from I's local group (y), and
to a person from a different country (z) from a token allotted to I's Personal, Local, or
World account, respectively. Reproduced from Buchan et al. (2009)

other countries were involved in the interaction in addition to the local
group. People now had the options of contributing to a local and to a
world account – in addition to the personal account. People were informed
that their partners lived in their same locality or in other parts of the
world – without specifying the countries where the research was actually
conducted. The intuition behind Decision W is depicted in Figure 9.1. Monetary incentives were exactly the same in Decision N and W. Each decision
was independent from the other two, and participants were matched with
different, randomly chosen groups of people in each decision. This was made
clear to subjects in order to minimize the risk that previous decisions affected
future decisions. All parameters are reported in Table 9.1.

The nested structure captures the multi-level nature that is common to
many problems of public goods in the real world. The MSR to either the
national account or the world account in Decisions N and W were larger
than the MSR of the local account. This was made to provide an appropriate
characterization of multi-level public goods. A contribution to a higher-order
public good typically benefits a larger number of people but at a smaller
rate than a contribution to a lower-order public good. This explains the
difference in MPCRs and MSRs between allocations to the local account
vis-à-vis the other two accounts. At the same time, the structure of incentives was unaltered between Decisions N and W, in order to have a direct
comparison between propensity to cooperate at the national and world level.
Since in this chapter we are mainly interested in assessing the relationships
between social capital and basic cooperation propensities, we focus on the
total level of contributions to collective accounts as our main variable of

Table 9.1 Typology and parameters of experimental decisions

Decision	Type of game	Type of interaction	Options available	Variables name	Parameters of the game
1	PGG at the Local level	Non-Nested	Personal account	Personal1	
			Local public good account	Local1	$N = 4$, $MPCR = 0.5$ $MLSR = 2$
2	PGG at the Local/National level	Nested	Personal account	Personal2	
			Local public good account	Local2	$N = 4$, $MPCR = 0.5$ $MLSR = 2$
			National public good account	Nation2	$N = 12$, $MPCR = 0.25$ $MLSR = 1$ $MNSR = 3$
3	PGG at the Local/World level	Nested	Personal account	Personal3	
			Local public good account	Local3	$N = 4$, $MPCR = 0.5$ $MLSR = 2$
			World public good account	World3	$N = 12$, $MPCR = 0.25$ $MLSR = 1$ $MWSR = 3$

interest. We will bear in mind, though, that in the first decision this boils down to cooperation at the local level only, and in the other two decisions this is cooperation at the national and global level – where national and global levels are not exclusive but include the local level, too.

3. Results

3.1. Definitions of trust

The literature abounds with definitions of trust. Several studies deploy a 'behavioural' definition, such as that proposed by Kollock (1994) 'An action demonstrates trust if it increases one's vulnerability [...] to another whose behavior is not under one's control. It refers to the conscious regulation of one's dependence on another'. The standard indicator used to measure this construct is the response to the General Social Survey (GSS) question *'Generally speaking, would you say that most people can be trusted or that you couldn't be too careful in dealing with people?'* (TRUST henceforth).

Even leaving aside the several reasons why we should not be satisfied with this indicator (see Glaeser et al. 2000; Putnam 2000), trust in others may take a broader view than the behavioral approach and refer more generically to the dependability and reliability of others in situations where an individual is still in a condition of *vulnerability* with respect to others, but this happens out of her will. For example, in scenario X person A might wonder whether her neighbor person B can be *trusted* in holding onto her house keys without intruding into her apartment while A is away. This is the case when it is A's choice to expose herself to a situation of vulnerability. In scenario Y, conversely, A happens to lose her keys accidentally in a street along with other documents making her address identifiable. In this case, A might wonder whether a stranger C could be *trusted* in not taking advantage of the situation. A might also wonder the extent to which C might be *trusted* in actively trying to help out A, picking up A's keys and documents with the purpose of tracking A down, rather than just ignoring the matter. Responses to the following two GSS questions can be used to measure trust in scenario Y-like situations: *'Do you think most people would try to take advantage of you if they got a chance, or would they try to be fair?'* (FAIR henceforth); *'Would you say that most of the people try to be helpful, or that they are mostly just looking out for themselves?'* (HELPFUL henceforth).

These three indicators can be expected to be positively correlated with each other. They all revolve around to what has been called an individual's *social intelligence* in detecting others' trustworthiness and dependability in situations of uncertainty (Yamagishi 2001). Nevertheless, it would not be surprising if they showed some deviations from each other. The reason has precisely to do with the fact that behavioral trust refers to actions willingly taken by the actor. These are then likely to be influenced by the actor's degree of risk or ambiguity aversion, whereas this is not the case for the kind of trust applicable to scenario Y situations. The FAIR and HELPFUL indicators thus appear to capture more closely the individual cognitive judgment over a stranger's propensity to be dependable in situations of vulnerability for the actor. For this reason, we consider the three indicators separately.[4]

3.2. Descriptive statistics

Table 9.2 reports descriptive statistics for our sample, broken down into the large metropolitan area – that is, Milan – and other locations. In addition to trust measures, we gathered information on the involvement of the participant in voluntary associations, divided into 13 types ranging from social welfare association to professional associations, as per the classification proposed in the most popular surveys such as GSS and WVS. Such index of association membership (ASSOC_MEMB) counts the number of *types* of associations to which an individual is a member, and as such it is a rather

Table 9.2 Descriptive statistics for trust measures by location

Variables	TRUST	FAIR	HELPFUL	ASSOC_MEMB	ENTRY	FOR_MIGR	EXPOS_GLOB	LOCAL SI	NATIONAL SI	GLOBAL SI	Contr. To Local (Decision 1)	Contr. To Local + National (Decision 2)	Contr. To Local + World (Decision 3)
	1 = Most people can be trusted	1 = Most people are fair	1 = Most people would be helpful	1 = Individual belongs to all 13 kind of voluntary associations listed	4 = Completely agree ENTRY of foreigners into country should be restricted	4 = more than 4 foreign immigrant communities live in subject's residential area	1 = Individual maximally exposed to globalization	1 = Maximum identification with local community	1 = Maximum identification with national community	1 = Maximum identification with global community			
Milan													
Mean	0.328	0.664	0.311	0.127	3.246	2.943	0.948	0.749	0.809	0.679	5.738	6.934	6.664
St. Dev.	0.471	0.474	0.465	0.136	0.826	1.093	0.063	0.224	0.188	0.193	2.840	2.590	2.868
Min	0	0	0	0	1	1	0.719	0	0.167	0.167	0	0	0
Max	1	1	1	0.615	4	4	1	1	1	1	10	10	10
N	122	122	122	122	122	122	122	121	121	122	122	122	122
Other locations													
Mean	0.272	0.598	0.280	0.124	3.049	3.000	0.898	0.665	0.738	0.638	6.566	7.494	7.446
St. Dev.	0.448	0.493	0.452	0.130	0.960	1.077	0.097	0.237	0.193	0.223	2.923	2.360	2.628
Min	0	0	0	0	1	1	0.636	0	0	0	0	2	0
Max	1	1	1	0.462	4	4	1	1	1	1	10	10	10
N	81	82	82	83	81	82	83	83	82	82	83	83	83
All													
Mean	0.305	0.637	0.299	0.126	3.167	2.966	0.927	0.715	0.780	0.662	6.073	7.161	6.980
St. Dev.	0.462	0.482	0.459	0.133	0.885	1.085	0.082	0.232	0.193	0.206	2.895	2.509	2.793
Min	0	0	0	0	1	1	0.636	0	0	0	0	0	0
Max	1	1	1	0.615	4	4	1	1	1	1	10	10	10
N	203	204	204	205	203	204	205	204	203	204	205	205	205
P-Value	−0.85	−0.964	−0.473	−0.127	−1.335	0.319	−4.14***	−2.841***	−3.160***	−1.162	1.68*	1.446	2.093**

Notes: Mann–Whitney test on H_0 = 'Observations from Milan and other group of locations generated by same distribution'.

imperfect measure of an individual's actual involvement in such organizations. In spite of this limitation, this indicator is one of the most widely used in the literature.

Neither generalized trust nor membership in voluntary associations appear to differ significantly between Milan and the other locations. Perhaps surprisingly, the same occurs with respect to our measure of aversion to racial/ethnic integration. As stated in the introduction, Italy is a country that is by far more homogenous from the ethnic/racial point of view than the US, as well as other European countries like Germany, France and the UK. For these reasons we used responses to a question drawn from the World Value Survey that seemed particularly suitable to be applied to the Italian situation. That is the response to the question *'We should restrict and control entry of people into our own country more than we do'*. The possible responses varied over a 4-point scale ranging from 'Strongly disagree' to 'Strongly agree' (ENTRY henceforth). Although Milan residents are more likely to experience sentiments of aversion to migrants than non-Milan residents, the difference is not statistically significant.

The number of locations where the research was conducted is so small that using a measure of ethnic or racial heterogeneity at the level of the urban area – the only aggregate where data would be available – does not appear to be meaningful. Moreover, the data available only break down the provenance of migrants by the continent where they come from, and as such they would probably supply too coarse a measure of ethnic fragmentation and a rather imprecise measure of racial fragmentation. We are then going to use a self-reported measure of the presence of migrants in the participant's area of residence. This is derived from responses to the question *'How many different immigrant communities live in the area where you live?'* (FOR_MIGR). Participants were given different options but in the following analysis we only consider the dichotomic variable signaling whether at least one foreign migrant community is present in the participant's residential area. It is perhaps surprising that this indicator does not detect a higher ethnical mix in residential areas in Milan vis-à-vis other towns. Since migrants are more numerous in Milan than in other areas, this result may either be due to a lack of sharpness in our instrument, or to the fact that most immigrants live in segregated areas within Milan. Also, we cannot rule out that the subjective character of the question lends itself to be influenced by an individual's attitudes toward foreign communities, with individuals more averse to immigration inflating the number of foreign migrant communities living in their areas.

Some significant differences across locations exist with respect to the other indicators we collected. First, people living outside Milan are consistently less exposed to globalization, as measured by our exposure to globalization index (GLOB_EXPOS). This is derived from the individual globalization index used in Buchan et al. (2009a), and measures an individual's ability to access several media of global connections, ranging from the Internet and mobile phones, to international news sources and multinational activities. It covers around 30 items. The higher the index, the higher an individual's exposure to global connections.

Second, social identity measures were constructed with the aim of measuring the degree to which an individual identifies him/herself with various territorially defined communities. The measure was derived from Yuki et al. (2005) and was constructed by asking subjects the extent to which they felt attachment and closeness to their local, national and world communities, and how strongly they would define themselves as members of such communities.[5] Perhaps surprisingly, the Milanese report stronger social identity ties with the local community than people from other areas. The same holds for national social identity and for global identity, but the difference is negligible in the latter case. Finally, contributions to the collective accounts are generally *lower* in Milan than in other locations, and the difference is statistically significant in two cases out of three.

3.3. Factors associated with generalized trust: The 'TRUST' question

We first ascertain the strength of the relationships between possible determinants and survey measures of generalized trust. This is carried out in three logit regressions that deploy as dependent variables the responses to the three survey questions. We start off with the TRUST variable (Table 9.3, columns 1–4).

All specifications deploy four basic individual-level demographic controls – income, level of education, gender and age – and one location-level control – the population size of the location where the session has been conducted. These controls are insignificant most of the time, apart from EDUCATION, which is significant in the first specification, albeit only weakly (see Table 9.3, column 1). The sign is positive, which means that an increase in one's education level is positively correlated to one's level of trust. This is consistent with other studies (see Helliwell and Putnam 1999; Yamagishi 2001). A participant's YEAR OF BIRTH is not significantly related to TRUST, and this contradicts other studies generally finding strong cohort effects, with youngest generations being less trusting (Putnam 2000). POPULATION, too, is largely insignificant. This contradicts the view that in smaller towns and villages the level of interpersonal generalized trust is higher than in larger cities. However, the close-knit nature of social relations in smaller towns/villages may manifest itself in larger levels of trust within *personalized* social relations (see e.g. Bacharach and Gambetta 2001), as many interactions of this kind are likely to characterize this kind of urban environments. A question addressing interactions with generic rather than specific individuals is obviously not well-suited to capture this aspect.

The other four different specifications test the correlation between TRUST and various possible determinants. First we are interested in verifying the linkages with ASSOC_MEMB. In spite of the possible coarseness of this variable (see previous section), the relationship appears strong – at less than the

Table 9.3 Analysis of factors associated with generalized trust

| | Dependent variable Trust | | | | Dependent variable Fair | | | | Dependent variable Helpful | | | |
| | Trust | | | | Fair | | | | Helpful | | | |
	(1)	(2)	(3)	(4)	(5)	(6)	(7)	(8)	(9)	(10)	(11)	(12)
INCOME	0.0770	0.0742	0.0543	0.0652	0.0694	0.0601	0.0326	0.0437	-0.101	-0.113	-0.133	-0.142
	(0.0601)	(0.0613)	(0.0646)	(0.0663)	(0.0647)	(0.0588)	(0.0805)	(0.0787)	(0.0887)	(0.0817)	(0.0948)	(0.0953)
EDUCATION	0.490*	0.454	0.476	0.312	0.116	0.0901	0.0530	-0.0460	0.315	0.213	0.192	0.225
	(0.297)	(0.279)	(0.298)	(0.242)	(0.243)	(0.236)	(0.257)	(0.249)	(0.212)	(0.227)	(0.217)	(0.224)
GENDER	-0.168	-0.378	-0.211	-0.336	0.339	0.128	0.306	0.221	-0.358	-0.463	-0.340	-0.677*
	(0.358)	(0.384)	(0.345)	(0.376)	(0.376)	(0.358)	(0.357)	(0.425)	(0.341)	(0.326)	(0.341)	(0.352)
YEAR OF BIRTH	0.00116	0.00133	-0.00144	-0.00162	-0.0297*	-0.0315**	-0.0330***	-0.0319***	-0.0393***	-0.0402***	-0.0432***	-0.0358***
	(0.0141)	(0.0147)	(0.0147)	(0.0156)	(0.0130)	(0.0126)	(0.0120)	(0.0127)	(0.0102)	(0.0105)	(0.0106)	(0.0127)
POPULATION	0.0155	0.0472	-0.0296	0.0220	0.0206	0.0506	-0.0434	-0.0260	0.00577	0.0345	-0.0400	-0.0362
	(0.0536)	(0.0694)	(0.0488)	(0.0880)	(0.0781)	(0.0818)	(0.0801)	(0.1000)	(0.0542)	(0.0666)	(0.0599)	(0.0817)
ASSOC_MEMB	1.956**				2.747*			2.404	-0.219			-1.532
	(0.965)				(1.583)			(1.746)	(1.346)			(1.537)
ENTRY		-0.604***		-0.428**		-0.706***		-0.494*		-0.449***		-0.349
		(0.195)		(0.209)		(0.216)		(0.269)		(0.160)		(0.233)
FOR_MIGR		0.0375		0.00826		0.107		-0.00173		0.194		0.164
		(0.145)		(0.171)		(0.138)		(0.168)		(0.155)		(0.173)
GLOB_EXPOS			3.808*	3.391			5.897***	4.295			5.610**	3.225
			(2.094)	(2.375)			(2.119)	(2.955)			(2.434)	(3.267)
LOCAL_SOC				-2.509***				-0.777				0.614
				(0.785)				(0.751)				(0.744)
NATIONAL_SOC				1.401*				2.290*				1.334*
				(0.777)				(1.204)				(0.792)
GLOBAL_SOC				2.664***				1.428				2.731***
				(0.968)				(0.888)				(0.889)
Constant	-2.917***	-0.652	-5.550***	-4.796	0.882	3.589*	-3.231*	-2.346	1.779*	2.996**	-2.462	-2.890
	(1.097)	(1.502)	(1.858)	(2.934)	(1.561)	(1.945)	(1.768)	(3.159)	(0.980)	(1.298)	(1.938)	(3.677)
Observations	185	185	185	183	186	186	186	184	186	186	186	184
Pseudo R2	0.0505	0.0857	0.0493	0.161	0.0659	0.0985	0.0773	0.164	0.0562	0.0883	0.0791	0.154
Number of clusters	16	16	16	16	16	16	16	16	16	16	16	16

Notes: Logit model. Robust standard errors clustered across research sessions. P-values reported in brackets

5 per cent level of significance – and the sign the one predicted. Thus, the AMBT hypothesis is not disconfirmed from our data, although admittedly we cannot prove the direction of causation.

Column 2 analyses the relationship between generalized trust and a participant's attitudes toward migratory inflows of foreign people. The analysis reveals a positive correlation between lack of trust and concern over migratory flows. The impact of this variable is strongly significant at less than the 1 per cent level. The coefficient sign implies that the more a person feels that entry of foreigners should be restricted or controlled, the more her trust in others decreases.

Other research has normally looked at aversion toward racial integration as an instrumental factor in influencing levels of trust. In particular, Alesina and La Ferrara (2002) show that people averse to racial integration in the US are those who are more reactive to their metropolitan area's racial fragmentation in bringing about a decrease in trust levels. A large body of empirical evidence from US metropolitan areas has been brought in support of the view that racial fragmentation acts as an important factor in reducing trust, as well as association membership and public goods provision. Putnam (2007) notes that in these areas people tend to be less trusting *both* toward people of a different race/ethnic group *and* toward people from the same race/ethnic group.

In our case the direction of causation is not clear. Northern Italy has been affected by a rapid flow of migration from abroad over the last three decades from different parts of the world. This has undoubtedly created social tensions that have led to demands for tighter controls on migratory flows. It is possible to conjecture that some people may feel their personal security to be endangered by these flows. This may breed a more general sense of insecurity toward others, which results in a decline of generalized trust. On the other hand, it may be the case that people having a general diffidence in others' trustworthiness may also feel more endangered by foreign immigrants than other people, thus demanding stronger controls on migratory flows. The fact that many Italians now living in Lombardy were themselves migrants from Southern Italy during the 1960 and 1970s, further complicates this picture, as at the time this process of migration caused some social tensions, too.

In order to shed light on this issue, we would want to look at contextual effects of racial fragmentation. That is, if it was aversion to migration causing a reduction of trust, we may expect this effect to be stronger in areas where migrants are more concentrated. As illustrated in the previous section, we lack a fine indicator of racial heterogeneity at the community level, so we resort to the self-reported measure FOR_MIGR. The results are shown in Table 9.3, column 2 by adding FOR_MIGR in the regression including ENTRY. However, this variable is not significant either in this regression or when being included in the regression without ENTRY (not reported). An interaction term would not be significantly different from zero, too (not reported).

This result seems to support the conjecture that the sense of direction may go from lower trust toward greater aversion toward migrant flows. However, the opposite conjecture may not be discarded. It may be the case that in Italy reactance toward heterogeneity is not territorially specific, as is the case for the US. The sense of insecurity induced by migration may instead be driven by mass media reports and political propaganda, rather than by direct contact with migrants, so that the migrant's actual geographical location does not heighten diffidence in others. Moreover, we cannot discard the possibility that our subjective measure of ethnic heterogeneity may lack sharpness (see previous section).[6] With the information currently in our possession it is not possible to disentangle fully this effect, which nonetheless highlights a crucial aspect for social-capital related policies.

Table 9.2, columns 3–4 are devoted to studying the possible interaction between generalized trust and global connectivity variables. Buchan et al. (2009a) finds a strong effect of global connectivity on cooperative patterns, which is likely to be mediated by a change in social identity (Buchan et al. 2009b). That is, global connectivity may foster a 'cosmopolitanism' sense of attachment to others, which may replace – or become more relevant – than more 'parochial' patterns of attachment. It is thus possible to conjecture that global connectivity and a more 'cosmopolitan' construal of the self may have some relevant effects on one's generalized trust. In column 3 we report the results of the analysis using GLOB_EXP. The analysis confirms, though only partially, the possible relevance of such link. The higher one's exposure to globalization, the higher the level of generalized trust in others. The effect is, however, only weakly significant.

Column 4 assesses the strength of the possible mediating effects of global connectivity, and includes our set of social identity measures. If social identity mediates the effect of global connectivity, then we should expect the global connectivity index to lose significance. We have also included the measure of aversion to migratory flows, as this variable may also have a possible mediating effect for globalization. The analysis reveals that the global exposure index effect is in fact fully mediated by the introduction of these two sets of variables. Interestingly, all of the three social identity variables exert a significant effect on trust, although this is only weak for national identity. What is more, the sign is positive for both global and national identity, and negative for local identity. This suggests an opposing impact on one's level of generalized trust, which depends on the type of group with whom an individual identifies. The more one identifies at the local level, the *lower* the level of generalized trust. The opposite holds for identification at the national and, even more so, at the global level.

This finding is particularly interesting and might open a different perspective on the literature on trust. It seems to suggest that more trusting individuals are more likely to construct their social self as a 'cosmopolitan' one rather than as a more 'local' one. Greater access to interactions on a global scale may spur a heightened confidence that a broad range of others, including both foreigners and fellow country people, are reliable. The expansion of the group of people whom an individual may trust may thus raise the overall confidence that a generic other is trustworthy. Yamagishi (2001) has stressed a possible 'virtuous circle' in the development of trusting attitudes, in that more socially intelligent people will enter risky interactions more frequently than less socially intelligent ones. This in turn has the effect of further improving their social skills. In the case of global interactions a similar virtuous cycle may operate, in that interacting with foreigners and learning that they can be trusted may bolster the belief that strangers in general may be trusted. Finally, it is also worth nothing that ENTRY, too, shows a significant and negative impact on the dependent variable. Hence, the two mechanisms highlighted above – that is, the 'cosmopolitan' sense of identity induced by global connectivity, and the reactance to migratory flows – seemingly exert independent effects on one's generalized trust in others.

3.4. Factors associated with generalized trust: The 'FAIR' and 'HELPFUL' question

Columns 5–8 and 9–12 of Table 9.2 replicate the analysis developed earlier with respect to FAIR and HELPFUL. The first major difference is that responses now vary quite strongly with age, and go in the expected direction of youngest cohorts being less confident in others being fair or helpful. Some age groups in the sample must have thus perceived the TRUST question as substantially different from the other two questions. Moreover, the predictive power of ASSOC_MEMB is now lower than for TRUST, being only weakly significant for FAIR and not significant (and with the wrong sign) for HELPFUL.

ENTRY is again a strongly significant predictor for both FAIR and HELPFUL, whereas the presence of migrant's group in the respondent's residence area is not. Finally, EXPOS_GLOB is now a strongly significant predictor of helping behavior, whereas it is only weakly so for FAIR. Its effect is fully mediated by the social identity measure for FAIR, whilst it maintains some predictive power – albeit weakly – with respect to HELPFUL. ENTRY again appears to have an autonomous relevance from globalization components.

3.5. Analysis of links between cooperation and trust

The social capital literature rightly emphasizes the relevance of trust in society as a medium to boost interpersonal cooperation, and thus public goods provision. In many pieces of research, trust is taken as the dependent variable of analysis, and it is somehow taken for granted that the higher the trust levels, the greater the civic-mindedness and cooperative spirit. Our experimental data enable us to test directly for this relationship.

Tables 9.4–9.6 report econometric analysis measuring the relationship between cooperation at the local, national and global level, and the three attitudinal trust measures considered above. We also report analysis regarding the interaction of the trust measures with some of the possible factors of trust reviewed in the previous section. This is done in order to check for possible mediating effects exerted by trust. In spite of the relevance of globalization variables in their relationship with cooperation at the global level (see Buchan et al. 2009a), we have omitted them from the analysis as the study of the linkages between trust and globalization variables will be object of future investigation.

We draw on an ordered logit model including the same four basic demographic controls used above. These controls generally have no predictive power individually, the only exception being YEAR OF BIRTH that is negatively related to cooperation at the world level (see Table 9.6). Hence, younger people appear to be less cooperative than older ones at the world level. It is also worth noting that urban size, too, matters in this decision, as cooperation is, *ceteris paribus*, generally *larger* in smaller urban centres than in larger ones, even after controlling for the demographic factors. This is an interesting result because it shows that what is deemed as a peculiar characteristic of smaller urban centres – namely, higher density of social connections leading to higher cooperation levels – is not limited to the local level but extends to broader levels of interaction. One may conjecture that the norms of reciprocal cooperation acquired in smaller-scale interactions can be carried over to larger levels of interaction, in a similar fashion to the mechanisms suggested in support of the AMBT hypothesis (see section 1). However, the fact that this difference is only significant at the world level in our econometric analysis probably requires a further explanation, that is, sentiments of aversion toward foreigners being particularly stronger in cities rather than smaller urban centres. This conjecture, too, will be object of further analysis.

Table 9.4 shows that the three attitudinal measures are poor overall predictors of cooperation at the local level only. TRUST is the only variable that is weakly correlated with local cooperation in the most basic econometric specification (Table 9.4, column 1), whereas the other two variables are not (Table 9.4, columns 4, 7). This is also the case when ASSOC_MEMB is introduced in the econometric model. The index itself is not significant in predicting cooperation at the local level,[7] thus failing to support the AMBER conjecture of a positive relationship between participation in associations and propensity to cooperate in the society at large.

The last specification includes ENTRY and FOR_MIGR. The former variable has a significant effect on cooperation (at the 5 per cent level), and its introduction reduces the predictive power of TRUST to outside the region of significance. FOR_MIGR does not exert significant effects. Therefore, not only do people asking for more migratory controls have lower levels of trust

Table 9.4 Analysis of possible determinants of cooperation at the local level only

	Dependent variable Contributions to local account (Decision L)								
	(1)	(2)	(3)	(4)	(5)	(6)	(7)	(8)	(9)
INCOME	0.0527	0.0532	0.0564*	0.0613*	0.0617*	0.0653**	0.0714**	0.0714**	0.0725**
	(0.0333)	(0.0329)	(0.0322)	(0.0330)	(0.0328)	(0.0320)	(0.0325)	(0.0319)	(0.0325)
EDUCATION	0.184	0.175	0.122	0.260	0.250	0.192	0.280	0.264	0.203
	(0.192)	(0.190)	(0.163)	(0.196)	(0.196)	(0.160)	(0.213)	(0.210)	(0.170)
GENDER	−0.0484	−0.0316	−0.0984	−0.150	−0.132	−0.187	−0.129	−0.103	−0.175
	(0.294)	(0.302)	(0.313)	(0.282)	(0.291)	(0.309)	(0.278)	(0.286)	(0.307)
YEAR OF BIRTH	−0.00990	−0.00968	−0.00870	−0.00684	−0.00683	−0.00673	−0.00710	−0.00686	−0.00701
	(0.00928)	(0.00931)	(0.00944)	(0.00839)	(0.00832)	(0.00850)	(0.00935)	(0.00935)	(0.00936)
POPULATION	−0.123	−0.121	−0.0961	−0.129*	−0.127*	−0.104	−0.132*	−0.129*	−0.105
	(0.0762)	(0.0776)	(0.0773)	(0.0701)	(0.0708)	(0.0701)	(0.0694)	(0.0709)	(0.0703)
TRUST	0.299*	0.292*	0.236						
	(0.166)	(0.173)	(0.165)						
ASSOC_MEMB		0.432			0.399			0.635	
		(0.901)			(0.802)			(0.835)	
FOR_MIGR			−0.131			−0.131			−0.127
			(0.110)			(0.120)			(0.114)
ENTRY			−0.349**			−0.366**			−0.380**
			(0.163)			(0.156)			(0.157)
FAIR				0.193	0.182	0.137			
				(0.142)	(0.150)	(0.157)			
HELPFUL							0.161	0.159	0.121
							(0.133)	(0.137)	(0.135)
Observations	185	185	185	186	186	186	186	186	186
Pseudo R2	13.17	13.89	26.14	11.58	13.14	24.94	16.48	17.59	27.35
Number of clusters	16	16	16	16	16	16	16	16	16

Notes: Ordered logit model. Robust standard errors clustered across research sessions. Standard errors reported in brackets.

Table 9.5 Analysis of possible determinants of cooperation at the local and national level

| | | | | Dependent variable | | | | | |
	(1)	(2)	(3)	(4)	(5)	(6)	(7)	(8)	(9)
			Contributions to local and national accounts (Decision N)						
INCOME	0.0743	0.0738	0.0786	0.0769	0.0761	0.0799	0.0878	0.0856	0.0884
	(0.0552)	(0.0546)	(0.0546)	(0.0568)	(0.0565)	(0.0560)	(0.0567)	(0.0565)	(0.0562)
EDUCATION	0.244*	0.240	0.175	0.205	0.199	0.135	0.222	0.208	0.146
	(0.143)	(0.151)	(0.128)	(0.156)	(0.165)	(0.132)	(0.162)	(0.175)	(0.139)
GENDER	0.156	0.161	0.117	0.153	0.161	0.125	0.181	0.198	0.151
	(0.270)	(0.270)	(0.277)	(0.255)	(0.254)	(0.267)	(0.270)	(0.269)	(0.279)
YEAR OF BIRTH	−0.0133	−0.0133	−0.0135	−0.0104	−0.0103	−0.0113	−0.00891	−0.00860	−0.00969
	(0.00900)	(0.00898)	(0.00863)	(0.00784)	(0.00781)	(0.00724)	(0.00909)	(0.00906)	(0.00901)
POPULATION	−0.114*	−0.113*	−0.0936	−0.0979	−0.0970	−0.0769	−0.100	−0.0986	−0.0790
	(0.0692)	(0.0687)	(0.0604)	(0.0756)	(0.0757)	(0.0658)	(0.0760)	(0.0768)	(0.0666)
TRUST	0.151	0.150	0.0971						
	(0.148)	(0.153)	(0.143)						
ASSOC_MEMB		0.130			0.181			0.451	
		(0.808)			(0.760)			(0.832)	
FOR_MIGR			−0.134			−0.149			−0.156
			(0.0968)			(0.103)			(0.108)
ENTRY			−0.351***			−0.374***			−0.366***
			(0.111)			(0.121)			(0.121)
FAIR				0.165	0.161	0.107			
				(0.208)	(0.216)	(0.219)			
HELPFUL							0.216**	0.220**	0.180*
							(0.0991)	(0.104)	(0.108)
Observations	185	185	185	186	186	186	186	186	186
Pseudo R2	22.73	23.64	40.91	13.56	18.14	53.23	19.97	23.19	55.62
Number of clusters	16	16	16	16	16	16	16	16	16

Notes: See Table 9.4.

Table 9.6 Analysis of possible determinants of cooperation at the local and global level

| | Dependent variable | | | | | | | | |
| | Contributions to local and world accounts (Decision W) | | | | | | | | |
	(1)	(2)	(3)	(4)	(5)	(6)	(7)	(8)	(9)
INCOME	0.115**	0.114**	0.115**	0.117**	0.117**	0.117**	0.131**	0.129**	0.128**
	(0.0531)	(0.0522)	(0.0555)	(0.0531)	(0.0525)	(0.0551)	(0.0520)	(0.0507)	(0.0545)
EDUCATION	0.211	0.173	0.164	0.195	0.172	0.165	0.229	0.188	0.185
	(0.153)	(0.168)	(0.141)	(0.141)	(0.157)	(0.133)	(0.157)	(0.173)	(0.146)
GENDER	−0.0463	0.00299	−0.123	−0.147	−0.112	−0.193	−0.0569	−0.00670	−0.126
	(0.355)	(0.355)	(0.388)	(0.364)	(0.373)	(0.390)	(0.354)	(0.354)	(0.385)
YEAR OF BIRTH	−0.0257***	−0.0252***	−0.0259***	−0.0233***	−0.0232***	−0.0240***	−0.0241***	−0.0236***	−0.0250***
	(0.00918)	(0.00923)	(0.00897)	(0.00820)	(0.00819)	(0.00809)	(0.00882)	(0.00886)	(0.00883)
POPULATION	−0.149**	−0.144**	−0.134**	−0.165**	−0.162**	−0.154**	−0.155**	−0.151**	−0.142**
	(0.0696)	(0.0708)	(0.0650)	(0.0727)	(0.0737)	(0.0679)	(0.0683)	(0.0687)	(0.0639)
TRUST	0.0812	0.0609	0.0376						
	(0.130)	(0.139)	(0.124)						
ASSOC_MEMB		1.250						1.305	
		(0.981)						(0.971)	
FOR_MIGR			0.0291			0.0310			0.0329
			(0.0926)			(0.0896)			(0.0916)
ENTRY			−0.268**			−0.188			−0.236*
			(0.124)			(0.119)			(0.129)
FAIR				0.351**	0.329*	0.308*			
				(0.167)	(0.189)	(0.167)			
HELPFUL							0.191***	0.197***	0.149**
							(0.0742)	(0.0754)	(0.0682)
Observations	185	185	185	186	186	186	186	186	186
Pseudo R2	0.0273	0.0295	0.0315	0.0383	0.0392	0.0404	0.0327	0.0350	0.0360
Number of clusters	16	16	16	16	16	16	16	16	16

Notes: See Table 9.4.

in others, but they are also significantly less inclined to cooperate with local others. We may infer, thus, that the motivational factors captured by ENTRY exhausts the possible incidence of TRUST. The variable ENTRY, therefore, helps identify a typology of individuals whose attitudes appear as being particularly harmful for public social capital and cooperation. Social policies addressing the views held by these individuals may boost a society's cooperation levels.

Table 9.5 conducts the same kind of analysis using COOP2 as dependent variable. This is the sum of cooperation at both the local and national level in the second experimental decision. The results of the analysis would not differ substantially were we to use contributions to the national account only as a dependent variable. The results are now quite different from those obtained for cooperation at the local level only. TRUST is now no longer a significant predictor of cooperation, and neither is FAIR. Conversely, HELPFUL turns out as having a significant effect on cooperation, which is significant at the 5 per cent level (Table 9.5, column 7). The positive sign indicates that – as expected – higher levels of expectation on others' propensity to be helpful are associated with higher levels of cooperation. Moreover, the same effects (or lack of) observed above holds here for ASSOC_MEMB, and the ENTRY variable. Interestingly, HELPFUL maintains some weak predictive power even when considered jointly with ENTRY.

The results only vary slightly with respect to cooperation at the world level (see Table 9.6). TRUST has no significant predictive power (see Table 9.6, columns 1–3), whereas HELPFUL does (see Table 9.6, columns 7–9). What is worth noting is that FAIR now has some significant predictive power when it enters as an individual regressor (Table 9.6, column 4), and when matched with either ASSOC_MEMB or ENTRY (Table 9.6, columns 5, 6).

4. Conclusions

As far as association membership is concerned, the results of our enquiry only show mixed support for the AMBT hypothesis, whereas they seem to disconfirm the AMBER hypothesis. They show a significant correlation with generalized trust only when this is measured by TRUST, but only weakly when this is measured by FAIR and no significance when this is measured by HELPFUL. Most importantly, ASSOC_MEMB does not exert any significant effect on cooperation at any level of interaction. If we interpret our experimental data as a measure of individual propensity to cooperate in anonymous 'depersonalized' situations of interaction, then there does seem to be very little evidence that people involved in associations manifest cooperative spirits in large-scale societies. It is true though that the paucity of observations prevents us from drawing firm conclusions.

Conversely, some support can be drawn for the TBER hypothesis, as individuals stating they trust others seemed more inclined to cooperate in our experiments than others. Substantial differences exist, though, across different measures of generalized trust. Of these, HELPFUL appears to be the most reliable predictor of cooperation, but only when this is at levels of interaction beyond the local. FAIR only predicts at the global level. A tentative explanation is that generalized trust is likely to be associated with a cosmopolitan sense of social identity, as suggested in section 3.3, by noting the significant correlation with globalization and social identity variables – though this varied somewhat across the three trust measures. As a consequence, people trusting others may be more inclined to cooperate at broader levels of interaction. Surprisingly enough, though, this is not true for the TRUST question, which only predicts – and weakly so – at the local level. At the minimum, this shows that the three measures do seem to capture different aspects of an individual's social attitudes (see section 3.1). More research on the relationship between social identity and trust is needed to understand why this proves to be the case.

Acknowledgements

Grants from the National Science Foundations #0652277 and #0652310 are gratefully acknowledged. We are also grateful to Giuseppe Attanasi, Emma Baldin, Giacomo Degli Antoni, Alessio D'Oria, Marco Faillo, Mara Gargatagli, Elena e Sabina Mazzucchelli, Cristina Nicotra, Elisa Portale, Niccolò Pozzi, Mariagrazia Ranzini and Nazaria Solferino, for their invaluable collaboration during fieldwork. We also thank Paolo Bertoletti, Carluccio Bianchi and Salvatore Grillo for the use of Pavia University and Bocconi University facilities. We also acknowledge support from Milan Sixth District Council, the Gallaratese public library, and the City Councils of Motta Visconti and Cilavegna. A special thanks goes to Lorenzo Sacconi and Econometica for the logistic support kindly offered and their encouragement throughout the research, and to Stefano Savoldi of Demoscopea for his excellent assistance to our research. Finally, we acknowledge the contribution of Nancy Buchan, Marilynn Brewer, Margaret Foddy, Enrique Fatàs and Rick Wilson, who, along with Gianluca Grimalda, conducted the project 'Globalization, Cooperation, and Trust', of which this study was part. All errors are our sole responsibility.

Notes

1. See e.g. Stolle (2001) and Degli Antoni (2009) for studies seeking to understand the impact of membership associations on trusting behavior.
2. For instance, greater economic output may *produce*, rather than being the outcome, of institutions better capable of enforcing contracts and prosecuting crimes, which in turn would increase interpersonal trust. This may then enable individuals to nurture more trust toward each other.

3. Note that a Trust Game is like a dynamic version of a cooperation problem, thus one should expect some consistency in patterns of behavior among the two interactions.
4. Glaeser et al. (2000) consider instead an index made up of the answers to the three questions.
5. The exact text of the three questions was as follows: How strongly do you feel attachment to / How strongly do you define yourself as a member of / How close do you feel to / other members of your community in [Name of local community], in the [Name of country], or to the world as a whole?
6. According to ISTAT, the percentage of migrant population over the whole resident population ranges from a maximum of 6.97 percent in Milan to a minimum of 1.25 percent in Motta Visconti. Obviously these statistics only take into account legal migrants, thus underestimating the actual number of immigrants.
7. The coefficient is not significantly different from zero even when it enters the model as a lone regressor without the trust measures (not reported).

References

A. Alesina and E. La Ferrara (2002) 'Who Trust Others?', *Journal of Public Economics*, 85, 207–234.

A. Alesina and E. La Ferrara (2000) 'Participation in Heterogeneous Communities', *Quarterly Journal of Economics*, August, 847–904.

L. Anderson, J. Mellor and J. Milyo (2004) 'Social Capital and Contributions in a Public-Goods Experiment', *American Economic Review*, 94(2), 373–376.

K. Arrow (1974) *The Limits of Organization* (New York: Norton).

Bacharach M. and D. Gambetta (2001) 'Trust in Signs', in K. Cook (ed.), *Trust in Society* (New York, NY: Sage), pp. 148–184.

C. Blackwell and M. McKee (2003) 'Only for My Own Neighborhood? Preferences and Voluntary Provision of Local and Global Public Goods', *Journal of Economic Behavior and Organization*, 52, 115–131.

N. Buchan, G. Grimalda, R. Wilson, M. Brewer, E. Fatas and M. Foddy (2009a) 'Globalization and Human Cooperation', *Proceedings of the National Academy of Sciences of the USA*, 106(11), 4138–4142.

N. Buchan, M. Brewer, G. Grimalda, R. Wilson, E. Fatas and M. Foddy (2009b) 'The Role of Social Identity in Global Cooperation', *mimeo*.

J. Coleman (1990) *Foundations of Social Theory* (Cambridge, MA: Harvard University Press).

G. Degli Antoni (2009) 'Intrinsic vs. Extrinsic Motivations to Volunteer and Social Capital Formation', *Kyklos*, 62(3), 359–370.

J. Delhey and K. Newton (2005) 'Predicting Cross-National Levels of Social Trust: Global Pattern or Nordic Exceptionalism?', *European Sociological Review*, 21, 311–327.

S. Durlauf (2002) 'On the Empirics of Social Capital', *Economic Journal*, 112, 459–479.

F. Farina, R. O'Higgins and P. Sbriglia (2008) 'Comparing Attitudinal and Behavioural Measures of Trust and Reciprocity', *mimeo*.

E. Fehr, U. Fischbacher, B. von Rosenbladt, J. Schupp and G. Wagner (2002) 'A Nation-Wide Laboratory – Examining trust and trustworthiness by integrating behavioral experiments into representative surveys', *Schmollers Jahrbuch*, 122(4), 519–542.

E. Glaeser, D. Laibson, J. Scheinkman and C. Soutter (2000) 'Measuring Trust', *Quarterly Journal of Economics*, 115(3), 505–531.

L. Guiso, L. Zingales and P. Sapienza (2007) 'Trusting the Stock Market', *SSRN Working paper* http://ssrn.com/abstract=973978.

J.F. Helliwell and R. Putnam (1999) 'Economic Growth and Social Capital in Italy', *Eastern Economic Journal*, 21, Reprinted Dasgupta and Serageldin (eds), *Social Capital: A Multifaceted Perspective* (Washington, DC: World Bank), pp. 253–268.

S. Knack and P. Keefer (1997) 'Does Social Capital Have an Economic Payoff? A Cross-Country Investigation', *Quarterly Journal of Economics*, 112, 1251–1288.

P. Kollock (1994) 'The Emergence of Exchange Structures: An Experimental Study of Uncertainty, Commitment and Trust', *American Sociological Review*, 100, 313–345.

R. La Porta, F. Lopez-de-Silanes, A. Shleifer A and R. Vishny (1999) 'The Quality of Government', *Journal of Law, Economics and Organization*, 15(1), 222–279.

B. Lahno (1995) 'Trust and Strategic Rationality', *Rationality and Society*, 7(4), 442–464.

E. Luttmer (2001) 'Group Loyalty and the Taste for Redistribution', *Journal of Political Economy*, 109(3), 500–528.

M. Paldam (2010) *infra* 'Generalized Trust: The Macro Perspective', in L. Sacconi and G. Degli Antoni (eds), *Social Capital, Corporate Social Responsibility, Economic Behaviour and Performance* (Basingstoke: Palgrave MacMillan).

P. Paxton (2007) 'Association Memberships and Generalized Trust: A Multilevel Model Across 31 Countries', *Social Forces* 86(1) 46–76.

R. Putnam (2007) 'E Pluribus Unum: Diversity and Community in the Twenty-first Century', *Scandinavian Political Studies*, 30(2), 137–174.

R. Putnam (2000) *Bowling Alone: The Collapse and Revival of American Community* (New York: Simon and Schuster).

R. D. Putnam, R. Leonardi and R. Y. Nanetti (1993) *Making Democracy Work: Civic Traditions in Modern Italy* (Princeton: Princeton University Press).

B. Rothstein and E. Uslaner (2005) 'All for All: Equality, Corruption, and Social Trust', *World Politics*, 58, 41–72.

R. Sampson, S. Raudenbush and F. Earls (1997) 'Neighborhoods and Violent Crime: A Multilevel Study of Collective Efficacy', *Science*, 277, 918–924.

R. Solow (1999) 'Notes on Social Capital and Economic Performance', in Dasgupta and Serageldin (eds), *Social Capital: A Multifaceted Perspective* (Washington, DC: World Bank), pp. 6–10.

D. Stolle (2001) 'Clubs and Congregations: The Benefits of Joining an Association', in K. Cook (ed.) *Trust in Society*, Russell Sage Foundation, pp. 202–244.

A. Wit and N. Kerr (2002) ' "Me Versus Just US Versus All" Categorization and Cooperation in Nested Social Dilemmas', *Journal of Personality and Social Psychology*, 83, 616–637.

T. Yamagishi (1988) 'The Provision of a Sanctioning System in the United States and Japan', *Social Psychology Quarterly*, 51(3), 265–271.

T. Yamagishi and M. Yamagishi (1994) 'Trust and Commitment in the United States and Japan', *Motivation and Emotion*, 18(2), 129–166.

T. Yamagishi (2001) 'Trust as a Form of Social Intelligence', in Cook K (ed.) *Trust in Society* (New York: Russell Sage Foundation).

M. Yuki, W. Maddux, M. Brewer and K. Takemura (2005) 'Cross-Cultural Differences in Relationship and Group-Based Trust', *Personality and Social Psychology Bulletin*, 31(1), 48–62.

L. Zucker (1986) 'Production of Trust: Institutional Sources of Economic Structure, 1840–1920', *Research in Organizational Behavior*, 8, 53–111.

10
Testing the Distributive Effects of Social Enterprises: The Case of Italy

Carlo Borzaga, Sara Depedri and Ermanno Tortia

1. Introduction

The debate on social enterprises has been stimulated by their spontaneous and haphazard emergence in many niches of activity and in various countries. Their initial appearance was driven by initiatives undertaken within civil society by social activists. The specialized literature has accordingly studied this new category of firms in a rather narrow way, whereas it may be more important to determine its general economic features. Different streams of analysis underline different advantages and disadvantages of social enterprises, mainly linking them to the literature on non-profit organizations. But they do so haphazardly, without a clear and comprehensive framework. The main contributions (Anheier and Ben-Ner 2003; Borzaga and Defourny 2001) have been based on industry studies, and on some specific features and types of social enterprises. Legislation has followed the same route by focusing on specific activities and organizational types. An example is the law on social cooperatives in Italy aimed at the regulation of social services and work integration, as well as the regulation of fair trade and micro-finance in various countries, etc.[1]

The first author to have attempted a convincing analysis of the social impact of entrepreneurial non-profit organizations is Burton Weisbrod (1977, 1988), who viewed nonprofits not as merely donative ventures, but as organizations explicitly undertaking productive activities in an independent way in order to satisfy both private and social needs. Weisbrod recognized that nonprofits produce (quasi)-public goods with a meritorious character, while distributing (implicitly or explicitly) benefits to non-paying demand. In this context, the bulk of the literature evidences the ability of social enterprises to produce public and quasi-public (collective and common) goods and services of a meritorious nature (Anheier and Ben-Ner 2003; Borzaga and Defourny 2001; Borzaga and Spear 2004). Social enterprises are, therefore, expected to complete existing markets and public welfare systems by complementing both public and private for-profit provision.

Given the quasi-public nature (Ben-Ner and Van Hoomissen 1991) and the high relational content (Borzaga and Musella 2003; Gui and Sugden 2005) of the services produced by social enterprises, traditional organizational forms would not be able to guarantee their production except at higher costs and/or lower effectiveness of supply, owing to market imperfections, contract incompleteness and government failures. The ability of social enterprises to achieve a high degree of efficiency and effectiveness in service delivery depends on fulfillment of the constraints imposed by economic sustainability in terms of an adequate endowment and renewal of resources. Economic sustainability can also be accomplished by drawing on non-market resources, such as voluntary labor and beneficent donations. The increased availability of resources and the change in the firm's objectives, which shift from profit maximization to the satisfaction of social needs, are supported by the absence of the profit motive, and they have major implications in terms of welfare effects as well. Higher supply and lower prices depend on the reduced exploitation of market power and on the pro-social motivations of the organization's patrons (Tortia 2010).

This study seeks to provide a more complete and coherent definition of the welfare effects of social enterprises. It will concentrate on the overproduction and distribution of resources for social aims by social enterprises. The second section illustrates our hypotheses concerning the distributive function of social enterprises, while the third section analyses the process of distribution and the supporting organizational mechanisms more thoroughly. The fourth section reports descriptive results from the ICSI 2007 survey, which was carried out on a representative sample of 320 Italian cooperatives. The fifth section concludes with concise policy implications.

2. Our hypotheses

The literature on social enterprises has paid insufficient attention to defining their distributive function, and it has often conflated all their beneficial effects under the heading of 'positive externalities'. The distributive function has been (partially) studied only in the case of donative non-profit organizations, such as grant-making foundations and associations, which often simply satisfy the demand for quasi-public goods and services expressed by their memberships (Ben-Ner 1994; Clotfelter 1992). Entrepreneurial nonprofits have not been taken into appropriate consideration. Bacchiega and Borzaga (2001) attempted the first analysis of the distributive impact of non-profit organizations when they are organized as social enterprises. In what follows we show that social enterprises are driven by an intentional attempt to solve social problems and that this attempt must be differentiated from unintentional external effects. Although the two kinds of effect may be complementary, they are substantially different. Both the intentional and the unintended effects are likely to be linked to the distinctive allocative and distributive mechanisms that characterize social enterprises. They are based, for example, on the distribution of goods and services free of charge or at below market prices to weak social groups (Tortia 2010). The distributive function can be considered an intentional effect insofar as it depends on the organization's explicit objectives and on the strategic decisions defining its operation. The intentional distribution of resources can be accomplished because social enterprises do not fully remunerate the production factors (labor and capital) and gather additional non-market resources, such as partial and complete labor donations and financial donations. They can also socialize part of their output through the asset lock or through expenses targeted at the solution of specific social problems usually concerning weak social groups or the community at large. In other words, part of the resources available to social enterprises are employed in the over-production and distribution of output relative to contractual commitments with the paying demand. This unique feature of social enterprises distinguishes them from traditional entrepreneurial organizations devoted to the satisfaction of private needs. Unintended effects are linked to positive externalities generated by the firm's operation in terms of positive impacts on the well-being of an entire local community achieved by diffusing voluntary actions and social norms, independently of the specific group of beneficiaries of the firm's services. Positive external effects and the accumulation of social capital (Coleman 1990) are indirect, but not secondary, effects of the operation of social enterprises. Specifically, as defined by political scientists (see Putnam 1996; Putnam et al. 1993), social capital concerns the advantages for collectivities by virtue of the civic norms prevailing among their members. Social cohesion and trust relations are crucial factors in defining social capital in general, and seem particularly relevant in social enterprises, since these organizations incur competitive advantages in developing trustworthiness, social norms, voluntary actions, cooperation among stakeholders and behaviors based on reciprocity (Depedri 2010). Furthermore, the development of social capital and positive externalities is linked to the ability of social enterprises to build networks among mutually dependent and co-motivated actors (Sacchetti and Sugden 2003), favoring the reduction of transaction costs and the expression of intrinsic and prosocial motivations. The ability to support the accumulation of social capital relates to the way in which social enterprises gather the necessary resources, define their objectives, and govern and involve the relevant patrons; but it should be interpreted as a by-product of the organization's objectives, not as its main aim.[2]

This framework also makes it possible to evidence the ability of social enterprises to internalize important external effects linked to the pursuit of entrepreneurial objectives. Our working hypothesis is that the commonality of the resources accumulated mainly through locked assets, the organization's public benefit aim, and its governance structure based on the involvement of different stakeholders, support the internalization of external effects that in more traditional organizational forms can be generated by both market imperfections and contract incompleteness. For example, the difficulties of managing contrasting interests in principal-agent relationships can be overcome or reduced if these relationships are managed through coordination mechanisms developed within the organizational boundaries and based on involvement, and not through mere contractual relations. Furthermore, the ability of social enterprises to socialize resources may help them overcome free-riding in the private production of public services.

Some of the effects generated by social enterprises would not have the same features and intensity in the case of other organizational forms, either public or for-profit. Public bodies must comply with rigid administrative procedures, which forestall the possibility of adequately involving the main patrons and enhancing their intrinsic motivations. The possibility of distributing resources for free is also forestalled if not in the presence of rigid regulation, which can by itself increase costs due to increased bureaucratization. On the other hand, incentives and strategic decision-making in for-profit firms are directed to the maximization of surplus and the organization's economic value for private appropriation. Social enterprises can instead pursue specific social objectives by using limited but dedicated resources. The institutional structure is designed to support this kind of behavior, because the non-profit constraint attenuates the importance of monetary incentives and curbs the quest for private appropriation. The same constraint also induces a high degree of the socialization of resources, whose utilization and distribution is defined by public-benefit objectives. By the same token, it enhances intrinsic motivations by favoring involvement in the organizational mission and decision-making (Valentinov 2007, 2008).

3. The distributive impact of social enterprises

A new interpretation of the economic nature of social enterprises and of its distributive consequences can be based on analysis of the relations between the motivational drives behind their creation and the definition of their social mission, on the one hand, and their distinctive institutional structure on the other. The allocation and distribution of resources in social enterprises takes place at the intersection between their pro-social nature, which is based on involvement and non-self-interested motivations, and orientation toward the production of social welfare. While the institutional structure and the motivational drives in social enterprises have already been analyzed in previous works (Borzaga and Depedri 2005; Borzaga and Tortia 2006, 2009), their distributive consequences have yet to be examined. Our argument starts from the finding that demand for the services usually produced by social enterprises is often greater than the supply provided by the state and by for-profit firms. We hypothesize that unmet demand can be satisfied through either one of two channels. First, social enterprises can intercept quotas of demand for niche public goods not satisfied by the public sector because of the preferences expressed by the median voter. Second, by increasing output and lowering prices, social enterprises can extend the consumption of collective and meritorious goods to weaker social groups. These outcomes arise because of distinctive allocative and distributive mechanisms that favor the fairer distribution of meritorious goods through the lesser exploitation of market power, which induces lower prices and increased production; and through an allocation of resources that by-passes the rule of equivalence characterizing market exchanges (Ben-Ner and Van Hoomissen 1991; Tortia 2010).

While the provision of quasi-public goods by entrepreneurial nonprofits has already been widely studied by the specialized literature at the empirical level as well, much work remains to be done in analyzing the beneficial and redistributive effects in the wider social context. Some studies have examined the distributive impact of non-profit organizations in favor of the poor in the USA (Clotfelter 1992; Ben-Ner 1994). However, they have obtained mainly negative results, because nonprofits prove to serve mainly the socio-economic groups that support them financially, with negligible or nil redistributive effects. They often behave as clubs that exclusively serve the collective objectives of their membership. The exceptions are mainly represented by public-sector subsidized nonprofits, which usually serve a larger number of low-income users. Nonprofits seem largely to serve demand for which financial support has been granted at the outset. These studies, however, have not considered such important elements as the specific features of the input markets, primarily the labor market, which in the case of nonprofits may be characterized by partial or complete work donations (volunteering) and by lower managerial remuneration (Leete 2000), which implies higher production and greater distributive fairness. Also not properly considered has been the ability of non-profit organizations to socialize resources through the accumulation of locked assets and to use these additional funds to increase supply. These effects are clearly reminiscent of the behavior of volunteers in donative non-profit and grant-making foundations. It has been shown that they are, at least partially, carried on to entrepreneurial nonprofits as well, in connection with their public benefit aim. Furthermore, the differences in governance structure and motivational drives between nonprofits and other organizational forms have not been considered either, while recent studies have paid greater attention to pro-social and relational aspects in not-for-profit firms relatively to the public sector and for-profit firms, concluding that they do indeed serve social objectives better (Borzaga and Depedri 2005; Borzaga and Tortia 2006). Finally, other institutional elements of a more formal nature should be added, because, under recent European legislation, social enterprises are obliged to serve social goals mainly in the communities where they operate. Hence, their surpluses and assets are often devoted to distributive aims as well.

When these additional elements are considered, the distributive function of social enterprises becomes apparent, and can also be studied empirically. Social enterprises can produce at lower costs by employing unused non-market resources, or by reducing the remuneration of production factors, both capital and labor, to below market levels. However, social enterprises can devote part of their surplus to social objectives even in the absence of donations and volunteering. This is possible because of reduced private appropriation and because of increased efficiency and effectiveness in service delivery. The absence of the profit motive supports the reduced exploitation of positional advantages on the market, the expansion of production and the fixing of lower prices. The public benefit aim instead favors the distribution of goods and services free of charge or under the cost level. Furthermore, social enterprises can discriminate on prices because of their non-profit nature by favoring the revelation of users' private information about their ability and willingness to pay (Ben-Ner and Van Hoomissen 1991). Though these processes may be only partially purposeful, they all allow a more equitable distribution of resources in favor of the less well-off.

The accomplishment of cost reduction and increased effectiveness in the absence of private appropriation and powerful monetary incentives requires that the actors involved, mainly managers and workers, but also clients, be guided not only by self-interest but also by pro-social, altruistic and relational preferences (Ben-Ner and Putterman 1998; Borzaga and Depedri 2005; Borzaga and Tortia 2006; Frey 1997; Grimalda and Sacconi 2005). In other words, the structure of behavioral propensities and decision-making attitudes becomes much more complex than traditional economic approaches used to assume. For all these reasons, social enterprises are able to increase the supply of public benefit goods beyond the levels achieved by for-profit firms and the public sector, and to reduce poverty and marginality by modifying the distribution of the social surplus. This is one of the cases in which the equivalence rule that regulates market exchanges is defeated in private organizations through the implementation of specific allocative mechanisms that support the expression of intrinsic and pro-social motivations.

4. Empirical analysis of survey data: the case of Italian social cooperatives

The aim of the following empirical analysis is to shed light on the distributive impact of social enterprises. A brief description is given of how social enterprises gather resources and distribute their economic surplus among different purposes, and the procedures followed to achieve these objectives.

Also analyzed is the contribution of social enterprises to the accumulation of social capital and its relation with the distributive mechanisms.

The analysis exploits the recent ICSI2007 database, which gathered data on a representative sample of 320 Italian social cooperatives, their managers and 4134 paid workers employed by the same organizations.[3] Most social cooperatives operate in the social service sector (71.8 per cent), while the rest have the work integration of disadvantaged workers as their main aim. Social cooperatives are on average rather small: specifically, 43.3 per cent of them employ fewer than 15 people, while only 26.3 per cent can be considered large. Social cooperatives also frequently employ volunteers (65.8 per cent of cases) because these represent an important resource for the organization and frequently compensate for the small amount of capital and financial resources.

Distinction by types of governance shows that one out of three cooperatives is multi-stakeholder – i.e. it is governed by different classes of patrons, such as employees, volunteers, other institutions and clients of the organization (although clients are involved only in the membership of one out of ten organizations). Another 30 per cent of cooperatives are hybrid organizations, where the membership also comprises other stakeholders, but only workers are members of the board of directors. The percentage of single-stakeholder cooperatives where workers constitute the entire membership is lower (21.2 per cent), although workers are always involved in the membership and are, therefore, the most represented class of patrons.

Most of the social cooperatives surveyed belonged to formal networks: 77.3 per cent of them were members of national associations; half of them were involved in horizontal networks based on mutual dependence, and specifically in local consortia of social cooperatives (45.7 per cent) or temporary associations of firms (TAF hereafter, in 45.8 per cent of cases). Only 13.3 per cent of the organizations surveyed did not belong to networks. Networks are important because they supply important services to their members, such as the means to access important economic information (as stated by more than 50 per cent of the sample) and financial support for research and innovation (Table 10.1) (about 50 per cent of consortia).[4]

Given these general characteristics of the sample, the following analysis focuses on the ability of social cooperatives to increase social well-being both intentionally by over-producing and distributing services, and unintentionally by influencing social capital development. The questionnaires administered comprised a section which collected information on the additional resources that social cooperatives are able to acquire and distribute over and above the equivalence rule represented by market exchanges. Specifically, the questionnaires gathered information on the resources employed and data on the tendency of social cooperatives to distribute part of their surpluses for the implementation of social programs and to the benefit of the

Table 10.1 Some characteristics of the sample (%)

	%
Type of activity	
Social services production	71.8
Work integration	28.2
Size	
Fewer than 15 employees	43.3
15–50 employees	30.4
More than 50 employees	26.3
Geographical area	
North-West	39.0
North-East	18.3
Centre	18.3
South	24.4
Governance	
Single-stakeholder	21.2
Multi-stakeholder of only workers and volunteers	15.8
Hybrid organizations (multi-membership, single-board)	29.2
Multi-stakeholder	33.8
Membership of networks	
Members of national associations	77.3
Members of consortia of social cooperatives	45.7
Members of temporary associations of enterprises	45.8
Involved in other networks with organizations operating in the sector	43.9
Involved in other networks with other organizations	14.7
Not involved in networks	13.3

Source: authors' calculations on ICSI 2007 data (*Indagine sulle Cooperative Sociali Italiane*).

needy, as opposed to traditional forms of distribution (e.g. wages and the cost of capital). Another section in the questionnaire concerned social capital, evaluated as the ability of social cooperatives to develop trust relations inside and outside the organization, and in terms of the sharing of values and adoption of practises of corporate social responsibility.

All these issues are likely to be intertwined, since the sharing of values and the adoption of a socially responsible behavior are necessary for social cooperatives to be able to gather the non-market resources needed to pursue social goals. By the same token, shared values and the fulfillment of a distributive function in pursuit of public benefit aims reinforce trust relations and reduce the transaction costs linked to private ends informed by self-interested preferences.

Hence, the empirical analysis first concentrates on the ways in which social cooperatives operate their distributive function, and specifically on how additional resources are distributed and services delivered for public benefit purposes and to improve the conditions of people unable to pay.

Second, estimation will be made of how social cooperatives gather additional resources beyond market transactions; the analysis will reflect on the presence of voluntary or underpaid labor, and on financial donations, but also on the accumulation of locked assets. Finally, the analysis will focus on the ability of social enterprises to increase trust and to improve relations (elements of social capital) both inside the organization and within the community of reference. Possible links between distributive effects and the accumulation of social capital will be then analyzed in order to determine the intentional and unintentional consequences of the operation of social enterprises.[5]

4.1. An estimation of the distributive effects of social cooperatives

The first step in determining whether social cooperatives are effective in producing and distributing resources at the community level consists in the evaluation of the quantity of services produced. However, mere comparison among the numbers of clients served by each organization is not enough, because a precise index should compare the organization's product against its resources, and then with the price fixed by the organization. Hence, managers' and directors' subjective evaluations of employed and distributed resources will be used, because these represent synthetic indexes summarizing numerous items of objective information. Subjective evaluations, of course, also have limitations as behavioral measures because they are not objective records. Nevertheless, they represent a rigorous and accepted methodology with which to compare different organizations of the same type, and they can deliver reliable results. Whether a linkage exists between the economic dimension of the organization in terms of net assets and value of the production and the distributive effects will be evaluated as the first step in the analysis.

Social cooperatives were requested to evaluate, first, their distributive effects defined as their ability to produce above the level of services financed by contracts stipulated with the public administration and/or with private enterprises and individuals, and second, if they direct this excess of production to public benefit aims. The data show that, although the majority of organizations do not acknowledge the presence of a distributive function (61.3 per cent), a significant percentage of social cooperatives do indeed recognize it. Specifically, 17 per cent of the organizations surveyed claimed that they produced distributive effects in a stable and continuous way, 16 per cent from time to time, while the remaining 5.7 per cent acknowledged a systematic distributive function, albeit with a weak economic impact. Surprisingly, the estimated monetary value of these distributive effects was very high: 58,000 Euros on average per enterprise with distributive effects. Furthermore, when this value was calculated as a percentage of the organization's total turnover, this index amounted to 9.4 per cent on average. This percentage

Table 10.2 Self-estimation of the distributive effects of cooperatives by membership of consortia (%)

	Non-members	**Members**	**Total**
No over-production	68.5	52.7	61.1
Sporadic over-production	12.1	20.6	16.1
Systematic but modest level of over-production	4.7	6.9	5.7
Systematic and substantial level of over-production	14.8	19.8	17.1

Source: authors' calculations on ICSI 2007 data (*Indagine sulle Cooperative Sociali Italiane*).

is quite high, and it acquires even more significance on considering that the universe of Italian social cooperatives is made up of more than 8000 organizations. Consequently, given that more than one third show a distributive function, the total value of the distributive effects on society is significant (Table 10.2).

Differences emerge when organizations are sorted by their characteristics. The distributive function characterizes more organizations in the north-east of Italy (25 per cent of which develop this activity stably and conspicuously), while in the south social cooperatives more frequently produce only in line with their funding (about 70 per cent). This situation is partially explained by differences in the stability of organizations, because, for example, the ability to distribute resources increases with the age of the organization (31.3 per cent of cooperatives born before the 1980s exhibit a stable and significant distributive function). Distributive effects characterize more organizations involved in networks (especially those cooperatives belonging to consortia), and this finding highlights the importance of networks in supporting the ability of organizations to respond to local needs. Furthermore, having a multi-membership social basis also increases the ability to develop a distributive function: 20.7 per cent of cooperatives controlled by a plurality of stakeholders have strong distributive effects and half a sporadic overproduction of resources, while about 80 per cent of single-stakeholder firms claim that they have no distributive effects. But the accomplishment of a distributive function does not significantly depend on the reliance of social cooperatives on public contributions. Moreover, when the majority of their revenues derive from sales to private citizens, cooperatives can achieve a distributive function in a stable way. These data support the hypothesis that distributive effects are frequently planned by organizations, in the sense that they enter formally in the organizational aim, while, at the same time, they depend prevalently on the cooperative own resources and not on subsidies and other public resources. This claim is consistent with the prevalence of altruistic aims in open-membership organizations and in cooperatives whose mission is enlarged thanks to higher assets and economic stability.

Few differences among cooperatives emerge, however, in the value of the distributive effects, when present. The highest values are estimated for the oldest cooperatives, for large organizations (i.e. enterprises employing more than 50 workers) and for enterprises which do not belong to consortia. Nevertheless, the ratio between the value of distributive effects and total revenues is higher in the smallest organizations (ratio equal to 18 per cent), in southern Italy (12.6 per cent), in organizations created during the 1980s (14 per cent) and in those involved in networks (13 per cent).

Inspection on organizations that have a distributive function reveals that the distribution of resources is, in half of the cases, implemented by supplying some services free of charge to all clients. Frequently, social cooperatives also require clients to pay proportionally to their income and they, therefore, supply free services to poor people (41.7 per cent), or they distribute resources to all clients at less than the costs (35 per cent). These various policies of distribution among clients are planned differently by cooperatives according to their characteristics. Single-stakeholders and cooperatives in central Italy frequently supply free services to all of their clients (respectively in 72.7 per cent and 57.9 per cent of cases). Social cooperatives in the south and small organizations distribute free services only to specific classes of clients (respectively 45.5 per cent and 42.9 per cent). The supply of services at less than cost price especially characterizes north-eastern (66.7 per cent) and multi-stakeholder cooperatives (48.4 per cent). Consortia instead encourage social cooperatives to distribute more services to people not directly involved in the organization (42.9 per cent), while the provision of services at less than cost price (a policy which characterizes only 14.3 per cent of cooperatives in consortia, against 38.2 per cent of independent cooperatives) is less frequent. Differences are also apparent between cooperatives financed mainly by sales of services to public authorities and cooperatives whose revenues derive mostly from private citizens and enterprises. The former mainly produce new types of services for all their clients (65.9 per cent of cases), while the latter tend more to supply services free of charge to non-clients (Table 10.3) (44.4 per cent).

Since many social cooperatives exhibit an effective distributive function exerted through non-market policies, it is possible to state that they have a significant impact on social well-being. Now to be evaluated are the possible explanations and sources for this function.

4.2. Possible sources of the distributive function

The first interesting point in understanding the intentionality of the distributive function consists in a cross-tabulation analysis with the organizational mission. The data show that social cooperatives with a stable and significant distributive function more frequently pursue social-interest aims (83 per cent of cases compared with 70 per cent in organizations not performing a distributive function) and are characterized by a democratic style of management (53 per cent against 27 per cent). It therefore seems that

Table 10.3 Distributive effects by size of social cooperative (%)

Distribution carried out through...	Small-sized (<15 employees)	Medium-sized (16–50 employees)	Large-sized (>50 employees)	Total
Services at less than their costs for all clients	19.0	38.6	36.4	33.2
Some extra services free of charge for all clients	47.6	54.5	57.6	52.4
Some free services for poorest classes	42.9	40.9	36.4	40.1
Some services at less than their costs to people other than clients	14.3	29.5	33.3	27.4
Other kinds of services and policies	14.3	20.5	3.0	13.3

More than one answer accepted.
Source: authors' calculations on the ICSI 2007 data (*Indagine sulle Cooperative Sociali Italiane*).

the broader the mission, and the more democratic the style of management, the more the distributive function is an explicit goal of the organization and has a significant impact on the community's social well-being. It is thus possible to conclude that the distributive function is a recognized method with which to increase the social impact required by the mission of social cooperatives.

But what explains the distributive function beyond the explicit or implicit decisions taken by individual organizations?

Generally speaking, the asset lock is a distinctive feature of social cooperatives and one of the possible sources for development of a distributive function. The relevant data therefore concern the structure of assets. Specifically, on average,[6] member's shares amount to 37,000 euros and locked assets to 130,000 euros per organization, for a total amount of 167,000 euros of owned capital resources. Most organizations have a capital worth less than 200,000 euros (66.7 per cent), and 26.8 per cent range from 50,000 to 200,000 euros, while only 18.5 per cent show a figure above 400,000 euros. The amount of capital worth is considered by 77.5 per cent of cooperatives as enough to ensure the ordinary management of the organization, while it is sufficient for planning the increase of their activities in 51.1 per cent of cases. Consequently, it is also possible to state that the level of capitalization of social cooperatives is a first explanatory factor for the adoption of distribution policies different from market provision.

This statement is confirmed by cross-tabulation analysis where the capacity to exert distributive effects seems to depend upon the financial dimension of organizations.[7] On average, capital worth amounts to 140,000 euros in cooperatives without a distributive function, while it progressively increases in organizations that claim to distribute resources, reaching more than 220,000 euros in cooperatives with a stable and high distributive function. Moreover, 52.2 per cent of these latter have a capital worth of over 200,000 euros, while 26.2 per cent of organizations without a distributive function have a capital worth of less than 20,000 euros. This significant difference is first explained by paid-up shared capital, the level of which is, on average, 30,000 euros in organizations without a distributive function, while it is 45,000 euros on average in other organizations. Also, loans from shareholders are double in cooperatives that develop a distributive function (33,000 against 18,000 euros in organizations not distributing services), but the main difference in absolute values emerges with regard to locked assets. While organizations with no distributive effects have locked assets of 115,000 euros, on average, organizations with a stable and significant distributive function have locked assets amounting to more than 185,000 euros.

The financing of the distributive function, therefore, depends on the accumulation of profits to locked assets. As regards the amount of profits, the variability of the data, measured by the standard deviation, is quite high,[8] since many small organizations frequently break even. Furthermore, the percentage of organizations with nil profits has increased in recent years, and 44.2 per cent of social cooperatives stated that in the three years before the interview their profits had diminished (although in one-third of cases profits had increased). These data can be partially explained by the distribution of free-of-charge services. In fact, the average amount of profits is higher in cooperatives not distributing services (over 9000 euros compared with a total average of 6000), while its absolute amount is negatively correlated with the distribution of resources. In the year before the survey, social cooperatives with distributive aims had assigned on average 93 per cent of their profits to locked assets, while the percentage decreased to 85 per cent in other organizations.[9] It is therefore possible to claim that a rate of accumulation of positive residuals to locked assets and an adequate availability of financial resources is functional to the accomplishment of distributive effects. Not so the level of profits, whose maximization appears instead detrimental to distributive aims.

Moreover, the financial capital allowing the development of a distributive function may also come from organizational liabilities. The amounts of debts are higher in social cooperatives that pursue distributive aims (about 550,000 euros on average, against less than 400,000 in other organizations). The trend of debts and investments for the period 2003 to 2005 shows a significant increase in both items of about 40 per cent in all cooperatives, but this percentage is higher in firms supplying free services, where debts grew significantly in 30 per cent of cases (against 12 per cent in organizations with no welfare effects), total investments increased significantly in 42 per cent of cases (compared with 20.6 per cent in other organizations), and innovations of services concerned 73 per cent of social cooperatives with a stable distributive function (compared with an average of 37.7 per cent in other organizations). The data seem, therefore, to support the idea that social cooperatives distributing conspicuous amounts of services free of charge tend also to invest more than others and to innovate their services. In other words, they show better adaptive and growth potential.

The information used heretofore concerns the subjective evaluation of the objective economic measure of the distributive effects of social enterprises.[10] It has allowed general conclusions to be drawn on the linkage between the organization's financial resources and its ability to implement a distributive function. Further results arise from the other subjective measures of a qualitative nature. They concern the different sources of the distribution of resources. Social cooperatives were first asked to evaluate the importance of profit-distribution policies in achieving distributive aims. The firms stated that an important source for their distributive effects was the forfeiting of their profits, since they distributed the economic value generated by the organization *ex ante* among their clients (Table 10.4).

Also, the analysis of different sources of cost savings is of interest in describing the capacity of these organizations to collect economic resources from the local community. When organizations were asked to single out the sources of their distributive function, the most important one cited was the contribution by voluntary workers (who on average contributed to the creation of 23 per cent of the total value). The presence of volunteers is especially important in southern Italy (with a contribution in value estimated at 32.3 per cent of turnover), in the youngest organizations (38.4 per cent), in cooperatives not involved in networks (34.7 per cent), in multi-stakeholder organizations (31 per cent) and in cooperatives whose

Table 10.4 Sources of the distributive function by membership of consortia (average weight of each aspect on the total value of production)

Distribution carried out through ...	Non-member	Member of consortia	Total
Voluntary work	34.7	18.7	23.0
Overtime not paid or under-paid	20.1	2.7	12.4
Wages below the market level	0.8	1.9	1.4
Donations from private citizens	0.5	4.2	2.7
Contributions from public and non-profit organizations	5.2	9.1	7.4
Resources accumulated to asset locks	35.5	25.4	33.9
Savings of costs in general	3.2	38.0	19.2

More than one answer accepted.
Source: authors' calculations on ICSI 2007 data (*Indagine sulle Cooperative Sociali Italiane*).

revenues derive only to a small extent from public bodies (33 per cent). Interestingly, the presence of non-remunerated workers is strictly correlated with the possibility of distributing services. Only 57.4 per cent of organizations which do not declare distributive aims employ volunteers, against 80 per cent of organizations with distributive effects.[11] Furthermore, the hours of work put in by volunteers are higher in cooperatives with a distributive function (on average 64 hours per week, against 28 hours in organizations with no distributive effects), and the turnover of volunteers is higher in the former than in the latter (amounting respectively to +5.5 persons and +3 persons in the year prior to the survey). Hence, firms distributing resources show a greater weight of intrinsic and pro-social motivations.

The contribution of remunerated workers is also essential to guarantee distributive effects. The organizations asked to evaluate this aspect stated that workers frequently forgo payment for overtime work, and they estimated this contribution at 12.3 per cent of the value of distributed resources. These data are particularly significant in social cooperatives of the south, in the youngest enterprises, and in those whose revenues derive mainly from the private consumption of their services. These findings are confirmed by the data on workers' activities. Although the percentage of people working overtime is largely the same in all types of organizations, independent of the level of their distributive function (about 40 per cent, which reaches 50.3 per cent only in social cooperatives with a stable but modest distributive function), the ways in which overtime work is performed differ significantly. In organizations with a stable distributive function, workers supply their overtime more frequently for free (about 18 per cent of the total against 8 per cent in social cooperatives without welfare effects) or by only partially recouping overtime hours or by only partially being paid for them (about 14 per cent against 10 per cent).

4.3. Social capital development

The contribution made by social cooperatives to the accumulation of social capital can be analyzed mainly in terms of relationships, trust with stakeholders and implementation of social norms. Descriptive figures have already shown that relationships with other organizations are important because of the involvement of cooperatives in networks. Furthermore, 80 per cent of the organizations interviewed stated that the networks in which they were involved were based on trust and long-term relationships, and half of them believed in the importance of geographical proximity with other member organizations. Consequently, networks are important sources of transaction cost reductions. However, they also support social capital development in other ways, because they diffuse information, develop skills and capabilities, improve training and increase trust among their members. The impact is greatest at the local level, where most organizations and networks operate.

However, an accurate description of social capital accumulation requires an examination of the qualitative dimension of relations, especially with users (both private citizens and the public administration). First, organizations stated that relationships were very important for ensuring effectiveness and efficiency of production in general (an average of 5.6 on a scale from 1 to 7). Social cooperatives mainly stressed the quality of relationships with users (6.4) and with public authorities (6.0), where both represent the clients of the services and require clear and cooperative transactions. Also, relationships with external stakeholders and in particular with other – both for-profit and non-profit – organizations are important, though less important than relations with users (average scores of respectively 4.8 and 5.4). These results shine a light on the ability of social cooperatives to produce external effects and to form networks, given that relations were perceived as very important by all organizations interviewed, regardless of their distributive effects.

Very similar results emerged from the analysis of trust. The organizations interviewed stated that it was very important to build trust relations with all their stakeholders (average score of 5.5 on a scale from 1 to 7) and especially with their clients (6.3), with public authorities (5.9) and also with other non-profit organizations (5.3). The linkage with the reputation enjoyed by cooperatives is evident, because all of them considered it important to have a good reputation, both among their clients (average score of 5.8), with public bodies (5.7) and with the local community in general (5.5). Furthermore, the correlation between the two groups of variables concerning trust and reputation is significant (Rho of Spearman Coefficient equal to .260). It is, therefore, possible to conclude that social capital, in terms of trust-based networking, has an important impact on the long-term sustainability of the service.

This is confirmed by the data on the advantages enjoyed by social cooperatives, because 44.6 per cent of the organizations interviewed stated that the reputation acquired in the local community was a major strength of the organization (for 49.8 per cent it was important). Among other advantages of social cooperatives, the exchange of information and trust with other organizations ranked second (with 34.5 per cent judging it a very important advantage and 59.5 per cent as an important one). Slightly less important were relationships with volunteers, friends and people irregularly involved in the organization (recognized as a major strength by only 18.4 per cent of the sample and as quite important by 48.4 per cent). By the same token, the ability of organizations to attract and motivate volunteers is quite or very important only for 43.6 per cent of interviewed organizations. Consequently, the data show the relevance of trust and reputation for social cooperatives, since they are regarded as competitive advantages that can increase their competitive potential. The effect on social capital is perceived indirectly, especially in terms of the enhancement of local values and conformism with the organization's social aims (Table 10.5).

Table 10.5   Strengths of social cooperatives (% of organizations considering the aspect as very important)

Factors	%
Reputation	44.6
Involvement in the local community	33.2
Network with other organizations based on trust and knowledge	34.5
Relationships with clients, volunteers, etc.	18.4
Organizational climate of trust and willingness to cooperate	42.0
Employee motivations	31.7

Source: authors' calculations on ICSI 2007 data (*Indagine sulle Cooperative Sociali Italiane*).

Furthermore, both trust and reputation are increased by the involvement of stakeholders in the organization's membership. As reported when the sample was described, 33.8 per cent of the organizations interviewed were multi-stakeholder. Although clients are involved in the membership of only one social cooperative out of ten, informal networks substitute formal ones in ensuring client involvement, the transmission of information, and the sharing of goals and social norms. Indeed, internal norms frequently have consultancy and informative roles (44.2 per cent of cases), and these cooperatives tend to promote advocacy activities and meetings more. Interestingly, the development of networks and the ability to diffuse information and social norms within the local community or specific classes of citizens also supports the possibility of becoming a member of the cooperative. Because of these results, social enterprises can be included among the main actors accumulating social capital at the local level (Borzaga and Tortia 2009).

When, instead, organizations are sorted by their internal characteristics, it emerges that the importance of reputation is emphasized especially by cooperatives in the north-east (where some social capital indexes are also over the national average, and consequently the network of trust-based relationships is widespread), by medium-to-large organizations and by enterprises belonging to local consortia. Also, relationships with other organizations are considered more important by cooperatives in the north than in the south of Italy, and their importance is greater for old and large organizations. As expected, the variable with the strongest impact on the importance of relationships with other organizations is involvement in networks, because organizations belonging to consortia or temporary associations of firms assign higher value to the development of relationships. Younger and small cooperatives instead pay more attention to the development of internal relations, and particularly to improving relationships with volunteers, friends and people involved in networks.

In order to determine whether the development of social capital is stronger in organizations that also perform a distributive function, the correlation between the two dimensions was first estimated by applying Spearman Rho indexes. Data showed a positive correlation only between distributive effects and the importance assigned to both trust-based (coefficient of 0.163) and good relationships (coefficients of 0.125). The importance of trust and good-quality relationships, especially with non-profit organizations, respectively receives values of 5.9 and 5.2 on a scale from 1 to 7 in enterprises with medium welfare effects, against 5.1 in organizations not distributing resources. This is also holds when considering other kinds of enterprises, where the indexed level of trust is 5.3 in organizations distributing resources and 4.8 in organizations without distributive effects. Furthermore, having a good reputation in the local community is considered more important by organizations with a systematic distributive function. Frequently, the organizations most sensitive to good relationships and trust are those with a low (although stable) distributive function. Consistently, enterprises showing positive distributive effects more frequently state that they have intensively sought to develop sentiments of trust, altruism and sharing of the mission in the local community, as asserted by 20 per cent of interviewed organizations against 10 per cent of cooperatives with no or low distributive effects. As for the presence of networks, this characterizes a greater number of enterprises performing a moderate distributive function, 60 per cent of which claim that relationships and trust with other organizations are very important. However, the correlation of distributive effects with the other dimensions of social capital was not significant. Nor was a significant correlation between the distributive function and social capital found when well-being was one of the main components of the organizational mission.

Instead, social cooperatives seem in most cases to have an important intended effect on the social well-being of their community. For 56.4 per cent of the enterprises surveyed, this was the primary aim of the organization, and another 34.6 per cent considered the well-being of the local community to be a very important aim (although not the primary one). The mission is totally endorsed by the members of 56.6 per cent and by the workers of 43.6 per cent of the organizations surveyed. Diffusion of the organization's ideals is stronger in the enterprises of southern Italy (where the mission was endorsed, respectively, by 74.6 per cent of members and 65.7 per cent of employees) and in small organizations (respectively 76.8 per cent and 66.2 per cent). Geographical differences seem to mean that, where social capital can be considered weak, as in southern Italy, social cooperatives have an important role in the diffusion of norms. This finding may open new avenues for the study of the generation of social capital in socio-economic contexts where its level is insufficient. The size of the organization instead supports the ability to diffuse social norms, especially in environments characterized by strict relationships and frequent communication. By way of conclusion, it may be stated that the accumulation of social capital is not explicitly planned by social cooperatives, even if it strictly depends on the internal workings of the organization and on the motivations of the actors involved. The distributive effects instead depend on the explicit decisions of the organization itself. The two aspects emerge as complementary and not as substitutes for each other. Hence, the importance explicitly given to social objectives also engenders unintended positive consequences.

5. Conclusions and policy implications

While the theory of social enterprises has studied their appearance in the presence of government and market failure, much work remains to be done in understanding the nature of their social and economic effects, and the institutional mechanisms supporting these effects. This chapter has sought to shed new light on these matters by exploring the way in which social enterprises over-produce and distribute resources for the satisfaction of social needs. The detailed description of the intentional social effects of social enterprises has yielded new insights also into their unintentional effects on the reinforcement of trust relations and on the accumulation of social capital.

In this chapter, the distributive effects of social enterprises have been tested by analyzing data collected by a recent survey carried out in Italy on a representative sample of social cooperatives. Their role emerges as significant, because half of the organizations interviewed stated that they have a distributive function, and a quarter of the total stably distributed resources for a value representing a non-marginal part of their revenues. The distribution mainly took place through the provision of services free of charge or at less than cost. This shows the importance of analyzing non-market allocation mechanisms governed within organizational boundaries. These mechanisms emerge as particularly important in organizations carrying out the private provision of public and quasi-public goods and services like social enterprises. Their ability to extract and distribute economic and social value mainly from non-market resources has been confirmed by analysis of the sources of their distributive function: on the one hand, capital resources are socialized to a great extent through locked assets and channeled to social and non-pecuniary aims, on the other hand, human capital (both volunteers and remunerated workers) are motivated to donate time and redistribute part (or the whole) of their wages to users and beneficiaries or to the community at large. Although the importance of these dynamics varies from organization to organization, it is possible to state that most cooperatives are able to gather resources in excess of the minimum necessary to survive, and that they distribute a conspicuous part of their resources to the benefit of weak socio-demographic groups. The unintentional effects on the accumulation of social capital appear weaker, and they enter mainly as indirect by-products of their operation in terms of improved relations, trust and recognition of common norms and values with the other main actors in the territory. Finally, social capital development and distributive effects appear to stand in a more complementary than substitutive relation.

Relevant policy implications are likely to ensue when the true contribution of social enterprises to the creation of economic and social welfare is highlighted. While social enterprises cannot be expected to operate in all sectors of activity, especially in the most traditional, industrial ones, a wide range of the service activities that represent a growing slice of contemporary market economies exhibit a high degree of compatibility with their institutional features. Where market imperfections are marked, social enterprises, more than profit-seeking and public organizations, can perform an important role in endogenous development patterns based on the delivery of quasi-public and social services thanks to their ability to increase the production of services characterized by a relational and meritorious character. Indeed, it is likely that national and local economic systems will be able to withstand increased international competition only if they are adequately equipped with a network of organizations able to improve the social performance of the industrial sector and to deal with the negative effects of economic downturns. Policy interventions and institutional reforms by governments should not overlook these development factors.

Notes

1. General legal frameworks for social enterprises have only recently been introduced in some European countries, examples being the Community Interest Company in the United Kingdom in 2005, and the Impresa Sociale in Italy in 2006 (law no. 118/2005 as implemented by legislative decree no. 158/2006). The aim of both reforms is to create a cross-ownership organizational form which acquires the legal status of traditional cooperatives, mutual societies and entrepreneurial non-profit organizations, but also investor-owned firms fulfilling the requirements and constraints imposed by law.
2. Given the paucity of studies that single out the determinants of social capital accumulation (Durlauf and Fafchamps 2005), social enterprises are a privileged organizational setting in which to analyze the generation of new social capital.
3. The questionnaires administered to workers, managers and organizations had different sections which, for workers, collected information about their level of well-being and attitudes toward the job, and, for the organization, both quantitative data (people employed and turnover, financial data and progress of budget items, etc.) and qualitative data on self-esteem concerning organizational aims, policies, social responsibility and social capital development.
4. Obviously, different types of networks respond differently to the needs of organizations. National associations usually supply services for training, planning and promotion, while TAF and consortia are also (and mainly) producers of financial and productive services.

5. The analysis concerns welfare effects more than their explanatory factors, since study of the precise causal linkages between individual and organizational factors, on the one hand, and their welfare consequences on the other is beyond the scope of this study. Future work needs to concentrate on the linkages among individual motivations, organizational patterns and the ability of the organization to distribute resources.

6. Elaborations exclude here some of the organizations interviewed, which must be considered outliers since their economic dimensions are significantly above the average (more than 1million euros of net property).

7. Also in this analysis outliers are excluded.

8. Furthermore, the average profit of social cooperatives changes significantly according to whether the outliers are included in the sample, with averages of respectively 12,000 and 1,400 Euros achieved in the year prior to the survey.

9. In general, the bulk of profits are not distributed to members. Over 60 per cent of social cooperatives have assigned all their profits to locked assets in recent years, while only 22 per cent reduced the accumulation of profits to locked assets to 50 per cent. This evidence reinforces the idea that the maximization of profits cannot be the objective of social enterprises, since the pursuit of social goals appears to entails lower distributable profits.

10. Another interesting finding derives from other indexes of the financial stability (and well-being) of organizations in that social cooperatives distributing resources also more frequently recorded an increase in their revenues from supply to private citizens (75 per cent of cases against 43 per cent in cooperatives without welfare effects), while less marked is their dependence on public bodies and contracting out. This evidence again testifies to the better dynamic adaptability in terms of independence from public finance of firms distributing resources.

11. Calculation of the opposite linkage shows that 46 per cent of organizations using volunteers achieve stable and high distributive effects, against only 22.2 per cent of organizations without volunteers.

References

H. K. Anheier and A. Ben-Ner (eds) (2003) *The Study of the Nonprofit Enterprise: Theories and Approaches* (New York: Kluwer Academic).

A. Bacchiega and C. Borzaga (2001) 'Social enterprise as an incentive structures', in C. Borzaga and J. Defourny (eds), *The Emergence of Social Enterprise* (London: Routledge), pp. 273–295.

A. Ben-Ner (1994) 'Who benefits from the nonprofit sector? Reforming law and public policy towards nonprofit organizations', *Yale Law Journal*, 104(3), 731–762.

A. Ben-Ner and L. Putterman (1998) 'Values and institutions in economic analysis', in A. Ben-Ner and L. Putterman (eds) *Economics, Values, and Organization* (Cambridge: Cambridge University Press), pp. 3–72.

A. Ben-Ner and T. Van Hoomissen (1991) 'Nonprofit organizations in the mixed economy: a demand and supply analysis', *Annals of Public and Cooperative Economics*, 62(4), 519–550.

C. Borzaga and J. Defourny (eds) (2001) *The Emergence of Social Enterprise* (London: Routledge).

C. Borzaga and S. Depedri (2005) 'Interpersonal relations and job satisfaction: some empirical results in social and community care services', in B. Gui and

R. Sugden (eds), *Economics and Social Interaction: Accounting for Interpersonal Relations* (Cambridge: Cambridge University Press), pp. 132–153.

C. Borzaga and M. Musella (eds) (2003) *Produttività ed Efficienza nelle Organizzazioni Nonprofit: il ruolo dei lavoratori e delle relazioni di lavoro*, Trento: Edizioni 31.

C. Borzaga and R. Spear (eds) (2004) *Trends and Challenges for Co-operatives and Social Enterprises in Developed and Transition Countries* (Trento: Edizioni 31).

C. Borzaga and E. Tortia (2006) 'Worker motivations, job satisfaction, and loyalty in public and non-profit social services', *Non-profit and Voluntary Sector Quarterly*, 35(2), 225–248.

C. Borzaga and E. Tortia (2009) "Social Enterprises and Local Economic Development", in A. Noya (ed.) *The Changing Boundaries of Social Enterprises*, Paris: OECD Publishing, pp. 195–228.

C. T. Clotfelter (ed.) (1992) *Who Benefits from the Nonprofit Sector?* (Chicago: University of Chicago Press).

J. Coleman (1990) *Foundations of Social Theory* (Cambridge Massachusetts: Harvard Univ. Press).

S. Depedri (2010) 'The competitive advantages of social enterprises', in L. Becchetti and C. Borzaga (eds), *The Economics of Social Responsibility. The World of Social Enterprises* (London: Routledge), pp. 33–54.

S. N. Durlauf and M. Fafchamps (2005) 'Social capital', in S. N. Durlauf and P. Aghion (eds), *Handbook of Economic Growth*, vol. 1B, (Amsterdam: Elsevier), pp. 1639–1693.

B. S. Frey (1997) *Not Just for the Money: An Economic Theory of Personal Motivation* (Cheltenham, UK: Elgar).

G. Grimalda and L. Sacconi (2005) 'The constitution of the not-for-profit organisation: reciprocal conformity to morality', *Constitutional Political Economy*, 16(3), 249–276.

B. Gui and R. Sugden (eds) (2005) *Economics and Social Interaction: Accounting for Interpersonal Relations* (Cambridge: Cambridge University Press).

L. Leete (2000) 'Wage equity and employment motivation in nonprofit and for-profit organizations', *Journal of Economic Behavior and Organization*, 43(4), 423–446.

R. Putnam (1996) 'The strange disappearance of civic America', *American Prospect*, 24, 34–48.

R. D. Putnam, R. Leonardi and R. Y. Nanetti (1993) *Making Democracy Work: Civic Traditions in Modern Italy* (Princeton: Princeton University Press).

S. Sacchetti and R. Sugden (2003) 'The governance of networks and economic power: the nature and impact of subcontracting relationships', *Journal of Economic Surveys*, 17(5), 669–691.

E. C. Tortia (2010) 'The impact of social enterprises on Output, employment and welfare', in L. Becchetti and Borzaga C. (eds), *The Economics of Social Responsibility. The World of Social Enterprises* (London: Routledge), pp. 54–73.

V. Valentinov (2007) 'The property rights approach to nonprofit organisations: the role of intrinsic motivation', *Public Organisation Review*, 7(1), 41–55.

V. Valentinov (2008) 'The economics of the non-distribution constraint: a critical reappraisal', *Annals of Public and Cooperative Economics*, 79(1), 35–52.

B. A. Weisbrod (1977) *The Voluntary Nonprofit Sector: An Economic Analysis* (Lexington, MA: Lexington Books).

B. A. Weisbrod (1988) *The Nonprofit Economy* (Cambridge, MA: Harvard University Press).

Part IV

Social Capital and Sustainable Economic Development: the Macro Approach

11
Social Assets, Technical Progress and Long-Run Welfare

Stefano Bartolini and Luigi Bonatti

1. Introduction

The scope of this chapter is to confute the idea that technical progress is necessarily welfare increasing. Indeed, we show that policies stimulating technical progress that augments the efficiency of the inputs used in the production of market goods can lead to an acceleration of output growth, but they may depress long-run individual well-being. At the root of this undesirable effect of growth-enhancing policies, we identify the detrimental impact of higher levels of consumption on social and environmental assets constituting important sources of people's welfare. In turn, the decline in the quantity and quality of these common property resources may feed the growth process by inducing the economic agents to intensify both the accumulation of private assets and the work effort, so as to have access to more market goods as substitutes for the declining quality of social and environmental assets. Conversely, we demonstrate that policies creating incentives for a more sober lifestyle improve long-run welfare, but they tend to depress productivity and output growth by inducing the economic agents to allocate less efforts and resources to enhance the production of market goods. Finally, we consider policies aimed at reducing the negative effects of consumers' activities on social and environmental assets, and we show that in the long run they lead to a lower rate of output growth and to a higher level of individual well-being.

The chapter relates to various strands of literature.

It is well known that the quality of many natural resources, like air or water, can hardly be the object of market transactions. Thus, it is often the case that natural capital is affected by negative externalities, which tend to increase with the expansion of market activities. Environmental economics is fully aware of the complex relationship linking economic growth to natural assets (see Smulders 2000, 2005). In particular, its focus is typically on the damaging impact that economic growth may have on the environment.

There is also a long tradition arguing that the evolution and success of the market economy leads to the progressive weakening of its cultural and ethical base, as a consequence of the erosion of community ties and the concomitant emergence of individualistic and competitive values systems that this success brings about (see Hirsch 1976; Hirschman 1982). Even the socio-economic transformations that, according to Putnam (2000), may have negatively affected the formation of social capital in the United States in the last decades can be considered a by-product of the process of marketization.[1] Indeed, he identifies some possible determinants of the decline in the US social capital in the rising female participation in the labor market, in the increase in geographical mobility, in 'the replacement of the corner grocery by the supermarket' and in the 'privatizing' or 'individualizing' of leisure time (mainly due to TV and, more in general, to the diffusion of home-entertainment technologies). This close relationship linking the growing prominence of modalities of consumption that atomize people to the decline of sociability and participation in community activities has been emphasized by analysts of modern consumerism (see Cross 2000; Schor 1998).[2]

The idea that community and inter-household mechanisms of trust and collaboration constitute precious intangible assets regulated by norms of reciprocity from which people can draw benefits is well known to anthropologists (see, e.g., Martin 1995; Peterson 1993). The people's possibility to access these social assets is very important for their well-being, especially if they are poorly endowed with privately owned assets (see Moser 1998, 2007). Particularly in urban settings, namely in contexts that are highly 'commoditized', the people's endowment of social assets is typically poor, and individuals are pushed to rely exclusively on what they can get through market transactions.

It is only recently that economic theory has started modeling the idea that the degradation of social and environmental assets may set the conditions for a further expansion of market transactions, thus stimulating economic growth. This idea was analyzed by Bartolini and Bonatti (2002, 2003), who model growth as a substitution process in which private goods progressively replace declining social and natural assets as sources of individual well-being. In the present chapter, we follow this line of research by assuming that consumption of market goods imposes negative externalities on a social (or environmental) asset, which enters positively the households' utility function. This captures the idea that an increase in individual consumption of market goods erodes those social ties and cultural values which are essential for the reproduction of community assets (or that this increase generates additional waste and pollution, thus damaging the environment). The specific contribution of this chapter to this class of models amounts to providing a set-up for analyzing two kinds of policy, one aimed at accelerating that endogenous technical progress, which enhances inputs efficiency in the production of market goods, and the other aimed at creating incentives to alleviate the negative impact of consumption on the common property resource. The latter can act by inducing households to devote some of their time to activities that increase social cohesion and community ties (in the case of a social asset), or to the experimentation and implementation of new technologies that reduce the negative effects of consumer activities on the natural resource (in the case of an environmental asset). In this way, we are able to investigate how public policies that affect the direction and pace of technical progress can have long-running effects on economic growth and individual welfare.

Another line of research related to this chapter is the theory of induced technical change (ITC) and the recent attempts to reformulate this theory in endogenous growth models. Originally suggested by Hicks (1932),[3] ITC was formally developed in the 1960s and integrated in a growth framework (see Drandakis and Phelps 1966; Kennedy 1964; Samuelson 1965) in order to explain why technical progress has been largely labor saving. Subsequent applications studied the degree to which the energy efficiency of production processes, machinery and consumer durable goods responded to changes in energy prices. At the core of the theory, which was criticized because of its weak micro-foundations (Ruttan 2001), it is the key role of relative prices in the allocation of private inventive activities. More recently, ITC was embodied in endogenous growth models of innovations and knowledge spillovers (Acemoglu 2002, 2003). These growth models, however, do not introduce social or environmental assets, although ITC has been also applied to the development of new technologies that can alleviate the impacts of human activities on the environment or act as a remedy for natural resource scarcity (see Bretschger 2005; Grübler et al. 2002). In this context, one can argue that given the incompleteness of markets – and especially in the lack of markets for open-access resources – price signals distort the direction of technical progress, with detrimental effects on the introduction of new technologies and organizational innovations aimed at reducing the negative impact of market production and consumer activities on the quality of social and environmental assets. In the absence of adequate incentives to develop technologies reducing the impact of producer and consumer activities on resources whose market price is zero – such as social and environmental ones – technical progress concentrates on technologies economizing the use of costly factors, such as labor. With regard to this important point, this chapter departs from endogenous growth models of technological spillovers that advocate policies allowing private agents to fully appropriate the fruits of their efficiency-enhancing activities. In the context of these models, indeed, policies that favor the internalization of those externalities that generate some overall efficiency gain in the production of private goods, boost long-run growth and are welfare-improving. In contrast, in the set-up presented here, these policies may reduce long-run welfare by determining an acceleration of technical progress in the production of private goods, which stimulates output growth but exacerbates the negative effects of consumer activities on social and environmental assets.

The chapter is organized as follows: section 2 presents the model, section 3 characterizes the balanced growth path emerging in the laissez-faire regime, section 4 studies alternative activist policies influencing long-run growth and steady-state levels of individual welfare, and section 5 concludes.

2. The basic model

We consider an economy in discrete time with an infinite time horizon. This economy is populated by a large number (normalized to unity) of identical households and by a large number (normalized to unity) of identical firms. For simplicity and without loss of generality, it is assumed that population is constant and that each household contains one adult, working member of the current generation. Thus, there is a fixed and large number of identical adults who take account of the welfare and resources of their actual and perspective descendants. Indeed, following Barro and Sala-i-Martin (1995) we model this intergenerational interaction by imaging that the current generation maximizes utility and incorporates a budget constraint over an infinite future. That is, although individuals have finite lives, we consider immortal extended families ('dynasties').[4] Expectations are rational (in the sense that they are consistent with the true processes followed by the relevant variables). In this framework, in which there is no source of random disturbances, this implies perfect foresight.

2.1. Households' utility

The period utility function of the representative household, U_t, is additively separable in consumption and leisure:

$$U_t = \beta u(x_t) + (1 - \beta)v(l_t), \; 0 < \beta < 1, \; u(x_t) = \begin{cases} \dfrac{(x_t)^{1-\xi}}{1-\xi} & \text{if } \xi > 0, \; \xi \neq 1 \\ \ln(x_t) & \text{if } \xi = 1, \end{cases}$$

$$v(l_t) = \begin{cases} \dfrac{(l_t)^{1-\zeta}}{1-\zeta} & \text{if } \zeta > 0, \; \zeta \neq 1 \\ \ln(l_t) & \text{if } \zeta = 1, \end{cases} \tag{1}$$

where x_t is the amount of service generated by a consumer activity in period t, and l_t are the units of time devoted to leisure in t. The preference parameter β captures the relative contribution that consumer service and leisure give to the households' utility. Households generate x_t by adopting a consumer technology that combines a resource to which all individuals have free access in every period and a consumer good that can be privately appropriated:

$$x_t = R_t C_t, \quad R_t \geq 0, C_t \geq 0, \tag{2}$$

where R_t is the endowment (or an index of the quality) in t of an open-access resource that cannot be produced, and C_t is the amount of the unique good produced in this economy that is devoted to consumption in t. Note that there is non-rivalry in the households' use of the resource R_t, from which no household can be excluded: it has the non-exclusive nature typical of a public good. Moreover, it is worth emphasizing that R_t and C_t are (Edgeworth) complements in consumption whenever $\xi < 1$ (thus implying that $\frac{\partial u(x_t)}{\partial C_t}$ is strictly increasing in R_t holding C_t fixed), and that they are (Edgeworth) substitutes whenever $\xi > 1$. They are independent whenever $\xi = 1$. Finally, both R_t and C_t are essential, since the consumer service can be produced only if the household has a strictly positive quantity of both R_t and C_t.

The model applies to a broad variety of situations. Interpreting R_t as a social asset, one may think that people's livelihoods and well-being have to increasingly depend on the market good C_t as the community assets from which people can draw benefits erodes or deteriorates. In the same time, people can derive some utility from C_t only if they have access to some social asset. Adopting an environmental interpretation of R_t, one may treat C_t as a man-made consumer good from which the households can draw some utility only if they are endowed with some amount of natural resources like air or water.[5] Although the consumer setup (1)–(2) can capture both the case in which R_t and C_t are (Edgeworth) complements and the case in which they are (Edgeworth) substitutes, one may think that the more diffuse and relevant situations are those in which reductions in the endowment of R_t makes C_t more valuable to households, namely in which the increasing limitation in the possibility of relying on commons as sources of welfare gives more subjective value to market goods. Therefore, the main results of the chapter are derived for the case in which R_t and C_t are substitutes.

2.2. Renewable resource

Common property resources tend typically to be accumulated or depleted. Hence, it makes sense to treat R_t as a renewable resource. Moreover, we assume that the ability of R_t to regenerate declines with the level of private consumption, so as to capture the idea that an increase in individual consumption of market goods erodes those social ties and cultural values which are essential for the reproduction of community assets ('the decline in social capital is the result of the triumph of consumerism'):

$$R_{t+1} - R_t = z(R_t, C_t), z_C < 0, \quad R_0 \text{ given.} \tag{3}$$

In particular, we specify a functional form for $z(.)$ by modifying the logistic model, which is one of the simplest and best-known functional specifications for the law of motion of a renewable resource (see Conrad 1987):

$$z(R_t, C_t) = \chi R_t \left(1 - \frac{R_t C_t}{E_0}\right), \quad \chi > 0, E_0 > 0, \tag{4}$$

where the parameter χ can be interpreted as the intrinsic growth rate of R_t, and E_0 is a parameter on which depends the impact of the consumers' activities on the future level of the common property resource. Note that each single household can ignore the negative effect of its consumer activity on the future level of R_t, since its own impact on the evolution of R_t is negligible. However, the aggregate impact of the consumers' activities on the future endowment of the renewable resource is significant because of the large number of households populating the economy. Moreover, it is worth emphasizing that equations (2)–(4) represent the engine driving the main results of the chapter: every household draws some benefit from the common property resource, but every household's consumption of market goods gives its own contribution to reduce the community's capacity of reproducing this resource. Finally, let us observe that one may also interpret (3)–(4) as the description of the dynamics of an environmental asset whose quality is negatively affected by the pollution generated by the consumers' activities.[6]

2.3. Production

The single good Y_t is produced by each firm, who produces it according to the technology

$$Y_t = K_t^{1-\alpha}(A_t L_t)^{\alpha}, \quad 0 < \alpha < 1, K_t \geq 0, A_t \geq 0, L_t \geq 0, \tag{5}$$

where K_t is the stock of capital existing in t, L_t are the units of time devoted in t to the production of Y_t and A_t represents the state of technical (or organizational) knowledge affecting labor productivity.

2.4. Labor-augmenting technical progress

The variable A_t is assumed to be a positive function of the stock of capital existing in the economy:

$$A_t = K_t \tag{6}$$

This assumption combines the idea that learning-by-doing works through each firm's use of capital equipment and machinery and the idea that knowledge and productivity gains spillover instantly across all firms (see Barro and Sala-i-Martin 1995). This implies that private agents cannot appropriate all the fruits of their activities. Thus, in accordance with Frankel (1962), it is supposed that although A_t is endogenous to the economy, each firm takes it as given, since a single firm's decision on K_t has only a negligible effect on the aggregate stock of capital. In its turn, the fact that a firm cannot appropriate all the fruits of the productivity gains that it contributes to generating reduces its demand for K_t, thus depressing the pace of technical progress and economic growth. Hence, one could advocate public policies aimed at inducing the private agents to take fully into account their actions' positive effects on productivity growth. However – as we shall see in next sections – these policies aimed at accelerating the pace of technical progress in the production of private goods may have surprising and perverse effects on long-run welfare.

2.5. Firms' objectives

At the beginning of each period t the representative firm hires labor and rents capital in order to maximize its period net profits, which are given by:

$$\pi_t = Y_t - w_t L_t - r_t K_t, \tag{7}$$

where w_t is the wage rate and r_t is the capital's rental rate.

2.6. Households' objective

Households supply labor, buy consumption and accumulate capital for renting it out to firms. Hence, in each t the representative household chooses $\{L_{t+i}\}_{i=0}^{\infty}$, $\{C_{t+i}\}_{i=0}^{\infty}$ and $\{K_{t+i+1}\}_{i=0}^{\infty}$ in order to maximize

$$\sum_{i=0}^{\infty} \theta^i U_{t+i}, \quad 0 < \theta < 1, \tag{8}$$

subject to

$$K_{t+i+1} + C_{t+i} \le w_{t+i} L_{t+i} + r_{t+i} K_{t+i} + \pi_{t+i} + (1 - \delta) K_{t+i},$$
$$0 \le \delta \le 1, K_0 \text{ given}, \tag{9}$$

$$l_{t+i} + L_{t+i} \le 1, \tag{10}$$

where θ is a time preference parameter and δ is a capital depreciation parameter. Note that the total time available to each household is normalized to unity, and that – for simplicity and without loss of generality – it is assumed that all households, being the firms' owners, are entitled to receive an equal share of the firms' net profits.

2.7. Market-clearing conditions

The product market, the labor market and the capital market are perfectly competitive. Equilibrium in the product market requires

$$K_{t+1} + C_t = Y_t + (1 - \delta)K_t, \tag{11}$$

equilibrium in the labor market requires

$$L_t = 1 - l_t, \tag{12}$$

and equilibrium in the capital rental market requires

$$K_t^d = K_t^s. \tag{13}$$

3. Laissez-faire

3.1. Firms-optimizing behavior

Profit-maximizing firms equalize the marginal productivity of labor to the wage rate:

$$\alpha K_t L_t^{\alpha - 1} = w_t. \tag{14}$$

Under laissez faire, the firms decide how much capital to rent by considering only the private returns that they can derive from this decision. Hence,

$$(1 - \alpha)L_t^{\alpha} = r_t. \tag{15}$$

3.2. Households-optimizing behavior

Under laissez faire each household has no interest in taking into account the negative externalities that it causes by its consumer activity.[7] Thus, the problem of the representative household in period t can be solved by maximizing

$$\sum_{i=0}^{\infty} \theta^i \left\{ \beta u(x_{t+i}) + (1 - \beta)v(1 - L_{t+i}) - \lambda_{t+i} \left[K_{t+i+1} + C_{t+i} \right. \right.$$
$$\left. \left. - r_{t+i}K_{t+i} - \pi_{t+i} - (1 - \delta)K_{t+i} - L_{t+i}w_{t+i} \right] \right\} \tag{16}$$

with respect to C_t, L_t, λ_t and K_{t+1}, where λ_t is a Lagrange multiplier. Therefore, one can use (3)–(7), (14), (15), together with the conditions obtained by maximizing (16), to derive the system of difference equations in $Z_t \equiv R_t K_t$

and L_t which governs the equilibrium path of the economy under laissez faire (see Appendix (i)):

$$\frac{Z_{t+1}}{1+\omega(L_t, Z_t)} - Z_t = \chi Z_t \left\{ 1 - \frac{1}{E_0} \left[\frac{\alpha\beta Z_t(1-L_t)^\varsigma}{(1-\beta)L_t^{1-\alpha}} \right]^{\frac{1}{\varsigma}} \right\}, \tag{17}$$

$$\frac{\theta L_{t+1}^{1-\alpha} \left[(1-\alpha)L_{t+1}^\alpha + 1 - \delta \right]}{(1-L_{t+1})^\varsigma} = \frac{[1+\omega(L_t, Z_t)]L_t^{1-\alpha}}{(1-L_t)^\varsigma}, \tag{18}$$

where

$$\omega(L_t, Z_t) = L_t^\alpha - \delta - \frac{1}{Z_t} \left[\frac{\alpha\beta Z_t(1-L_t)^\varsigma}{(1-\beta)L_t^{1-\alpha}} \right]^{\frac{1}{\varsigma}}. \tag{19}$$

An equilibrium path of the economy must also satisfy the transversality condition (see Appendix)

$$\lim_{i\to\infty} \theta^i \frac{(1-\beta)L_{t+i}^{1-\alpha}}{\alpha(1-L_{t+i})^\varsigma} = 0. \tag{20}$$

Along a balanced growth path (BGP) one must have $Z_{t+1} = Z_t = Z$ and $L_{t+1} = L_t = L$ in (17)–(18), where

$$Z = \frac{(1-\beta)L^{1-\alpha}}{\alpha\beta(1-L)^\varsigma} \left\{ \frac{E_0(1+\chi)}{\chi} - \frac{E_0}{\theta\chi[(1-\alpha)L^\alpha + 1 - \delta]} \right\}^\varsigma$$

and L satisfies $f(L) = 0$,

$$f(L) = (L^\alpha + 1 - \delta)(1 - \theta) + \theta\alpha L^\alpha$$
$$- \frac{\alpha\beta(1-L)^\varsigma}{(1-\beta)L^{1-\alpha}} \left\{ \frac{E_0(1+\chi)}{\chi} - \frac{E_0}{\theta\chi[(1-\alpha)L^\alpha + 1 - \delta]} \right\}^{1-\varsigma}.$$

One can easily check that $\varsigma \geq 1$ – implying that R_t and C_t are not (Edgeworth) complements in consumption – is sufficient for insuring the uniqueness of a BGP pair (Z^*, L^*),[8] where '*' denotes the BGP value of a variable under laissez faire. In this case, one can also verify that L^* increases with β: as the households give more importance to consumption, they tend to work harder. Hence, a large β is likely to be consistent with unbounded growth. Indeed, there are parameter values such that $\rho^* = \omega(L^*, Z^*) > 0$, $\rho_t \equiv \frac{Y_{t+1}-Y_t}{Y_t}$.[9]

Finally, along a BGP the period utility of the representative household is given by

$$U^* = \beta u(x^*) + (1-\beta)v(1-L^*), \quad x^* = \left[\frac{\alpha\beta Z^*(1-L^*)^\varsigma}{(1-\beta)(L^*)^{1-\alpha}} \right]^{\frac{1}{\varsigma}}. \tag{21}$$

Notice that the steady-state utility level of the representative household is constant even when the steady-state rate of output growth is strictly positive. This is because, along a BGP displaying perpetual growth, the renewable resource entering the households' utility function is asymptotically depleted. Therefore, the positive impact on the households' welfare of the steady increase in per capita output and per capita (private) consumption is offset along a BGP by the diminishing endowment of R_t. Long-run growth is fed by a substitution process in which the private good progressively replaces the declining renewable resource as a source of individual well-being.

4. Activist policies

4.1. Internalization of the positive externality

Under laissez faire the benefits of labor-augmenting technical progress are not appropriated by those paying for it. Suppose now that there is a policy authority that has the instruments to induce the economic agents to internalize the technological spillovers generated by their use of capital. For instance, one may think that the authority subsidizes the firms' renting of capital. Consistently, we can rewrite (7) as

$$\pi_t = Y_t - w_t L_t - r_t K_t + q_t K_t - T_t, \tag{7'}$$

where q_t is the subsidy for unit of capital paid by the authority in period t, and T_t is the (lump-sum) tax that each firm must pay to the authority in t. In the presence of the subsidy, the firms' optimality condition with respect to the choice of K_t can be rewritten as

$$(1 - \alpha)L_t^\alpha + q_t = r_t. \tag{15'}$$

It is assumed that this authority balances its budget in each period:

$$q_t K_t = T_t, \tag{22}$$

and that it determines the subsidy so as to induce the firms to fully internalize the positive externality that they generate:

$$q_t = \alpha L_t^\alpha. \tag{23}$$

If the representative household maximizes (16) in the presence of such authority, one can derive the system of difference equations that governs the motion of the economy under full internalization of the positive externality (see Appendix (ii)). This system consists of (17) and

$$\frac{\theta L_{t+1}^{1-\alpha}(L_{t+1}^\alpha + 1 - \delta)}{(1 - L_{t+1})^\varsigma} = \frac{[1 + \omega(L_t, Z_t)]L_t^{1-\alpha}}{(1 - L_t)^\varsigma}, \tag{18'}$$

where $\omega(L_t, Z_t)$ is given by (19). An equilibrium path must also satisfy the transversality condition (20).

Along a BGP, $Z = \frac{(1-\beta)L^{1-\alpha}}{\alpha\beta(1-L)^\xi}\left[\frac{E_0(1+\chi)}{\chi} - \frac{E_0}{\theta\chi(L^\alpha+1-\delta)}\right]^\xi$ and L satisfies $g(L) = 0$,

$g(L) = (L^\alpha + 1 - \delta)(1 - \theta) - \frac{\alpha\beta(1-L)^\xi}{(1-\beta)L^{1-\alpha}}\left[\frac{E_0(1+\chi)}{\chi} - \frac{E_0}{\theta\chi(L^\alpha+1-\delta)}\right]^{1-\xi}$. Again, $\xi \geq 1$ is sufficient for insuring the uniqueness of (Z°, L°),[10] where '°' denotes the BGP value of a variable under full internalization of the positive externality. Moreover, $\xi \geq 1$ is sufficient for proving that $\rho^\circ = \omega(L^\circ, Z^\circ) > \rho^* = \omega(L^*, Z^*)$ and $x^\circ = \left[\frac{\alpha\beta Z^\circ(1-L^\circ)^\xi}{(1-\beta)(L^\circ)^{1-\alpha}}\right]^{\frac{1}{\xi}} > x^* = \left[\frac{\alpha\beta Z^*(1-L^*)^\xi}{(1-\beta)(L^*)^{1-\alpha}}\right]^{\frac{1}{\xi}}$.[11]

It is not surprising that when private agents can fully appropriate all the benefits that they generate by using their capital stock, labor-augmenting technical progress and economic growth tend to accelerate. Although this accelerates the depletion of the renewable resource, in the long run the amount of consumer service is higher. However, the steady-state utility level of the representative household may be lower than under laissez faire: it is possible to have $U^\circ < U^*$.[12] Facing a more rapid decline of that source of welfare represented by R_t, the households have to rely more heavily on private goods. Hence, they may be induced to intensify both the accumulation of private assets and the work effort. In this case, they tend to sacrifice leisure ($L^\circ > L^*$), and households' long-term welfare may be lower than under laissez faire even if $x^\circ > x^*$. It is only when households attach much importance to leisure (small β) that they allocate part of the faster economic growth to reduce the work effort: in this case $L^\circ < L^*$ (see Appendix (iii)), thus entailing $U^\circ > U^*$.[13]

4.2. Internalization of both externalities (Pareto-optimal policies)

We assume here that – together with the authority subsidizing the firms' renting of capital – there is also a regulatory authority which can optimally tax the households' consumer activities. Consistently, one can write (9) as

$$K_{t+i+1} + C_{t+i} \leq w_{t+i}L_{t+i} + r_{t+i}K_{t+i} + \pi_{t+i} + (1-\delta)K_{t+i}$$

$$-\tau_{t+i}\frac{R_{t+i}C_{t+i}}{E_0} + G_{t+i}, \quad K_0 \text{ given}, \qquad (9')$$

where τ_t is the tax rate in period t (taxes are proportional to the impact of the household's consumer activities on the growth rate of R_t),[14] and G_t are the net transfers that each household receives from the regulatory authority in t. This authority balances its budget in each period:

$$\tau_t\frac{R_tC_t}{E_0} = G_t, \qquad (24)$$

and determines τ_t optimally.

Hence, the problem of the representative household in the presence of both authorities can be solved by maximizing

$$\sum_{i=0}^{\infty} \theta^i \left\{ \beta u(x_{t+i}) + (1 - \beta)v(1 - L_{t+i}) - \lambda_{t+i} \left[K_{t+i+1} + C_{t+i} - r_{t+i}K_{t+i} \right. \right.$$

$$\left. \left. - \pi_{t+i} - (1 - \delta)K_{t+i} - L_{t+i}w_{t+i} + \tau_{t+i} \frac{R_{t+i}C_{t+i}}{E_0} - G_{t+i} \right] \right\} \tag{25}$$

with respect to C_t, L_t, λ_t and K_{t+1}. Therefore, one can use (5), (6), (7′), (14), (15′), (22), (23), (24), together with the conditions obtained by maximizing (25) under the assumption that τ_t is determined optimally, to derive the system of difference equations in Z_t, $V_t \equiv \frac{C_t}{K_t}$ and L_t which governs the Pareto-optimal path of the economy (see Appendix (iv)). This system consists of

$$\frac{Z_{t+1}}{1 + \psi(L_t, V_t)} - Z_t = \chi Z_t \left(1 - \frac{Z_t V_t}{E_0} \right), \tag{26}$$

$$\frac{\theta L_{t+1}^{1-\alpha}(L_{t+1}^\alpha + 1 - \delta)}{(1 - L_{t+1})^\varsigma} = \frac{[1 + \psi(L_t, V_t)]L_t^{1-\alpha}}{(1 - L_t)^\varsigma}, \tag{27}$$

$$\left(1 + \chi - \frac{2\chi V_{t+1}Z_{t+1}}{E_0} \right) \frac{\theta E_0}{\chi Z_{t+1}} \left[\frac{\beta}{(V_{t+1}Z_{t+1})^\xi} - \frac{(1 - \beta)L_{t+1}^{1-\alpha}}{\alpha Z_{t+1}(1 - L_{t+1})^\varsigma} \right]$$

$$+ \frac{\theta \beta V_{t+1}}{(V_{t+1}Z_{t+1})^\xi} = \frac{E_0}{\chi Z_t[1 + \psi(L_t, V_t)]} \left[\frac{\beta}{(V_t Z_t)^\xi} - \frac{(1 - \beta)L_t^{1-\alpha}}{\alpha Z_t(1 - L_t)^\varsigma} \right], \tag{28}$$

where

$$\psi(L_t, V_t) = L_t^\alpha - \delta - V_t. \tag{29}$$

A Pareto-optimal path must also satisfy the transversality conditions (20) and

$$\lim_{i \to \infty} \theta^i \frac{E_0}{\chi} \left[\frac{\beta}{(V_{t+i}Z_{t+i})^\xi} - \frac{(1 - \beta)L_{t+i}^{1-\alpha}}{\alpha Z_{t+i}(1 - L_{t+i})^\varsigma} \right] = 0. \tag{30}$$

Along a BGP, one must have $Z_{t+1} = Z_t = Z$, $V_{t+1} = V_t = V$ and $L_{t+1} = L_t = L$ in (26)–(28), where

$$Z = \frac{E_0}{(L^\alpha + 1 - \delta)(1 - \theta)\chi} \left[1 + \chi - \frac{1}{\theta(L^\alpha + 1 - \delta)} \right],$$

$V = (L^\alpha + 1 - \delta)(1 - \theta)$ and L satisfies $g(L) + n(L) = 0$, $n(L) = (L^\alpha + 1 - \delta)\theta$ $[(1 + \chi)\theta(L^\alpha + 1 - \delta) - 1]$, $n' > 0$. Again, $\xi \geq 1$ is sufficient for insuring the uniqueness of (Z^{**}, V^{**}, L^{**}), where '**' denotes the BGP value of a variable when both externalities are fully internalized. Moreover, $\xi \geq 1$ is sufficient for having $L^{**} < L^\circ$,[15] which entails $\rho^{**} = \psi(L^{**}, V^{**}) < \rho^\circ$ and $x^{**} = V^{**}Z^{**} < x^\circ$:[16] along the BGP, the level of labor supply, the rate of output growth and the amount of consumer service tend to be lower under a Pareto-optimal policy than when only the positive externality is internalized. Facing a less rapid decline of the common property resource thanks to the 'conservationist' policy implemented by the public authorities, the households have to rely less heavily on private goods, thus tending to reduce the accumulation of private assets, the rate of (labor-augmenting) technical progress and the work effort. In the long run, the households' well-being tends to be higher because of the larger amount of leisure that they enjoy: $U^{**} > U^\circ$.[17] It is also typically the case that both $L^{**} < L^*$ and $x^{**} > x^*$, thus implying $U^{**} > U^*$:[18] the BGP emerging under a Pareto-optimal policy tends to exhibit both a lower level of work effort and a higher level of consumer service than the BGP emerging under laissez faire.

4.3. 'Resource-saving technical progress'

Let us introduce the possibility of also having activities that reduce the detrimental impact of a certain level of consumption of market goods on the future quality of social assets. To model this possibility we rewrite (3) as $R_{t+1} - R_t = z(R_t, C_t, E_t)$, R_0 and E_0 given, where

$$z(R_t, C_t, E_t) = \chi R_t \left(1 - \frac{R_t C_t}{E_t}\right), \quad \chi > 0, \quad E_t > 0. \tag{4'}$$

Note in (4') that an increase in E_t reduces the negative effect on R_{t+1} of any given level of consumption. We may interpret this increase in E_t as 'resource-saving technical progress'. Moreover, we assume that this kind of 'technical progress' occurs if some households' time is devoted to social activities, i.e. to activities that increase social cohesion and community ties:

$$E_{t+1} - E_t = \gamma E_t N_t, \gamma > 0, \tag{31}$$

where N_t are the units of households' time devoted in t to social activities, and γ is a parameter measuring the extent to which the households' time devoted to social activities can generate 'resource-saving technical progress'. Note also that N_t in (31) should be interpreted as the aggregate amount of households' time that is devoted to social activities, since a single household can give only a negligible contribution to reduce the erosion of social assets due to the increased consumption of market goods. Alternatively, in accordance with an environmental interpretation of the renewable resource, we may consider N_t as the society's time devoted to the experimentation and implementation of new resource-saving technologies: an increase in E_t is a technological improvement that reduces the environmental impact of the consumers' activities.

To derive the optimal rate of 'resource-saving technical progress', one may think that the same authority taxing the households' consumer activities subsidizes the social activities by paying for the households' time devoted to social activities. For simplicity, we assume that this time is paid by the authority at the market wage. If we interpret the renewable resource as an environmental asset, the authority can be also conceived as a public agency employing workers who undertake R&D activities aimed at generating resource-saving technological improvements, which are made available for free to all consumers. In other words, we model the generation of 'resource-saving technical progress' as the provision of a pure public good by a governmental authority. Finally, we still assume that this public authority balances its budget in each period. Consistently, one can rewrite (9), (10), (12) and (24), respectively, as

$$K_{t+i+1} + C_{t+i} \leq w_{t+i}H_{t+i} + r_{t+i}K_{t+i} + \pi_{t+i} + (1 - \delta)K_{t+i}$$

$$- \tau_{t+i}\frac{R_{t+i}C_{t+i}}{E_{t+i}} + G_{t+i}, \quad K_0 \text{ given}, \tag{9''}$$

$$l_{t+i} + H_{t+i} \leq 1 \tag{10'}$$

$$L_t + N_t = H_t, \tag{12'}$$

$$\tau_t\frac{R_t C_t}{E_t} = G_t + w_t N_t, \tag{24'}$$

where H_t is labor supply in period t and the policy instruments q_t, τ_t, and N_t are determined optimally.

Hence, the problem of the representative household under these circumstances can be solved by maximizing

$$\sum_{i=0}^{\infty} \theta^i \left\{ \beta u(x_{t+i}) + (1 - \beta)v(1 - H_{t+i}) - \lambda_{t+i} \left[K_{t+i+1} + C_{t+i} - r_{t+i}K_{t+i} \right. \right.$$

$$\left. \left. - \pi_{t+i} - (1 - \delta)K_{t+i} - H_{t+i}w_{t+i} + \tau_{t+i}\frac{R_{t+i}C_{t+i}}{E_{t+i}} - G_{t+i} \right] \right\} \tag{32}$$

with respect to C_t, H_t, λ_t and K_{t+1}. Therefore, one can use (5), (6), (7'), (12'), (14), (15'), (22), (23), (24'), together with the conditions obtained by maximizing (32) under the assumption that τ_t and N_t are determined optimally, to derive the system of difference equations which governs the Pareto-optimal path of the economy in the presence of 'resource-saving technical progress' (see Appendix (v)). The equations in Z_t, V_t, N_t, E_t and L_t governing the Pareto-optimal path are (31),

$$\frac{Z_{t+1}}{1 + \psi(L_t, V_t)} - Z_t = \chi Z_t \left(1 - \frac{Z_t V_t}{E_t}\right), \tag{33}$$

$$\frac{\theta L_{t+1}^{1-\alpha}(L_{t+1}^{\alpha} + 1 - \delta)}{(1 - N_{t+1} - L_{t+1})^{\varsigma}} = \frac{[1 + \psi(L_t, V_t)]L_t^{1-\alpha}}{(1 - N_t - L_t)^{\varsigma}}, \tag{34}$$

$$\left(1 + \chi - \frac{2\chi V_{t+1}Z_{t+1}}{E_{t+1}}\right)\frac{\theta E_{t+1}}{\chi Z_{t+1}}\left[\frac{\beta}{(V_{t+1}Z_{t+1})^{\varsigma}} - \frac{(1-\beta)L_{t+1}^{1-\alpha}}{\alpha Z_{t+1}(1 - N_{t+1} - L_{t+1})^{\varsigma}}\right] +$$
$$\frac{\theta\beta V_{t+1}}{(V_{t+1}Z_{t+1})^{\varsigma}} = \frac{E_t}{\chi Z_t[1 + \psi(L_t, V_t)]}\left[\frac{\beta}{(V_t Z_t)^{\varsigma}} - \frac{(1-\beta)L_t^{1-\alpha}}{\alpha Z_t(1 - N_t - L_t)^{\varsigma}}\right], \tag{35}$$

$$\frac{\theta V_{t+1}}{E_{t+1}}\left[\frac{\beta Z_{t+1}}{(V_{t+1}Z_{t+1})^{\varsigma}} - \frac{(1-\beta)L_{t+1}^{1-\alpha}}{\alpha(1 - N_{t+1} - L_{t+1})^{\varsigma}}\right] + \frac{\theta(1-\beta)(\gamma N_{t+1} + 1)}{E_{t+1}\gamma(1 - N_{t+1} - L_{t+1})^{\varsigma}}$$
$$= \frac{(1-\beta)}{E_t\gamma(1 - N_t - L_t)^{\varsigma}}, \tag{36}$$

where $\psi(L_t, V_t)$ is given by (29). This Pareto-optimal path with 'resource-saving technical progress' must also satisfy the transversality conditions

$$\lim_{i \to \infty} \theta^i \frac{(1-\beta)L_{t+i}^{1-\alpha}}{\alpha(1 - N_{t+i} - L_{t+i})^{\varsigma}} = 0, \tag{37}$$

$$\lim_{i \to \infty} \theta^i \frac{E_{t+i}}{\chi}\left[\frac{\beta}{(V_{t+i}Z_{t+i})^{\varsigma}} - \frac{(1-\beta)L_{t+i}^{1-\alpha}}{\alpha Z_{t+i}(1 - N_{t+i} - L_{t+i})^{\varsigma}}\right] = 0, \tag{38}$$

$$\lim_{i \to \infty} \theta^i \frac{(1-\beta)}{\gamma(1 - N_{t+i} - L_{t+i})^{\varsigma}} = 0. \tag{39}$$

Along a BGP, one must have $Z_{t+1} = Z_t = Z$, $V_{t+1} = V_t = V$, $N_{t+1} = N_t = N$, $E_{t+1} = E_t = E$ and $L_{t+1} = L_t = L$ in (31) and (33)–(36), where for $\xi \neq 1$ $Z = \frac{E}{(L^{\alpha}+1-\delta)(1-\theta)\chi}\left[\frac{(1+\chi)(L^{\alpha}+1-\delta)\theta-1}{\theta(L^{\alpha}+1-\delta)}\right]$, $V = (L^{\alpha} + 1 - \delta)(1 - \theta)$, $N = 0$, $E = e(L) = \frac{(L^{\alpha}+1-\delta)\theta\chi}{[(1+\chi)(L^{\alpha}+1-\delta)\theta-1]}\left\{\frac{(1-\beta)(L^{\alpha}+1-\delta)[(1+\chi)(L^{\alpha}+1-\delta)\theta^2+1-2\theta]}{\alpha\beta(1-L)^{\varsigma}L^{\alpha-1}}\right\}^{\frac{1}{1-\xi}} > E_0$ and L satisfies $d(L) = 0$, $d(L) = \frac{(L^{\alpha}+1-\delta)\theta^2[(1+\chi)(L^{\alpha}+1-\delta)\theta-1]}{(1-\theta)\alpha L^{\alpha-1}} - \frac{1}{\gamma}$. One can easily prove for $\xi \neq 1$ that the BGP characterized by $(Z^{\circ\circ}, V^{\circ\circ}, E^{\circ\circ}, N^{\circ\circ}, L^{\circ\circ})$ is unique,[19] where '$\circ\circ$' denotes the BGP value of a variable when policies are Pareto optimal and there is 'resource-saving technical progress'.[20] Comparing this BGP to the BGP emerging when policies are Pareto optimal but no 'resource-saving technical progress' is possible, one can check that $\xi > 1$ is sufficient for having both $L^{\circ\circ} < L^{**}$ (see Appendix (vi)) and $x^{\circ\circ} = V^{\circ\circ}Z^{\circ\circ} > x^{**}$ (see Appendix (vii)), which entail $\rho^{\infty\infty} = \psi(L^{\infty\infty}, V^{\infty\infty}) < \rho^{**}$ and $U^{\infty\infty} > U^{**}$.[21] The implementation of a policy achieving the optimal rate of 'resource-saving technical progress' tends to lead the economy along a BGP characterized by a lower rate of economic growth and a higher level of households' utility.

5. Conclusion

An important implication of endogenous growth models displaying unbounded growth is that the individuals' utility grows forever because of ever increasing consumption opportunities. This implication appears to be at odds with the evidence indicating that the perceived well-being stagnates in the advanced economies in spite of spectacular technical progress and economic growth (see Easterlin 1974, 1995; Oswald 1997). We have presented a model that reconciles unceasing labor-augmenting technical progress and unbounded growth with this evidence by emphasizing the negative externality that consumers' activities may have on social and environmental assets that are important sources of people's well-being. In the model, these assets are treated as a renewable resource and households combine this resource and market good to produce a consumer service that gives them utility. Long-run growth is fed by a substitution process in which the market good progressively replaces the declining common property resource as a source of individual well-being.

In most of the endogenous growth literature, markets are incomplete (given that there are positive externalities like those due to activities that generate new knowledge and productivity advances whose fruits cannot be privately appropriated), and growth is suboptimally low under laissez faire. Hence, regulatory interventions aimed at internalizing this kind of positive externalities should raise long-term utility. We show that this may not be the case and that these policies may depress steady-state welfare. Indeed, they lead to a higher steady-state rate of (labor-augmenting) technical progress, of capital accumulation and of output growth, and – possibly – to an increase of the individuals' work effort, thus raising permanently the pace at which the production of market goods grows. In the same time, however, they exacerbate the negative effects that consumers' activities have on the renewable resource.

In our model, Pareto-optimal policies are those policies that lead to the internalization of both externalities. In the presence of such policies, the private agents face a less rapid decline of the common property resource and have to rely less heavily on market goods. As a consequence, along a balanced growth path, the level of individual utility is higher, while the accumulation of capital, the rate of (labor-augmenting) technical progress, the rate of output growth and the work effort tend to be lower under a Pareto-optimal policy than under a policy internalizing only the positive externality. Moreover, the balanced growth path emerging under a

Pareto-optimal policy tends to exhibit both a lower level of work effort and a higher level of consumption than the BGP emerging under laissez faire, thus implying a higher steady-state level of utility.

Finally, we introduce the possibility of generating 'resource-saving technical progress', namely of subsidizing activities that reduce the damaging impact of consumers' activities on the renewable resource. In this context, we study policies that – beside leading to the internalization of both externalities – devote the optimal amount of effort to resource-saving technical progress: the balanced growth path emerging under such policies tends to be characterized by a lower rate of labor-saving technical progress, a lower rate of output growth, and a higher level of households' utility than the balanced growth path emerging when policies are Pareto optimal but no 'resource-saving technical progress' is possible.

The results of this chapter suggest that policies aimed at stimulating that kind of technical progress that enhances efficiency in the production of market goods may not lead, in the long run, to welfare improvements if they are not accompanied by other policies directed to safeguard social and environmental assets that tend to be damaged in the growth process of a market economy. Without these other policies, the introduction of public subsidies that appear justified by the differential between private and social returns to efforts generating productivity advances, or the enforcement of property rights increasing the appropriability of the fruits of these efforts, may boost economic growth but may also end up lowering people's quality of life.

Appendix

(i) Derivation of the equations characterizing a competitive-equilibrium path under laissez faire

By maximizing (16) with respect to C_t, L_t, λ_t and K_{t+1}, and by using (3)–(7), (14) and (15), one obtains the conditions that a competitive equilibrium must satisfy under laissez faire:

$$\beta R_t (C_t R_t)^{-\xi} = \lambda_t, \tag{A1}$$

$$(1 - \beta)(1 - L_t)^{-\zeta} = \lambda_t \alpha L_t^{\alpha - 1} K_t, \tag{A2}$$

$$K_{t+1} = K_t L_t^\alpha + (1 - \delta)K_t - C_t, \tag{A3}$$

$$\lambda_t = \lambda_{t+1} \theta [(1 - \alpha)L_{t+1}^\alpha + 1 - \delta]. \tag{A4}$$

A competitive-equilibrium path must also satisfy the transversality condition:

$$\lim_{i \to \infty} \theta^i \lambda_{t+i} K_{t+i} = 0. \tag{A5}$$

Therefore, (A1)–(A5) characterize a competitive equilibrium path under laissez faire. By rearranging this set of equations, one can derive the equations (17)–(20).

(ii) Derivation of the equations characterizing a competitive-equilibrium path under full internalization of the positive externality

By maximizing (16) with respect to C_t, L_t, λ_t and K_{t+1}, and by using (3)–(6), (7′), (14), (15′), (22) and (23), one obtains that when the positive externality is fully internalized a competitive-equilibrium path must satisfy (A1)–(A3) and

$$\lambda_t = \lambda_{t+1}\theta(L_{t+1}^\alpha + 1 - \delta). \tag{A4′}$$

In the presence of full internalization of the positive externality, a competitive-equilibrium path must also satisfy the transversality condition (A5). Therefore, (A1)–(A3), (A4′) and (A5) characterize a competitive equilibrium path under full internalization of the positive externality. By rearranging this set of equations, one can derive the equations (17), (18′), (19) and (20).

(iii) Proof that a small β is necessary for having $L° < L^*$

To see that when $\xi \geq 1$, a small β is necessary for having $L° < L^*$, write
$b(L, \varepsilon) = L^\alpha + 1 - \delta - (\varepsilon L^\alpha + 1 - \delta)\theta - \frac{\alpha\beta(1-L)^\xi}{(1-\beta)L^{1-\alpha}}\left[\frac{E_0(1+\chi)}{\chi} - \frac{E_0}{\theta\chi(\varepsilon L^\alpha + 1 - \delta)}\right]^{1-\xi}$, where

$b(L, \varepsilon) = \begin{cases} f(L) & \text{if } \varepsilon = 1-\alpha \\ g(L) & \text{if } \varepsilon = 1. \end{cases}$

Since $\xi \geq 1$, one can easily check that $\frac{\partial b(L,\varepsilon)}{\partial L} > 0$. Given the implicit function theorem, this implies that $\frac{dL}{d\varepsilon}\big|_{b(L,\varepsilon)=0} < 0$, thus entailing $L° < L^*$, if and only if $\frac{\partial b(L,\varepsilon)}{\partial \varepsilon}\big|_{b(L,\varepsilon)=0} > 0$. Consider that $\frac{\partial b(L,\varepsilon)}{\partial \varepsilon}\big|_{b(L,\varepsilon)=0} = -L^\alpha\theta -$

$\frac{(1-\xi)E_0 L^\alpha[L^\alpha+1-\delta-\theta(\varepsilon L^\alpha+1-\delta)]}{\theta\chi(\varepsilon L^\alpha+1-\delta)^2}\left[\frac{E_0(1+\chi)}{\chi} - \frac{E_0}{\theta\chi(\varepsilon L^\alpha+1-\delta)}\right]^{-1} > 0$ if and only if $c(L,\varepsilon) = -\theta -$

$\frac{(1-\xi)E_0[L^\alpha+1-\delta-\theta(\varepsilon L^\alpha+1-\delta)]}{\theta\chi(\varepsilon L^\alpha+1-\delta)^2}\left[\frac{E_0(1+\chi)}{\chi} - \frac{E_0}{\theta\chi(\varepsilon L^\alpha+1-\delta)}\right]^{-1} > 0$. Since $\frac{\partial c(L,\varepsilon)}{\partial \varepsilon} \leq 0$ for $\xi \geq 1$,

$c(L,\varepsilon)\big|_{\varepsilon=1} = -\theta - \frac{(1-\xi)E_0(1-\theta)}{\theta\chi(L^\alpha+1-\delta)}\left[\frac{E_0(1+\chi)}{\chi} - \frac{E_0}{\theta\chi(L^\alpha+1-\delta)}\right]^{-1} > 0$ entails $c(L,\varepsilon) > 0$ for any value of ε such that $0 < \varepsilon \leq 1$. In its turn, a necessary condition for having $c(L,\varepsilon)\big|_{\varepsilon=1} > 0$ is that $\xi > 1$. Moreover, since $\frac{\partial c(L,\varepsilon)\big|_{\varepsilon=1}}{\partial L} < 0$ whenever $\xi > 1$, one knows that – other things being equal – $c(L,\varepsilon)\big|_{\varepsilon=1} > 0$ is likely to be satisfied for low values of L. Considering that for $\xi \geq 1$ the value of L satisfying $b(L,\varepsilon) = 0$ increases with β, one can conclude that a small β is necessary for having $L° < L^*$.

(iv) Derivation of the equations characterizing a competitive-equilibrium path in the presence of Pareto-optimal policies

In the absence of resource-saving technical progress, one can characterize the Pareto-optimal path by maximizing $\sum_{i=0}^{\infty} \theta^i \{\beta u(x_{t+i}) + (1-\beta)$
$v(1 - L_{t+i}) - \lambda_{t+i} [K_{t+i+1} - K_{t+i}L_{t+i}^\alpha - (1-\delta)K_{t+i} + C_{t+i}] - \eta_{t+i} [R_{t+i+1} - \chi R_{t+i}$
$\left(1 - \frac{C_{t+i}R_{t+i}}{E_0}\right) - R_{t+i}]\}$ with respect to C_t, L_t, λ_t, η_t, K_{t+1} and R_{t+1}, where λ_t
and η_t are Lagrange multipliers. Hence, a Pareto-optimal path in the absence of resource-saving technical progress must satisfy (A2), (A3), (A4′),

$$\beta R_t (C_t R_t)^{-\xi} = \lambda_t + \eta_t \chi \frac{R_t^2}{E_0}, \tag{A6}$$

$$R_{t+1} - R_t = \chi R_t \left(1 - \frac{C_t R_t}{E_0}\right), \tag{A7}$$

$$\eta_t = \eta_{t+1}\theta \left(1 + \chi - \frac{2\chi C_{t+1}R_{t+1}}{E_0}\right) + \theta\beta C_{t+1}(C_{t+1}R_{t+1})^{-\xi}. \tag{A8}$$

A Pareto-optimal path must also satisfy the transversality conditions (A5) and

$$\lim_{i \to \infty} \theta^i \eta_{t+i} R_{t+i} = 0. \tag{A9}$$

To decentralize this allocation, one can maximize (25) and use (5)–(7), (14), (15′), (22), (23) and (24), thus obtaining that a competitive-equilibrium path must satisfy (A2), (A3), (A4′), (A5) and

$$\beta R_t (C_t R_t)^{-\xi} = \lambda_t + \lambda_t \tau_t \frac{R_t}{E_0}. \tag{A1′}$$

By comparing (A6) with (A1′), one can verify that a competitive-equilibrium path is Pareto optimal if in each period t the tax per unit of pollution is set by the authority so as to satisfy

$$\tau_t = \chi \eta_t \frac{R_t}{\lambda_t}. \tag{A10}$$

Therefore, (A1′), (A2), (A3), (A4′) and (A5) – together with (A7)–(A10) – must hold along a competitive-equilibrium path in the presence of Pareto-optimal policies. By rearranging this set of equations, one can derive the equations (20) and (26)–(30).

(v) Derivation of the equations characterizing a competitive-equilibrium path in the presence of Pareto-optimal policies and resource-saving technical progress

In the presence of resource-saving technical progress, one can characterize the Pareto-optimal path by maximizing $\sum_{i=0}^{\infty} \theta^i \{\beta u(x_{t+i}) + (1-\beta)$
$v(1 - L_{t+i} - N_{t+i}) - \lambda_{t+i} \left[K_{t+i+1} - K_{t+i}L_{t+i}^{\alpha} - (1-\delta)K_{t+i} + C_{t+i}\right] - \mu_{t+i} \left[E_{t+i+1} - \gamma E_{t+i}\right.$
$\left.(1 - L_{t+i} - N_{t+i}) - E_{t+i}\right] - \eta_{t+i} \left[R_{t+i+1} - \chi R_{t+i} \left(1 - \frac{C_{t+i}R_{t+i}}{E_{t+i}}\right) - R_{t+i}\right]\}$ with respect
to C_t, L_t, N_t, λ_t, μ_t, η_t, K_{t+1} R_{t+1} and E_{t+1} where λ_t, μ_t, and η_t are Lagrange multipliers. Hence, a Pareto-optimal path in the presence of resource-saving technical progress must satisfy (A3), (A4'),

$$(1 - \beta)(1 - N_t - L_t)^{-\zeta} = \lambda_t \alpha L_t^{\alpha-1} K_t, \tag{A2'}$$

$$\beta R_t (C_t R_t)^{-\xi} = \lambda_t + \eta_t \chi \frac{R_t^2}{E_t}, \tag{A6'}$$

$$R_{t+1} - R_t = \chi R_t \left(1 - \frac{C_t R_t}{E_t}\right), \tag{A7'}$$

$$\eta_t = \eta_{t+1}\theta \left(1 + \chi - \frac{2\chi C_{t+1}R_{t+1}}{E_t}\right) + \theta\beta C_{t+1}(C_{t+1}R_{t+1})^{-\xi}, \tag{A8'}$$

$$(1 - \beta)(1 - N_t - L_t)^{-\zeta} = \mu_t \gamma E_t, \tag{A11}$$

$$E_{t+1} - E_t = N_t E_t, \tag{A12}$$

$$\mu_t = \eta_{t+1}\theta\chi \frac{C_{t+1}R_{t+1}^2}{E_{t+1}^2} + \mu_{t+1}\theta(\gamma N_{t+1} + 1). \tag{A13}$$

A Pareto-optimal path must also satisfy the transversality conditions (A5), (A9) and

$$\lim_{i \to \infty} \theta^i \mu_{t+i} E_{t+i} = 0. \tag{A14}$$

To decentralize this allocation, one can maximize (32) and use (5), (6), (7'), (12'), (14), (15'), (22), (23), (24'), thus proving that a competitive-equilibrium path must satisfy (A2'), (A3), (A4') and

$$\beta R_t (C_t R_t)^{-\xi} = \lambda_t + \lambda_t \tau_t \frac{R_t}{E_t}, \tag{A1''}$$

By comparing (A6') with (A1''), one can verify that a competitive-equilibrium path is Pareto optimal if in each period t the tax per unit of pollution is set by the authority so as to satisfy (A10). Therefore, (A1''), (A2'), (A3), (A4') and (A5) – together with (A7'), (A8'), (A9) and (A11)–(A14) – must hold along a competitive-equilibrium path in the presence of Pareto-optimal policies and resource-saving technical progress. By rearranging this set of equations, one can derive the equations (29) and (33)–(39).

(vi) Proof that $L^{\circ\circ} < L^{**}$ for $\xi > 1$

Consider that L^{**} is that value of L that satisfies $m(L, E)\big|_{E=E_0}$, while $L^{\circ\circ}$ is that value of L that satisfies $m(L, E)\big|_{E=E^{\circ\circ}}$, where $m(L, E) = (L^\alpha + 1 - \delta)(1 - \theta) + \alpha L^\alpha - \frac{\alpha\beta(1-L)^\xi}{(1-\beta)L^{1-\alpha}} \left\{ \frac{E(1+\chi)}{\chi} - \frac{E}{\theta\chi[(1-\alpha)L^\alpha+1-\delta]} \right\}^{1-\xi} + (L^\alpha + 1 - \delta)\theta[(1 + \chi)\theta(L^\alpha + 1 - \delta) - 1]$. Since $E^{\circ\circ} > E_0$, and both $m_L > 0$ and $m_E > 0$ with $\xi > 1$, it is necessarily the case that $L^{\circ\circ} < L^{**}$ for $\xi > 1$.

(vii) Proof that $x^{\circ\circ} > x^{**}$ for $\xi > 1$

Consider that x^{**} is that value of x that satisfies $j(L)\big|_{L=L^{**}}$, while $x^{\circ\circ}$ is that value of x that satisfies $j(L)\big|_{L=L^{\circ\circ}}$, where $j(L) = \left\{ \frac{(1-\beta)(L^\alpha+1-\delta)[(1+\chi)(L^\alpha+1-\delta)\theta^2+1-2\theta]}{\alpha\beta(1-L)^\xi L^{\alpha-1}} \right\}^{\frac{1}{1-\xi}}$. Since $L^{\circ\circ} < L^{**}$, and $j' < 0$ with $\xi > 1$, it is necessarily the case that $x^{\circ\circ} > x^{**}$ for $\xi > 1$.

Notes

1. For Putnam's definition of social capital as those features of social organizations that facilitate coordination and cooperation (specifically, values and norms of reciprocity inhering in informal and horizontal social networks), see also Putnam et al. (1993). For a review of the concept years after Putnam's original definition, see Woolcock and Narayan (2000).
2. The implications that high levels of television consumption have on sociality and life satisfaction have been recently investigated by Frey et al. (2007) and by Bruni and Stanca (2008).
3. 'The real reason for the predominance of labor saving inventions is surely that which was hinted at in our discussion of substitution. A change in the relative prices of the factors of production is itself a spur to invention and to inventions of a particular kind – directed at economizing the use of a factor which has become relatively expensive'. (Hicks 1932: 124–125).
4. As Barro and Sala-i-Martin (1995: 60) point out, 'this setting is appropriate if altruistic parents provide transfers to their children, who give in turn to their children, and so on. The immortal family corresponds to finite-lived individuals who are connected via a pattern of operative intergenerational transfers that are based on altruism'.
5. The household production function approach can be used to measure the demand for environmental attributes (e.g. Kerry Smith 1991) by treating the quality of a household's personal environment as a function of both the quality of the collective environment and the goods that can be privately appropriated.
6. Consistently with this interpretation, one may rewrite (4) as $z(R_t, C_t) = \chi R_t (1 - p_t)$, where $p_t \equiv \frac{x_t}{E_0}$ is the total level of pollution generated in t by all the households' consumption activities. An alternative approach leading to the same result amounts to use (2) and (4) in order to rewrite the consumer production function as $x_t = \min(R_t C_t, E_0 p_t)$ (see Smulders 2000). In this way, it is more immediately apparent that consumers treat the renewable resource as an input entering their production function, and that E_0 measures the efficiency with which the consumers utilize this resource.

7. Giving an environmental interpretation to the model, laissez faire entails free disposal: each consumer can dispose of its waste at no (private) cost.

8. Indeed, $\xi \geq 1$ is sufficient for having $f' > 0$, thus implying that L which satisfies $f(L) = 0$ is unique. One can also verify that the unique BGP pair (Z^*, L^*) is saddle-path stable.

9. In particular, with $\xi \geq 1$ one has $\rho^* = [(1-\alpha)(L^*)^\alpha + 1 - \delta]\theta - 1 > 0$ if and only if

$$(D^\alpha + 1 - \delta)(1 - \theta) - \alpha D^\alpha - \frac{\alpha\beta(1-D)\zeta}{(1-\beta)D^{1-\alpha}} \left\{ \frac{E_0(1+\chi)}{\chi} - \frac{E_0}{\theta\chi[(1-\alpha)D^\alpha + 1 - \delta]} \right\}^{1-\xi} < 0, \text{ thus imply-}$$

ing $L^* > D \equiv \left[\frac{1 - (1-\delta)\theta}{\theta(1-\alpha)}\right]^{\frac{1}{\alpha}}$. As a numerical example, let $\xi = 2$, $\zeta = 1$, $\alpha = 2/3$, $\beta = 1/3$, $\chi = 0.2098127$, $\delta = 0.1$, $\theta = 0.95$ and $E_0 = 0.7$. Given these parameter values, one can obtain $L^* = 0.3642128$, $Z^* = 1.9167338$ and $\rho^* = 0.0165$.

10. Indeed, $\xi \geq 1$ is sufficient for having $g' > 0$, thus implying that the value of L that satisfies $g(L) = 0$ is unique. Again, one can verify that the unique BGP pair (Z°, L°) is saddle-path stable.

11. Comparing (18) with (18′), one can check that $\rho^\circ = \omega(L^\circ, Z^\circ) = \theta[(L^\circ)^\alpha + 1 - \delta] - 1$, while $\rho^* = \omega(L^*, Z^*) = \theta[(1-\alpha)(L^*)^\alpha + 1 - \delta] - 1$. Thus, $\rho^\circ > \rho^*$ if and only if $(L^\circ)^\alpha > (1-\alpha)(L^*)^\alpha$. One can verify that this is actually the case whenever $\xi \geq 1$ by considering that $(L^\circ)^\alpha \leq (1-\alpha)(L^*)^\alpha$ is inconsistent with the fact that L° and L^* are those values of L that satisfy, respectively, $g(L) = 0$ and $f(L) = 0$. Indeed, one can check that $g(L)\big|_{L=L^\circ} = 0$ and $(L^\circ)^\alpha \leq (1-\alpha)(L^*)^\alpha$ would imply $f(L)\big|_{L=L^\circ} > 0$. Hence, since $f' > 0$, one can have both $g(L)\big|_{L=L^\circ} = 0$ and $f(L)\big|_{L=L^*} = 0$ if and only if $(L^\circ)^\alpha > (1-\alpha)(L^*)^\alpha$.

12. Given $\xi = 2$, $\zeta = 1$, $\alpha = 2/3$, $\beta = 1/3$, $\chi = 0.2098127$, $\delta = 0.1$, $\theta = 0.95$ and $E_0 = 0.7$, one can verify that $L^\circ = 0.6132925$, $L^* = 0.3642128$, $Z^\circ = 23.071671$, $Z^* = 1.9167338$ and $U^\circ = -0.811555 < U^* = -0.7439$.

13. As a numerical example, let $\xi = 2$, $\zeta = 1$, $\alpha = 2/3$, $\beta = 0.1615108$, $\chi = 0.2$, $\delta = 0.15$, $\theta = 0.8810652$ and $E_0 = 1$. Given these parameter values, one can verify that $L^\circ = 0.2$, $L^* = 0.3$, $Z^\circ = 8.7404185$, $Z^* = 0.769915$ and $U^\circ = -0.3174 > U^* = -0.801385$.

14. Consistently with an environmental interpretation of the model, one may think of τ_t as the tax per unit of pollution in period t.

15. Indeed, $\xi \geq 1$ entails $f' > 0$, which – together with $n(L) > 0$ – implies $L^{**} < L^\circ$.

16. Since $\rho^{**} = [(L^{**})^\alpha + 1 - \delta]\theta - 1$ and $\rho^\circ = [(L^\circ)^\alpha + 1 - \delta]\theta - 1$, $L^{**} < L^\circ$ entails $\rho^{**} < \rho^\circ$. Since $x^{**} = \frac{E_0(1+\chi)}{\chi} - \frac{E_0}{\theta\chi[(L^\circ)^\alpha + 1 - \delta]}$ and $x^\circ = \frac{E_0(1+\chi)}{\chi} - \frac{E_0}{\theta\chi[(L^{**})^\alpha + 1 - \delta]}$, $L^{**} < L^\circ$ entails $x^{**} < x^\circ$.

17. Given $\xi = 2$, $\zeta = 1$, $\alpha = 2/3$, $\beta = 1/3$, $\chi = 0.2098127$, $\delta = 0.1$, $\theta = 0.95$ and $E_0 = 0.7$, one can verify that $Z^{**} = 18.277171$, $V^{**} = 0.0595755$, $L^{**} = 0.1573925$ and $U^{**} = -0.4202966 > U^\circ = -0.811555$.

18. Again, given $\xi = 2$, $\zeta = 1$, $\alpha = 2/3$, $\beta = 1/3$, $\chi = 0.2098127$, $\delta = 0.1$, $\theta = 0.95$ and $E_0 = 0.7$, one can verify that $U^{**} = -0.4202966 > U^* = -0.7439$.

19. Indeed, one has $d' > 0$, thus implying that there is a unique value of L which satisfies $d(L) = 0$.

20. We consider parameter values such that $E^{\circ\circ} = e(L^{\circ\circ}) > E_0$, implying that along the transition path it is optimal to devote some households' time to social activities that generate 'resource-saving technical progress'.

21. Since $\rho^{**} = [(L^{**})^\alpha + 1 - \delta]\theta - 1$ and $\rho^{\circ\circ} = [(L^{\circ\circ})^\alpha + 1 - \delta]\theta - 1$, $L^{**} > L^{\circ\circ}$ entails $\rho^{**} > \rho^{\circ\circ}$. Since $U = \beta u(x) + (1-\beta)v(l)$, where $l = 1 - L - N$, $x^{**} < x^{\circ\circ}$, $L^{**} > L^{\circ\circ}$ and $N^{**} = N^{\circ\circ} = 0$ entail $U^{**} > U^{\circ\circ}$.

References

D. Acemoglu (2002) 'Directed Technical Change', *Review of Economic Studies*, 69, 781–810.

D. Acemoglu (2003) 'Labor- and Capital-Augmenting Technical Change', *Journal of European Economic Association*, 1, 1–40.

R. J. Barro and X. Sala-i-Martin (1995) *Economic Growth* (New York: McGraw-Hill).

S. Bartolini and L. Bonatti (2002) 'Environmental and Social Degradation as the Engine of Economic Growth', *Ecological Economics*, 43, 1–16.

S. Bartolini and L. Bonatti (2003) 'Endogenous growth and Negative Externalities', *Journal of Economics*, 79, 123–144.

L. Bretschger (2005) 'Economics of Technological Change and the Natural Environment: How Effective Are Innovations as a Remedy for Resource Scarcity?', *Ecological Economics*, 54, 148–163.

L. Bruni and L. Stanca (2008) 'Watching Alone: Relational Good, Television and Happiness', *Journal of Economic Behavior and Organization*, 65, 506–528.

J. M. Conrad (1987) *Natural Resource Economics* (Cambridge: Cambridge University Press).

G. Cross (2000) *An All-Consuming Century: Why Commercialism Won in Modern America* (New York: Columbia University Press).

E. Drandakis and E. S. Phelps (1966) 'A Model of Induced Innovation, Growth and Distribution', *Economic Journal*, 76, 823–840.

R. Easterlin (1974) 'Does Economic Growth Improve the Human Lot? Some Empirical Evidence', in P. A. David and M. W. Reder (eds), *Nations and Households in Economic Growth: Essays in Honour of Moses Abramowitz* (New York and London: Academic Press).

R. Easterlin (1995) 'Will Raising the Income of All Increase the Happiness of All?', *Journal of Economic Behavior and Organization*, 27, 35–48.

M. Frankel (1962) 'The Production Function in Allocation and Growth: A Synthesis', *American Economic Review*, 52, 995–1022.

B. S. Frey, C. Benesch and A. Stutzer (2007) 'Does Watching TV Make Us Happy?', *Journal of Economic Psychology*, 28(3), 283–313.

A. Grübler, N. Nakicenovic and W. D. Nordhaus (eds) (2002) *Technological Change and the Environment* (Washington DC: Resources for the Future Press).

J. Hicks (1932) *The Theory of Wages*, 1st ed. (London: Macmillan) (2nd ed., 1963).

A. O. Hirschman (1982) 'Rival Interpretations of Market Society: Civilizing, Destructive or Feeble', *Journal of Economic Literature*, 20, 1463–1484.

F. Hirsch (1976) *Social Limits to Growth* (Cambridge: Harvard University Press).

C. Kennedy (1964) 'Induced Bias in Innovation and the Theory of Distribution', *Economic Journal*, 74, 541–547.

Kerry Smith V. (1991) 'Household Production Functions and Environmental Benefit Estimation', in J. B. Braden and C. D. Kolstad (eds), *Measuring the Demand for Environmental Quality* (Amsterdam: North Holland).

D. Martin (1995) 'Money, Business and Culture: Issues for Aboriginal Economic Policy', Discussion Paper No. 101/1995, Center for Aboriginal Economic Policy Research, Australian National University, Canberra.

C. O. N. Moser (1998) 'The Asset Vulnerability Framework: Reassessing Urban Poverty Reduction Strategies', *World Development*, 26(1), 1–19.

C. O. N. Moser (2007) 'Asset Accumulation Policy and Poverty Reduction', in C. O. N. Moser (ed) *Reducing Global Poverty. The Case for Asset Accumulation* (Washington, DC: Brookings Press).

A. J. Oswald (1997) 'Happiness and Economic Performance', *Economic Journal*, 107, 1815–1831.

N. Peterson (1993) 'Demand Sharing: Reciprocity and the Pressure for Generosity among Foragers', *American Anthropologist*, 95, 860–874.

R. D. Putnam (2000) *Bowling Alone: The Collapse and Revival of American Community* (New York: Simon&Schuster).

R. D. Putnam, R. Leonardi and R. Y. Nanetti (1993) *Making Democracy Work: Civic Traditions in Modern Italy* (Princeton: Princeton University Press).

V. W. Ruttan (2001) *Technology, Growth and Development: An Induced Innovation Perspective* (Oxford: Oxford University Press).

P. Samuelson (1965) 'A Theory of Induced Innovations along Kennedy-Weisacker Lines', *Review of Economics and Statistics*, 47, 444–464.

J. Schor (1998) *The Overspent American* (New York: Basic Books).

S. Smulders (2000) 'Economic Growth and Environmental Quality', in H. Folmer and H. L. Gabel (eds) *Principles of Environmental and Resource Economics* (Cheltenham, Edward Elgar).

S. Smulders (2005) 'Endogenous Technical Change, Natural Resources and Growth', in D. Simpson, M. Toman and R. Ayres (eds), *Scarcity and Growth Revisited* (Washington, DC: Resources for the Future Press).

M. Woolcock and D. Narayan (2000) 'Social Capital: Implications for Development Theory, Research and Policy', *The World Bank Research Observer*, 15(2).

12
Generalized Trust: The Macro Perspective

Martin Paldam

1. Introduction: The *G-trust* variable

One of the key variables in the social capital discussions is generalized trust.[1] To save words, the average generalized trust for a country is termed: *G-trust*. Table 12.1 gives the formulation and the aggregate of all answers in the World Values Survey,[2] which cover 188 pools in 83 countries during the last two decades of the twentieth century. Almost 30 per cent of the 255,399 answers say that 'most people can be trusted'. The individual country *G-trusts* are listed in the Appendix.

Justified trust reduces transaction and monitoring costs. It saves time and trouble the higher it is in society. It is thus a factor of production – however, it will be demonstrated that it is not a powerful one.

Any country has a level of justifiable or rational trust, *RT*. If you have more trust than *RT*, you are a 'sucker' that other people exploit. If you have less trust than *RT*, you are a 'cynic', who creates costs and trouble for other people. Most prefer to deal with reasonable people, who are realistic by being close to *RT*. By the law of large numbers the *G-trust* $\approx$ *RT* for a country:

> **Thesis 1**: The *Rationality Theorem of Trust*: Trust is rational for society at large.

We may measure it poorly and individuals deviate to both sides, but the *G–trust* is rational and an important characteristic of a society.

The *G-trusts* of the 188 polls are depicted in Figure 12.1, which shows that they have a strong correlation to income. Figure 12.2 shows an almost equally strong correlation of *G-trust* and *LiSa*, high life satisfaction used in happiness research as a welfare measure (see Frey and Stutzer 2002). The two – rather similar – figures allow us to make three observations about *G-trust*:

> Obs 1: It varies widely between countries, from close to 0 per cent to almost 70 per cent.

331

Obs 2: It is related to other important matters in society as income and welfare – that is, to economic development.

Obs 3: It contains a 'cultural' element so that some groups of countries cluster.

As *G-trusts* from a wide variety of countries are considered, an organizing principle is necessary. For this purpose I use the theory of the Grand Transition – GT-theory, as discussed in section 2. It is the process whereby poor countries become wealthy, and thus has the relation between the *G-trust* and economic development as the underlying theme.

The newest survey of the literature on growth and trust is Bjørnskov (2007). It appears that the variables in Table 12.2 are the main ones that

Table 12.1   The *G-trust* item in the World Values Survey: 1980–2000

Item A165: Generally speaking, would you say that most people can be trusted or that you need to be very careful in dealing with people?

Answer	Frequency	Per cent
Most people can be trusted	75,466	**29.55**
Can't be too careful	179,933	70.45
Sum	255,399	100.00

Note: The WVS covers 188 polls covering 267,870 people in 83 countries in 4 waves. The *G-trust* item is included in all 188 polls.

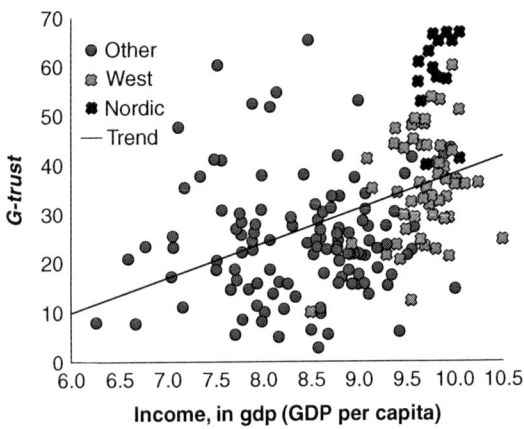

Figure 12.1   Scatter of the 188 *G-trust* and *income* (logarithm to GDP per capita)

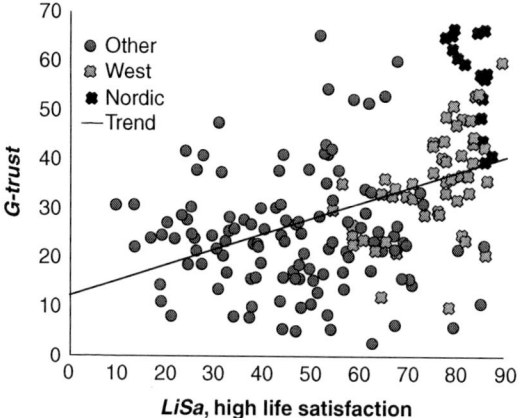

Figure 12.2 Scatter of the 187 *G-trust* and *LiSa,* high life satisfaction
Note: Life satisfaction is missing in one of the 188 polls.

Table 12.2 The six variables considered in the chapter

Variables	Definition	Source, see also netsources
G-trust	Generalized trust (see Table 12.1)	World Values Survey
Income	Natural logarithm to gdp[a]	Maddison (2003)
LiSa	High life satisfaction	World Values Survey
TI-hc	Honesty/corruption measure	Transparency International
-Gini	Minus the Gini coefficient	World Development Indicators
Polity	*Polity* index for democracy/dictatorship	Peace Research Institute, Univ. of Maryland

[a] gdp is GDP per capita. It is measured in PPP-prices.

enter in the family of models tried, but a handful of other variables have been tried as well, though with less success, see e.g. Delhey and Newton (2005) and Bjørnskov (2006).

Section 2 offers a few notes on GT-theory. Figure 12.1 suggests that the Grand Transition is associated with a change from a *G-trust* of 10 per cent to about 40 per cent, i.c. by 30 points. Section 3 discusses the time dimension: Is trust a stable factor in the society? Section 4 looks at a set of the main variables – listed in Table 12.2 – which are related to the *G-trust* and discusses causality. Section 5 discusses the problematic relations between the *G-trust* and on one side development and on the other democracy. Section 6 contains concluding remarks.

2. A note on the Grand Transition and the GT-theory

The GT is the path of a country going from a low to high income, i.e. from a poor LDC to a wealthy DC. At present the difference in gdp (in PPP prices) is about 40 times. Most socio-political and institutional variables also have large changes when countries go through the GT. Tables 12.5–12.7 below show that this is indeed the case with the six variables we consider in the chapter.

For example: The *TI-hc* index (from Transparency International) for honesty-corruption has a range of 7.9 from about 1.8 in the most corrupt country to about 9.7 in the most honest. If we compare the *TI-hc* of the 10 per cent poorest to that of the 10 per cent richest countries, they differ by almost seven points, so the GT is somehow associated with a transition of corruption of about 85 per cent of the observed range for the index, and also the correlation between income and the *TI-hc* is 0.81 in the data sample of Table 12.5. Thus the two variables are strongly connected. Paldam (2002) argues that the main direction of causality is from the GT to corruption, and these arguments are supported by the causality analysis in Gundlach and Paldam (2009).[3]

The key idea of the GT-theory is that development is a path where the whole society changes in much the same way in all countries.[4] Thus the GT consists of a set of transitions in all proportions and institutions in society. The GT is not a unique path, but rather a zone around such a path. All countries deviate somewhat, but the GT does give a lot of convergence.[5] Thus, if we compare two countries that have both gone through the full transition, they are much more alike after the transition than they were before.

Poor countries have little physical and human capital, mortality is high, people live in the countryside, religiosity and corruption are high, etc. Development changes all of that, and we speak of the urban transition, the demographic and the democratic transitions, the sectoral transition, the religious transition (or secularization), the transition of corruption, etc. Here the GT-claim is that all these transitions are basically endogenous, but if one of them does not occur, it turns into a development barrier.

Consequently, the GT is a highly simultaneous dynamic process, where everything depends upon everything else, resulting in much multicollinearity that makes it difficult to untangle causality as illustrated by a comparison of Figures 12.1 and 12.2.

GT-theory takes income/production as the most representative 'catch all' variable for the Grand Transition, and thus says that the key causal link expected is from the income level to the other variable. This is obviously a reduced form relation as it covers the full web of simultaneity. All variables that are within the GT-complex can be used to explain each other – see e.g. Table 12.5 below. From nearly all sets of three variables from that Table, it is easy to present a model where any two of them explain the third in a seemingly convincing way.

Thus the key variable is income/production. We use the natural logarithm to gdp, which is the GDP (gross domestic product) per capita, as the best income variable.

Income is ln gdp, where we use the gdp-data, from Maddison (2001, 2003).

The concept of the Grand Transition thus implies that everything depends upon everything else. The big simultaneity has caused many researchers to look for a key: something that is *primary*, in the sense that it causes development, but is not caused by development. In order to work, such a key has to be reasonably stable and must differ substantially between countries.

3. The time dimension: Are *G-trusts* stable?

The book that pushed the concept of social capital into its present status was Putnam et al. (1993).[6] Two of its main ideas are:[7]

> **Claim 1**: *Stability*: Social capital stays stable for centuries. At present we take this claim to mean that the *G-trusts* are stable.
> **Claim 2**: *Primacy*: Social capital is primary to institutional and economic development.

Putnam's first claim is that social capital came first and hereby it fills a crucial role. Claim two states that social capital is primary with respect to institutions – or at least to the effectiveness of institutions.[8]

The same claim is also made – though in a different context – by Uslaner (2002) as regards *G-trust*. Uslaner takes *G-trust* back to the 'moral' foundation of society. It is thus something basic that deserves to be primary.

To the extent that *G-trust* is a factor of production, the idea that *G-trust* changes slowly is a troubling idea, especially if it has to do with the moral foundation. Putnam's claim is that poor countries are deemed to remain poor for a long time to come due to something that was formed slowly centuries ago. Uslaner's idea leads to the conclusion that rich countries are – and maybe even deserve to be – richer *because* they have a sounder moral foundation.

Below, we show that *G-trust* does move more than enough to be endogenous, and that it is – at least in one important case – endogenous.[9]

3.1. The changes ΔG and numerical changes |ΔG|

Thus it is crucial whether a country's *G-trust* is stable. The data contains 161 changes of the *G-trust* of a country, as seen in Table 12.3. The first three columns show average changes over five years, then the next two columns show

Table 12.3 All changes ΔG and numerical changes |ΔG| calculated from the 188 polls

About	5 years			10 years			15 years	20 years
Waves	W2–W3	W3–W4	All	W1–W2	W2–W4	All	W1–W3	W1–W4
App. Years	1990–95	1995–00	5 years	1982–90	1990–00	10 years	1982–95	1982–00
Number	31	41	72	20	39	59	11	19
(A) Average ΔG	−4.49	1.10	−1.31	3.08	−3.54	−1.30	−4.50	−0.57
(B) Average |ΔG|	**5.76**	**6.73**	**6.91**	**5.44**	**7.25**	**7.39**	**5.68**	**8.74**
Fraction of |ΔG| > 10	19.4%	14.6%	16.7%	10.0%	23.1%	18.6%	18.2%	42.1%

Note: The table covers all 161 pairs of *G-trusts* for the same country that can be calculated from the 188 polls. The numbers in bold in the (B) row are shown on Figure 12.3.

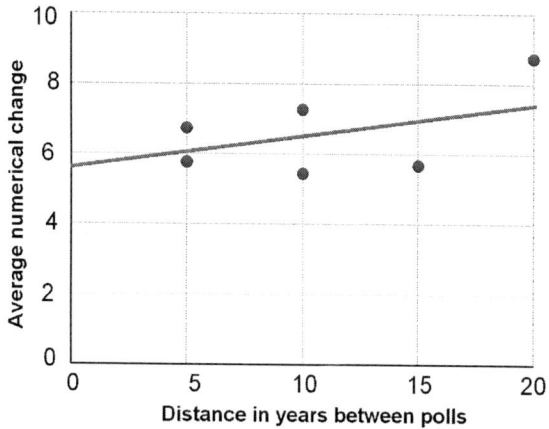

Figure 12.3   Average numerical changes |ΔG| from Table 12.3 (bold)

average changes over ten years, etc. The averages in row (A) are for the plain changes, while the averages in row (B) are for the numerical changes.

We first consider the numerical changes in row (B) of the table. Two points are immediately obvious: (1) The five-year changes are rather large. (2) The changes are not much larger as the span increases to ten, 15 and 20 years.

This suggests that a good deal of the movement is due to measurement error, which includes short-run reactions to 'random' events. Figure 12.3 gives an estimate of the orders of magnitude. The six dots are the **unshaded** averages, from Table 12.3. If the average line is weighted with the number of observations it tilts marginally upward only.

Thus Figure 12.3 suggests that the measurement error is of the order of magnitude of at least 5 percentage points:

> **Thesis 2**: The *measurement error* in national polls of the *G-trust* is about 5 points

Hence, the 'true' average movement in the *G-trust* is about 2 points over the 20 years or 0.1 points per year. This is rather modest – much as suggested by Thesis 2. But if the movement adds up over two centuries, it does reach 20 points. Note also than no less that 42 per cent of the 19 first differences that extend 20 years change more than 10 points, which is twice the likely measurement error. Consequently this measure of social capital is not stable.

If we take into account that the Grand Transition in most cases takes two to three centuries and that it is associated with a change of about 20 points in the *G-trust*, there is really nothing in these orders of magnitude that prevents the full change in the *G-trust* shown on Figure 12.1 being endogenous.

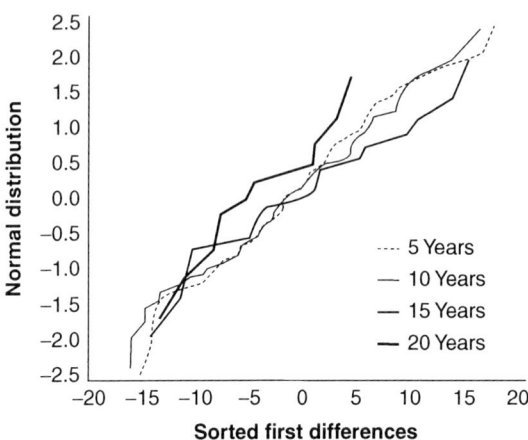

Figure 12.4   The distribution of the changes, ΔG

3.2. The distribution of the changes

With such a large measurement uncertainty, it is difficult to determine how much the results change. However, it may help to look at the absolute changes.

Figure 12.4 shows all the 161 changes drawn as four probit diagrams; i.e. for each lag length the observations are sorted and depicted with the standardized normal distribution at the vertical axis. If these observations are normally distributed, the four lines should be approximately straight – precisely as they are. However, we note that the lines for the five years' and the ten years' lag show some truncation. That is, changes are rarely larger than 15 points for five years and for ten years. Given the near-normality, we also note that the slopes of the four lines are approximately the same, so that the variance is the same. Also, the intersection with the vertical axis for the zero-change is close, so the averages are close too.

In fact, Table 12.4 shows that we are unable to reject that either pair of averages or either pair of variances are different at the 5 per cent level of significance. Hence, we know that these data show little *systematic* movement, but Figure 12.4 shows that large changes take place in the *G-trusts*. In fact, no less that 25 per cent of the observations are in excess of 1.8 times the likely measurement error (of 5 per cent). So, surely there are countries with big changes in the *G-trust*.

3.3. A large scale social experiment: The transition from socialism[10]

The period from 1982 to 2000 contains a large social experiment: the collapse of communism in East and Central Europe and the transition to a

Table 12.4 Pair-wise two-group tests for differences between averages and variances of the absolute changes, ∆G, from Table 12.3

Samples		Observations		Averages		Variance	
S1	S2	N1	N2	A1 < A2	A1 = A2	V1 < V2	V1 = V2
y5	y10	71	60	45%	91%	31%	62%
y5	y15	71	11	92%	17%	69%	62%
y5	y20	71	19	33%	66%	7%	14%
Y10	y15	60	11	91%	17%	77%	47%
Y10	y20	60	19	37%	73%	14%	28%
Y15	y20	11	19	10%	20%	10%	19%
Result should be:				<50%	<5%	<50%	<5%
Result is:				Mostly	Never	Mostly	Never

Note: Going from sample 1 of the 71 5-year changes to sample 2 of the 60 10-year changes should increase the average and its variance. The average and variance should further increase when going from the 71 5-year averages to the 11 15-year averages, etc. The predicted signs normally occur, but not always.

Western (capitalist/democratic) society. The collapse happened very fast in 1988–1990. It came unpredicted, and it caused a large U-shaped economic crisis, where the full recuperation has only taken place after 2000 in most of the countries, and is not even complete yet in some of the transition countries. It seems reasonable to treat the transition as a large, sudden, exogenous chock to the system. It is documented rather well in the WVS data, with two to three observations from 19 countries for waves two to four. However, there is only one observation from 1982, namely from Hungary, which was a unique communist country (Figure 12.5).[11]

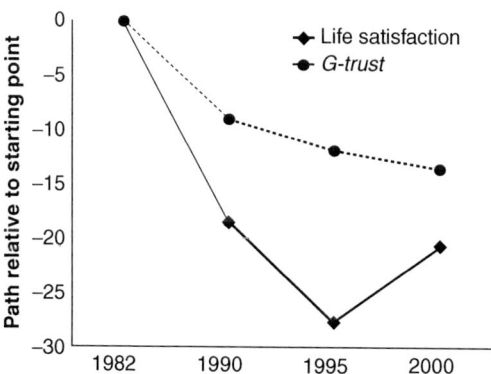

Figure 12.5 The *G-trust* and life satisfaction during the transition from communism

The figure is calculated by taking the (one) change from 1982–1990 and adding the change from 1990 to 1995 (that is for 12 countries), and finally adding the change from 1995 to 2000 (for 19 countries). So it includes all the available information, and the last two sections of the curve are reasonably well determined. 1989/90 was the year of the big political collapse and the starting year of the transition downswing, so it is unfortunate that the change out of the old system is only indicated by one observation.

It builds trust in the data that the path of the life satisfaction variable is similar to the one of the *G-trust*, though the *G-trust* moves a little less and turns a little slower. If we take these data to be representative, they show a large effect on the *G-trust* of the transition from communism. Also, we predict that (most of) the return to the previous levels of life satisfaction and trust will take place in the first decade of the century.

We know only the level of *G-trust* in one old communist country and in two Asian communist countries. However, we also have three polls for the *G-trust* in Belorussia, which is the ex-communist country that has changed the least, so perhaps we can assess that the level in the old communist block in Eastern and Central Europe was between 35 and 40. Thus the fall was about 30 per cent due to transition that generated a fall of income that peaked at about 30 per cent in the average country. This suggests a strong endogenous reaction of *G-trust* to the economy.

The greatest 'social experiment' in our data consequently shows that the *G-trust* can have large endogenous movements. Thus we are not able to say that *G-trust* is fully primary – perhaps it is not primary at all.

4. The web of connections between the *G-trust* and other variables

The research on trust has found several variables that are related to the *G-trust*. The five main ones included are, as defined in Table 12.2:

Income or production is (the natural) logarithm to gdp, as explained; *LiSa*, high life satisfaction; *TI-hc*, Transparency International's honesty/corruption index, which is scaled from 10 for full honesty to 0 for full corruption. Here, only data for the last period are available. *Gini* is the Gini coefficient (measuring the distribution of income). Here, the data has many gaps, and time series are not available. As it should be negatively correlated to the *G-trust*, the sign has been reversed, and we thus use –*Gini*. *Polity* is the *Polity* index of democracy/dictatorship. It is scaled from 10 for a perfect democracy to −10 for a perfect dictatorship. An average for the last 10 years is used.

The expected result from Grand Transition theory is that the variables contain much simultaneity, in the sense that all other variables contribute somewhat to explaining income, and the income contributes much to explaining all other variables. However, we hope to find that some variables

Table 12.5 Correlation matrix – pure cross-country

N = 80	G-trust	Income	LiSa	TI-hc	-Gini	Polity
G-trust	1	**0.38**	**0.45**	**0.49**	**0.52**	0.13
Income, Ln gdp	**0.38**	1	**0.73**	**0.81**	**0.33**	**0.71**
LiSa, High Life satisfaction	**0.45**	**0.73**	1	**0.71**	0.07	**0.46**
TI-hc, index for corruption	**0.49**	**0.81**	**0.71**	1	**0.29**	**0.57**
−1 x Gini coefficient	**0.52**	**0.33**	0.07	**0.29**	1	**0.25**
Polity index, last 10 years	0.13	**0.71**	**0.46**	**0.57**	**0.25**	1
Average correlation	0.39	0.59	0.48	0.57	0.29	0.42

Note: The bolded variables are significant at the 5 per cent level.

are only indirectly related to income. That is, if *A*, *B* and *C* are used to explain income, then *C* is not needed, if *C* is insignificant when included together with A and B, and contributes nothing to the R^2 when it is adjusted for degrees of freedom. Even if C is very significant when included without A and B. In this case we say that *A* and *B* encompass *C*.

4.1. The correlations

Table 12.5 is a correlation matrix between these variables. Due to the scaling all coefficients of correlation and thus all regression coefficients in Table 12.7 (below) should be positive.

It is satisfactory that all coefficients in the table have the positive sign predicted, and that only two are insignificant. The least significant is the one between the *Gini* and *LiSa*. This is puzzling, but not central to our argument. It is much more important for that argument that the correlation between the *G-trust* and the *Polity* index is insignificant.

Income is the variable that is most correlated to all the others, as it should be by the Grand Transition theory. The variable that has the least correlation to the others is the *Gini*. This is not unexpected given the quality of measurement for that variable, and the literature. The second least correlated coefficient is *G-trust*, which also has a large measurement problem.

The tools of causality testing demand time series of a considerable length that depend on the stochastic element in the series. Above, we have demonstrated that the *G-trust* has considerable measurement error/short-run instability, relative to the longer-run movements. As, at most, four observations are available, it is difficult to establish causality. Many of the cells in the table have been researched, and some of this research has reached agreement.

4.2. The links to income via growth

By far the most researched connections are the ones to income via growth, dealt with in Table 12.6. The effects of hundreds of variables on the growth

Table 12.6   The links to income, the central variable

(1)	(2)	Correlation	Size in % of range	(1) ⇒ (2) Via growth	Comments to growth connection	(2) ⇒ (1) GT-pattern
G-trust	Income	0.38	50%	Some	Social capital is a factor of production	Yes?
LiSa	Income	0.73	70%	No?	Perhaps a link via productivity	Yes
TI-hc	Income	0.81	85%	Weaker	Weak effect from TI ➔ investment ➔ growth	Yes
Gini	Income	0.33	50%	Dubious	Much researched, but weak results	Yes
Polity	Income	0.71	60%	Weak	Borderline significant	Yes

Note: Column (4) considers the difference between the value of the said index in the poorest 10 per cent and in the richest 10 per cent of the countries relative to the range observed for the index.

rate have been studied by a range of methods, and large scale attempts have been made to determine which of these variables have a robust impact.[12] This literature shows that a little more than ten variables have a robust effect on growth, while another five to ten are borderline robust. None of our variables are among the robust ones, but a couple are in the borderline group. These results are helpful when it comes to untangling a pattern such as the one we consider.

Consider the observation that income and democracy have a correlation of no less than 0.71. The growth literature tells us that the many attempts to find an effect of democracy on growth have only led to a weak effect, see Doucouliagos and Ulubasoglu (2008) for a new meta study covering the literature. At least ten other effects are stronger, and there is a considerable residual factor. So there is no way the causality from democracy to income can explain more than a small fraction of the correlation. Thus the large correlation has to be mainly a GT-effect, i.e. a Grand Transition effect.

This is only a reduced form conclusion, for there are a number of possible channels whereby the Grand Transition may lead to democracy. One may be a pure demand effect saying that the income elasticity of people's demand for democracy is larger than one. Another explanation goes via the vast expansion in education that is associated with the GT, etc. However, our analysis contains no education variable. This allows us to start with the causal connections from/to income as drawn on Figures 12.6 and 12.7.

Table 12.7 OLS-regressions between the six variables (N = 80)

	(1) G-trust			(2) Income		(3) LiSa		
	(a)	(b)	(c)	(a)	(b)	(a)	(b)	(c)
Constant	63.90	38.77	40.15	7.73	7.52	−92.61	−114.01	−43.93
	(2.9)	(5.9)	(6.0)	(23.7)	(27.7)	(−4.0)	(−7.0)	(−2.2)
(1) G-trust				−0.057		0.41	0.47	0.19
				(−1.2)		(3.4)	(4.4)	(1.7)
(2) Income	−3.34					11.68	14.58	9.57
	(−1.2)					(4.2)	(9.5)	(3.7)
(3) LiSa	0.34	0.29	0.32	0.016	0.015			
	(3.4)	(3.2)	(4.8)	(4.2)	(4.0)			
(4) -Gini	0.84	0.80	0.80	0.017	0.012	−0.71	−0.74	
	(5.8)	(5.7)	(5.7)	(2.4)	(2.1)	(−4.1)	(−4.4)	
(5) TI-hc	2.01	1.53		0.15	0.14	1.50		1.99
	(2.4)	(2.0)		(4.7)	(4.6)	(1.6)		(1.9)
(6) Polity	−0.67	−0.84		0.049	0.054	−0.02		
	(−2.2)	(−3.2)		(4.2)	(5.0)	(−0.1)		
R² adj	0.49	0.49	0.43	0.79	0.78	0.64	0.64	0.57

Table 12.7 (Continued)

	(4) -Gini			(5) TI-hc		(6) Polity		
	(a)	(b)	(c)	(a)	(b)	(a)	(b)	(c)
Constant	-72.18 (-5.6)	-77.62 (-8.8)	-46.13 (-23.5)	-11.26 (-4.1)	-11.67 (-6.7)	-26.08 (-3.2)	-33.57 (-7.8)	-32.00 (-7.4)
(1) G-trust	0.37 (85.8)	0.35 (5.9)	0.32 (5.4)	0.035 (2.4)	0.030 (2.5)	-0.09 (-2.2)	-0.06 (-2.0)	
(2) Income	4.39 (2.4)	5.14 (4.2)		1.54 (4.7)	1.64 (6.8)	4.00 (4.2)	4.58 (9.0)	4.20 (8.8)
(3) LiSa	-0.26 (-4.1)	-0.27 (-4.4)		0.021 (1.6)	0.023 (1.9)	-0.002 (-0.1)		
(4) -Gini				(-0.4) (-0.4)		(1.1) (1.1)		
(5) TI-hc	-0.22 (-0.4)					0.25 (0.8)		
(6) Polity	0.23 (1.1)			0.03 (0.8)				
R^2 adj	0.41	0.41	0.26	0.69	0.70	0.50	0.51	0.49

Note: The bolded coefficients are significant at the 5 per cent level. The gray cells are the ones where wrong signs appear.

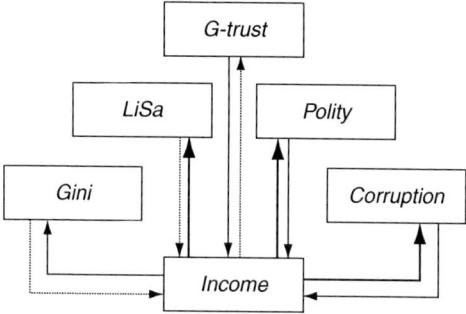

Figure 12.6 The causal links from/to income

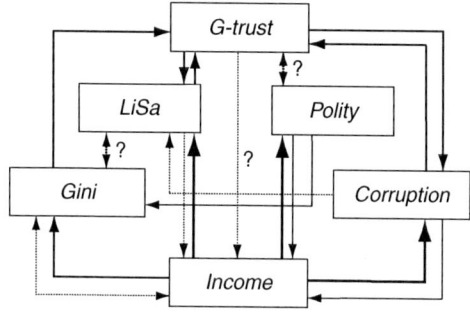

Figure 12.7 All causal links between the six variables

Income influences all the other variables, but they do in turn all influence income a little, as per the theory of the Grand Transition.

4.3. The other links: Regressions looking for encompassing

The next step is then to find the important parts of all the other causal links. In principle, all boxes may be connected to all others. In order to assess the causal direction, we should run causality tests on all connections. This is not possible for most of the links as time series of the necessary length are not available, so we have just run all the OLS-regressions between the six variables to obtain an expanded version of Table 12.5.

The regressions are run in two or three versions. Version (a) in Table 12.7 includes all six variables. Version (b) is reached by testing down; that is, first the least significant of the insignificant variables is deleted, and the regression is re-run. Then the process is repeated till only significant variables remain. Version (c) is reached by first deleting variables with wrong signs and then testing down.

4.4. Including regional/cultural country groups

Appendix Tables 12.2 and 12.3 re-run Table 12.7 with a set of five regional/cultural dummies, which are one if the country is in the group and zero otherwise. The five groups are *Western, Muslim, Oriental*, in *TraSoc* (in transition from socialism) and *Nordic*. The variable name is in italics. *Oriental* means Far Eastern, *Nordic* is the five Nordic/Scandinavian countries.

Once again the sign on the *Gini* has been reversed, so that all signs in the table should be positive. Of the 49 signs, only 13 are negative, and of these five are insignificant. So there are only $8 = 4 \times 2$ problems in the table. And they are, not surprisingly, 2×2 symmetrical, so we shall say that the said effects are *dominated* by the other variables. They are: (i) the two coefficients between *G-trust* and *Polity*, and (ii) the two coefficients between the *Gini* and *LiSa* (life satisfaction). These two sets of coefficients were the same two that had insignificant correlations in Table 12.5. So we conclude that the strong GT-correlation between all the variables have pulled them into the negative. This is what happens with high multicollinearity. In some cases it does matter if the variables with wrong signs are deleted, but in most it does not.

By and large the results are the same for the six variables covered in Tables 12.7 a and b, but in a few cases something happens. For the *G-trust* variable, we see that it is high in the *West* and in the *Orient*, and particularly high in the *Nordic* countries. Since these countries are the richest and the most democratic, it has effects on the two variables with wrong signs. The effect on *Polity* disappears, but the income effect becomes even more wrong.

The effects on income are almost unchanged, but the effect of the *Gini* disappears. Here the expected high growth in the *Orient* and the *TranSoc* countries (around the year 2000) appears. The analysis of high life satisfaction, *LiSa*, is interesting as a highly significant pattern in the regional/cultural groups appears. Three groups appear with low life satisfaction: Muslims, Orientals and, as expected, East and Central Europeans in the transition countries.

For the *Gini* it is interesting to note that when the regional/cultural variables are included, they replace the effect of income, but instead a significant effect of democracy appears, while the effect of the *Gini* on *Polity* is dubious. On the *TI-hc* variable, the regional/cultural variables replaced the *G-trust*, as *West* and *Nordic* become positive while *Transition* becomes negative. Finally, for *Polity*, most of the regional/cultural variables become significant with the expected signs, but at the same time the income variable becomes even more significant.

4.5. Summing up: The causal net

Thus we have reached the pattern of causality shown in Figure 12.7. There are still some uncertain links, which are indicated with a question mark and, of course, more variables may be included.

How much can we trust the causal directions indicated? I am fairly confident that the ones on Figure 12.6 are trustworthy. Also the causal links from the *Gini, LiSa* and *TI-hc* to *G-trust* on Figure 12.7 seem reasonably well justified.[13]

However, the two key causal relations in the policy debates on social capital both end with a question mark on the figure. Thus, they need a separate section.

5. Two dubious links: Social capital, development and democracy

Three links to *G-trust* are indicated to be dubious in Figure 12.7. We shall not discuss the dubious link between *LiSa* (high life satisfaction) and the *Gini*. The correlation is only 0.07 in Table 12.5 and has the wrong sign in all four regression tables. Thus it appears that there is no connection between *LiSa* and the *Gini*. This is certainly against the beliefs of most social reformers.

However, the really puzzling and worrying result for the policy discussions about social capital is that the two-times two links between the *G-trust* and *income* on the one side and between *G-trust* and *Polity* both appear weak and dubious in the analysis.

5.1. The links between the *G-trust* and income

We expect to find a positive connection between *income* and *G-trust*, and the correlation is 0.38 in Table 12.5 – also, it looks convincing in Figure 12.1. There is no doubt that the two variables are connected. However, the *income/G-trust* coefficients in all four regression tables have the wrong sign and some are even significant. Thus we have to conclude that the connections are indirect and more of a general GT-nature than due to direct causality. Let us look at each link.

The causality: *G-trust* → *income*.[14] A substantial literature from Putnam et al. (1993), Dasgupta and Seargeldin (2000) and, in particular, Grootaert and Bastelaer (2002) argues that social capital plays a role for development. It is easy to argue that social capital is a factor of production. Social capital – certainly trust – makes transactions faster and cheaper, it reduces monitoring costs, etc.

Above, Thesis 2 and Thesis 3 claim that *G-trust* is *the* primary factor that explains development. This should give a clear causal link from the *G-trust* to income, but our finding is that the link is encompassed by other links. It must mean that the causal link operates through other variables. Thus, it is difficult to believe that social capital is *the* primary factor for development we are all looking for. It rather appears as another endogenous factor in the complex causal net of the Grand Transition. However, this does not mean that it is not an important variable to study.

The causality: *income* ➜ *G-trust*. Here it appears that the link goes via other variables, and has a typical GT-effect. It is interesting that the link goes via two seemingly independent variables, the *Gini* and *LiSa*, so that *income* ➜ *Gini* ➜ *G-trust* and *income* ➜ *LiSa* ➜ *G-trust*. As the two intermediate variables are independent, we are dealing with a complex web where the influence of additional variables is likely to be involved.

5.2. The links between the *G-trust* and *Polity*, the degree of democracy

We then turn to the links between *G-trust* and *Polity*. Here the correlation is only 0.13 in Table 12.5, and Figure 12.8 shows a picture corresponding to Figures 12.1 and 12.2. It looks much less convincing. Also, it is strange that the line through *Other* countries has a negative slope, while the line through all points (not included) has almost the same slope, but positive. Neither slope is significant. Also, the *Polity/G-trust* coefficients in all four regression tables have wrong signs and some are significant.

The causality: *G-trust* ➜ *Polity*. A considerable literature discusses social capital as an important prerequisite for democracy, in particular see Deth et al. (2002). Also, many development aid agencies argue that it is important for development to build civic society and social capital. Thus we expect a positive link from *Polity* to *G-trust*. Our findings suggest that this link must be indirect and weak.

The causality: *Polity* ➜ *G-trust*. It is one of the cornerstones in the argument in Putnam et al. (1993) that the difference in social capital in the north and south of Italy is due to the political history of the two parts of the country in the previous 500 years. Especially the dictatorship in the kingdom of

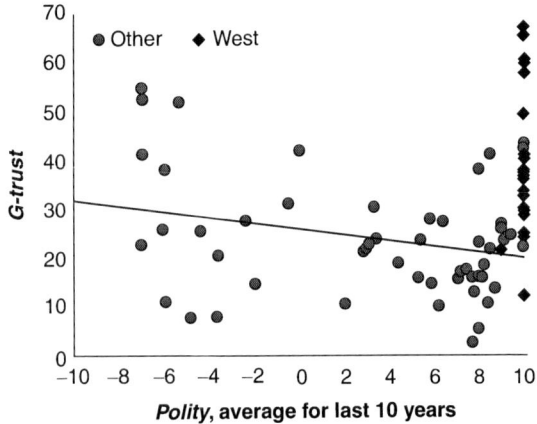

Figure 12.8   Scatter of the 80 *G-trust* and the *Polity* index for the degree of democracy

the two Sicilies in the south prevented the development of social capital, while the north of Italy had a complex set of regimes that were often less oppressive, and hence permitted the building of social capital.

This idea has been developed in Paldam and Svendsen (2000, 2002) to explain the difference between West and East Europe, due to the democratic history of the West and the communist dictatorship in the East. This led to the dictatorship theory of social capital: that dictatorial regimes fear voluntary cooperation between their citizens and thus try to bring such cooperation under the control of the political system. Also, it is well known that many dictators use fear as a deliberate instrument.

Thus, I expected to find a clear connection from *Polity* to *G-trust*. However, this did not work.[15] Part of the reason may be that the transition from communism in East and Central Europe was associated with a rather large depression, a chaotic period of rent grabbing, and a wave of high inflation that caused a large drop in life satisfaction. So perhaps something may still appear in a longer perspective.

6. Conclusion: The trust transition

This chapter is a mixture of a survey and a basic exposition of the macro data on generalized trust, *G-trust*. It covers only one of the main series used to measure social capital. However, a great deal of data has been collected on this variable. The chapter has looked at the dynamics of the measured *G-trusts*, and at its relation to five other series.

The organizing framework is the theory/empirics of the Grand Transition, which sees the process of development as a broad transition of all socio-political and economic variables in society. All these transitions add up to the Grand Transition. It is not helpful to say that everything depends on everything else, so the literature on development has searched for *the* key to development: something that is primary to all other factors. Since Putnam et al. (1993) it has been frequently claimed that social capital is that key.

It is clear from the results in the chapter that the data show a transition from low trust in poor societies to high trust in rich societies. Thus, there is a transition of trust. The chapter discusses how the transition of trust relates to development.

The chapter demonstrates that the measures of *G-trust* have a considerable element of measurement error, and though it normally changes slowly it does change enough so that it is perfectly possible that the trust transition is fully endogenous. Thus, the Putnam claim that social capital is a deep constant in society and hence primary does not appear to hold as regards the *G-trusts*.

In the analysis of the relation between generalized trust and other variables, a number of connections were found strongly significant. The main variables that appear to be causal to social capital are the *Gini* and *LiSa* (high life satisfaction), but corruption also matters. My interpretation of the literature (including my own research) is that these variables all have income as a key causal factor. Thus it is clear that *G-trust* enters into the complex.

So whereas *G-trust* is an interesting variable that plays a role in the Grand Transition, it is hardly the key causal factor for the transition.

Acknowldegements

The paper on which this chapter is based has been presented at the workshop and summer school on 'Social Capital, Corporate Social Responsibility and Sustainable Economic Development'. I am grateful to the discussants, especially to Giacomo Degli Antoni, Leonardo Becchetti and Felix Roth. I have also benefited from discussions with Gert Tinggaard Svendsen and Christian Bjørnskov. A short version is published as Paldam (2009).

Appendix Table 12.1 All *G-trusts* in the World Values Survey – first four waves

	Country	1982	1990	1995	2000
1	Albania			27.0	24.4
2	Algeria	26.1	23.3		11.2
3	Argentina			17.6	15.9
4	Armenia			24.7	
5	Australia	48.2		40.1	
6	Austria		31.8		33.4
7	Azerbaijan			20.5	
8	Bangladesh			20.9	23.5
9	Belarus		25.5	24.1	41.9
10	Belgium	29.2	33.5		29.2
11	Bosnia			28.3	15.8
12	Brazil		6.5	2.8	
13	Bulgaria		30.4	28.6	26.8
14	Canada	48.5	53.1		37.0
15	Chile		22.7	21.4	23.0
16	China		60.3	52.3	54.5
17	Colombia			10.8	
18	Croatia			25.1	20.5
19	Czech Re		27.4	28.5	24.6
20	Denmark	52.7	57.7		66.5
21	Dominican Re		19.8	26.5	
22	Egypt		30.8		37.9

	Country	1982	1990	1995	2000
23	El Salvador			14.6	23.5
24	Estonia		27.6	21.5	57.4
25	Finland		62.7	48.8	57.4
26	France	24.8	22.8		21.4
27	Georgia			18.7	
28	Germany	32.3	32.9	33.3	37.5
29	Greece				23.7
30	Hungary	33.6	24.6	22.7	22.4
31	Iceland	39.8	43.6		41.1
32	India		35.4	37.9	41.0
33	Indonesia				51.6
34	Iran				65.4
35	Iraq				47.6
36	Ireland	41.1	47.4		36.0
37	Israel	26.8			23.5
38	Italy	41.5	35.3		32.6
39	Japan		41.7	42.3	43.1
40	Jordan				27.7
41	Korea S	38.0	34.2	30.3	27.3
42	Kyrgyzstan				16.7
43	Latvia		19.8	24.7	17.1
44	Lithuania		30.8	21.9	25.9

Appendix Table 12.1 (Continued)

	Country	1982	1990	1995	2000		Country	1982	1990	1995	2000
45	Luxemburg				24.8	66	Slovakia		22.0	27.0	15.9
46	Macedonia			8.2	13.7	67	Slovenia		17.4	15.5	21.7
47	Malta		23.8		20.8	68	South Africa		29.1	15.9	13.1
48	Mexico		33.5	31.2	21.8	69	Spain	35.1	34.2	29.7	36.3
49	Moldova			22.2	14.6	70	Sweden	56.7	66.1	59.7	66.3
50	Morocco				22.8	71	Switzerland		42.6	37.0	
51	Netherlands	44.8	53.5		60.1	72	Taiwan			38.2	
52	New Zealand			49.1		73	Tanzania				8.1
53	Nigeria		23.2	17.3	25.6	74	Turkey		10.1	5.5	16.0
54	Norway	60.9	65.1	65.3		75	Uganda				7.8
55	Pakistan			18.8	30.8	76	UK	43.1	43.7	29.6	28.9
56	Peru			5.0	10.7	77	Ukraine			31.0	27.8
57	Philippines			5.5	8.6	78	Ulster	44.0	43.6		39.5
58	Poland		31.8	17.9	18.4	79	Uruguay			21.6	18.4
59	Portugal		21.7		12.3	80	USA	40.5	51.1	35.9	36.3
60	Puerto Rico			6.0	22.6	81	Venezuela			13.8	15.9
61	Romania		16.1	18.7	10.1	82	Vietnam				41.1
62	Russia		37.5	23.9	24.0	83	Zimbabwe				11.2
63	Saudi Arabia				53.0		Number	21	43	54	70
64	Serbia			30.2	25.8		Average	38.9	34.8	25.8	25.8
65	Singapore				14.7		Standard deviation	11.5	14.5	13.2	14.7

Note: Every poll in the WVS includes this item. The list thus also covers the 188 pools of the WVS data set.

Appendix Table 12.2 OLS-regressions with regional/cultural dummies (N = 80)

	(1) G-trust			(2) Income		(3) LiSa		
	(a)	(b)	(c)	(a)	(b)	(a)	(b)	(c)
Constant	56.90 (2.6)	66.39 (3.9)	33.57 (5.6)	6.85 (17.3)	6.39 (31.1)	−88.01 (−3.8)	−85.99 (−4.3)	−35.65 (−2.6)
Western	10.06 (2.1)	8.40 (2.1)		0.27 (1.4)		5.71 (1.1)		
Muslim	6.34 (1.3)			0.44 (2.2)	0.42 (2.3)	−12.45 (−2.3)	−14.67 (−3.0)	−14.32 (−3.0)
Orient	15.75 (3.3)	15.55 (3.9)	11.94 (3.2)	0.73 (4.0)	0.60 (3.9)	−9.93 (−1.8)	−13.38 (−3.0)	−8.60 (−2.0)
Transition	4.91 (1.2)			0.40 (2.7)	0.40 (3.2)	−10.20 (−2.4)	−12.28 (−3.6)	−15.20 (−4.9)
Nordic	17.47 (3.5)	18.03 (3.9)	19.56 (4.2)	−0.30 (−1.4)	−0.39 (−2.2)	6.25 (1.1)		
(1) G-trust				−0.01 (−1.4)		0.32 (2.5)	0.39 (3.8)	0.31 (3.3)
(2) Income	−4.31 (−1.4)	−4.19 (−2.1)				14.40 (5.1)	14.32 (7.0)	10.09 (6.4)
(3) LiSa	0.26 (2.5)	0.25 (2.5)	0.23 (3.6)	0.019 (5.1)	0.019 (5.4)			
(4) -Gini	0.42 (2.4)	0.54 (3.6)	0.55 (4.2)	0.0065 (0.9)		−0.48 (−2.4)	−0.38 (−2.1)	
(5) TI-hc	0.79 (0.9)			0.16 (4.9)	0.18 (6.3)	−0.73 (−0.7)		
(6) Polity	−0.21 (−0.6)			0.065 (5.9)	0.071 (6.9)	−0.73 (−2.0)	−0.74 (−2.1)	
R² adj	0.59	0.58	0.56	0.84	0.83	0.71	0.71	0.67

Note: Corresponds to top half of Table 12.7.

354

Appendix Table 12.3 OLS-regressions with regional/cultural dummies (N = 80)

	(4) -Gini			(5) TI-hc		(6) Polity		
	(a)	(b)	(c)	(a)	(b)	(a)	(b)	(c)
Constant	-55.49	-44.54	-52.41	-10.09	-7.91	-28.67	-31.86	-24.52
	(-4.2)	(-13.2)	(-26.2)	(-3.7)	(-4.5)	(-3.8)	(-7.2)	(-4.0)
Western	10.45	10.75	8.54	1.35	1.38	-1.11		-2.82
	(3.6)	(4.3)	(3.4)	(2.2)	(3.1)	(-0.6)		(-1.8)
Muslim	8.25	9.07	10.56	-0.46		-5.82	-5.07	-5.27
	(2.6)	(3.1)	(3.6)	(-0.7)		(-3.5)	(-3.3)	(-3.2)
Orient	4.95	6.11	4.92	-0.25		-6.69	-6.44	-7.17
	(1.5)	(2.2)	(1.8)	(-0.4)		(-4.1)	(-5.0)	(-4.8)
Transition	9.98	10.82	12.31	-0.82	-0.71	-3.41	-2.23	-2.62
	(4.4)	(5.2)	(6.2)	(-1.6)	(-2.0)	(-2.5)	(-2.1)	(-2.0)
Nordic	6.50	5.88		1.64	1.75	0.85		
	(1.9)	(1.8)		(2.5)	(3.3)	(0.4)		
(1) G-trust	0.17	0.16	0.20	0.013		-0.027		
	(2.4)	(2.3)	(3.2)	(0.9)		(-0.6)		
(2) Income	1.70			1.65	1.42	5.21	4.99	4.14
	(0.9)			(4.9)	(6.9)	(5.9)	(8.4)	(6.6)
(3) LiSa	-0.16	-0.14		-0.010		-0.08	-0.10	
	(-2.4)	(-2.5)		(-0.7)		(-2.0)	(-2.9)	
(4) -Gini				-0.02		0.10		0.11
				(-0.6)		(1.5)		(1.9)
(5) TI-hc	-0.38					-0.26		
	(-0.6)					(-0.8)		
(6) Polity	0.31	0.41	0.39	-0.03				
	(1.5)	(2.6)	(2.4)	(-0.8)				
R² adj	0.55	0.56	0.52	0.76	0.77	0.63	0.64	0.61

Note: Corresponds to bottom half of Table 12.7.

Notes

1. See Fukuyama (1995). The present chapter does not discuss the definitions of social capital, see Paldam (2000).
2. For easy replicability the WV-survey data are used throughout this chapter. The data are documented in Inglehart et al. (1998, 2004). I used the full data set as available from http://www.worldvaluessurvey.org.
3. Some other authors claim that the reverse causality dominates, see e.g. Lambsdorff (2007). People who have worked with these things have not yet managed to agree on the causal structure explaining the strong correlation.
4. See Paldam and Gundlach (2008) for a discussion of GT-theory, and the relation between this theory and the main alternative, the Primacy of Institutions theory.
5. We do not observe convergence in cross-country samples because countries are at very different stages in the GT.
6. Putnam's definition of social capital is network density, though he discusses its relation to trust. Thesis 3 is defended in Helliwell and Putnam (1995).
7. I should state that this is the standard interpretation of Putman's book, and that it does not speak of *G-trust*, but of network density. Also, Putnam (2000) describes a large fall in social capital in the US over a couple of decades.
8. Consequently, Putnam's claim encompasses the *primacy of institutions hypothesis* claim by Acemoglu, Johnson and Robinson (see 2005).
9. The argument contradicts the results cited in Uslaner (2002) and Bjørnskov (2009) arguing the trust is primary.
10. This subsection uses the term *transition* for the transition from socialism.
11. Hungary was the communist country that was allowed the most market institutions and the most contacts with the West; it also had a relatively easy transition to a market system.
12. See Doppelhofer, Miller and Sala-i-Martin (2004) and Sturm and Haan (2005).
13. The significant coefficient to the *Gini* is common in this research, see e.g. Uslaner (2004) and Leigh (2006).
14. See also Berggren, Elinder and Jordahl (2007) for a study of the robustness of the relation.
15. An alternative way to study this connection is to analyze the relation between *G-trust* and economic freedom directly, as done by Berggren and Jordahl (2006), who do find considerable correlation.

References A

D. Acemoglu, S. Johnson and J. Robinson (2005) 'Institutions as the fundamental cause of long-run growth', in P. Aghion and S. Durlauf (eds), *Handbook of Economic Growth* (Amsterdam: North-Holland), pp. 385–472.

P. Aghion and S. Durlauf (eds) (2005) *Handbook of Economic Growth* (Amsterdam: North-Holland).

N. Berggren, M. Elinder and H. Jordahl (2007) *Trust and Growth: A Shaky Relationship*, IFN Working Paper No. 705, Stockholm, Sweden.

N. Berggren and H. Jordahl (2006) 'Free to trust: Economic freedom and social capital', *Kyklos*, 59, 141–169.

C. Bjørnskov (2006) 'Determinants of generalized trust: A cross-country comparison', *Public Choice*, 130, 1–21.

C. Bjørnskov (2009) 'Economic growth' Cpt 20, 337-53, in G. L. H. Svendsen and G. T. Svendsen (eds), *Handbook of Social Capital. The Troika of Sociology, Political Science and Economics* (Cheltenham: Edward Elgar).

P. Dasgupta and I. Serageldin (eds) (2000) *Social Capital: A Multifaceted Perspective* (Washington, DC: World Bank).

J. Delhany and K. Newton (2005) 'Predicting cross-national levels of social trust: Global pattern or Nordic exceptionalism?', *European Sociological Review*, 21, 311–327.

J. W. V. Deth, M. Maraffi, K. Newton and P. F. Whiteley (eds) (2002) *Social Capital and European Democracy* (Abingdon: Routledge).

G. Doppelhofer, R. I. Miller and X. Sala-i-Martin (2004) 'Determinants of long-term growth: A Bayesian Averaging of Classical Estimates (BACE) approach', *American Economic Review*, 94, 813–835.

H. Doucouliagos and M. Ulubasoglu (2008) 'Democracy and economic growth: A meta-analysis', *American Journal of Political Science*, 52, 61–83.

B. S. Frey and A. Stutzer (2002) *Happiness and Economics: How the Economy and Institutions Affect Human Well-being* (Princeton, N.J.: Princeton UP).

F. Fukuyama (1995) *Trust* (New York: Simon and Schuster/Free Press).

C. Grootaert and T. V. Bastelaer (eds) (2002) *The Role of Social Capital in Development* (Cambridge, UK: Cambridge UP).

E. Gundlach and M. Paldam (2009) 'Farewell primacy. The political system and the economy', *European Journal of Political Economy*, 25, 340–354.

J. F. Helliwell and R. Putnam (1995) 'Economic growth and social capital in Italy', *Eastern Economic Journal*, 21, 295–307.

R. Inglehart, M. Basáñez, J. Díez-Medrano, L. Halman and R. Luijks (eds) (2004) *Human Beliefs and Values. A Cross-Cultural Sourcebook Based on the 1999–2002 Values Survey* (México, DF: Siglo XXI Editiones).

R. Inglehart, M. Basáñez, M. and A. Moreno (eds) (1998) *Human Values and Beliefs. A Cross-Cultural Sourcebook* (Ann Arbor, M. I.: University of Michigan Press).

J. G. Lambsdorff (2007) *The Institutional Economics of Corruption and Reform* (Cambridge, UK: Cambridge UP).

A. Leigh (2006) 'Does equality lead to fraternity?', *Economics Letters*, 93, 121–125.

A. Maddison (2001) *The World Economy: A Millennial Perspective* (Paris: OECD).

A. Maddison (2003) *The World Economy: Historical Statistics* (Paris: OECD).

M.Paldam (2000) 'Social capital: one or many?', *Journal of Economic Surveys*, 14, 629–653.

M. Paldam (2002) 'The big pattern of corruption. Economics, culture and the seesaw dynamics', *European Journal of Political Economy*, 18, 215–240.

M. Paldam (2009) 'The macro perspective on generalized trust', in G. L. H. Svendsen and G. T. Svendsen (eds), *Handbook of Social Capital. The Troika of Sociology, Political Science and Economics* (Cheltenham: Edward Elgar), pp. 354–375.

M. Paldam and E. Gundlach (2008) 'Two views on institutions and development: The grand transition vs the primacy of institutions', *Kyklos*, 61, 65–100.

M. Paldam and G. T. Svendsen (2000) 'An essay on social capital: Looking for the fire behind the smoke', *European Journal of Political Economy*, 16, 339–366.

M. Paldam, G. T. Svendsen (2002) 'Missing social capital and the transition in Eastern Europe', *Journal for Institutional Innovation, Development and Transition (IB Review)*, 5, 21–34.

R. D. Putnam, R. Leonardi and R. Y. Nanetti (1993) *Making Democracy Work. Civic Traditions in Modern Italy* (Princeton, NJ: Princeton University Press).

R. D. Putnam (2000) *Bowling Alone: The Collapse and Revival of American Community* (New York: Simon & Schuster).

J.-E. Sturm and J. D. Haan (2005) 'Determinants of long-term growth: New results applying robust estimation and extreme bounds analysis', *Empirical Economics*, 30, 597–617.

G. L. H. Svendsen and G. T. Svendsen (eds) (2009), *Handbook of Social Capital. The Troika of Sociology, Political Science and Economics* (Cheltenham: Edward Elgar).

E. M. Uslaner (2002) *The Moral Foundation of Trust* (Cambridge UK and New York: Cambridge UP).

References B: Net links

Author's working papers are at: http://www.martin.paldam.dk

Maddison's data set is at: http://www.ggdc.net/maddison/

Polity is at: http://www.cidcm.umd.edu/inscr/polity

Transparency International is at: http://www.transparency.org/

World Values Survey is available from: http://www.worldvaluessurvey.org

World Development Indicators are at: http://devdata.worldbank.org/dataonline/

13
The Local Path to Sustainable Development: Social Capital in Naples

Raffaella Nanetti, Robert Leonardi and Catalina Holguin

1. Introduction: a changed context

When the analyses and conclusions which now inform this chapter were first presented as preliminary findings of an ongoing research project in 2007[1] the world was a very different place indeed than it is today. Yet, the introduction to the 2007 paper is still valid in the way in which it profiled the transformative trends of the world economy over the previous two decades and, at the same time, cautioned about them. Thus, it was pointed out, that driven by accelerating technological and communication innovations the rapidity and scale of economic development and social change around the world had been and still were astounding. Developed as well as developing countries were profoundly affected, as their economies and cities were pulled directly into multiple and denser networks of external relationships which defined this phase of globalization, fuelled by its aim of achieving ever higher levels of growth (Lechner and Boli 2004; Sassen 1998; Streeten 2001; Taylor 2006). Only marginalized countries, it was said, were left partially unscathed by this process of change, although they too often had to pay a high cost of dependency, particularly in terms of increased outflows of human capital and natural resources toward the world's core areas (Brecher and Costello 1994; Clark 1996; Przeworski 1992; Smith 1984).

The introduction underlined how, in those two decades, the policy paradigm of growth had overtaken the paradigm of development in most of the world, the People's Republic of China being the exemplary and macroscopic example. However, the paper warned that the territorial significance and sustainability of gains made by those advanced countries where more comprehensive development policies had been adopted were also threatened by change. Competition principles and economic forces hetero-directed and controlled were seen as profoundly influencing the future prosperity and cohesiveness of developed countries, more than ever before, so that no economic and social gains could be considered permanent. Rather, countries' improvements in their safety nets and increases in their stocks of 'public goods' were under threat, while domestic policies to counter the trend were limited in their impact.

Two years later, in 2009, no lesser contextual change than a worldwide economic crisis of great proportion has abruptly materialized, one which in its causes is compared by many to the Great Depression. It started in the core countries, the United States first, with the unravelling of their financial sector, which had prospered to oversized proportions through the creation and sale of mortgage-backed securities, facilitated by the loosening of regulations and controls over capital mobility. From them, the financial crisis – and related credit crunch – has expanded to the rest of the world's financial system and then, very rapidly, to the world's 'real economy', where it has devastated the construction, car manufacturing and consumer products industries, causing the loss of millions of jobs and escalating unemployment. As we write, this has forced many governments into action, borrowing heavily to fund 'stimulus' packages which can inject capital into their stalled and shrinking economies and hoping that the downward spiral can thus be reversed. No movement, so far, has been observed in the realm of adopting elements of a new international system of governance for the world's economy, save for the stated acknowledgement by several national leaders that countries' cooperation and financial market regulation are priority principles.

An implication of the world economic crisis is the compelling reflection which it requires on two levels: ethics and policy responses. On the level of ethics, many ask who are those to carry the moral responsibility for this crisis and how should their behavior change? Were they the politicians who pushed through neoliberal tenets of deregulation, bankers who devised risky financial products, financial institutions operating on maximum short-term rewards, investors eager to accrue such gains, regulators who failed to regulate, consumers who took on too much debt? On the policy response level of the debate, it is asked: what are the macro and micro policies that need to be put in place to begin to counter the crisis? What makes development sustainable rather than haphazard and wasteful? The content of this book could not be more important and timely, in terms of the contribution it provides to both aspects of the ongoing debate.

The essence of our chapter is to concentrate on a policy path to sustainable development that incorporates a clear ethical dimension provided by the community orientation proper of the concept of social capital. To this end, we begin with a discussion of the changing policy paradigm in the developed countries, as they have been moving from 'growth'-based policies to 'development'-based policies. In the pre-crisis period, this move meant to face up to the challenge that globalization posed to their prosperity, while in the current crisis they are challenged to prove the validity of their sustainable paths to development. We then focus on the concept of social capital, revisiting and updating the debate on it, most of all on the relationship between an engaged civil society and its institutions, and ultimately drawing out the nexus between social capital and development outcomes.

Central to this discussion is the 'how' question, that is which strategies are apt to promote the increase in the stock of social capital in a particular community and yield sustainable development outcomes. Our work focuses on this very issue by introducing a significant example of a social capital building strategy aimed at development, through the case study of the multi-year, integrated development program in Naples' peripheral neighborhood of Pianura. The experimental program, co-financed by the city of Naples and the European Commission, has been empirically monitored throughout the period and its development outcomes have been measured, together with the variations in the levels of social capital in Pianura and the city at large. The empirical evidence shows the ignition of a process of meaningful civic society participation in planning, a responsive learning curve impacting on institutional performance, and a social climate more suitable to private investments.

2. The paradigm of sustainable development

The process of worldwide profound economic and social transformation, which the relevant literature of the last few decades has identified as a new historical wave of globalization,[2] is underpinned by a neoliberal economic philosophy that translates into principles of free-trade, capital mobility, fiscal discipline and decreased role for the state, a reduced role of fiscal policy, and reliance on monetary policy to control inflation. Conceptually first and then widely adopted, the free-trade model erupted onto the world scene in the 1980s, prompted by the urgency to find a new and effective path to growth. It follows that the free-trade model is predicated on the objective of generating higher levels of growth for countries, which in turn would or could trickle down and diffuse throughout their sub-national territorial communities and social groups (Carnoy 1993; Castells 1993; Peet and Hartwick 1999; Przeworski 1992). Therefore, the model is not directly concerned with issues of growth distribution, so that in this as well as other regards, it supplants the Keynesian economic model of the post-war period, which is associated with the creation of welfare state policies and with principles of cohesion, particularly in the developed countries of Western Europe.

One response around the world to the advance of this wave of globalization has been to give way to the emergence of multi-state regional economic blocs, adopting common rules in trading with the rest of the world and similar principles in pursuing growth. Beyond NAFTA, ASEAN, MERCOSUR and the European Union (EU), the phenomenon of regional aggregative blocs has been expanding to Africa and other parts of Latin America. But, while this institutional behavioral response appears to be the same in its prompting, it is instead significantly different in terms of the content of the policies adopted by different blocs. We have argued forcefully (Leonardi 2005; Leonardi and Nanetti 2008; Nanetti and Leonardi 2002) that the case of the European Union is most significant in this regard, because it is the only regional bloc that has been creating an alternative model, focused on 'development', to the free-trade model, focused on 'growth', that has prevailed elsewhere.[3]

In contrast to growth, which is measured by aggregate wealth creation, development is a complex, multidimensional concept that has come onto its own in the last couple of decades,[4] and has profoundly impacted our understanding of people's quality of life, of what private behaviors contribute to it, and of what public policies are necessary to insure it and maintain it (Nanetti 1988; Woolcock 1998; World Bank 2002). Since the 1990s particularly there has been a significant shift by the major international development organizations in their approach to the reduction of poverty and the pursuit of growth, moving toward more comprehensive strategies, which incorporate human resources development policies and the recognition of the importance of communities, institutions and social relations.[5] Distilling from the growing development literature, we articulate the following definition of the concept (Leonardi and Nanetti 2008). Development is:

- Politically a *project*, underpinned by its own policy commitment, as much as growth creation is a political project;
- Territorially *significant*, in that it seeks to add value and not consume the environmental assets of a territory;
- Generationally *important*, since it aims for longitudinal sustainability;
- Territorially *specific*, because it acknowledges that every territory (locus) has its own significant and multiple assets to build upon, in the pursuit of improved living conditions;
- Comprehensively *targeted*, in that it draws on human, cultural, natural, historical and economic-financial assets;
- Longitudinally *pursued*, for it is a process unfolding through time;
- Normatively *guided*, by principles and rules to insure convergence of private and public efforts;
- Individually *accepted*, as the vision of development is to be shared by citizens;
- Socially *inclusive*, in that it pursues the improvement in the living conditions of all people across the territory;
- Socially *acted upon*, because the project of development is to be contributed to by organized social actors.

3. Social capital in development: concepts and strategies

Social capital is a concept that has emerged in the social science literature in a powerful manner over the last couple of decades. On the heels of
Coleman's classic conceptual piece (Coleman 1988) and of Putnam, Leonardi
and Nanetti's empirical and longitudinal study that extracted and opera-
tionalized the notion of social capital as a collective asset (Putnam et al.
1993), significant theoretical and methodological work has been done on
the refining of the concept and the selection of indicators and measures, as
well as comparative work to measure the levels of social capital in different territorial contexts (Inkeles 2000; Lyberaki and Paraskevopoulos 2002;
Narayan and Cassidy 2001; Paraskevopolous et al. 2006). Nevertheless, no
other longitudinal study has been carried out to challenge the key findings of the Italian study, whereby social capital was empirically uncovered.
In relation to the investigation of 'institutional performance', social capital
was found to have three necessary dimensions that enhance the efficiency
of society because they facilitate coordinated action, increase its impact
on policy, and produce relevant outcomes and public 'goods' (Leonardi
1995).[6]

Diffused social trust is the dimension of social capital that expresses the
widespread and mutual confidence in others, on the part of people not
related by family ties. Therefore, diffused social trust, when present, is
evidenced across different spheres of people's lives, in multiple societal relationships such as those among neighbors, between vendors and customers,
between the electorate and politicians, or between students and teachers.

Solidarity norms of reciprocity are the dimension of social capital underlining the extent to which, within a society, normative principles of equality
and fairness are valued, rooted and shared by the members. When solidarity
norms prevail, they underpin an inclusive and common vision of societal
improvement benefiting all, and balance an individualistic set of norms that
are also present in society.

Engaged associational behavior is the dimension of social capital that establishes the capacity of people to act in a concerted fashion in the public realm,
on the basis of the solidarity norms that they share as members of that
society. When social and civic engagement occurs in society, it facilitates
the formulation and adoption of policies in pursuit of a common vision of
development.

All three dimensions are *conditio sine qua non* for sustained institutional
performance, including public policy formulation and implementation in
support of private investment. The existence of social networks, attitudes
of reciprocity, solidarity and cooperation reinforce the efficiency of markets
and contribute to the improvement of institutional performance, ultimately
leading to higher economic and social development. Within the fields of
development planning and public policy particularly, studies conducted in

both rural and urban settings concur in the view that developed countries and regions benefit from higher levels of social capital as a collective asset than underdeveloped areas of the world (Bebbington 1997; Grootaert 1998, 1999; Narayan 1999).

A key question asked in policy and academic circles, since the concept of social capital has entered the policy-making arena with force, has been 'how to build it', when and where social capital is in short supply (Ostrom 1996; Gittel and Vidal 1998; Nanetti and Leonardi 2002). The debate on social capital generation has seen the prevalence in the development and public policy fields of the thesis that social capital stocks are not pre-determined by the communities' history but can be augmented by inclusive public policies and a participatory governance style (Harding 2005; John 2001; Skocpol 1995, 1996; Woolcock and Narayan 2000). Ultimately, how to generate social capital in different communities is also an empirical question, whose answer, or more appropriately answers, are to be found through empirical *trial and error* approaches.

Conceptually, we have articulated a preliminary taxonomy of 'social capital building strategies', focusing on the element of *leadership* and drawing from our own work as well as from the literature[7] to identify different sources of strategic initiative, modalities of action and continuity of commitment which may be effective in different communities:

- *Institutional/political leadership*: examples range from 'trust building measures' in the Middle East, to project-based trust building measures in Pianura, Naples.
- *Religious leadership*: examples include interfaith communication initiatives and the essential role of parishes in civic engagement in Pianura, Naples.
- *Secular/civil society leadership*: examples are partnerships between the Soros Foundation and local NGOs in the Balkans, and trade unions' and parents associations' role in Pianura, Naples.
- *Economic/institutional leadership*: examples include 'economic capacity building' projects by the sustainable development unit of the World Bank in Kosovo and East Timor, and project building capacity in Borgo Orefici, Naples.

4. The local path to sustainable development: Naples' social capital building strategy in Pianura

The EU and development planning in Naples

The 1988 reform of the European Community's Structural Funds culminated a long period of gestation, characterized by trial and error experimentation with development approaches that dated back to the creation in 1975 of the principal fund, the European Regional Development Fund. Adopting the principle of geographically targeting development resources where they are mostly needed,[8] the reform placed at its center the newly defined concept of *'integrated development'*. It was a multidimensional notion, based on the interconnection between its economic and social defining elements, which was to substitute what previously had been a sectoral approach to development. Therefore, the goals and objectives of any Commission-sponsored development program had to be mutually reinforcing across sectors to create synergies of impact, and had to avoid working at cross purposes from one sector to another. Operationally, it followed that such objectives would yield a program of integrated measures, whereby the 'outputs' of one measure would contribute to more than one development outcome. The reform also provided the basis for a new, integrated approach to funding, so that the three Structural Funds could contribute to the whole of the program budget, rather than to isolated parts.

Likewise, the reform changed the temporal horizon of development planning, moving it from a short- to a *medium-term perspective*, by adopting planning cycles stretching over several years, the current one being 2007–2013. The change in time perspective of the planning programs was accompanied by a redefinition of who should be involved in decision-making and implementation. An increase in the number of participants became mandatory, together with partnerships cutting across vertical institutional boundaries and sectoral boundaries, which traditionally had separated the public institutional and the private sector spheres. In this manner, the principle was established that a partnership between the public and private spheres had to be encouraged in EU-funded programs. Wherever possible, this principle extended to the private sector sharing in the responsibility of contributing to the overall development budget, thereby building further on the principle of 'additionality', which had already required the co-financing of EU programs on the part of national and sub-national governments. Finally, the reform incorporated into the development planning process the 'accountability of impact' principle, by mandating both *ex ante* and *ex post* evaluations in addition to the monitoring of the implementation of measures (Nanetti 1990).

In Italy, the 1988 reform provided new development opportunities, particularly for the country's less developed – or Objective 1 – areas: the regions and cities of the south. The two main funding sources for regional and local government programs were those provided by the 5-year development plans of the Community Support Frameworks (CSF) and the Commission's Community Initiatives based on the Article 10 provisions of the reform, designed to stimulate networking among local and regional governments across national borders. The first development cycle, 1989–1993, was not satisfactorily implemented in Italy. The country's Objective 1 regions were ranked last in the EU in being able to spend development funds according to the provisions set out in the national CSF and regional 'operational programs'. In the second cycle, 1994–1999, an additional opportunity was provided to the three large cities in the south, in the form of a 'global funding initiative'. These cities – Naples, Palermo and Catania – are those where significant social and economic problems were manifest in the context of particularly severe conditions of urban decay and social exclusion. The mechanism envisioned by the global funding initiative was to be an innovative program of sectorally integrated investments, financed through a co-financing scheme developed by the city, national authorities and the Commission. Afforded the opportunity, the eligible cities had to come up with and propose a convincing approach that would spark the ignition of a cycle of development, thus reversing in time long-standing negative socio-economic trends (Nanetti and Leonardi 1997).

The strategy of social capital formation

In 1996, the mayor of Naples took the initiative to seize the opportunity provided by the Commission.[9] The strategic concept put forward by the city was that of *sustainable and endogenous development activated and maintained by the formation and accumulation of social capital*. What distinguished the development proposal that ensued, was its deliberate attempt to use the city planning process not just to include existing groups – as in the models of 'advocacy', 'participatory' and, currently, 'stakeholder' planning[10] – but to initiate the creation of new groups, to set the premises for their sustained cooperative behavior and to secure their continued involvement in development planning to produce both public and private goods.

We define this cycle of expected results of the experimentation in Naples as 'social capital formation'. The development planning process entailed repeated iterations of such *'virtuous cycle'*. Conceptually, the cycle in Naples began with the mayor as the initiator and the Commission as an external agent. The mayor made the political investment into the concept of sustainable development and shared with the Commission the initial commitment of resources. In the community selected, existing groups were approached; their number at the beginning was limited. The existing groups were involved in the planning process through the preparation of the development proposal, according to the principles mandated by the Commission.

The broad-based scope of the planning process is to nurture and attract others, whose interests are solicited by the prospects of the specific proposal, as well as by the feasibility of further development opportunities when a track record of accomplishments is established. As a result, new groups emerge and new cooperative attitudes and behavior are induced because no part of the development program is operable without inter-group cooperation. The implementation of the program produces public and private goods, while the accountability that the participants share with the mayor feeds back to the city in terms of new inputs to begin a new iteration. In the second iteration, the number of 'existing groups' is expected to be larger and the 'production of public goods' expands to incorporate the 'production and maintenance of goods' function; the process continues over the life of the program and well beyond.

The Pianura neighborhood development Program

The site chosen in 1996 for the experimental program was Pianura, one of Naples 20 'quartieri'[11] (neighborhoods), located in the north-western periphery of the city. Four principal reasons led to the selection of Pianura, the first two of which encapsulate the logic of development planning based on the assessment of local needs, assets and potentials. Pianura was a particularly deprived neighborhood: in fact, it was the one with the highest incidence of illegal housing and a related deficit of public infrastructure and services. It typified the essence of the 'dormitory' community, suffering from problems of social exclusion, unemployment and the impact of organized crime ('camorra').

Yet, Pianura was also a neighborhood with potential for economic and social improvement, which could be realized by building on its relatively stable base of young families, its endowment of naturally precious hillside areas and volcanic craters, its institutional past as an autonomous commune,[12] and, moreover, its location near the Bagnoli area, which was scheduled for massive re-development, from the status of 'brownfield' into a service and tourism hub.

The other two reasons for choosing Pianura responded to the Commission's and the mayor's political logic of searching for complementarity and synergy, rather than overlap, in development planning efforts. From locality ('frazione') of less than 10,000 people in 1951, Pianura had accounted for over 60,000 residents in the 2001 census (and up to 80,000 according to unofficial counts). Demographic growth over the decades has been spurred by immigration flows first from the provinces around Naples, then by out-migration from the historical center, which had accelerated after the earthquake of 1980. Young families were attracted to Pianura by the relatively low cost of its mostly high density housing stock, much of it built without permits ('edilizia abusiva') by speculators and 'camorra'. Estimates in the mid 1990s put the stock of illegal housing at around five/sixth of the total, a phenomenon with its accompanied illegal electrical and sewer connections to systems unable to sustain the load. More recently, immigration into Pianura has been fuelled by illegal migrants from Africa and Eastern Europe.

This type of unchecked residential growth has not spawned economic growth in Pianura. Unemployment levels in 1996 were high, and penalized severely women and youth, thus accounting for the low numbers of the active population statistics. The neighborhood still reflected its recent past of agricultural community with some people employed in agriculture and several more producing quality products for their own consumption, products (for example, honey) which had the potential of being marketed externally. Jobs in industry and services in Pianura were scarce, so that the majority of its residents who worked in these sectors were employed outside the community. Yet educational levels in Pianura were higher than in other peripheral neighborhoods, and private elementary schools and middle schools were numerous. Because of these assets, Pianura was spared the problem of overcrowded schools and of the double school shifts which plagued other areas of the city. Not unexpectedly, school attendance was higher than in other neighborhoods.

The impetuous residential growth had created a shapeless and amorphous dormitory community, so atypical of traditional Italian settlements of the past that it even lacked a market area and a public square. Indeed, many of the 'public goods' normally expected in an urban community of the 1990s were absent in Pianura. The neighborhood lacked a health care facility, a high school and a fire station. Its endowment of sport facilities was limited to vacant lots and a few private gyms, and its potentially large acreage of green public space was not developed as parkland or recreation space.

The Pianura neighborhood development Program (Comune di Napoli 1996) set out to reverse these conditions by designing a set of integrated measures[13] to maximize their economic impact in terms of new economic activities generated, while at the same time creating public goods and increasing the neighborhood's endowment of social capital. The technical content of the Program covered five interrelated sub-programs – transport, environmental safety, community services, production and commercial activities, and the mandated evaluation – constructed around nine operational measures.[14]

To the eye of the visitor, the physical isolation and the lack of perceptible visual identity of Pianura were astounding. This situation called for measures to improve the accessibility to and around the neighborhood, by means of mass transit as well as by automobile. The continuous problems of street flooding and hillside soil erosion required urgent intervention to repair the existing sewer system and to prevent further erosion of the hillside. This, in turn, would justify the undertaking of measures to expand, among others, an industrial park for artisan enterprises, create a market hall, a parking area, a health clinic, and a pedestrian walk of green and sport spaces out of vacant land present in the community, much of which was publicly owned. The quality of life in Pianura and the sense of place identity of its residents would also be strengthened by the creation of a metropolitan park in the Pisani area, partly to be reserved for open space and partly equipped with an 18-hole golf course and other open air sports facilities, on the site of what had been an illegal dump. Underlining all these efforts in the Program was the promotion of economic activities in the form, for example, of new and expanded artisan shops, service cooperatives to manage sports facilities, new producers of value-added agricultural products, and new medical and other professional facilities.

The logic of the Program was to work with operational measures which would be mutually interactive so that each measure would contribute to the fulfillment of one or more of the Program's objectives. Thus, for example, the objective to improve the health services in Pianura was to be directly pursued by the comprehensive health clinic ('poliambulatorio'), which was one of the projects of the sub-program on community service infrastructure. However, the railroad mass transit and inter-modal and local road system measures were also to contribute to the objective by facilitating residents' access to the clinic, while the completion and improvement of the sewer system were to better the liveability of the whole neighborhood and promote better health conditions for the residents of Pianura. Another example is the objective of increasing the value of local products whose area marketing potential was to be facilitated by the new and improved transport connections with the city of Naples and whose production capacity was to be enhanced by the availability of new production areas, the presence of new producers and the protection of the hillside areas as sites of the original production.

5. Social capital formation and sustainable economic development: empirical evidence

Our research work of monitoring the implementation of the Program and longitudinally measuring the stock of social capital in Pianura began right after the approval of the Program in 1997.[15] Our research calendar, using multiple methods, has followed the Program on a systematic basis. Over the 10-year period, we have completed three full waves of in loco assessments, backed by intermediate assessments. The three waves of survey interviews were conducted in early 2000, late 2002 and late 2006/early 2007. Each full phase consisted of a telephone survey of a representative sample of adult residents of the 20 neighborhoods of Naples, to measure social capital changes in Pianura in comparison to similar peripheral neighborhoods and the city as a whole. It also included focus group interviews with a range of groups[16] to assess views, norms and patterns of behavior and personal interviews with an inclusive sample of Pianura's 'observers'.[17] Finally, 'participant observer' interviewing of difficult to reach residents included young mothers at home and street youth. In the third wave the number of focus groups was increased to incorporate new ones, either not present or inactive in the first two rounds. Throughout the life of the Program the research evaluated the mode and level of involvement of the mayor and key assessors and systematically collected documentation on the Program's changes and delays in implementation.[18]

Based on the responses from the various samples of interviews, for each sample we have constructed three indices to measure the dimensions of social capital: a 'trust' index, a 'solidarity' norms index and an 'engagement' (acting on the norms) index. Moreover, because the research is at the level of the neighborhood of Pianura, we constructed two other indices of neighborhood 'identity' and 'participation' in the life of the neighborhood. Finally, we constructed a contextual index at the neighborhood level, measuring the perception of the 'quality of life'.[19] The three measurements (2000, 2002, 2007) give us a longitudinal perspective of the changes in the views and behavior of our respondents over the period of the implementation of the Program, that is the changes which may have occurred in the stock of social capital. Pianura is the test case, while the other similar neighborhoods and the city are terms of comparison.

In the Figures that follow, we report on significant selected findings from a massive body of data, which are largely converging in supporting the trends of the incremental growth of the social capital stock and of the improvement in the quality of life in Pianura (Leonardi and Nanetti 2008). We comment first on the trend in social capital, focusing on the dimensions of 'trust' and 'engagement' (participation), which were absolute lows in 2000. We proceed to assess the changes in the neighborhood 'quality of life' index, specifically related to improvements in infrastructure and economic conditions. Finally, we discuss the significance of the changes which occurred in Pianura by comparing them with city-wide changes in residents' perception of 'quality of life' and sense of neighborhood 'identity'.

Over the period (Figures 13.1–13.4), diffused 'trust' increased generally in Naples, and it grew more in Pianura where it had started lower; in early 2007 almost 30 per cent of Pianura's residents expressed themselves in this regard, in comparison to about 13 per cent in 2000. Similarly, the 'engagement' dimension of social capital doubled in Pianura, with one in ten residents indicating so by 2007, which is close to the city's norm. When data are assessed for 'observers' – the most attentive group of residents and/or people working in Pianura and most knowledgeable of the Program – (and focus groups), not unexpectedly but nonetheless significantly, the growth in 'trust' reached beyond 50 per cent and below 40 per cent of the respondents, while for 'engagement' it was above 20 per cent and 12 per cent respectively; hefty increases vis à vis 2000. The commentary to the answers given in the interviews by the various respondents indicates the novelty and importance in the lives of people of the bottom-up aspects of the implementation of the Pianura Program. For the first time, in the experience of many, a public program had been attentive to and recipient of residents' input. Particularly the observers in terms of their life and work interests, together with residents who had shown a keen interest in neighborhood change by agreeing to participate in focus groups discussions, were positively affected by the Program implementation. In essence, this peripheral neighborhood showed

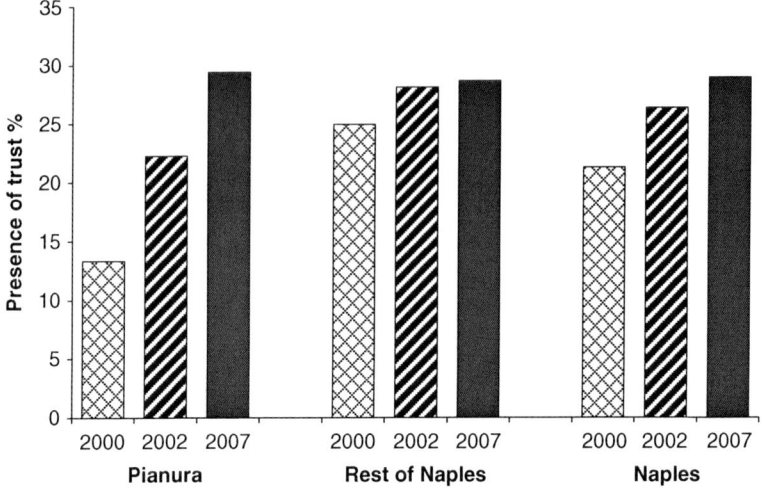

Figure 13.1 Comparative 'trust' index

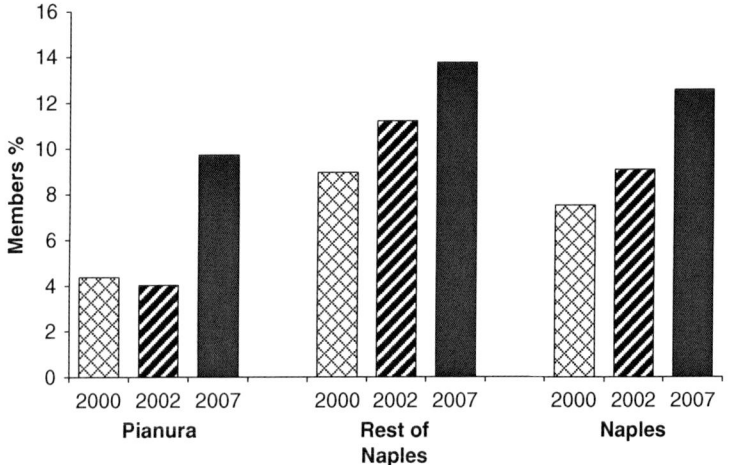

Figure 13.2 Comparative 'engagement' index

a trend in social capital stock that was upward and faster than that of the city of Naples.

Insights into the significance of the Program to explain these results come from the other Figures (13.5–13.8). The observers' (and focus groups') 'quality of life' index, expressed a marked improvement in the neighborhood infrastructure, with 60 per cent of focus group respondents (all residents of

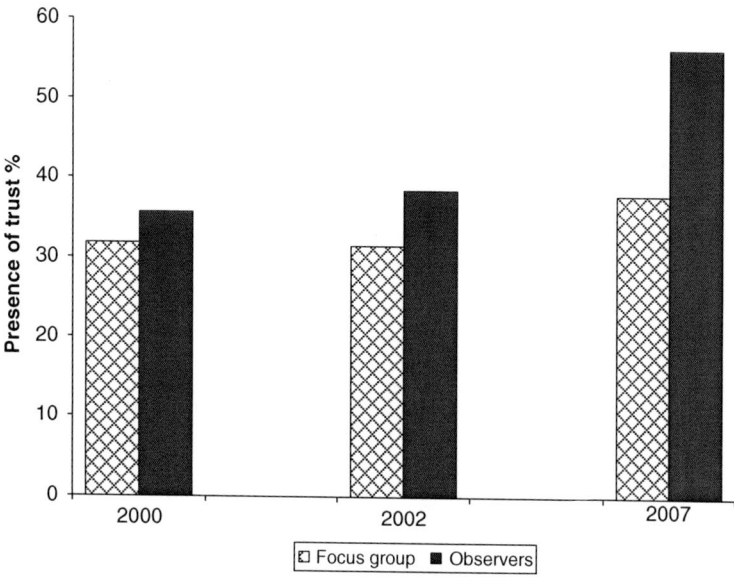

Figure 13.3   Observers' 'trust' index

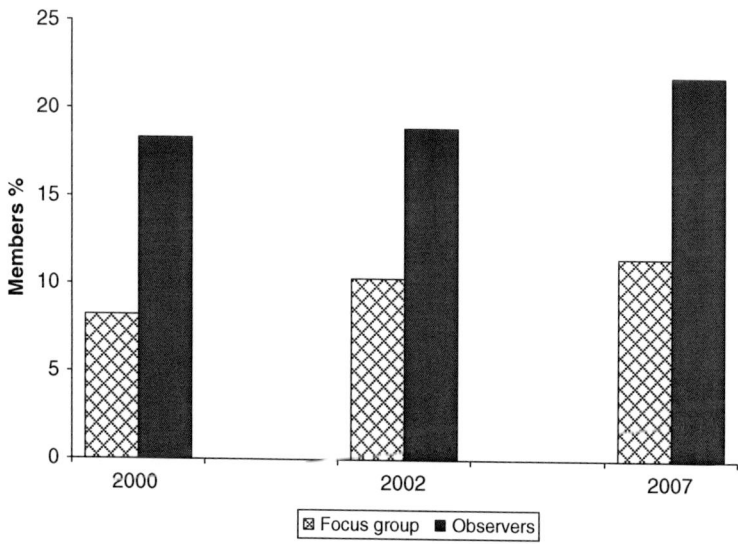

Figure 13.4   Observers' 'engagement' index

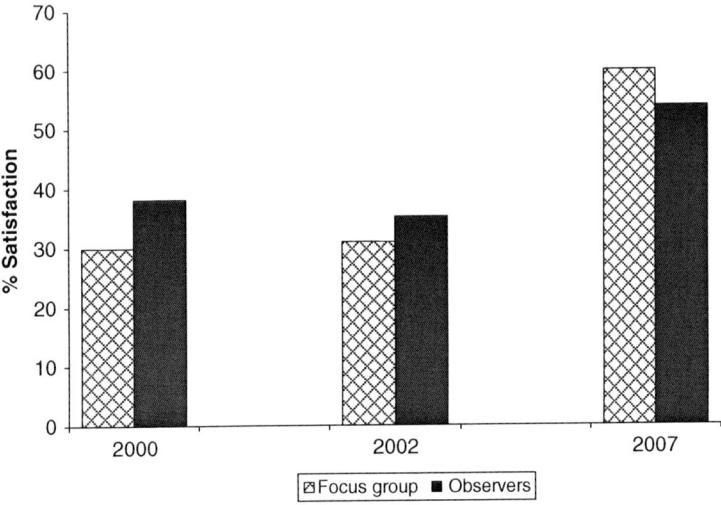

Figure 13.5   Observers' 'quality of life' index: infrastructure

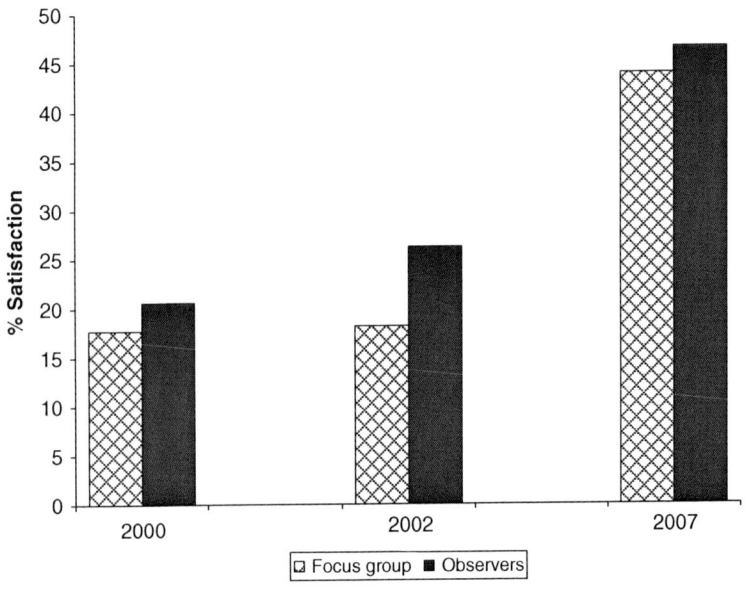

Figure 13.6   Observers' 'quality of life' index: economy

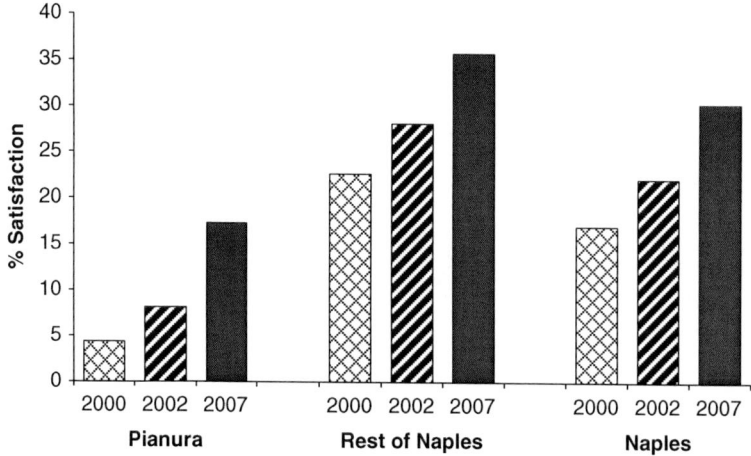

Figure 13.7 Comparative 'quality of life' index

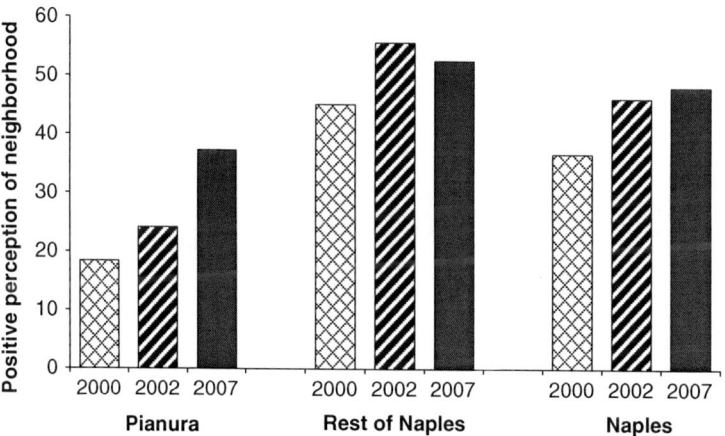

Figure 13.8 Comparative 'identity' index

Pianura) and over 50 per cent of observers being satisfied. The other indicator of positive change comes from the assessment that observers (and
focus groups) made of the condition of the neighborhood economy, with
a tripling of consensus (at around 45 per cent) by 2007. Likewise, the positive trend in the 'quality of life' and sense of 'identity' expressed by the
residents of Pianura when compared with city residents is quite remarkable,
a tripling and doubling over the period. The commentary offered by respondents to the open-ended questions asked during the interviews underlines

two aspects of uniqueness of the Pianura Program. One is the fact that it was a 'first' ever in the life of this once small and cohesive neighborhood, which had grown rapidly and massively in size but certainly not in liveability, and had felt marginalized and forgotten by institutions. The second aspect of distinctiveness is that the Pianura Program not only sought inputs from the residents through meetings held during its formulation phase but also continued this interaction with residents and associations throughout its life.

6. Conclusions

Naples' Pianura neighborhood development Program, an experiment aimed at pursuing economic and social development while simultaneously increasing the community's stock of social capital, has shown the validity of the strategy combining participation and investments. The data clearly indicate the incremental growth of social capital in Pianura over the life of the Program, together with significant improvements in the neighborhood's physical and service infrastructure and economic opportunities. There is also evidence of a more solid growth of social capital in Pianura in comparison to other peripheral neighborhoods where no such program was experimented. The positive conclusion of social capital formation through an ad hoc policy strategy and Program comes not just from the quantitative data but also from the wealth of qualitative data, relating comments of respondents during the life of the Program.

But, as we started in the introduction to the chapter, we want to update its conclusions as well. In the 2007 paper, we reported on an important story about Pianura as a positive test case, a story which on 10 July 2007 had also been told on a national TV program, 'Viva l'Italia diretta'. One key lesson learned in Pianura is that a social capital oriented strategy/program needs to be longitudinal in order to weather inevitable delays in its implementation and events which may convey a message of unfulfilled promises. This is what happened in Pianura when the aftermath of the flooding of 1999 required re-programming and, therefore, delays in implementation. More meetings were called for it and people got a sense that the Program was being lost. Then an event happened, which in its horror helped to consolidate the community against the 'camorra' hold and take greater advantage of the resources offered by the Program: the killing of two innocent young men, Gigi and Paolo, turned the tide. It brought about, among other changes, the organizing of shopkeepers into a 'basta camorra' campaign ('enough with camorra'), an active association and movement supported by the local and municipal institutions, which has stopped the racket of extortion on Pianura's main commercial street and become a main participant in the expansion of the Program to create, for example, a police station in Pianura.

Then, in January 2008, the city of Naples experienced one of its worst downturns when the 'garbage collection crisis' unfolded, burying the city under mounds of uncollected waste when the magistrates imposed the closing of waste disposal sites in and around the city. The assault on the city's image began. Pictures in national and world media outlets generically and unjustifiably portrayed Naples as being 'on the ropes'; no overall information was given of why so suddenly the crisis had occurred. A few and repeated television images of a bus being turned and burned in Pianura by, presumably, irate citizens 'taking the law into their hands', became the icon of the 'crisis'; national politics played into it, leading to the fall of the center-left coalition government in Rome. Instead, for example, no coverage of mothers of school children, teachers, local school administrators and parish priests active in demanding the removal of waste in the streets and around the schools of Pianura and the safeguarding of the Pisani natural area made the news. Since then, it has been learned that the 'citizens' were a handful of political extremists and the 'crisis' dated back to the ineffective management structure for waste collection in the region of Campania put in place by the national law in 1994 (Leonardi and Nanetti 2008).

Notes

1. This chapter builds and expands upon a paper presented at the workshop on 'Social Capital, Corporate Social Responsibility (CSR) and Sustainable Economic Development', EconomEtica – University of Milano–Bicocca and LaSER – Department of Economics, University of Trento, 24–25 July 2007 (Trento).
2. Its beginnings are often ascribed to coincide with the momentous events of the collapse of the Bretton Woods agreements in 1971 when the United States abandoned the 'gold standard', followed by the two 'oil embargoes' that hit the world's economy during that decade, and further prompted by the significant processes of de-industrialization and restructuring that ensued in the developed countries. This wave is contrasted with other globalization experiences of the past which were characterized by different causes and consequences, such as the military and cultural expansion of the Roman Empire, the discovery and conquest of the New World, or the colonial empires of the Industrial Revolution (Hopkins 2002).
3. Actually, the EU model embraces the 'development' paradigm (for example, in its 'regional development policy' and its member countries' welfare state provisions) without rejecting the 'growth' paradigm (for example, in its Lisbon agenda of competitiveness and cohesion). In the Southern Cone of the Americas, the MERCOSUR regional bloc has been inspired by the EU model, but with not much progress so far.
4. Adding to the sociological, anthropological, planning and other social science literature, the economic literature has greatly contributed through the work, among others, of authors such as Amartya Sen (1999).
5. The periodic crises of the 1990s (Mexico, South East Asia, Argentina and Brazil) had led to the questioning by the World Bank and the International Monetary Fund of the 'Washington Consensus', on which the neoliberal growth approach was based (Stiglitz 2002).

6. In the works of other authors, social capital has been investigated as a different kind of social asset, often with a more limited or nil policy impact or even with a negative social impact (Levi 1996). By now, three kinds of social capital have conceptualized: 'bonding', 'linking' and 'bridging'. In a related fashion, studies have been conducted, for example by the World Bank, which have focused on social capital in conflict-ridden societies and in relation to issues of mere survival. Social capital of the 'bonding' kind is thus seen as a coping mechanism against others on the part of the basic societal group struggling for survival (Baranyi et al. 1997).

7. Including International Relations, Development Planning, Political Science, NGO and Foundations, International Agencies.

8. The reform identified six priority objectives, three of which are 'regional' (area-wide) and three others are 'national' (nation-wide) in scope. Almost four fifths of the development budget was targeted for the areas of the three regional objectives, and uppermost for Objective 1 areas defined as those overall less developed in the Community. Since then, revisions of the objectives have not touched this latter priority principle while adding and consolidating it. This is seen in the allocation of large resources to the new accession states for the period 2007–2013.

9. It is appropriate to notice that Antonio Bassolino, elected in 1993, had been successful in other endeavors, including the participation in the Commission's Initiative URBAN, the decision by the national government to pay for the dismantling and environmental clean up of the site of the former Bagnoli steel complex, and the involvement in the national government's historical preservation program, all of which contributed to establish a track record which was very important at the time of the negotiations over the 'global funding initiative'.

10. Reference is made here to the North American and also European planning literature, which since the 1960s has argued for the direct or indirect – that is, through professional consultancy – participation in the planning process. The classic work is Davidoff (1968).

11. In 2006, continuing on a decentralization trend, they were re-organized into 10 'municipalità' (municipalities) with greatly expanded functions, including the policy areas of education, social services, sports and culture.

12. This tradition was considered a particularly important asset in Pianura, in making it possible to create a new sense of place identity. Pianura was a rural town and autonomous commune until 1926 when it was annexed by Naples, first becoming a low density community surrounded by a large agricultural area, before the demographic explosion of the post-war period.

13. In the terminology used in development planning by the Commission, 'program' refers to the overall plan, 'sub-program' to its main sectoral components, 'measure' to the set of sectoral interventions, and 'action' to a specific project.

14. The operational measures or set of sectoral interventions which informed the five sub-programs targeted for either construction or completion or improvement were Pianura's: railroad mass transit and inter-modal transport, local road system, hydro-geological securing of the hillside, sewer system, parks and green space, community service infrastructure, artisan/industrial parks and markets, and new enterprise spin-offs.

15. We were confident at the time that Bassolino would be the mayor of Naples for a second term, thereby giving the Pianura program the chance to succeed and our research the horizon of a decade. Such was the scenario we adopted for the work we organized. While Bassolino was re-elected in 1998, with ever more popular support, in 2000 he decided to run for president of the Campania region,

and won that higher office. But the city of Naples retained a center-left coalition and mayor, when it elected with a convincing majority Rosa Russo Iervolino as mayor in 2001 and again in 2006. The new mayor has strongly supported the implementation of the Pianura Program (Nanetti 2001).

16. Focus group interviews were conducted with constructed groups of residents of Pianura, by age and gender and by family/social status. Therefore, among others the groups included: after school-age young women (age 18–29), after school-age young men, adult working women, adult working men, immigrant women, immigrant men, senior citizens and mothers at home.

17. In our research on the Italian regions we called such informed participants 'observers', in that context regional residents who were particularly attuned to what was happening at the regional level. In today's planning and institutional phrasing the term 'stakeholders' is used, while in the social science phraseology a term with similar meaning is 'key respondent'. Therefore, observers in Pianura included representatives of trade unions, artisan, commerce and professional associations, senior citizens and sports clubs, cultural and civic associations, parishes and schools. In most cases the observers lived in Pianura while in fewer cases they worked in the neighborhood.

18. For example, in 1999 the program went through a partial re-programming agreed to by the Commission, and involving a few important measures. Reasons for the changes and delays in implementation were a blend of technical and political events. The main reason was the catastrophic rainfall which eroded the hillside and flooded Pianura, mandating a partial revision of the program's priorities and relative scale of projects. Another reason was the significant street confrontations organized by the illegal street vendors and supported by the rightist opposition parties, against the project of the market hall, which was scaled down. A third one was the opposition led by the radical leftist parties against the golf course on the area Pisani.

19. The 'Trust' index measures the level of diffused trust that is exchanged through the relationships occurring among the residents of Pianura in the different spheres of their lives, that is as buyers and traders, parents and teachers, doctors and patients, voters and elected officials, priest and faithful, neighbors and neighbors, etc. The 'Solidarity' index measures the level of solidarity values and norms shared by the residents of Pianura; the 'Engagement' index measures the capacity of Pianura's residents to engage themselves with public institutions/officials for the purpose of pursuing community objectives. The 'Identity' index measures the sense of belonging expressed at the neighborhood level; while the 'Participation' index measures the dimension of associational capacity strictly in formal and informal groups at the neighborhood level. Ad hoc questions in the questionnaires provided the basis for the construction of the indices.

References

S. Baranyi, S. Kibble, A. Kohen and K. O'Neill (1997) Making Solidarity Effective: Policy Advocacy and the Promotion of Peace in Angola and East Timor (Washington, DC: The World Bank).

A. Bebbington (1997) 'Social Capital and Rural Intensification: Local Organizations and Islands of Sustainability in the Rural Andes', *The Geographical Journal*, 163(2), 189–197.

J. Brecher and T. Costello (1994) *Global Village or Global Pillage* (Boston: South End).

M. Carnoy (1993) 'Multinationals in a Changing World Economy', in M. Carnoy, M. Castells, S.S. Cohen and F.H. Cardoso (eds), *The New Global Economy and the Information Age* (University Park, PA: Pennsylvania State University Press), pp. 45–96.

M. Castells (1993) 'The Informational Economy and the New International Division of Labor', in M. Carnoy, M. Castells, S.S. Cohen and F.H. Cardoso (eds), *The New Global Economy and the Information Age* (University Park, PA: Pennsylvania State University Press), pp. 14–43.

D. Clark (1996) *Urban World/Global City* (London and New York: Rutledge).

J. Coleman (1988) 'Social Capital in the Creation of Human Capital', *American Journal of Sociology*, 94(Supplement), 95–120.

Comune di Napoli (1996) *Programma di sviluppo socio-economico e riqualificazione ambientale del quartiere di Pianura* (Napoli: Comune di Napoli).

Comune di Napoli (1997) *Programma integrato di riqualificazione e sviluppo urbano. Area metropolitana di Napoli. San Giovanni a Teduccio* (Napoli: Comune di Napoli).

P. Davidoff (1968) 'Advocacy and Pluralism in Planning' in S. Campbell and S. Fainstein (eds), *Readings in Planning Theory* (New York: Blackwell), pp. 305–322.

R. Gittell and A. Vidal (1998) *Community Organizing: Social Capital as a Development Strategy* (Newbury Park, CA: Sage).

C. Grootaert (1998) 'Social Capital: The Missing Link?', Social capital initiative working paper series, www.worldbank.org/socialdevelopment.

C. Grootaert (1999) 'Social Capital, Household Welfare, and Poverty in Indonesia', Local Level Institutions Working Paper 6. World Bank, Social Development Department, Washington, DC.

A. Harding (2005) 'Governance and Socio-Economic Change in Cities', in: N. Buck, I. Gordon, A. Harding and I. Turok (eds), *Changing Cities: Rethinking Urban Competitiveness, Cohesion and Governance* (London: Palgrave).

A. G. Hopkins (ed.) (2002) *Globalization in World History* (London: Pimlico).

A. Inkeles (2000) 'Measuring Social Capital and its Consequences', *Policy Sciences*, 33(3–4), 245–268.

P. John (2001) *Local Governance in Western Europe* (London : SAGE).

F. J. Lechner and J. Boli (eds), (2004) *The Globalization Reader* (Malden, MA: Oxford and Blackwell).

R. Leonardi (1995) 'Regional Development in Italy: Social Capital and the Mezzogiorno', *Oxford Review of Economic Policy*, 11(2), 165–179.

R. Leonardi, and R. Nanetti (2008) *La sfida di Napoli: capitale sociale, sviluppo e sicurezza* (Milan: Guerini).

M. Levi (1996) 'Social and Unsocial Capital: A Review Essay of Robert Putnam's "Making Democracy Work" ', *Politics and Society*, 24, 45–55.

A. Lyberaki and C. Paraskevopoulos (2002) 'Social Capital measurement in Greece', Paper presented at OECD-ONS International Conference on Social Capital Measurement. London, September 25–27.

R. Nanetti (1988) *Growth and Territorial Policies: The Italian Model of Social Capitalism* (London and New York: Pinter and Columbia University Press).

R. Nanetti (1990) 'Integrated Development Planning: The Reform of the Structural Funds', paper presented at the American Political Science Conference.

R. Nanetti (2001) 'Adding Value to City Planning: The European Union's Urban Programs in Naples', *South European Society and Politics*, 6(3), 33–57.

R. Nanetti and R. Leonardi (1997) 'Betting on Naples: Institutional Change, Development Planning and Social Capital', paper presented at the ECPR workshop on 'Social Capital and Politico-Economic Performance', Berne, February 28–March 4.

R. Nanetti and R. Leonardi (2002) *Reconciliation for Development Program (RDP) for Gorizia (I), Nova Gorica (SL) and Sempeter-Vrtojba (SL), 2000–2006* (Strasbourg: European Parliament).

D. Narayan (1999) 'Bonds and Bridges: Social Capital and Poverty', Policy Research Working Paper 2167, World Bank, Poverty Reduction and Economic Management Network, Washington, DC.

D. Narayan and M. F. Cassidy (2001) 'A Dimensional Approach to Measuring Social Capital: Development and Validation of a Social Capital Inventory', *Current Sociology*, 49(2), 59–102.

E. Ostrom (1996) 'Crossing the Great Divide: Coproduction, Synergy and Development', *World Development*, 24(6), 1073–1087.

C. J. Paraskevopolous, P. Getimis and N. Rees (eds) (2006) *Adapting to EU Multi-Level Governance : Regional and Environmental Policies in Cohesion and CEE Countries* (Burlington, VT: Ashgate).

R. Peet and E. Hartwick (1999) *Theories of Development* (New York and London: The Guilford Press).

A. Przeworski (1992) 'The Neoliberal Fallacy', *Journal of Democracy*, 3(3), 45–59.

R. D. Putnam, R. Leonardi and R. Y. Nanetti (1993) *Making Democracy Work: Civic Traditions in Modern Italy* (Princeton: Princeton University Press).

S. Sassen (1988) *The Mobility of Labor and Capital* (Cambridge, MA: Cambridge University Press).

A. Sen (1999) *Development as Freedoms* (New York: Alfred Knopf).

T. Skocpol (1995) *Protecting Soldiers and Mothers: The Political Origins of Social Policy in the United States* (Cambridge, Mass.: Harvard University Press).

T. Skocpol (1996) 'Unraveling from Above', *The American Prospect*, 25, 20–25.

M. P. Smith (ed.) (1984) *Cities in Transformation* (Beverly Hills, CA: Sage).

J. Stiglitz (2002) *Globalization and Its Discontents* (New York: W.W. Norton & Company).

P. Streeten (2001) *First Things First. Meeting Basic Human Needs in Developing Countries* (Oxford: Oxford University Press).

P. Taylor (2006) *World City Network: A Global Urban Analysis* (London and New York: Routledge).

M. Woolcock and D. Narayan (2000) 'Social Capital: Implications for Development Theory, Research and Policy', *The World Bank Research Observer*, 15(2), 225–249.

M. Woolcock (1998) 'Social Capital and Economic Development: Toward a Theoretical Synthesis and Policy Framework', *Theory and Society*, 27, 151–208.

World Bank (2002) *Building Institutions for Markets* (Oxford: Oxford University Press).

Index